ベルセルク
BERSERK 26

BY
KENTARO MIURA
三浦建太郎

TRANSLATION
DUANE JOHNSON
LETTERING AND RETOUCH
REPLIBOOKS

DARK
HORSE
MANGA

PRESIDENT AND PUBLISHER
MIKE RICHARDSON

US EDITORS
CHRIS WARNER
FRED LUI

COLLECTION DESIGNER
DAVID NESTELLE

BERSERK vol. 26 by KENTARO MIURA

Dark Horse Manga
A division of Dark Horse Comics LLC
10956 SE Main Street
Milwaukie OR 97222

DarkHorse.com

To find a comics shop in your area, go to comicshoplocator.com

First edition: November 2008

ISBN 978-1-59307-922-2

20 19 18 17 16 15 14 13 12
Printed in the United States of America

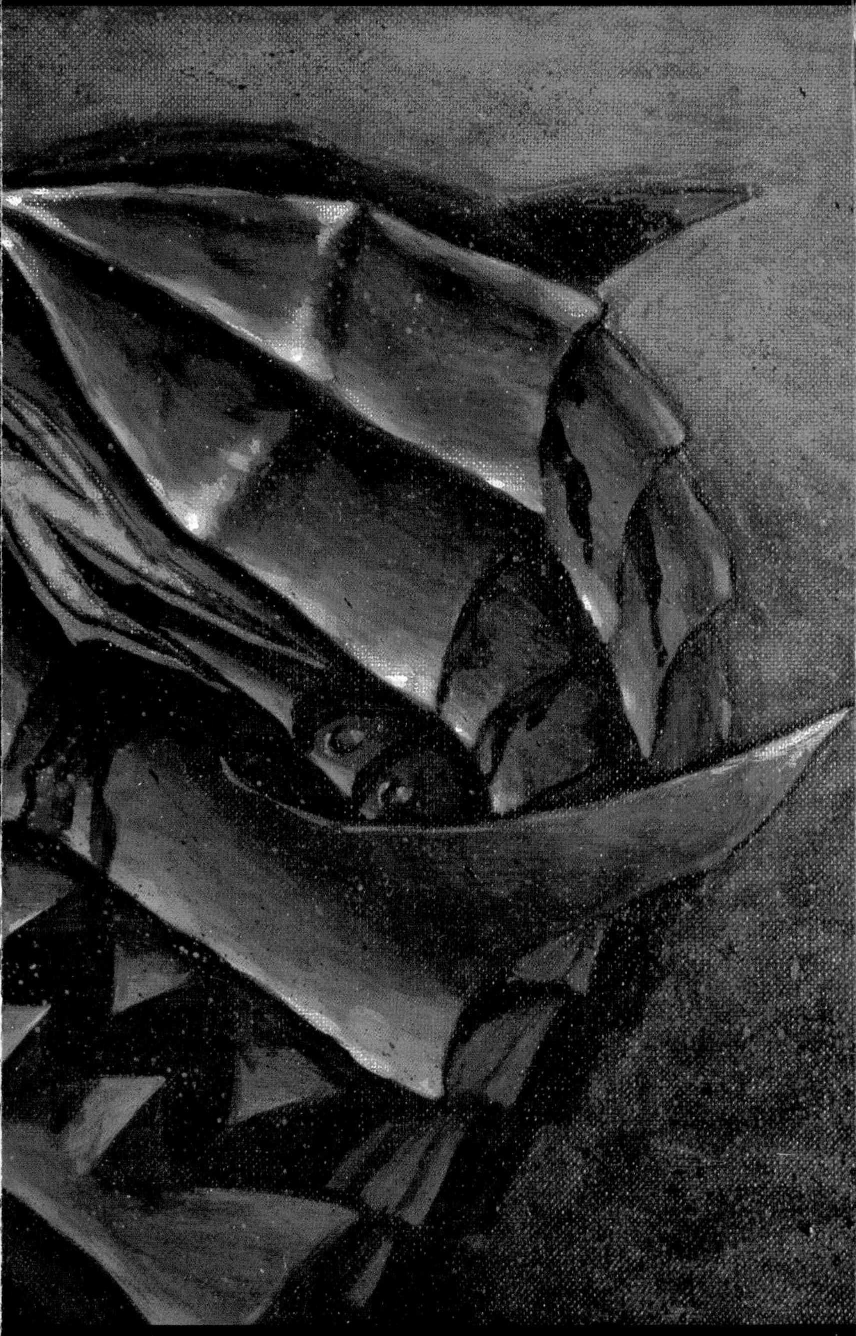

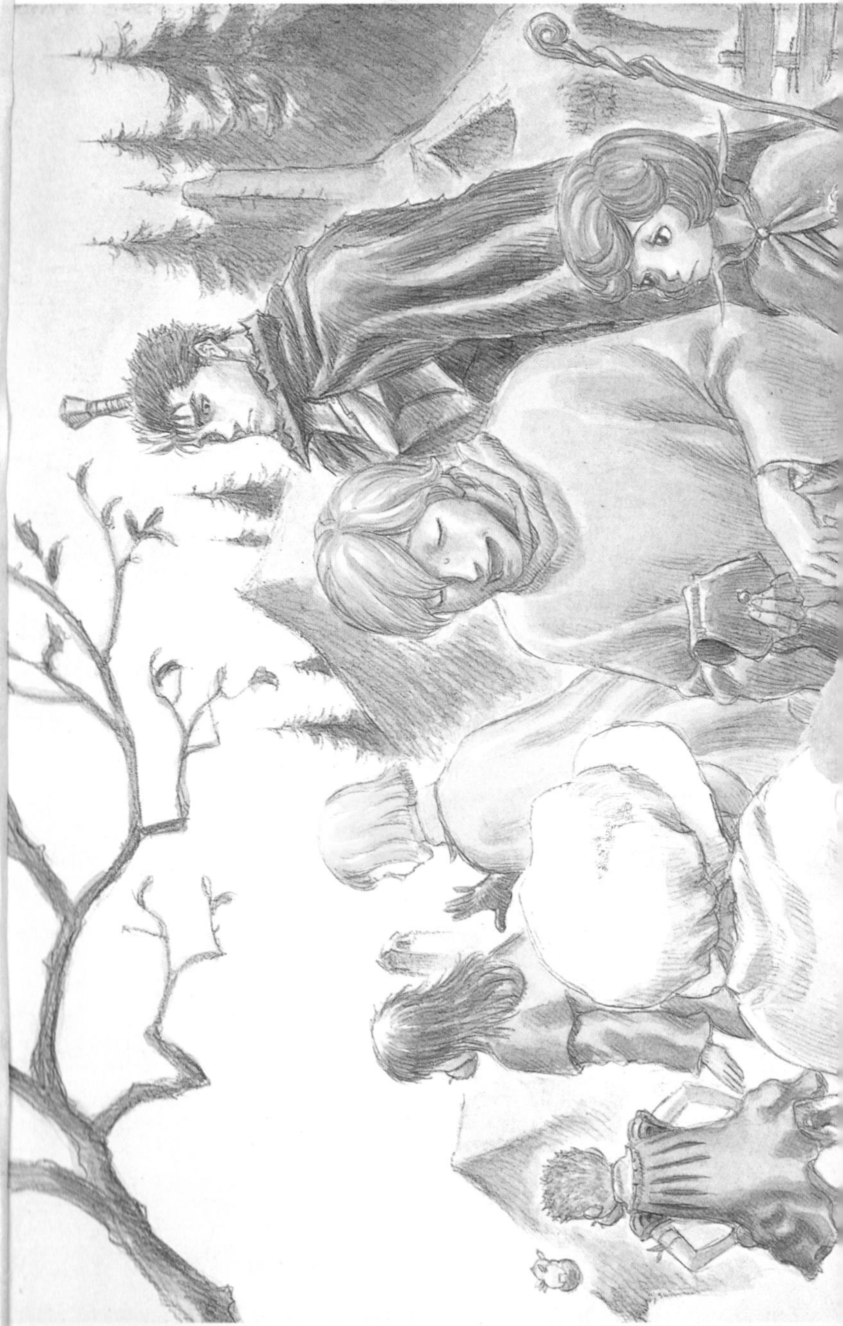

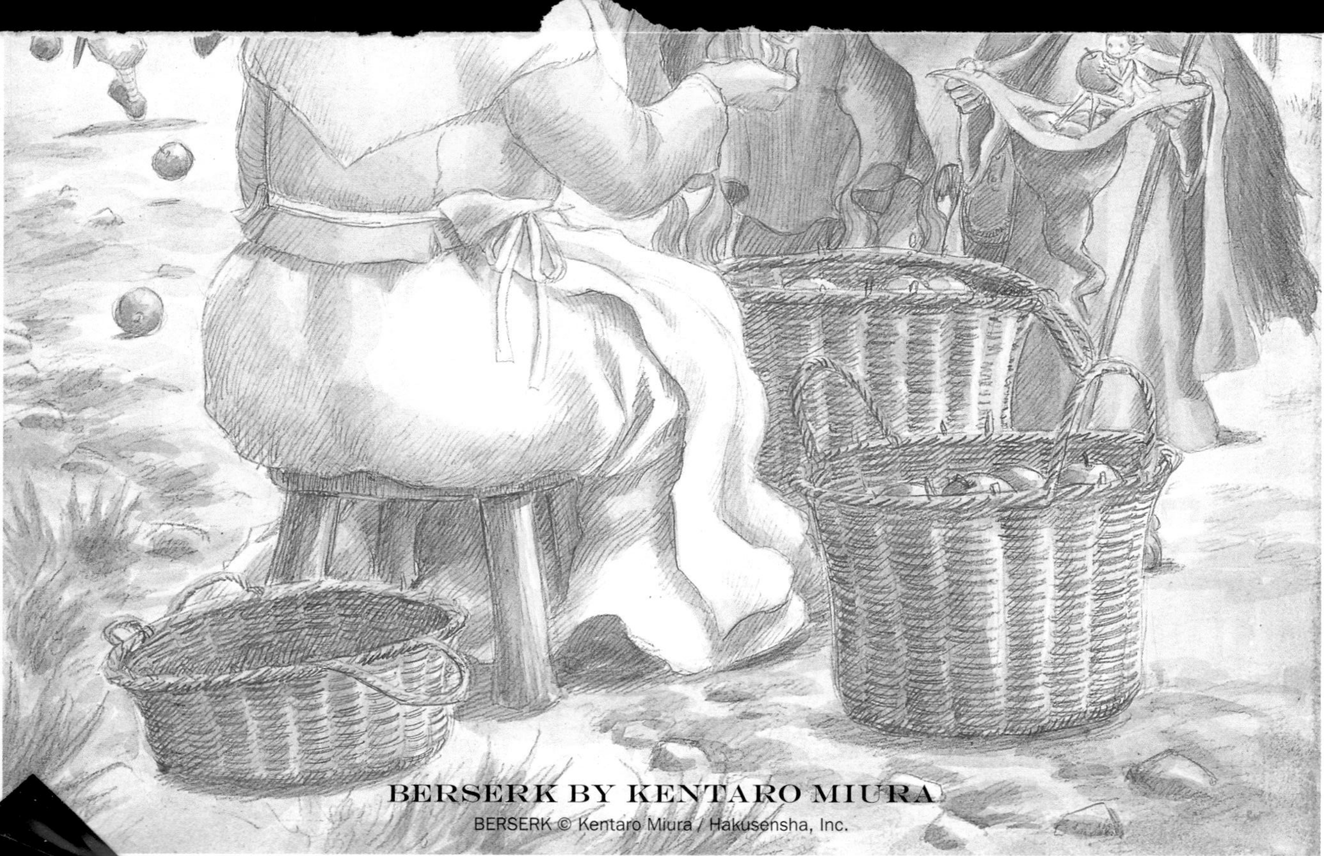
BERSERK BY KENTARO MIURA
BERSERK © Kentaro Miura / Hakusensha, Inc.

BERSERK

ベルセルク㉖

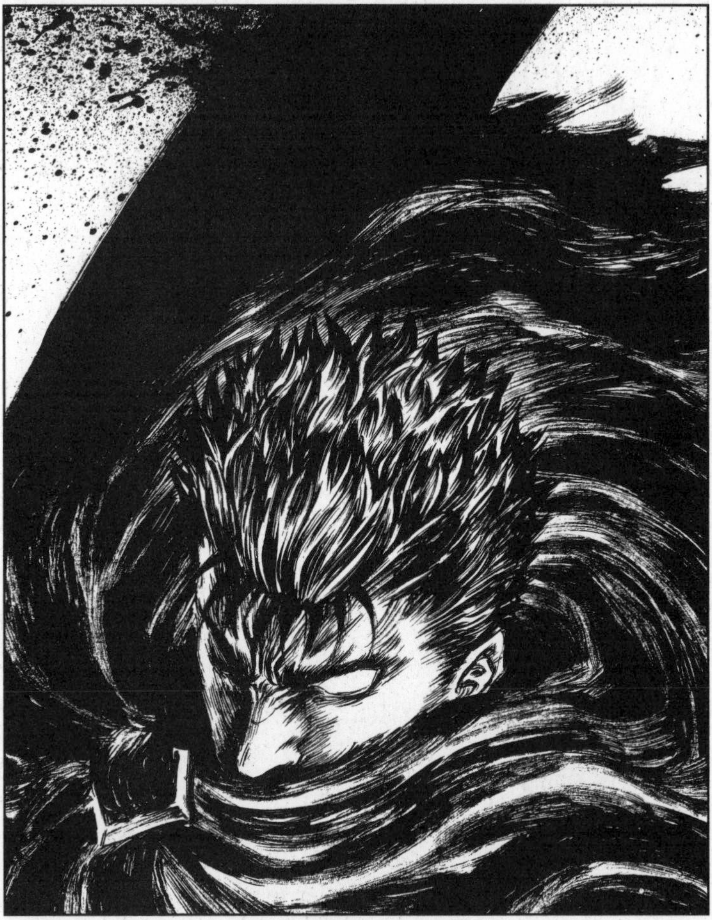

三浦建太郎

CONTENTS

FALCON OF THE MILLENNIUM EMPIRE ARC
THE HOLY EVIL WAR CHAPTER

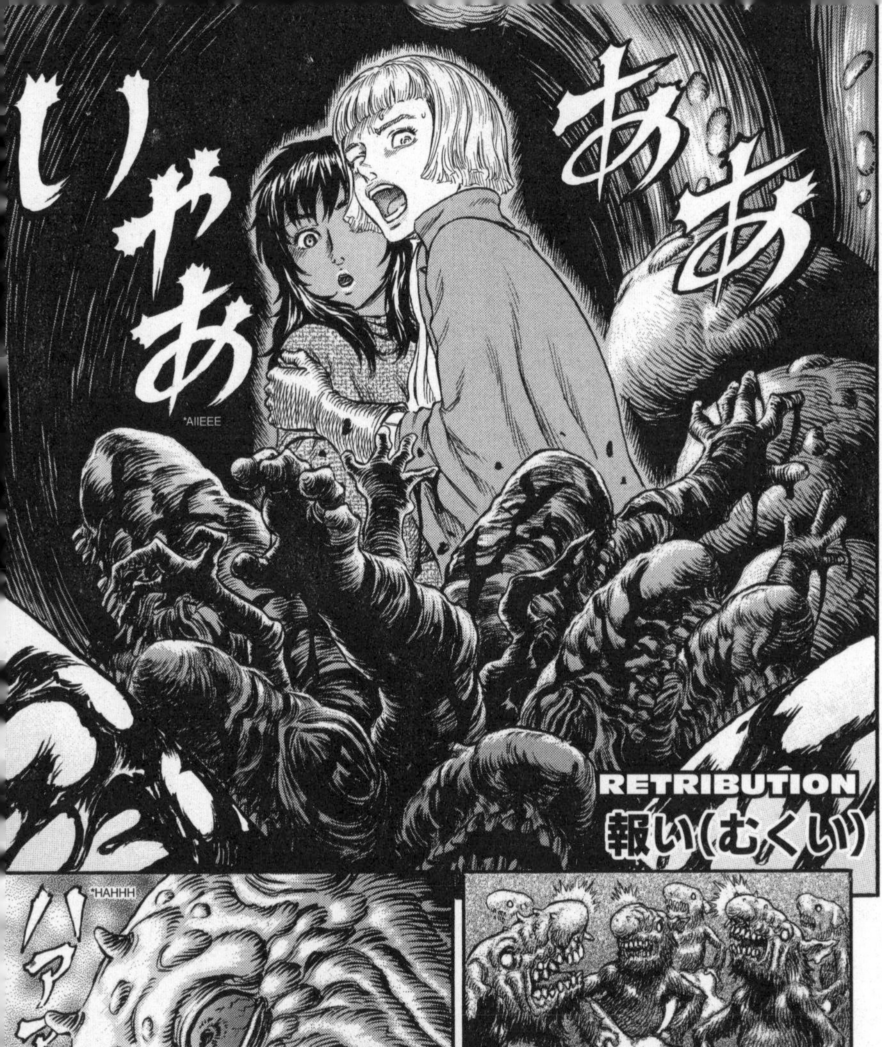
ああ
いやあ
*AIIEEE

RETRIBUTION
報い(むくい)

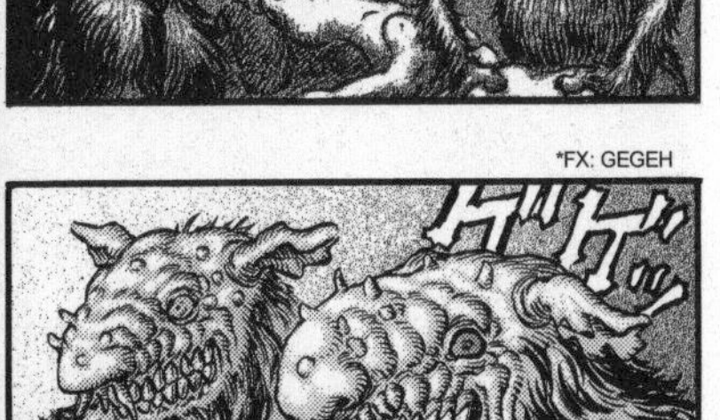

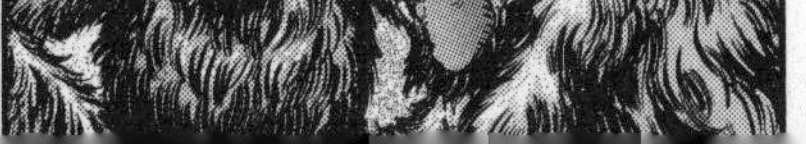
*FX: GEGEH
ゲゲッ

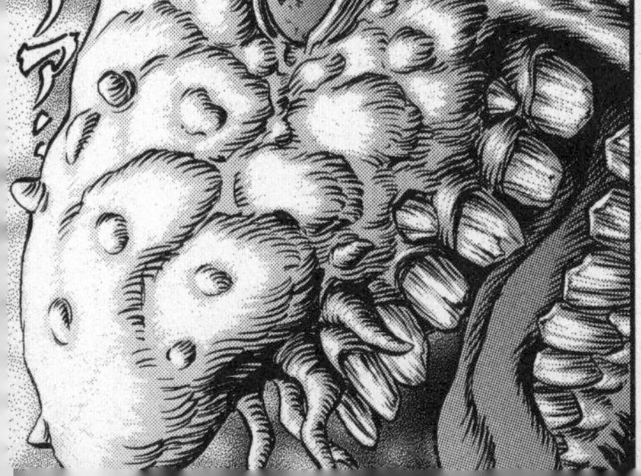
*HAHHH
ハァアア…

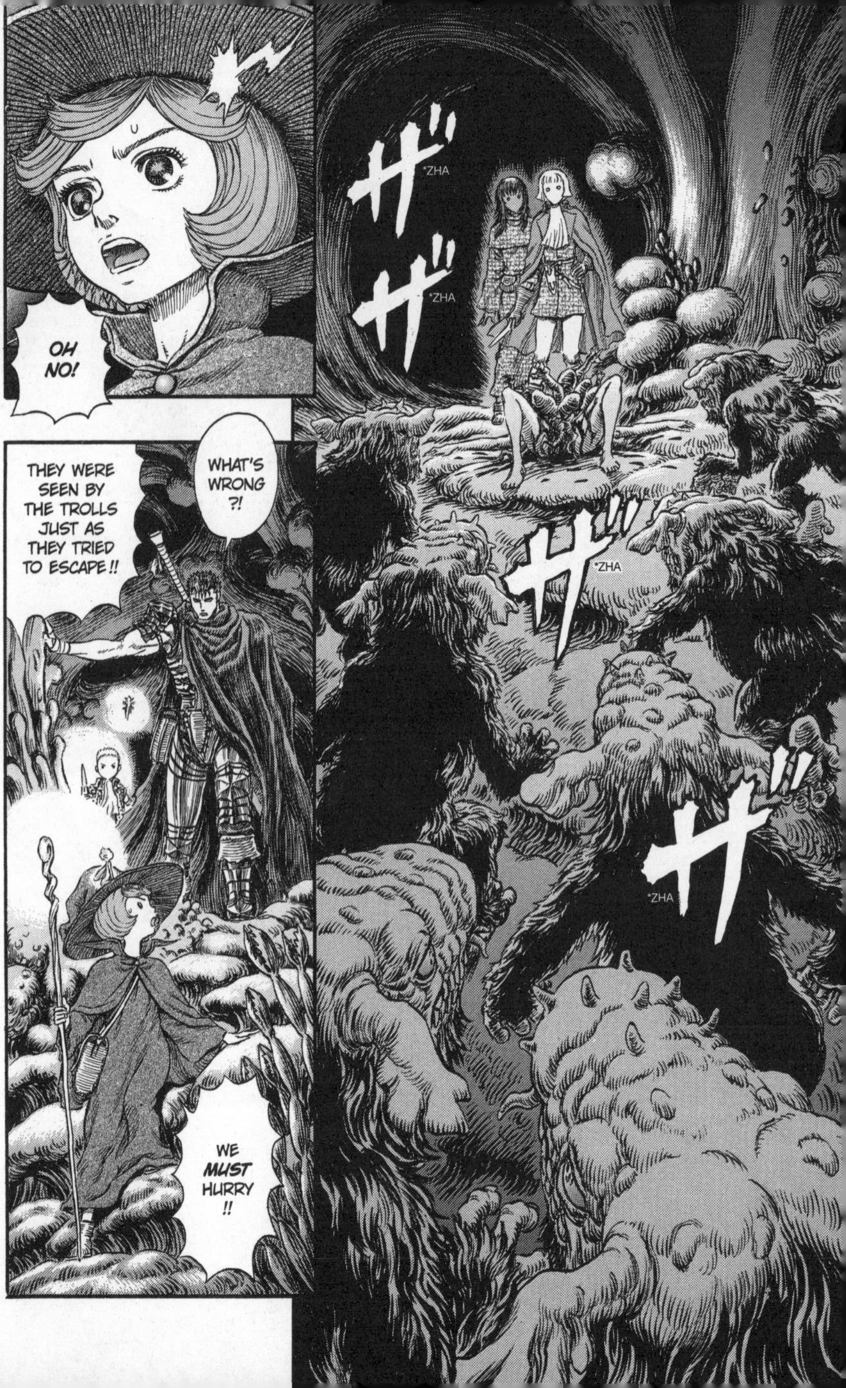
ザ
*ZHA
ザ
*ZHA
ザ
*ZHA
ザ
*ZHA
OH NO!
WHAT'S WRONG ?!
THEY WERE SEEN BY THE TROLLS JUST AS THEY TRIED TO ESCAPE !!
WE MUST HURRY !!

TROLL OD IS CONCENTRATED OFF AT AN ANGLE...
THIS WAY!
THREE TO THE LEFT!
IT'S ALL RIGHT, THEIR OD IS NOT DIRECTED TOWARD US!
STOP!
I WILL TRICK THEIR OD.
NOW!
?
?

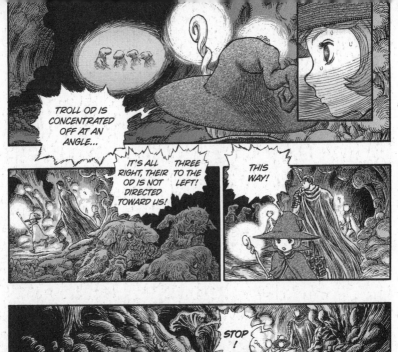

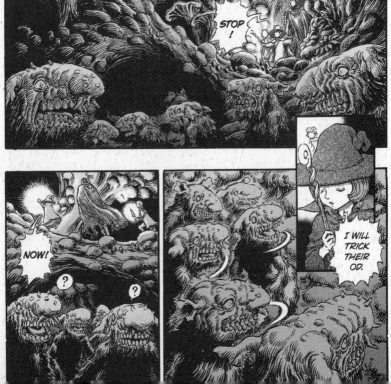

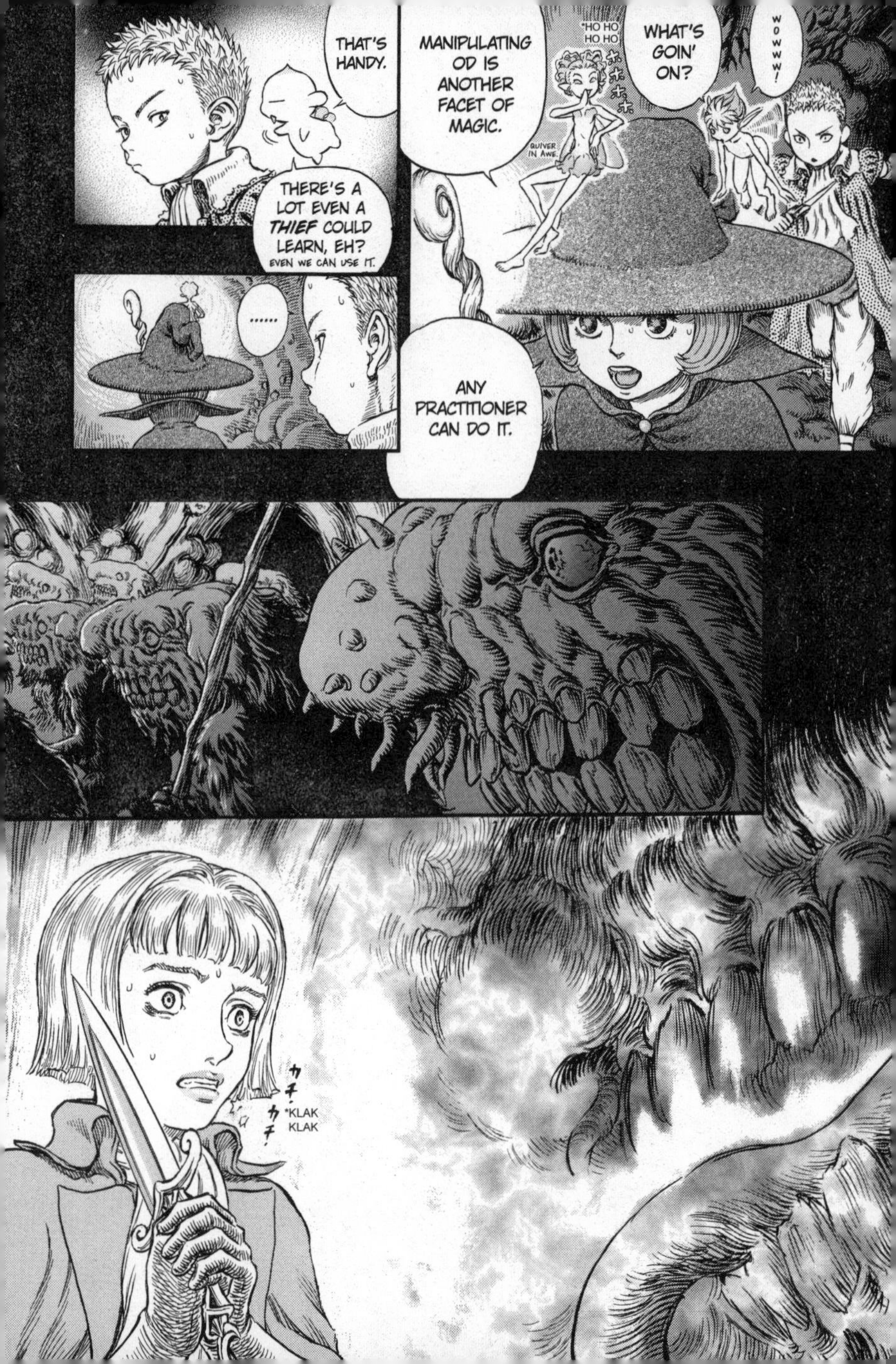
WOWWW!
WHAT'S GOIN' ON?
*HO HO HO HO
QUIVER IN AWE.
MANIPULATING OD IS ANOTHER FACET OF MAGIC.
ANY PRACTITIONER CAN DO IT.
THAT'S HANDY.
THERE'S A LOT EVEN A *THIEF* COULD LEARN, EH?
EVEN WE CAN USE IT.
......
*KLAK KLAK

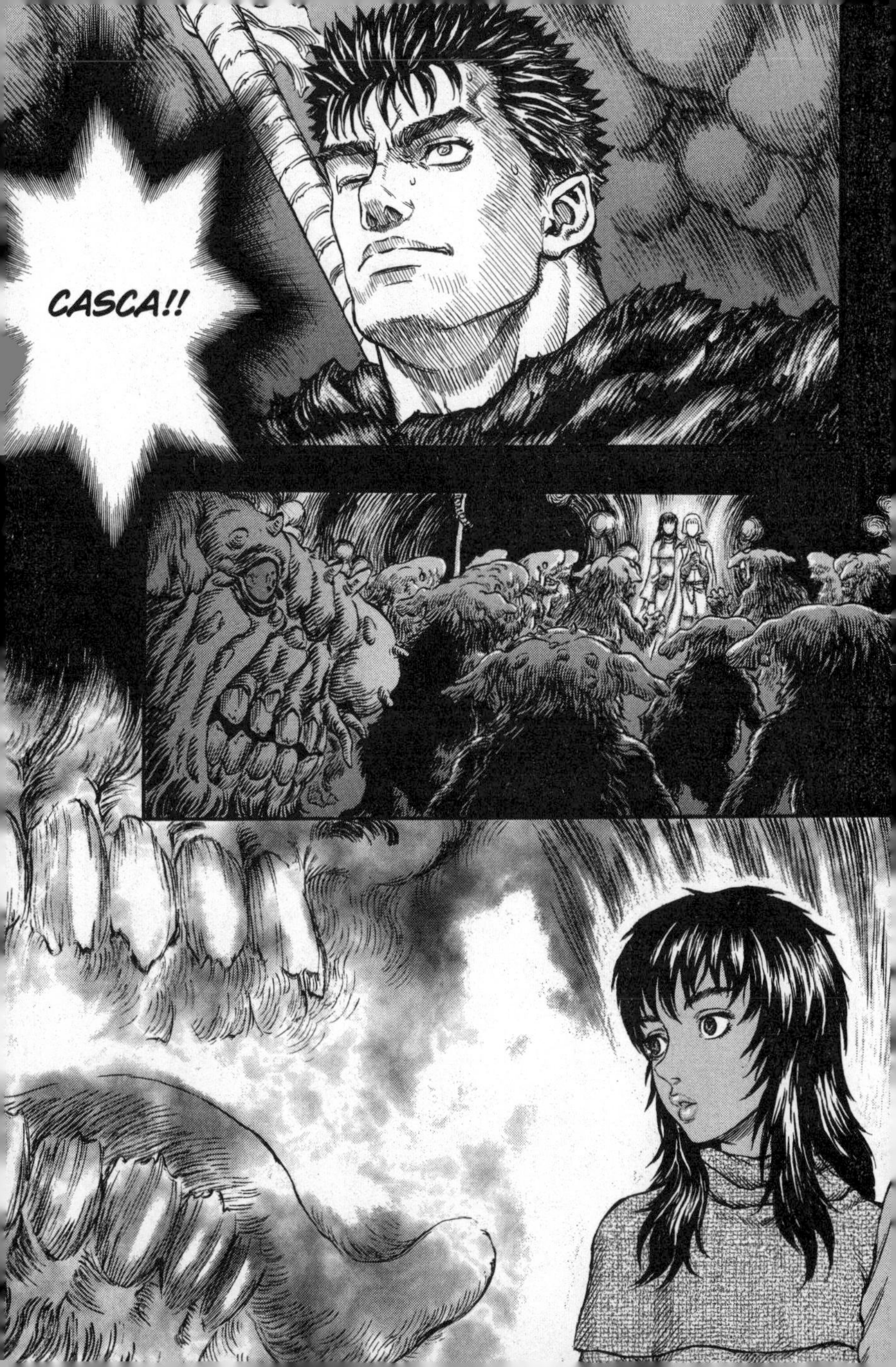
CASCA!!

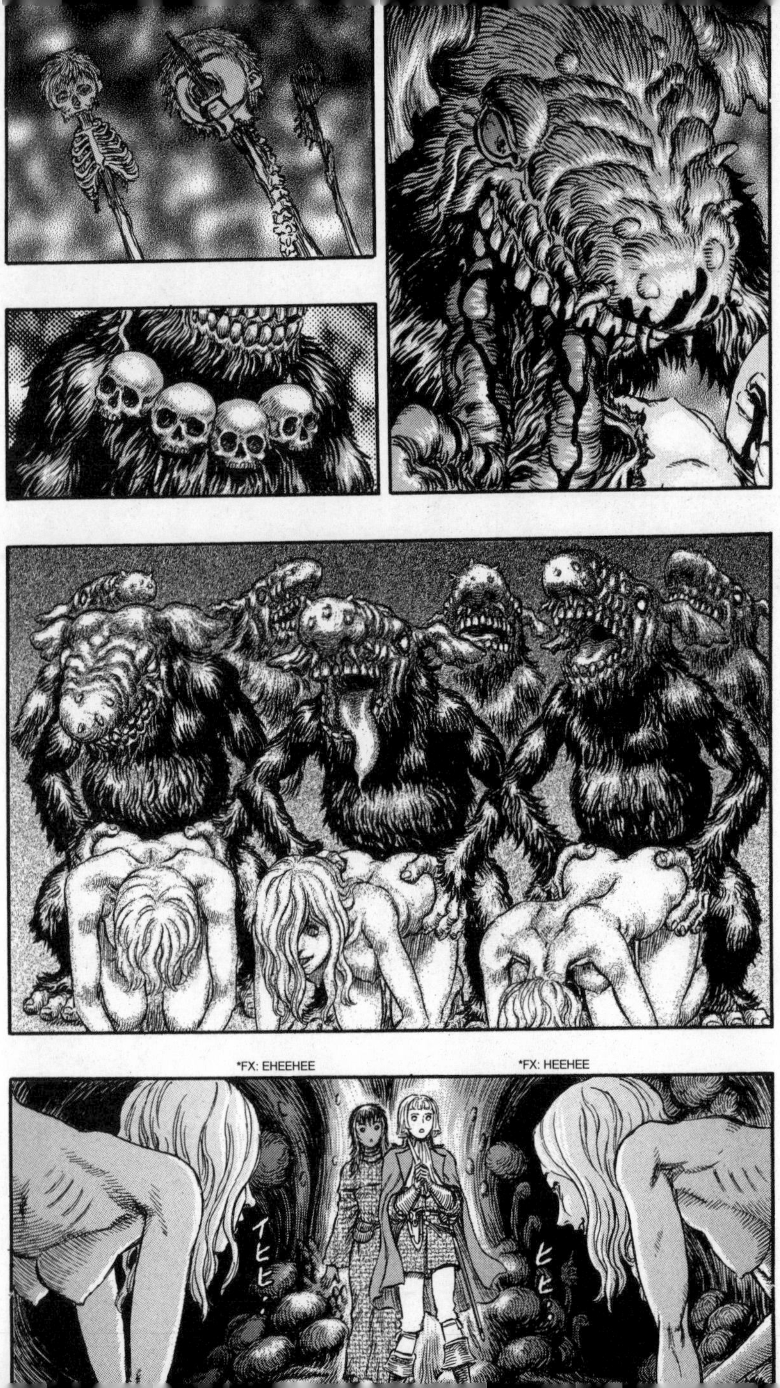
*FX: HEEHEE
ヒヒ・・
*FX: EHEEHEE
イヒヒ・・

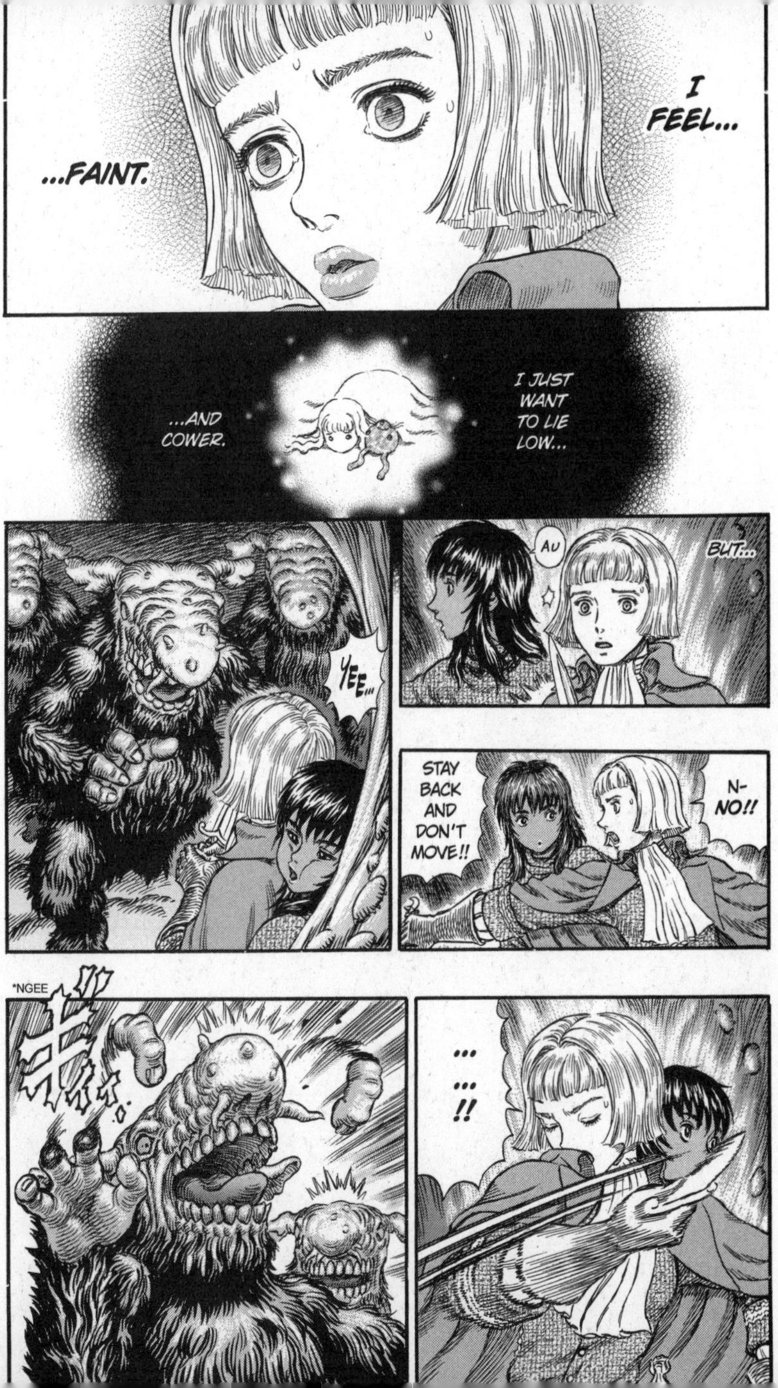
I FEEL...
...FAINT.
I JUST WANT TO LIE LOW...
...AND COWER.
BUT...
AU
STAY BACK AND DON'T MOVE!!
N- NO!!
YEEE...
...
...
!!
*NGEE

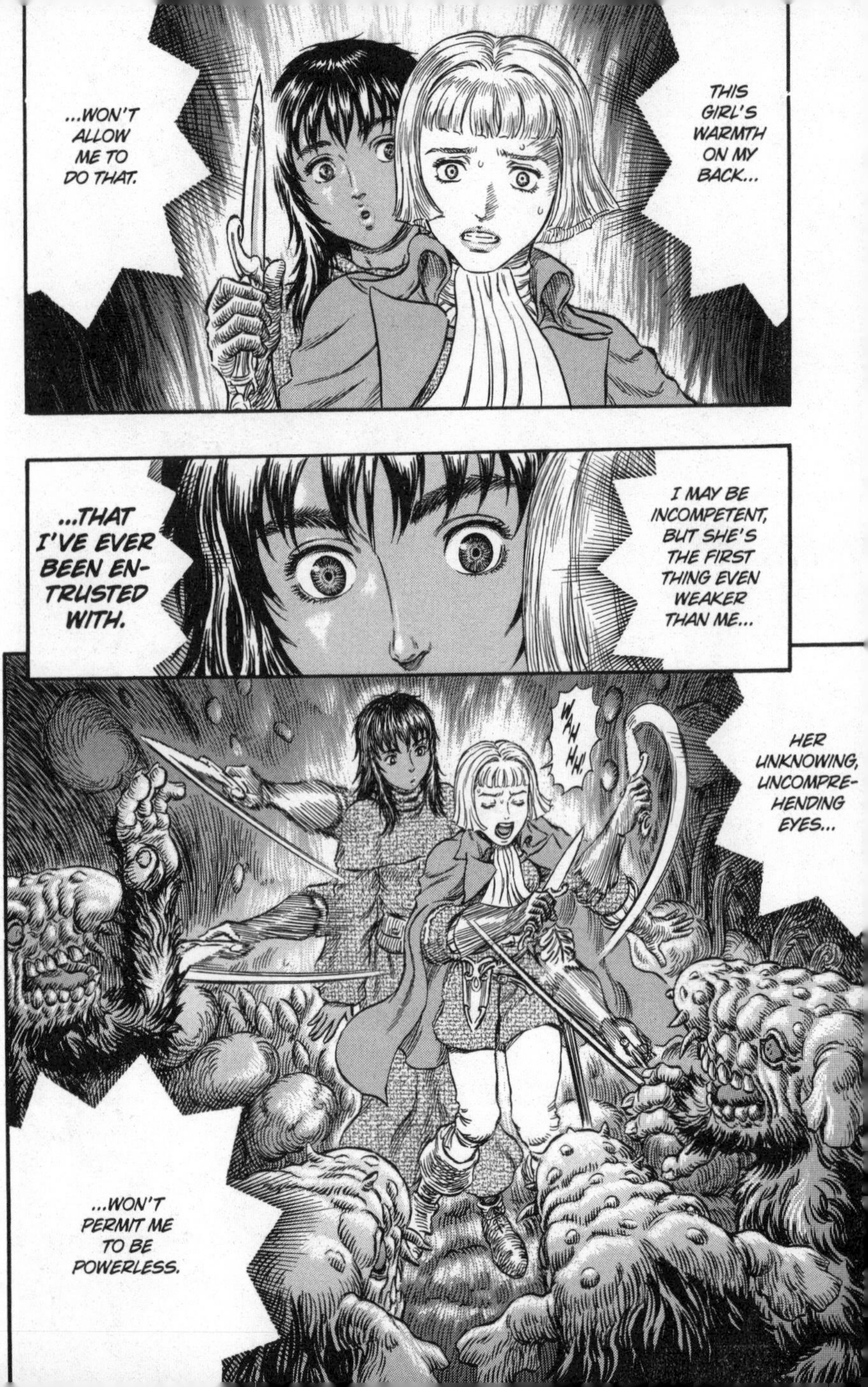
THIS GIRL'S WARMTH ON MY BACK...
...WON'T ALLOW ME TO DO THAT.
I MAY BE INCOMPETENT, BUT SHE'S THE FIRST THING EVEN WEAKER THAN ME...
...THAT I'VE EVER BEEN ENTRUSTED WITH.
HER UNKNOWING, UNCOMPREHENDING EYES...
WAHHH!
...WON'T PERMIT ME TO BE POWERLESS.

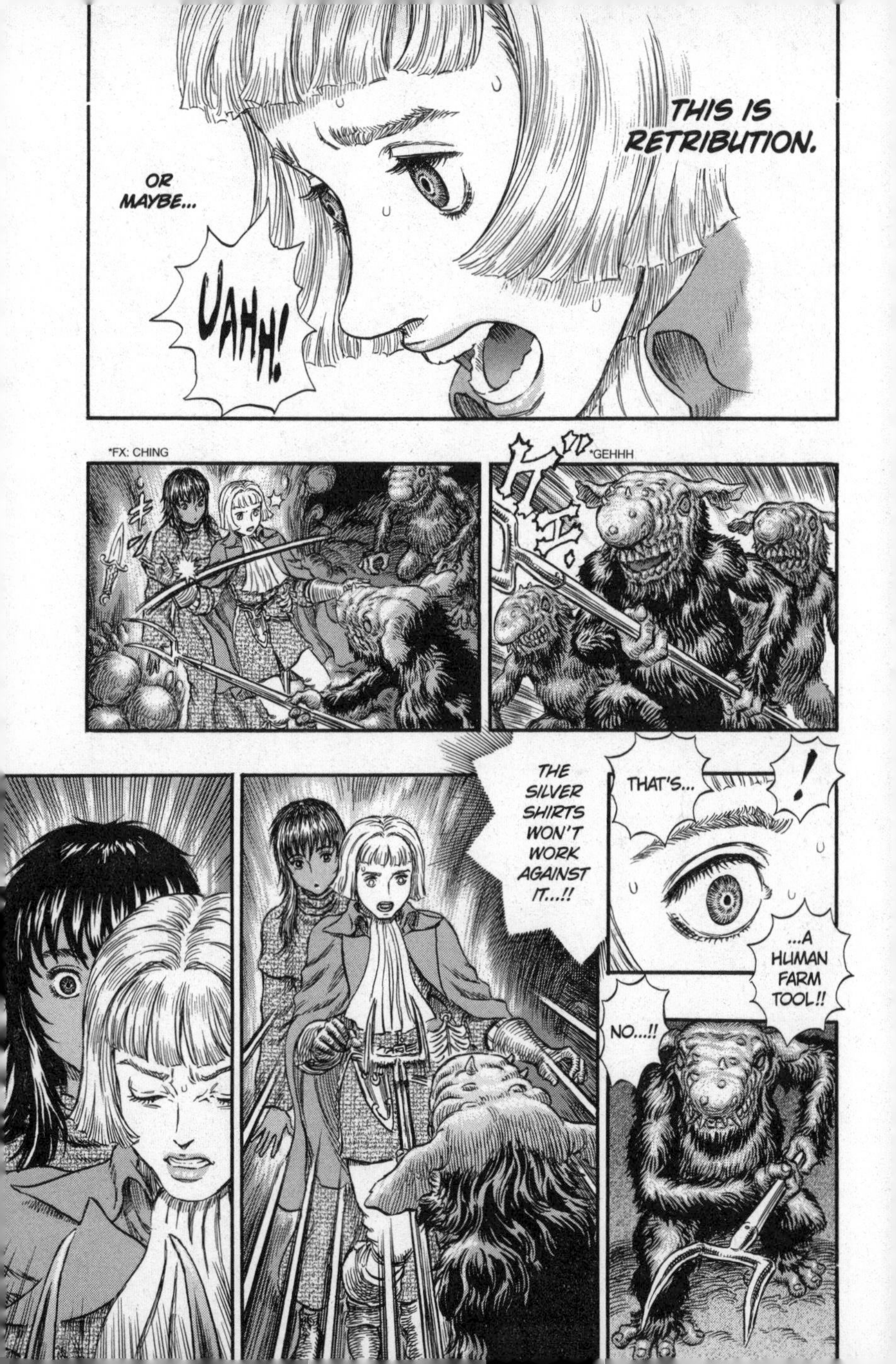
THIS IS RETRIBUTION.
OR MAYBE...
UAHH!
*GEHHH
*FX: CHING
!
THAT'S...
...A HUMAN FARM TOOL!!
NO...!!
THE SILVER SHIRTS WON'T WORK AGAINST IT...!!

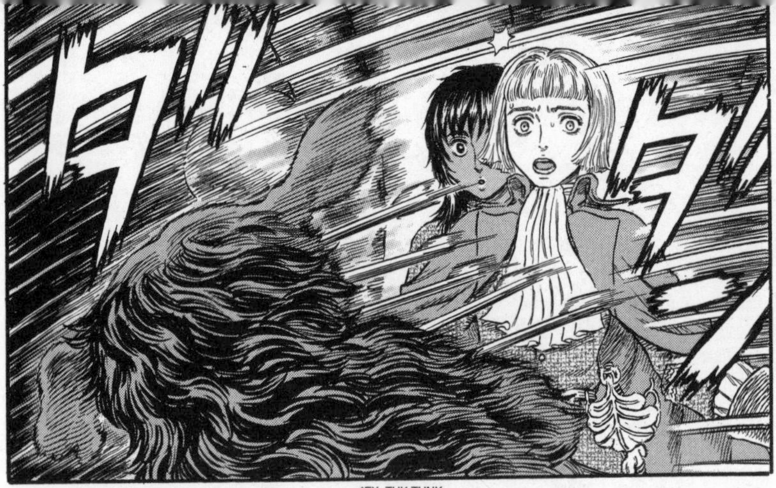

*FX: THK THNK

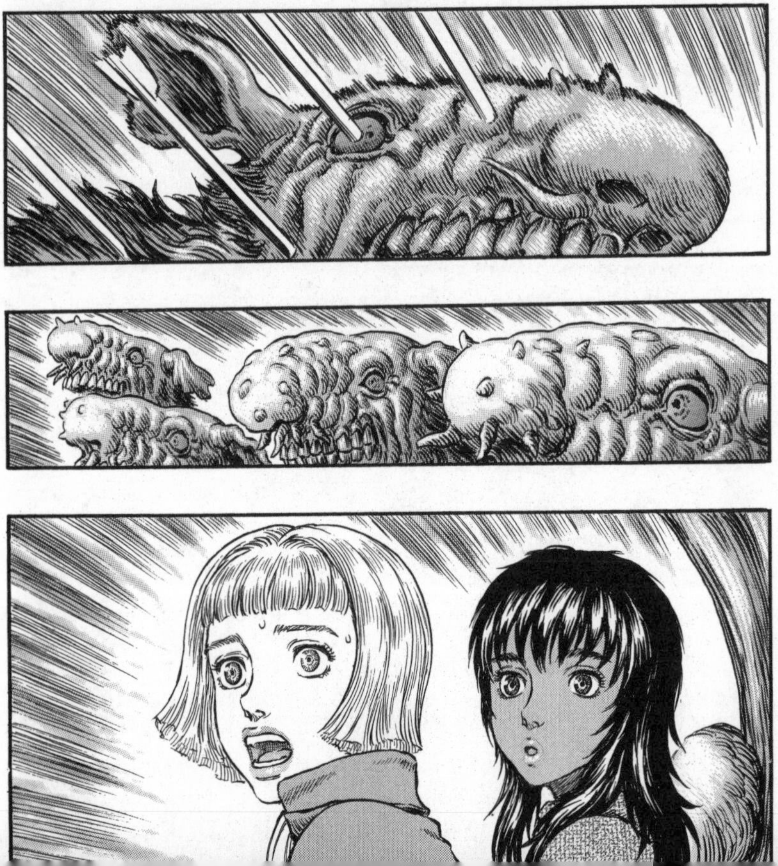

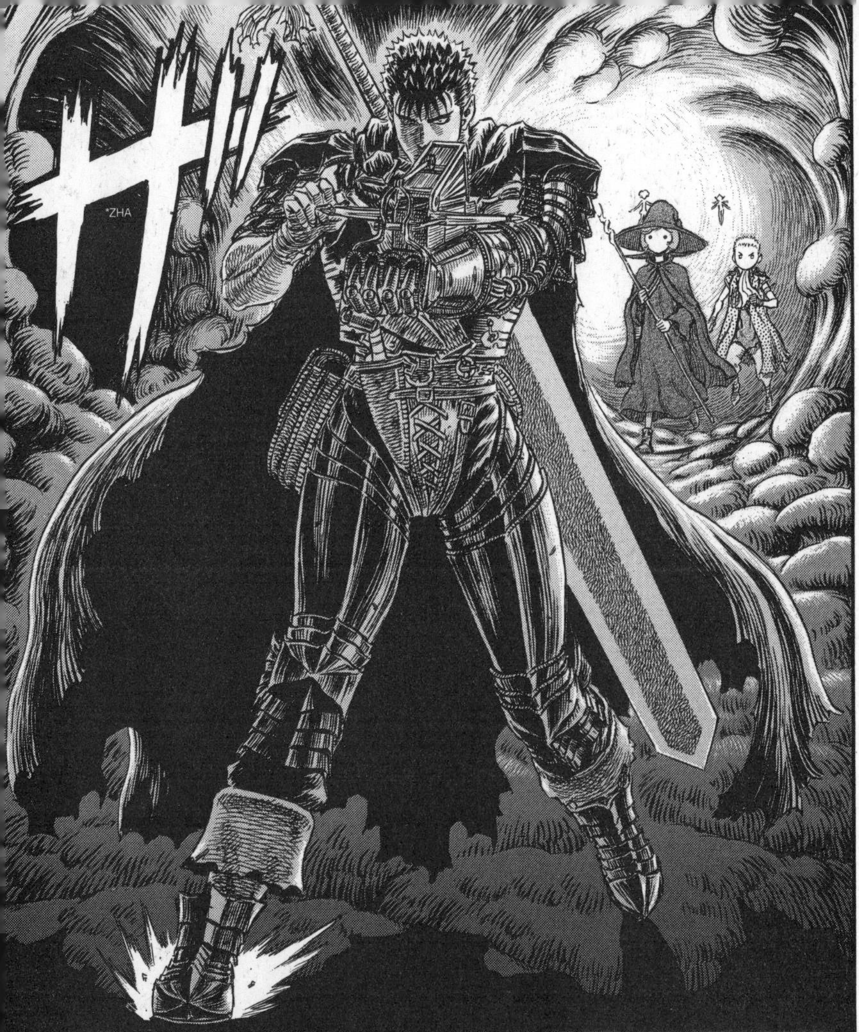
*ZHA
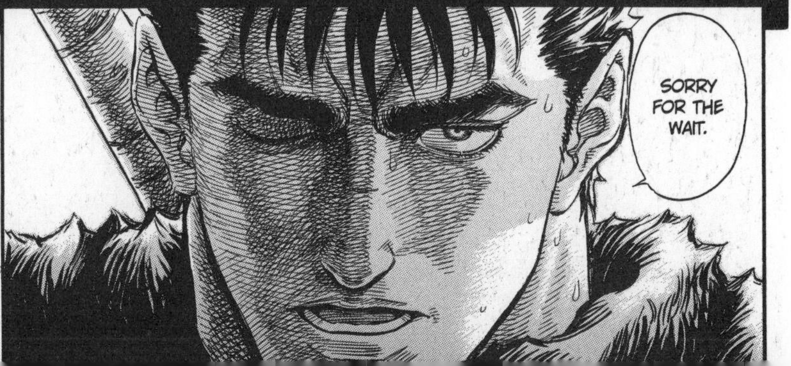
SORRY FOR THE WAIT.

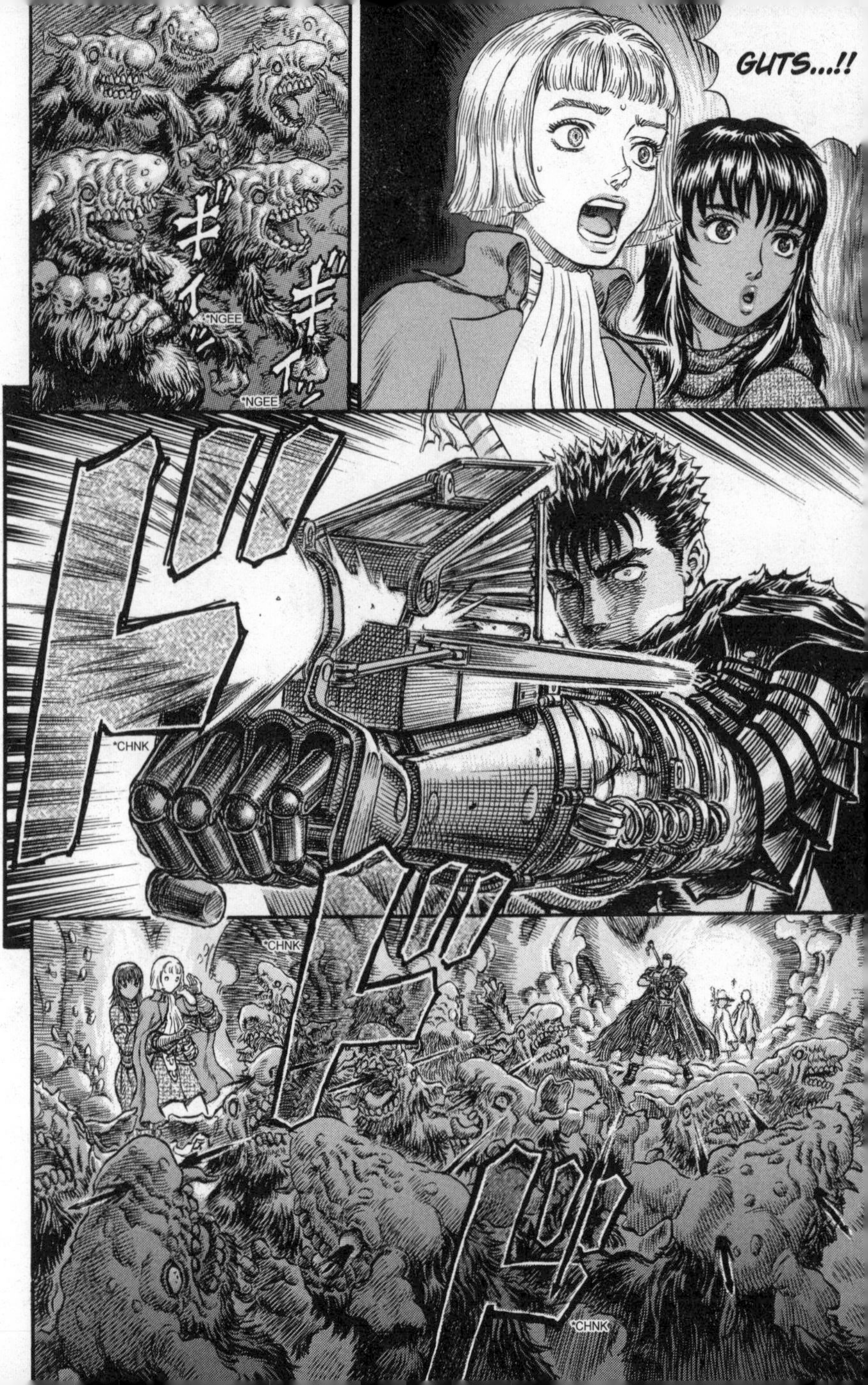
GUTS...!!
*NGEE
*NGEE
*CHNK
*CHNK
*CHNK

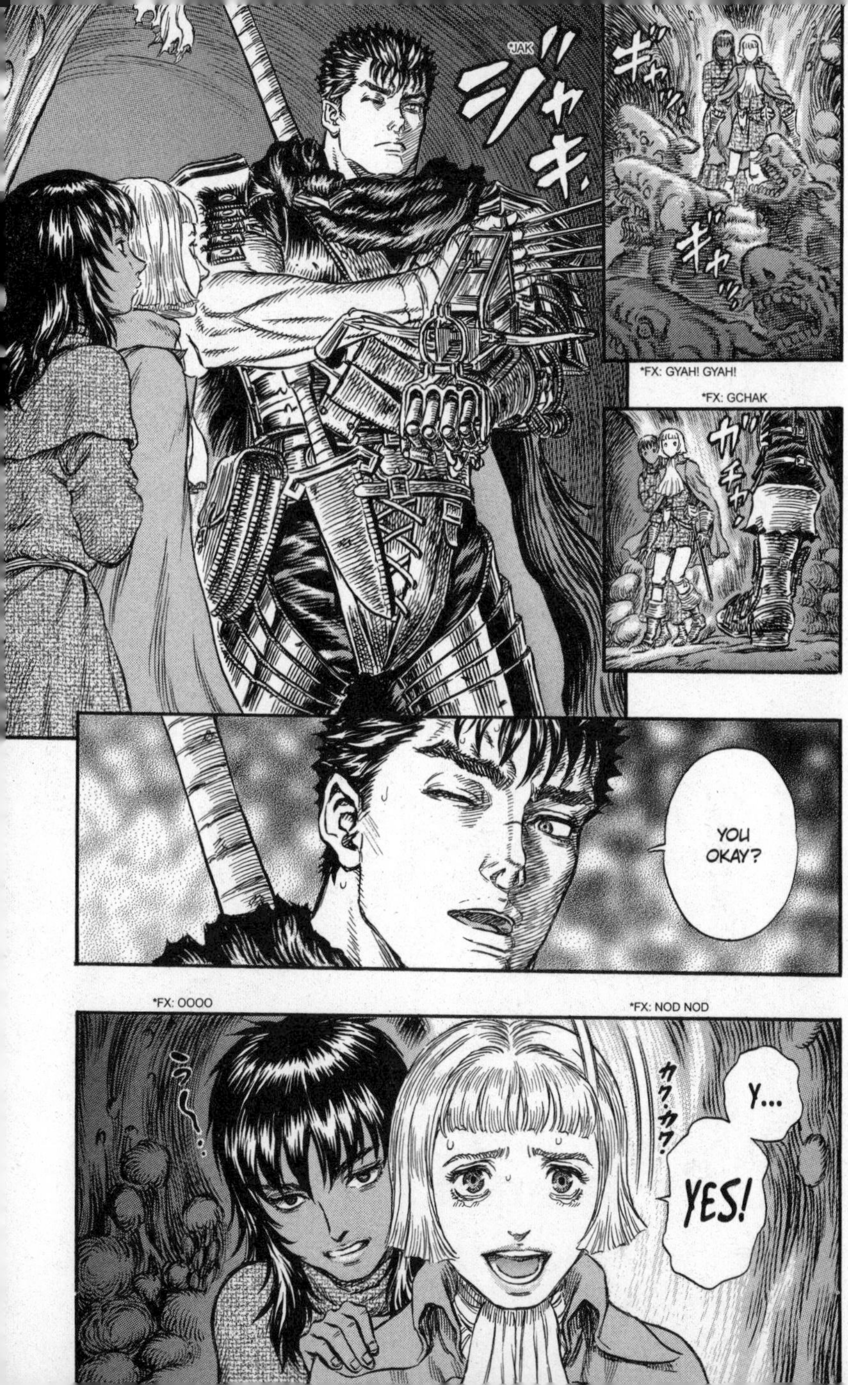
ギャッ
ギャッ
*FX: GYAH! GYAH!
ガチャッ
*FX: GCHAK
ジャキ
*JAK
YOU OKAY?
Y...
YES!
カクカク
*FX: NOD NOD
*FX: OOOO

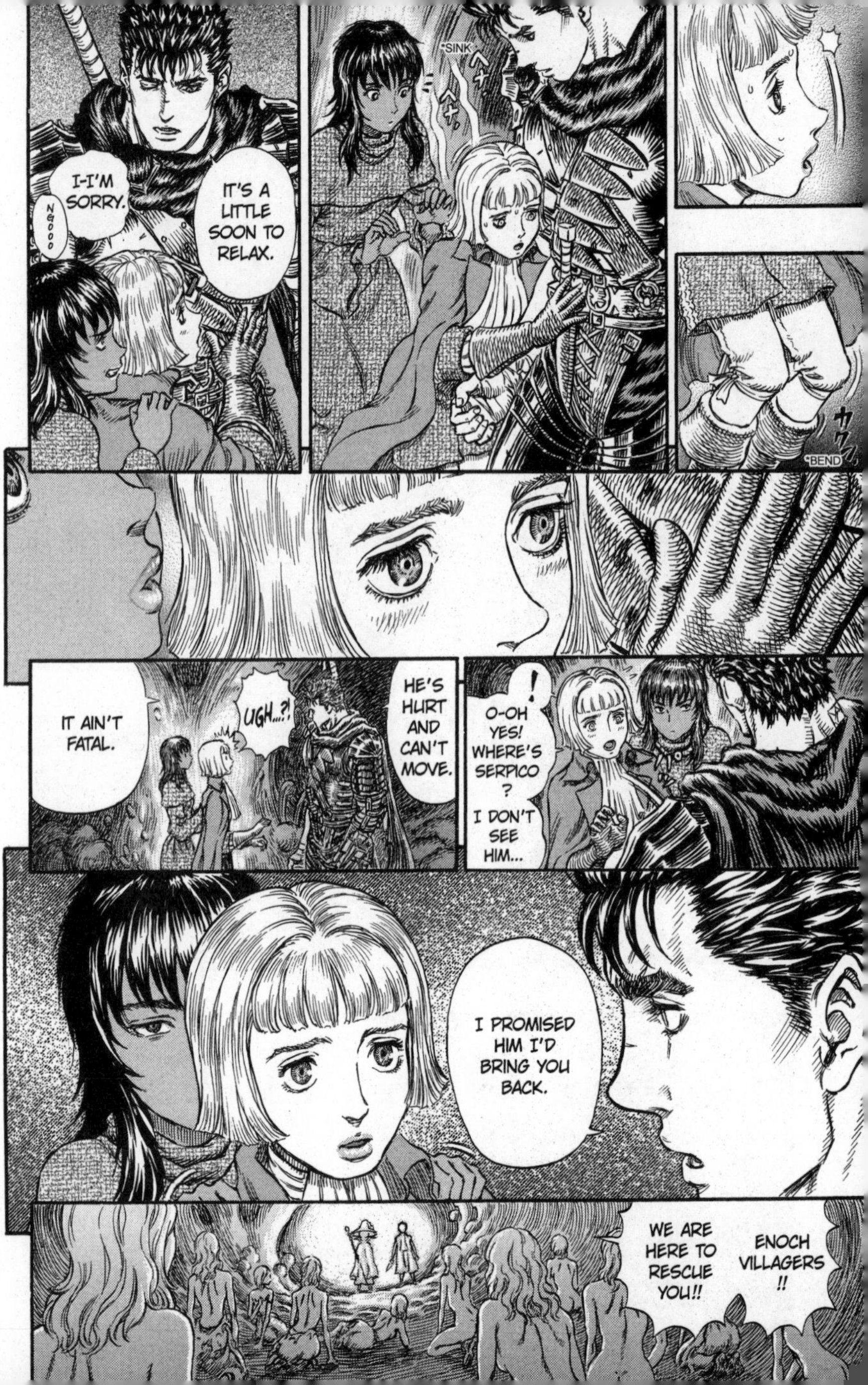

カク
*BEND
*SINK
IT'S A LITTLE SOON TO RELAX.
I-I'M SORRY.
NGOOO
!
O-OH YES! WHERE'S SERPICO?
I DON'T SEE HIM...
HE'S HURT AND CAN'T MOVE.
UGH...?!
IT AIN'T FATAL.
I PROMISED HIM I'D BRING YOU BACK.
ENOCH VILLAGERS!!
WE ARE HERE TO RESCUE YOU!!

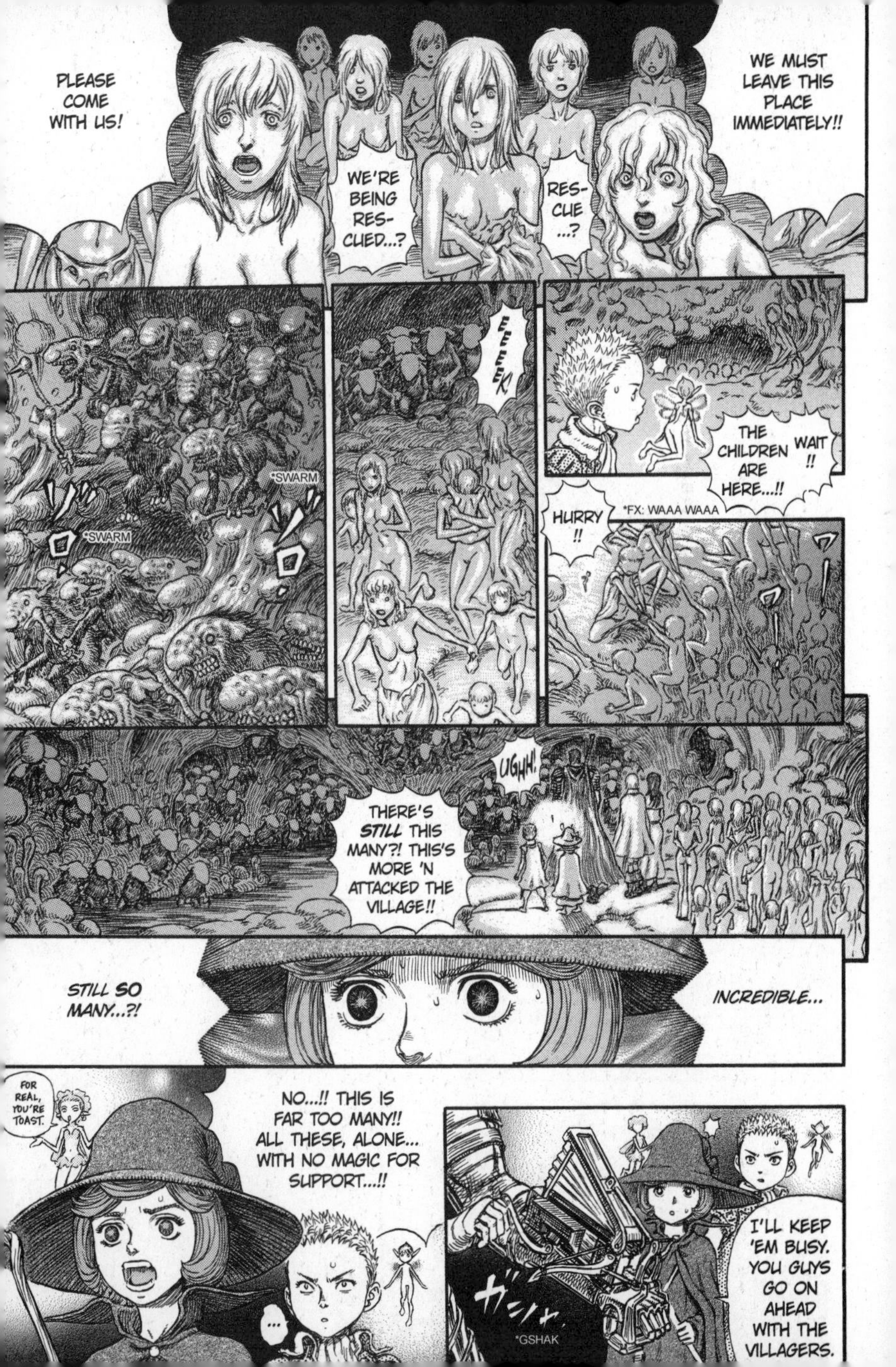

WE MUST LEAVE THIS PLACE IMMEDIATELY!!
RES-CUE ...?
WE'RE BEING RES-CUED...?
PLEASE COME WITH US!
WAIT !!
THE CHILDREN ARE HERE...!!
HURRY !!
*FX: WAAA WAAA
EEEEEK!
*SWARM
*SWARM
UGHH!
THERE'S STILL THIS MANY?! THIS'S MORE 'N ATTACKED THE VILLAGE!!
INCREDIBLE...
STILL SO MANY...?!
I'LL KEEP 'EM BUSY. YOU GUYS GO ON AHEAD WITH THE VILLAGERS.
*GSHAK
NO...!! THIS IS FAR TOO MANY!! ALL THESE, ALONE... WITH NO MAGIC FOR SUPPORT...!!
FOR REAL, YOU'RE TOAST.
...

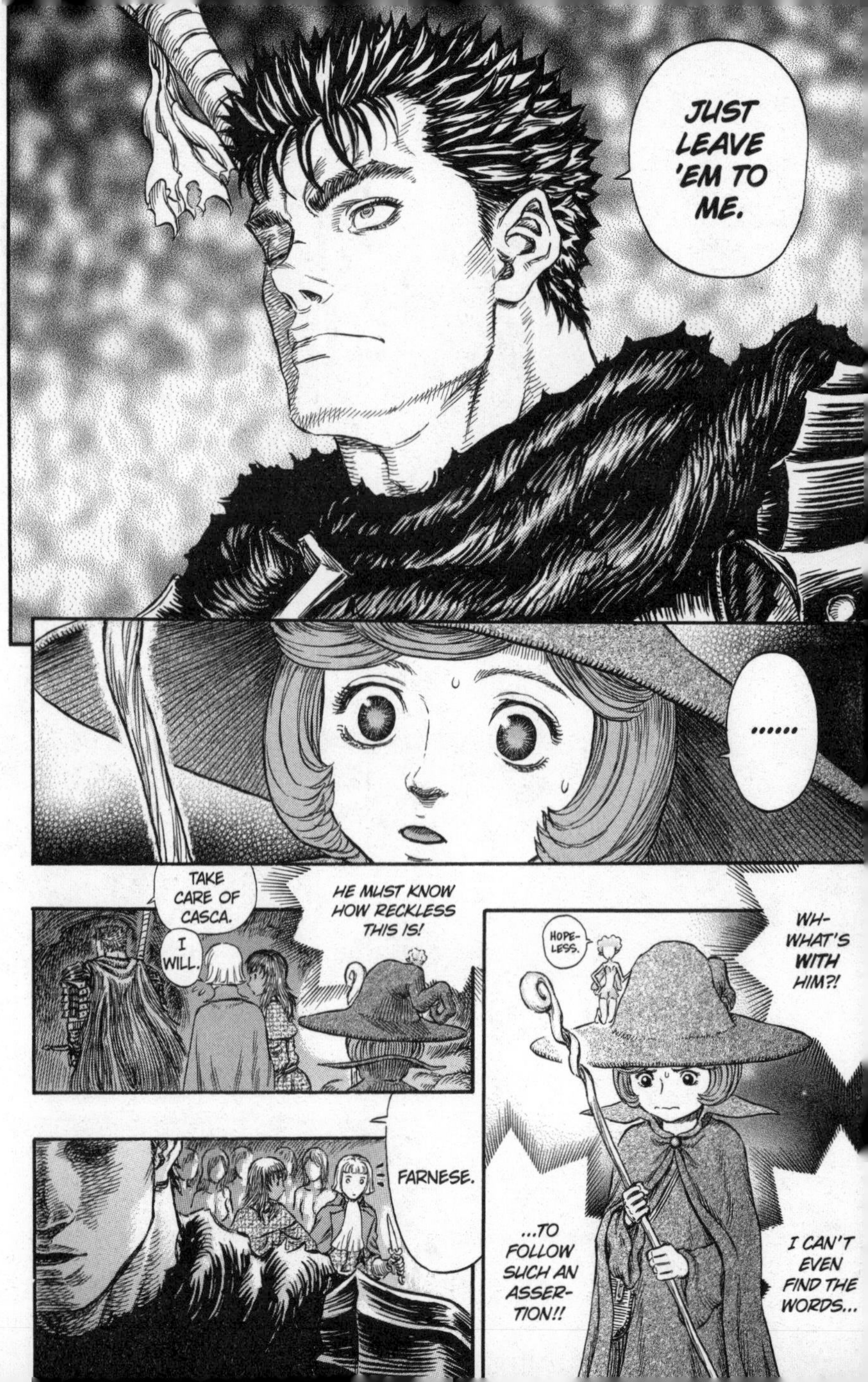
JUST LEAVE 'EM TO ME.
......
WH-WHAT'S WITH HIM?!
HOPE-LESS.
I CAN'T EVEN FIND THE WORDS...
...TO FOLLOW SUCH AN ASSER-TION!!
HE MUST KNOW HOW RECKLESS THIS IS!
TAKE CARE OF CASCA.
I WILL.
FARNESE.

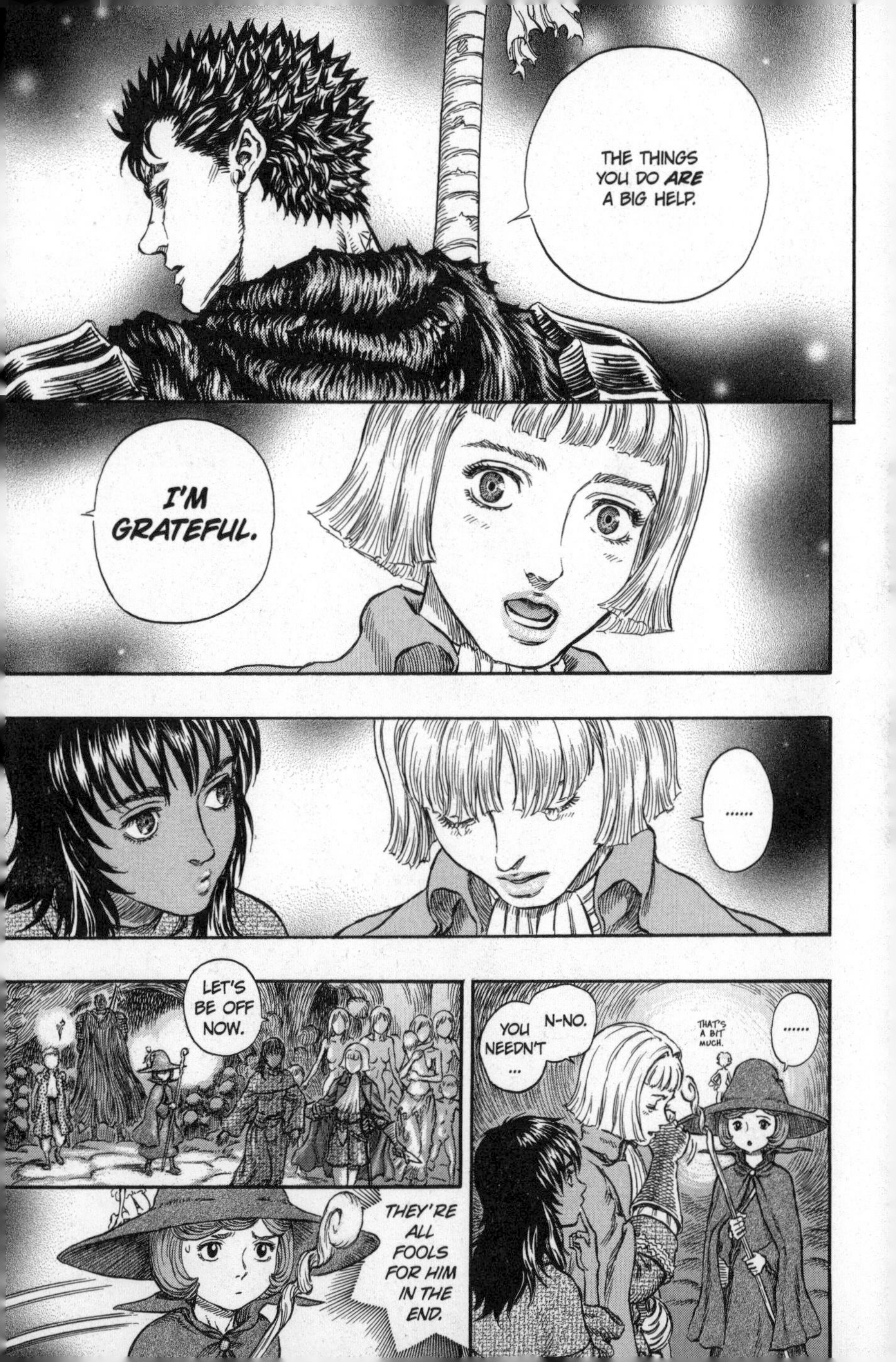
THE THINGS YOU DO *ARE* A BIG HELP.
I'M GRATEFUL.
......
......
THAT'S A BIT MUCH.
N-NO. YOU NEEDN'T ...
LET'S BE OFF NOW.
THEY'RE ALL FOOLS FOR HIM IN THE END.

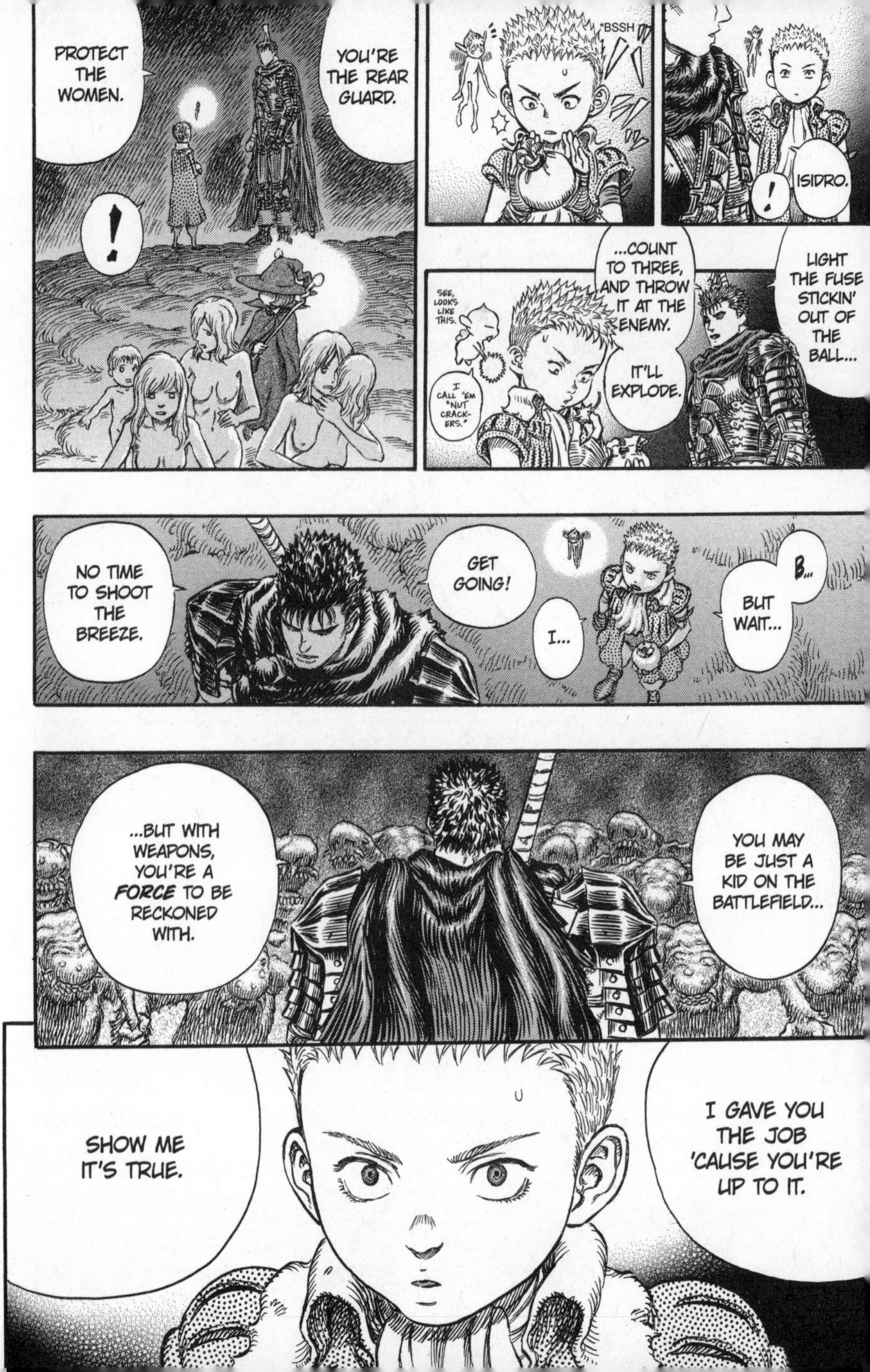
ISIDRO.
!
*BSSH
LIGHT THE FUSE STICKIN' OUT OF THE BALL...
...COUNT TO THREE, AND THROW IT AT THE ENEMY.
IT'LL EXPLODE.
SEE, LOOKS LIKE THIS.
I CALL 'EM "NUT CRACKERS."
YOU'RE THE REAR GUARD.
PROTECT THE WOMEN.
!
B...
BUT WAIT...
I...
GET GOING!
NO TIME TO SHOOT THE BREEZE.
YOU MAY BE JUST A KID ON THE BATTLEFIELD...
...BUT WITH WEAPONS, YOU'RE A FORCE TO BE RECKONED WITH.
I GAVE YOU THE JOB 'CAUSE YOU'RE UP TO IT.
SHOW ME IT'S TRUE.

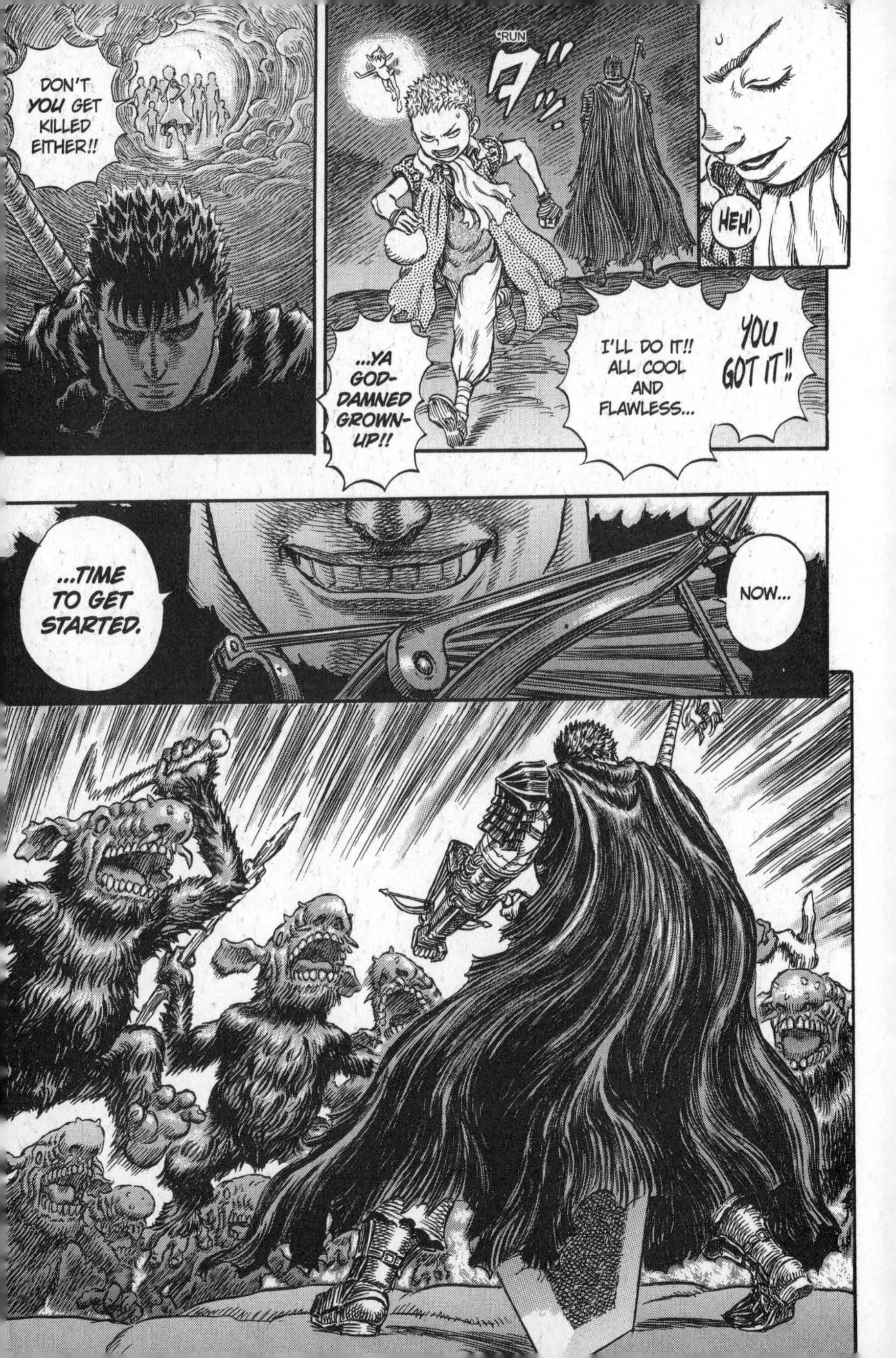
HEH!
*RUN
ダッ
YOU GOT IT!!
I'LL DO IT!! ALL COOL AND FLAWLESS...
...YA GOD-DAMNED GROWN-UP!!
DON'T YOU GET KILLED EITHER!!
NOW...
...TIME TO GET STARTED.

REDEMPTION
報い（すくい）

BERSERK

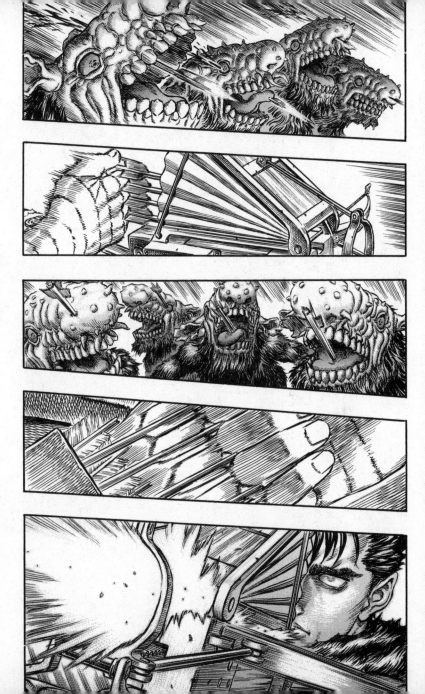

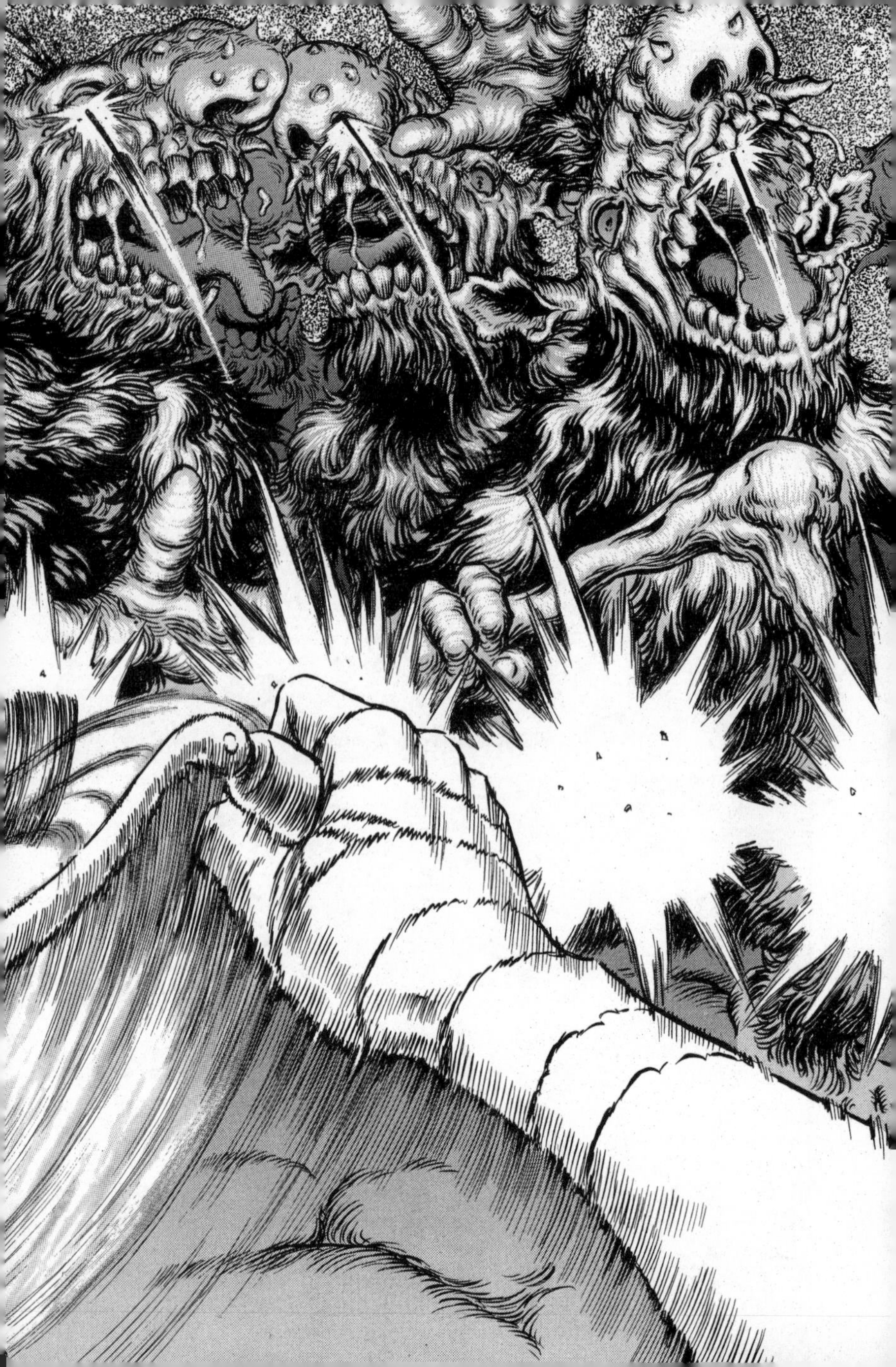

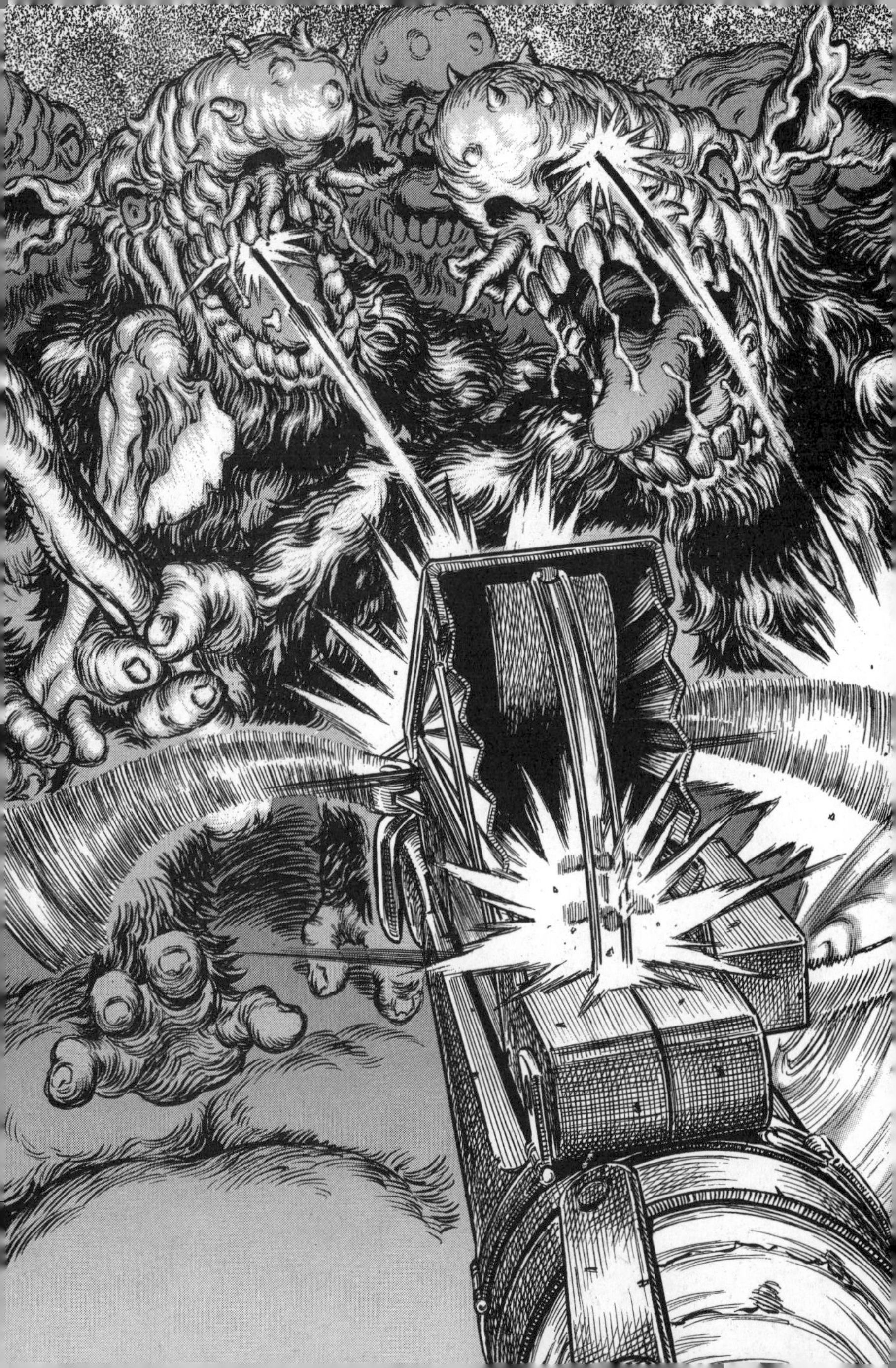

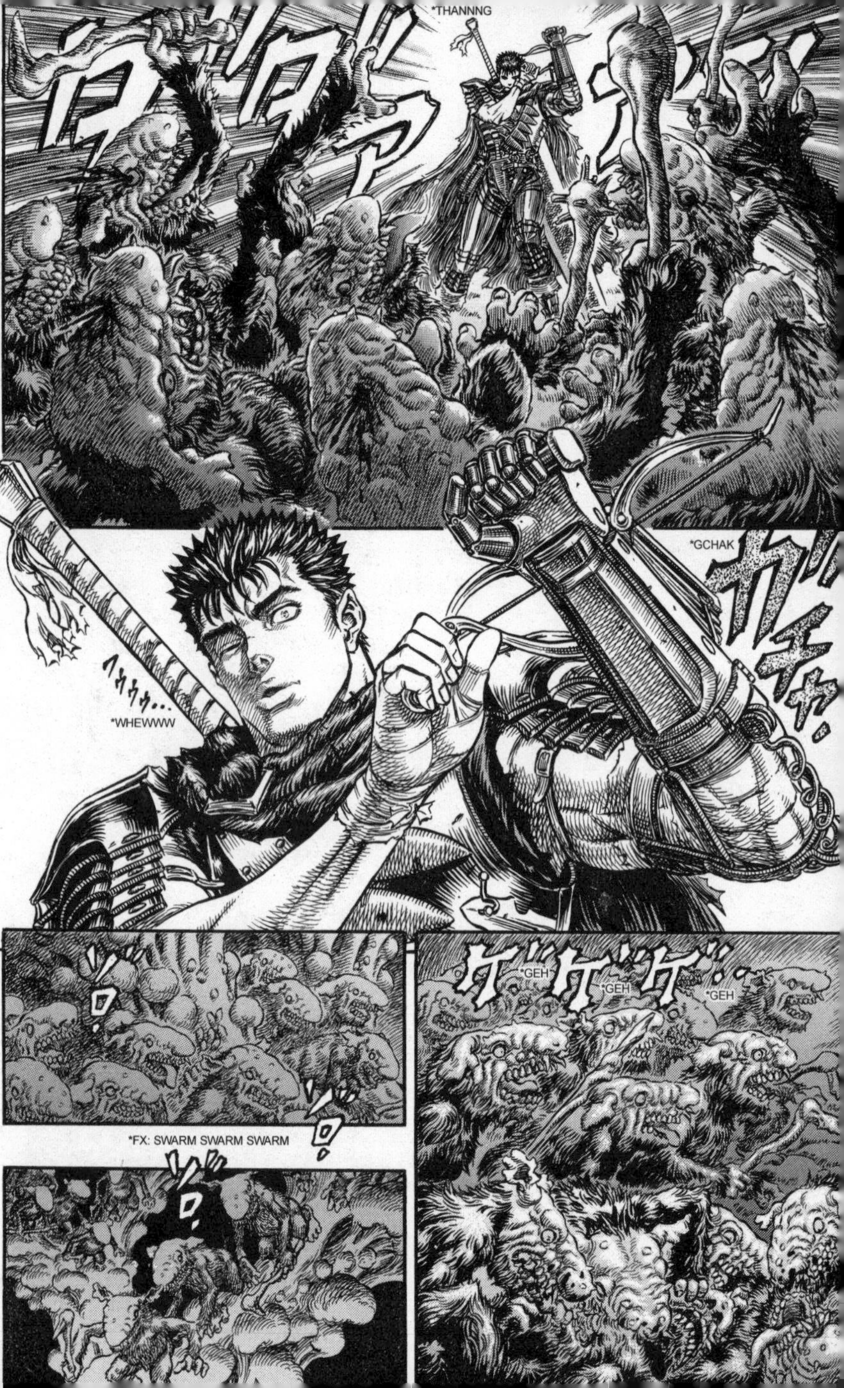
*THANNNG
*GCHAK
*WHEWWW
*GEH
*GEH
*GEH
*FX: SWARM SWARM SWARM

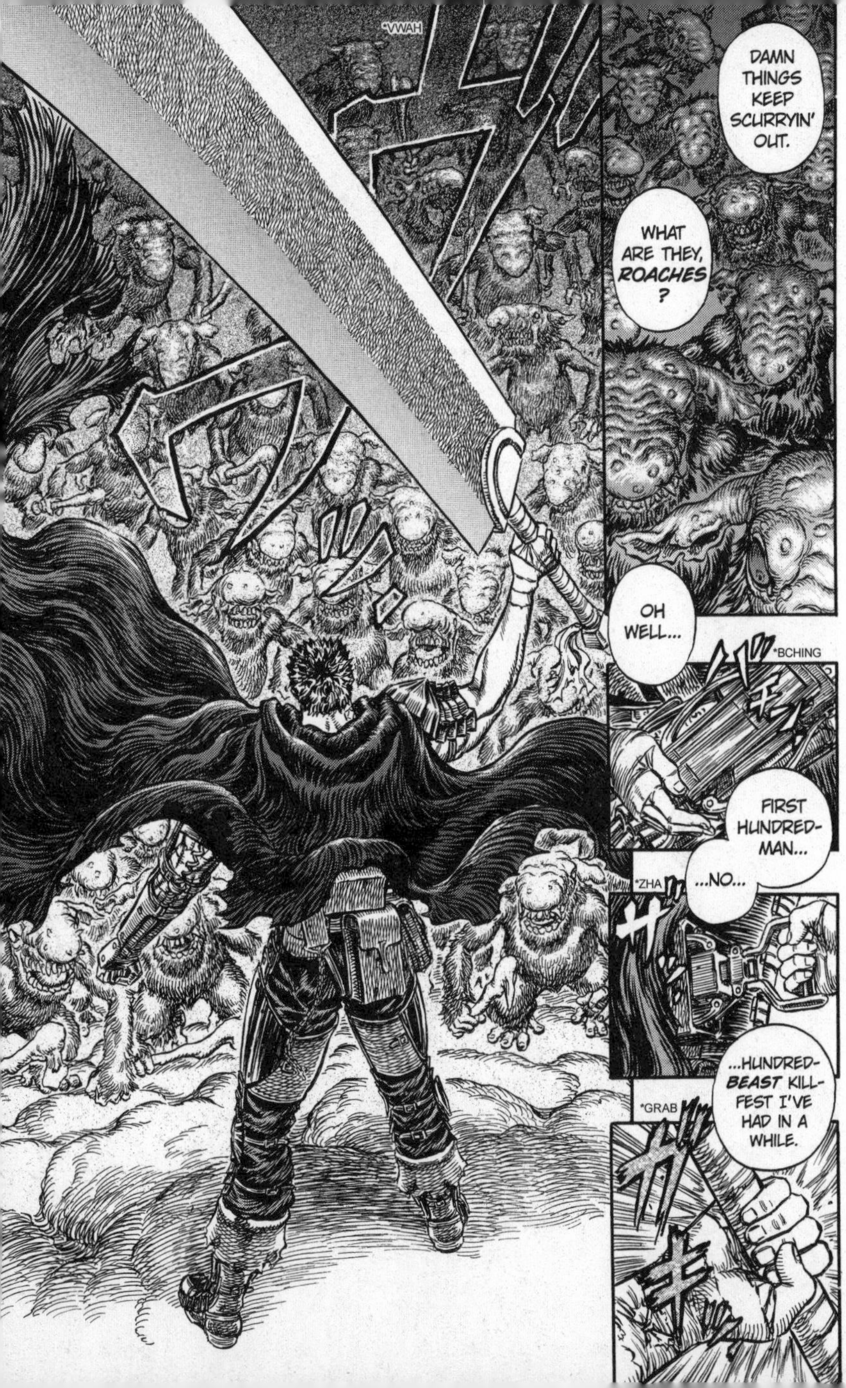
DAMN THINGS KEEP SCURRYIN' OUT.
WHAT ARE THEY, *ROACHES*?
OH WELL...
*BCHING
FIRST HUNDRED-MAN...
*ZHA
...NO...
*GRAB
...HUNDRED-*BEAST* KILL-FEST I'VE HAD IN A WHILE.
*VWAH

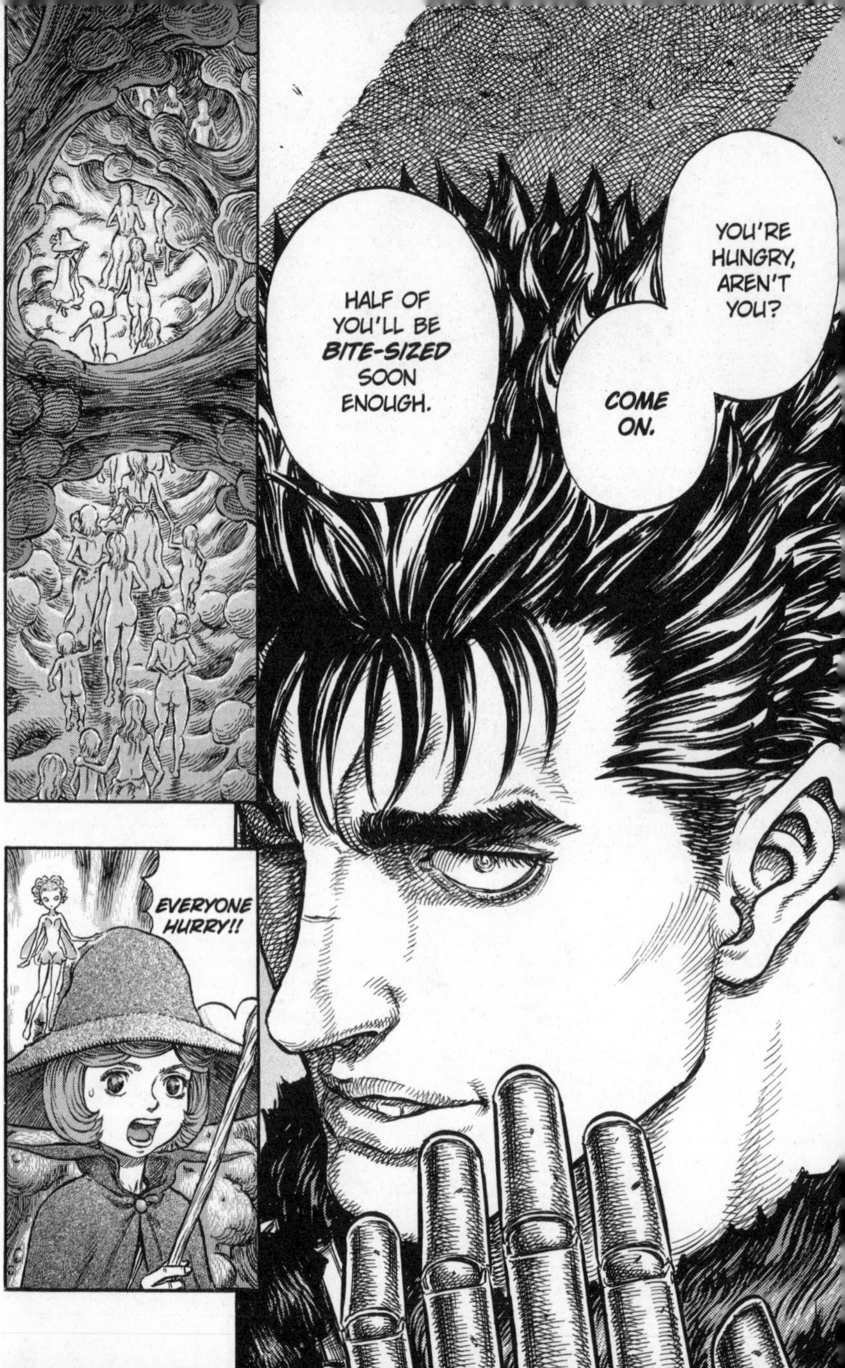
YOU'RE HUNGRY, AREN'T YOU?
COME ON.
HALF OF YOU'LL BE BITE-SIZED SOON ENOUGH.
EVERYONE HURRY!!

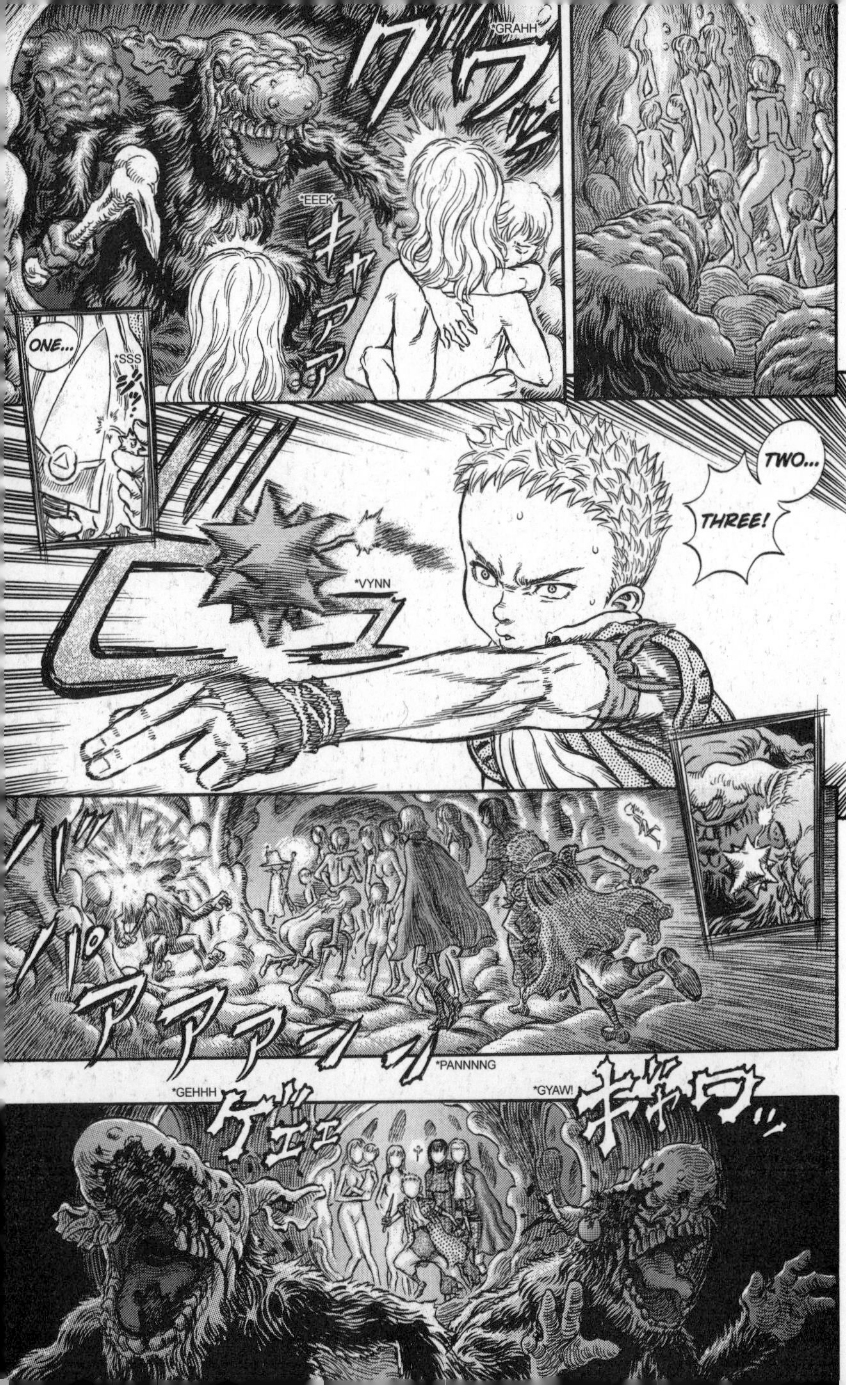

*GRAHH
*EEEK
ONE...
*SSS
TWO...
THREE!
*VYNN
*PANNNG
*GYAW!
*GEHHH

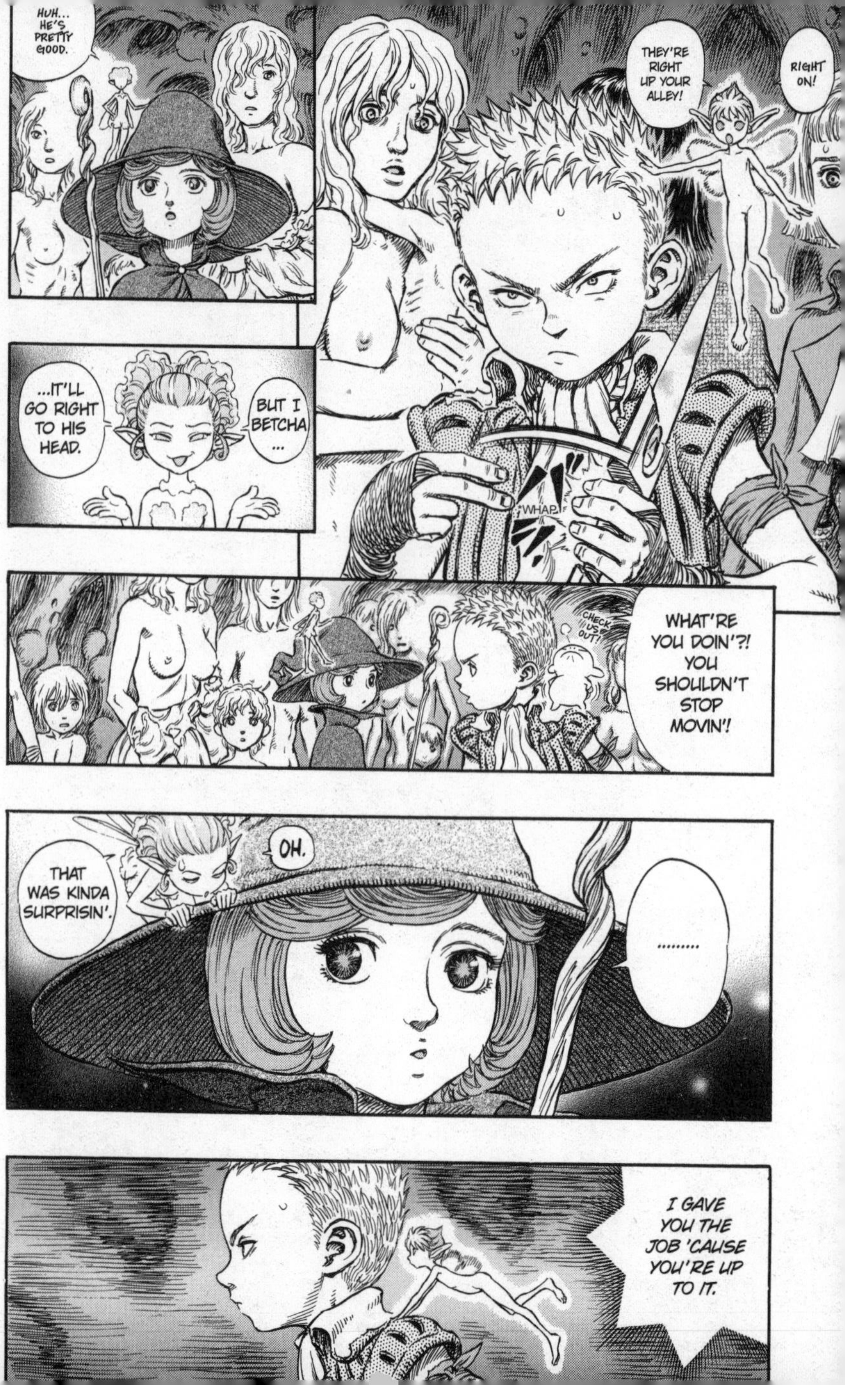
THEY'RE RIGHT UP YOUR ALLEY!
RIGHT ON!
WHAP
HUH... HE'S PRETTY GOOD.
BUT I BETCHA ...
...IT'LL GO RIGHT TO HIS HEAD.
WHAT'RE YOU DOIN'?! YOU SHOULDN'T STOP MOVIN'!
CHECK US OUT!
OH.
THAT WAS KINDA SURPRISIN'.
....
I GAVE YOU THE JOB 'CAUSE YOU'RE UP TO IT.

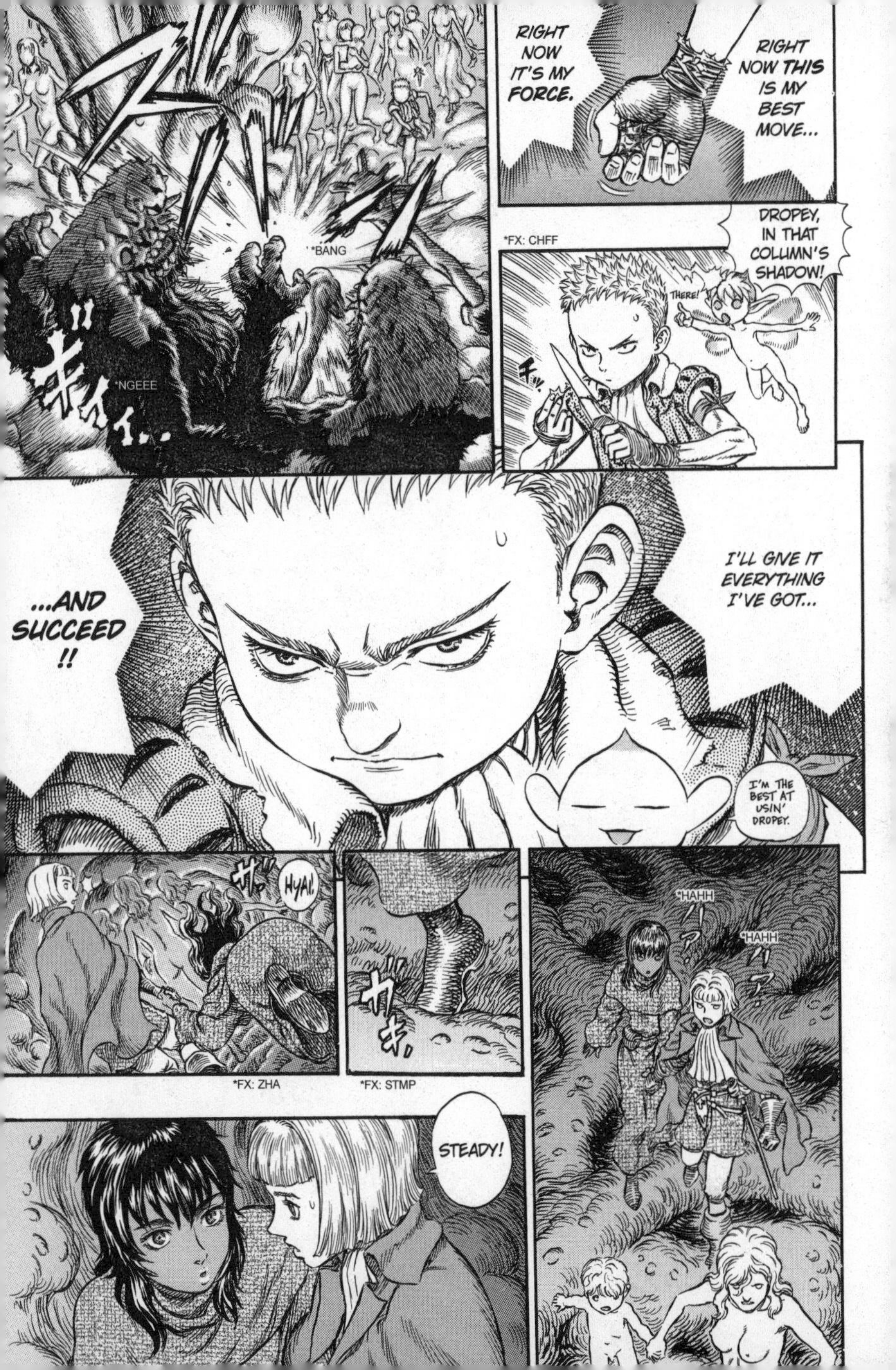
RIGHT NOW THIS IS MY BEST MOVE...
RIGHT NOW IT'S MY FORCE.
*FX: CHFF
DROPEY, IN THAT COLUMN'S SHADOW!
THERE!
*BANG
*NGEEE
I'LL GIVE IT EVERYTHING I'VE GOT...
...AND SUCCEED !!
I'M THE BEST AT USIN' DROPEY.
*HAHH
*HAHH
*FX: STMP
HYA!
*FX: ZHA
STEADY!

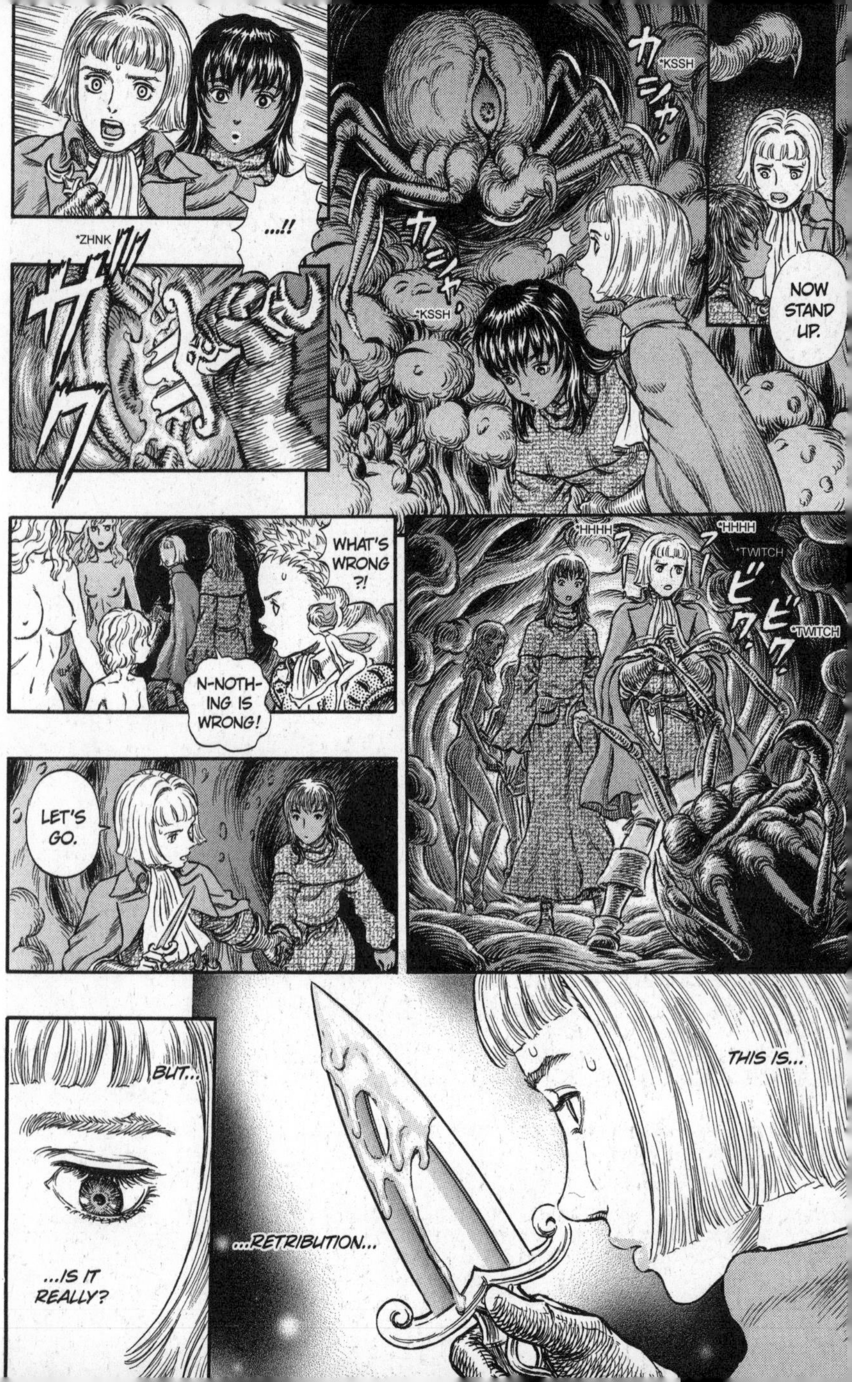
NOW STAND UP.
*KSSH
*KSSH
...!!
*ZHNK
*HHHH
*HHHH
*TWITCH
*TWITCH
WHAT'S WRONG?!
N-NOTHING IS WRONG!
LET'S GO.
THIS IS...
...RETRIBUTION...
BUT...
...IS IT REALLY?

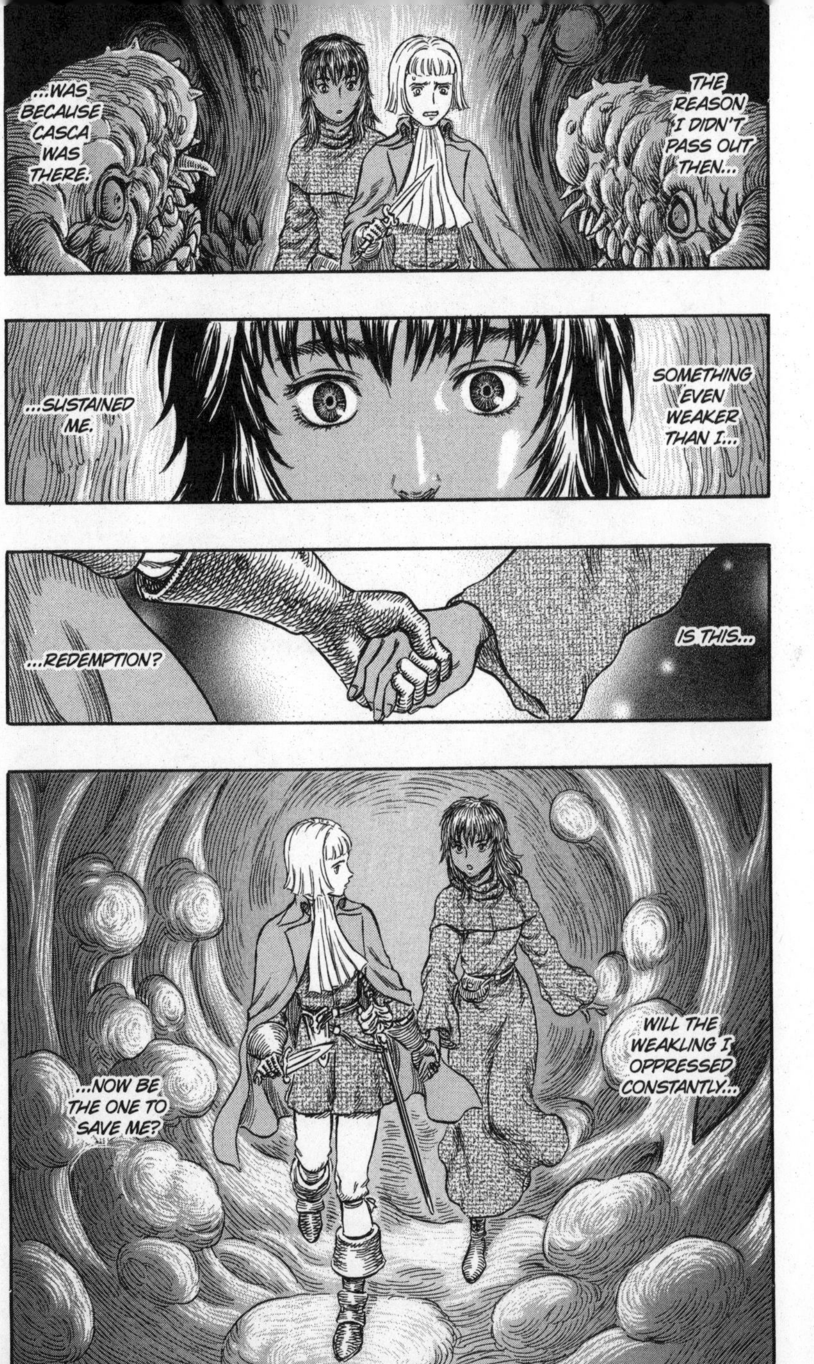
THE REASON I DIDN'T PASS OUT THEN...
...WAS BECAUSE CASCA WAS THERE.
SOMETHING EVEN WEAKER THAN I...
...SUSTAINED ME.
IS THIS...
...REDEMPTION?
WILL THE WEAKLING I OPPRESSED CONSTANTLY...
...NOW BE THE ONE TO SAVE ME?

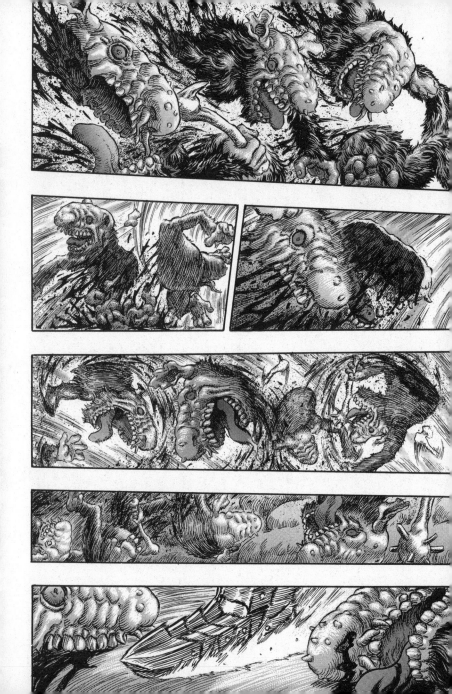

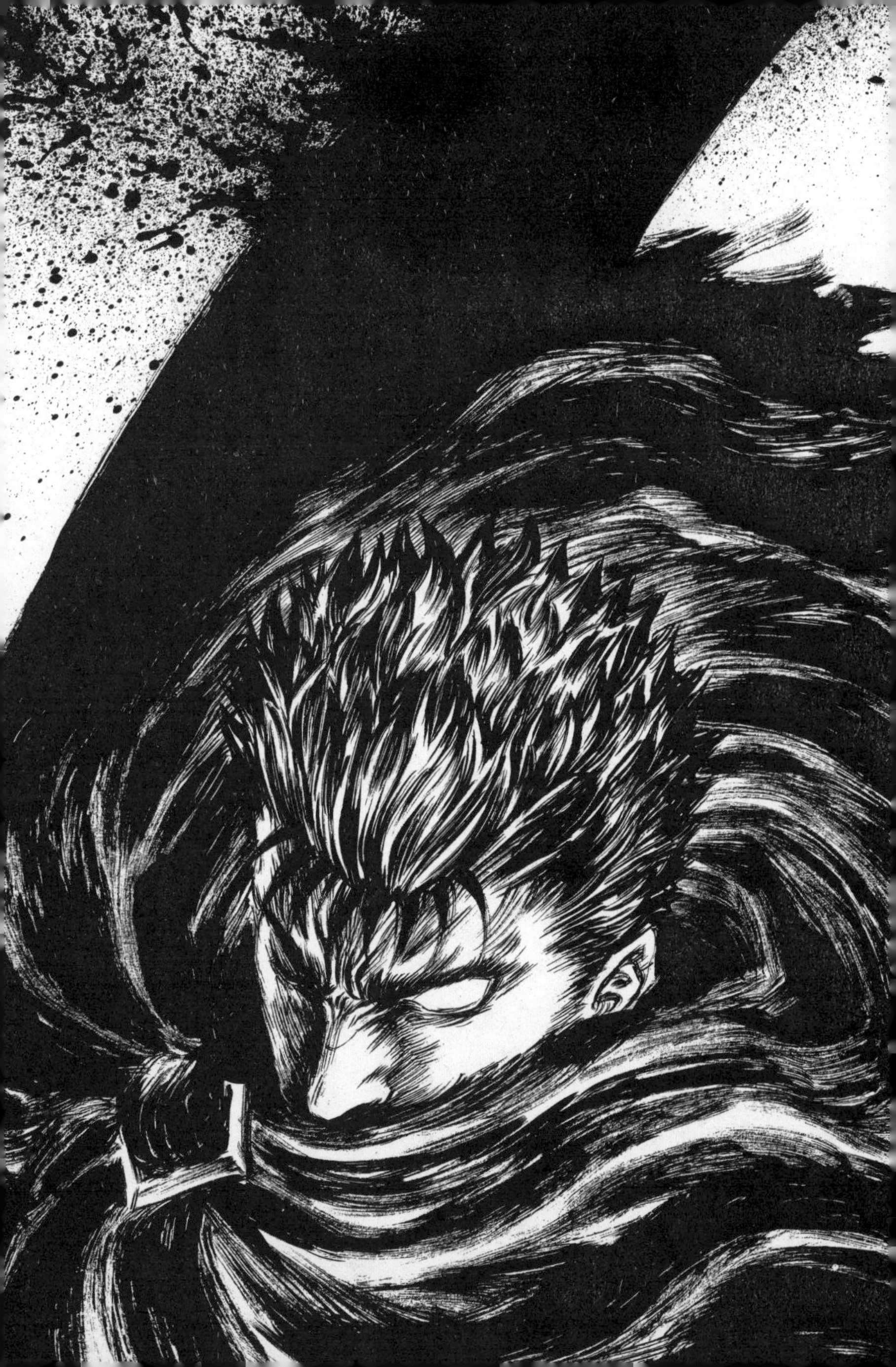

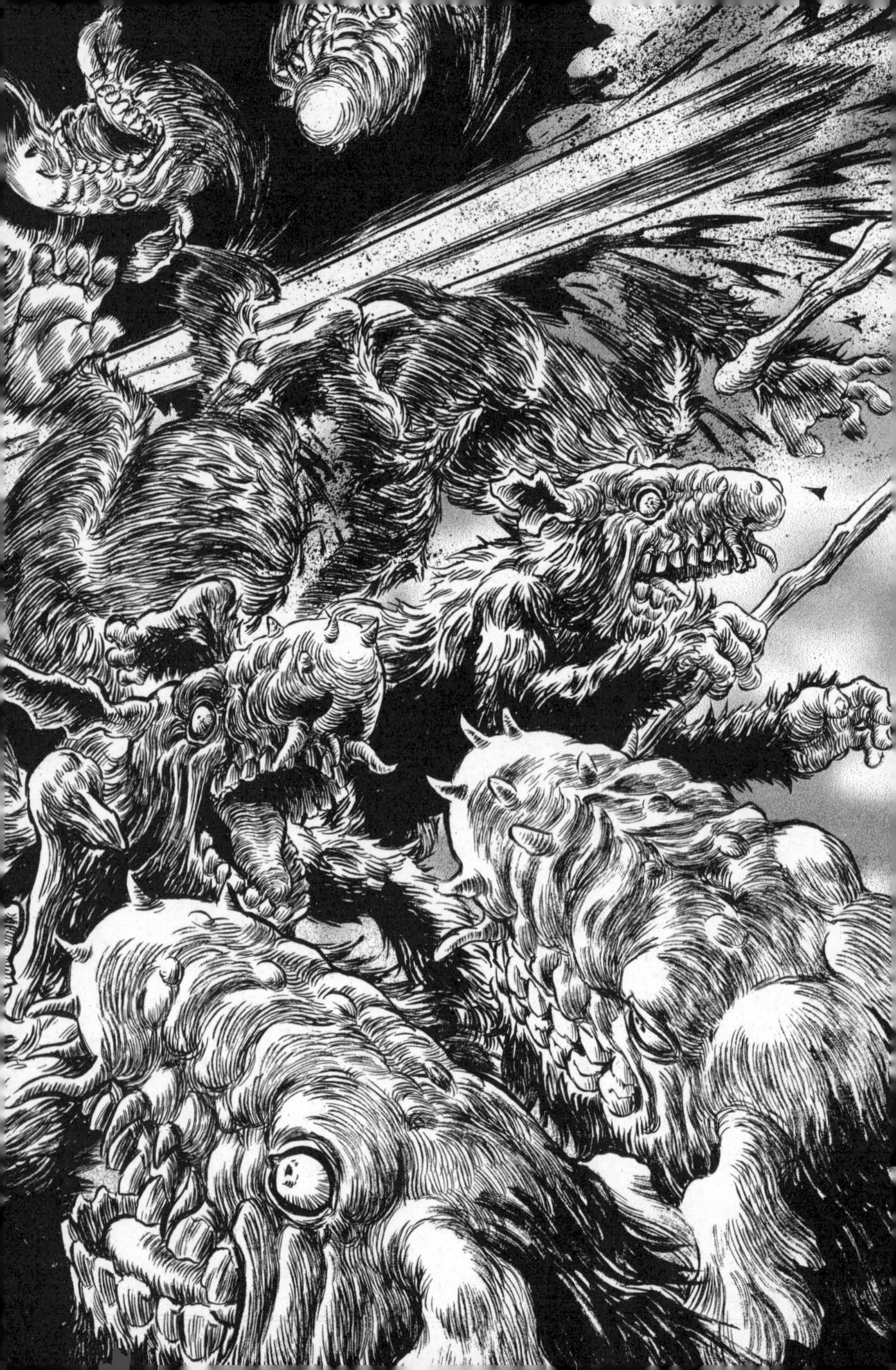

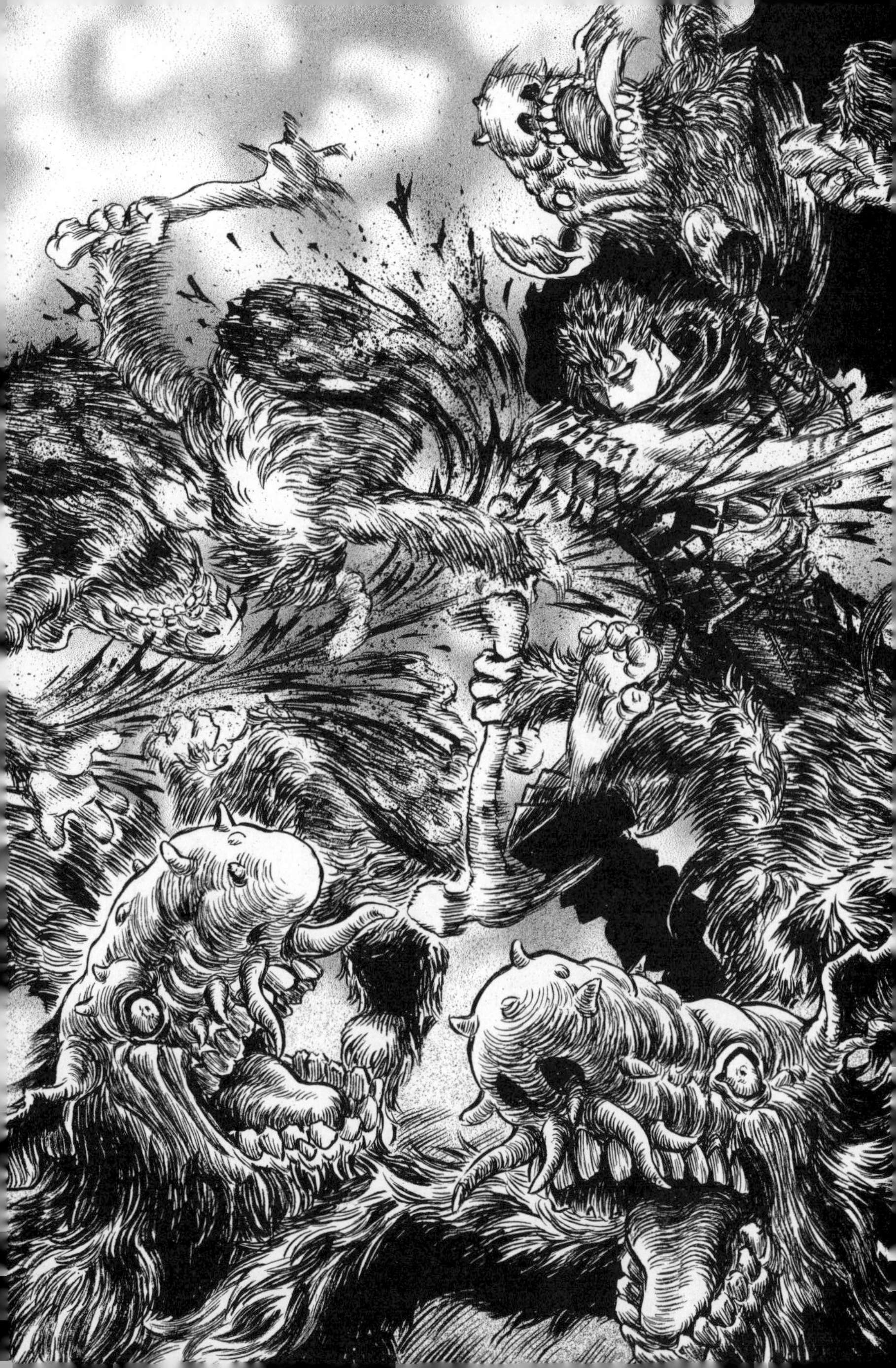

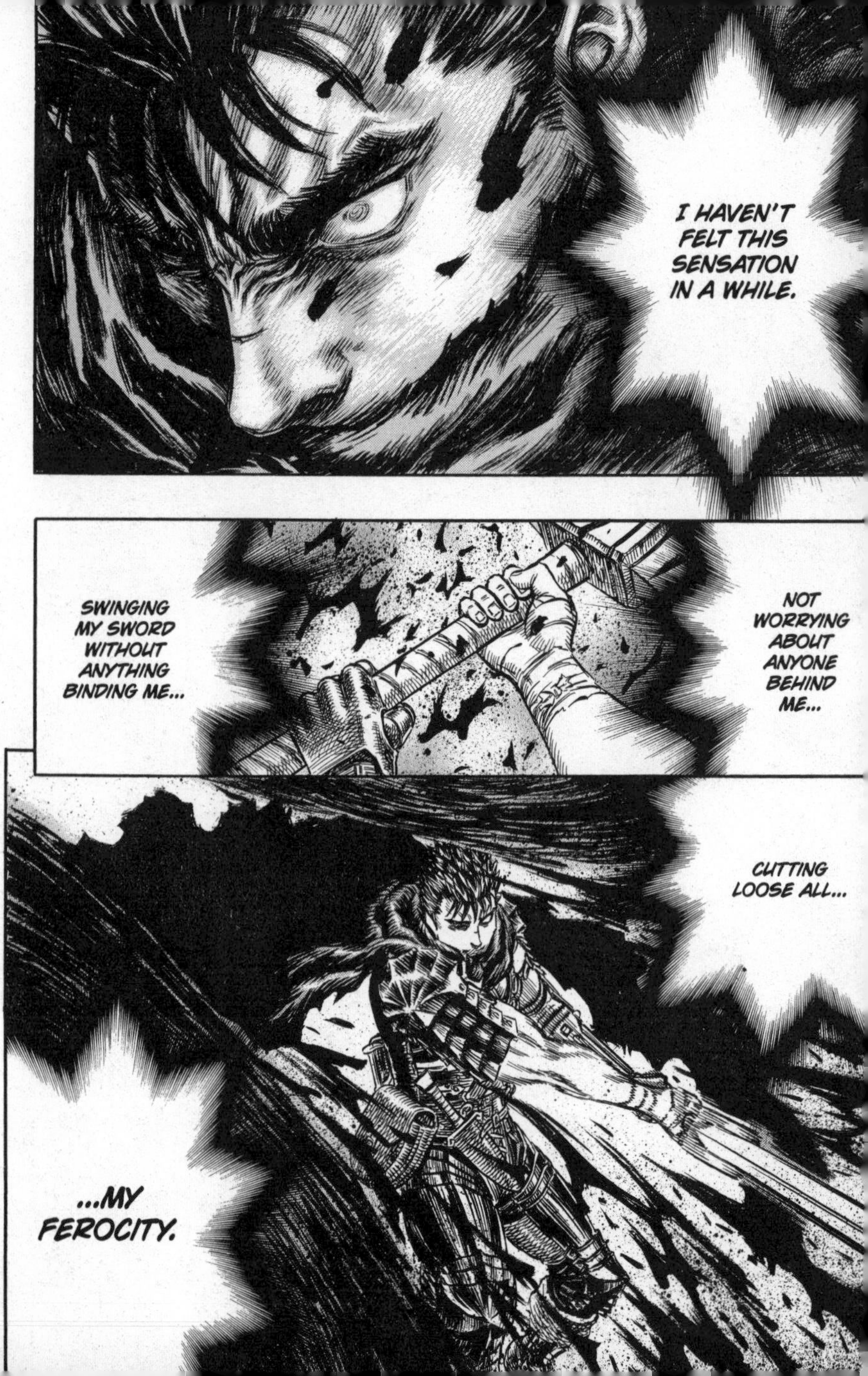
I HAVEN'T FELT THIS SENSATION IN A WHILE.
NOT WORRYING ABOUT ANYONE BEHIND ME...
SWINGING MY SWORD WITHOUT ANYTHING BINDING ME...
CUTTING LOOSE ALL...
...MY FEROCITY.

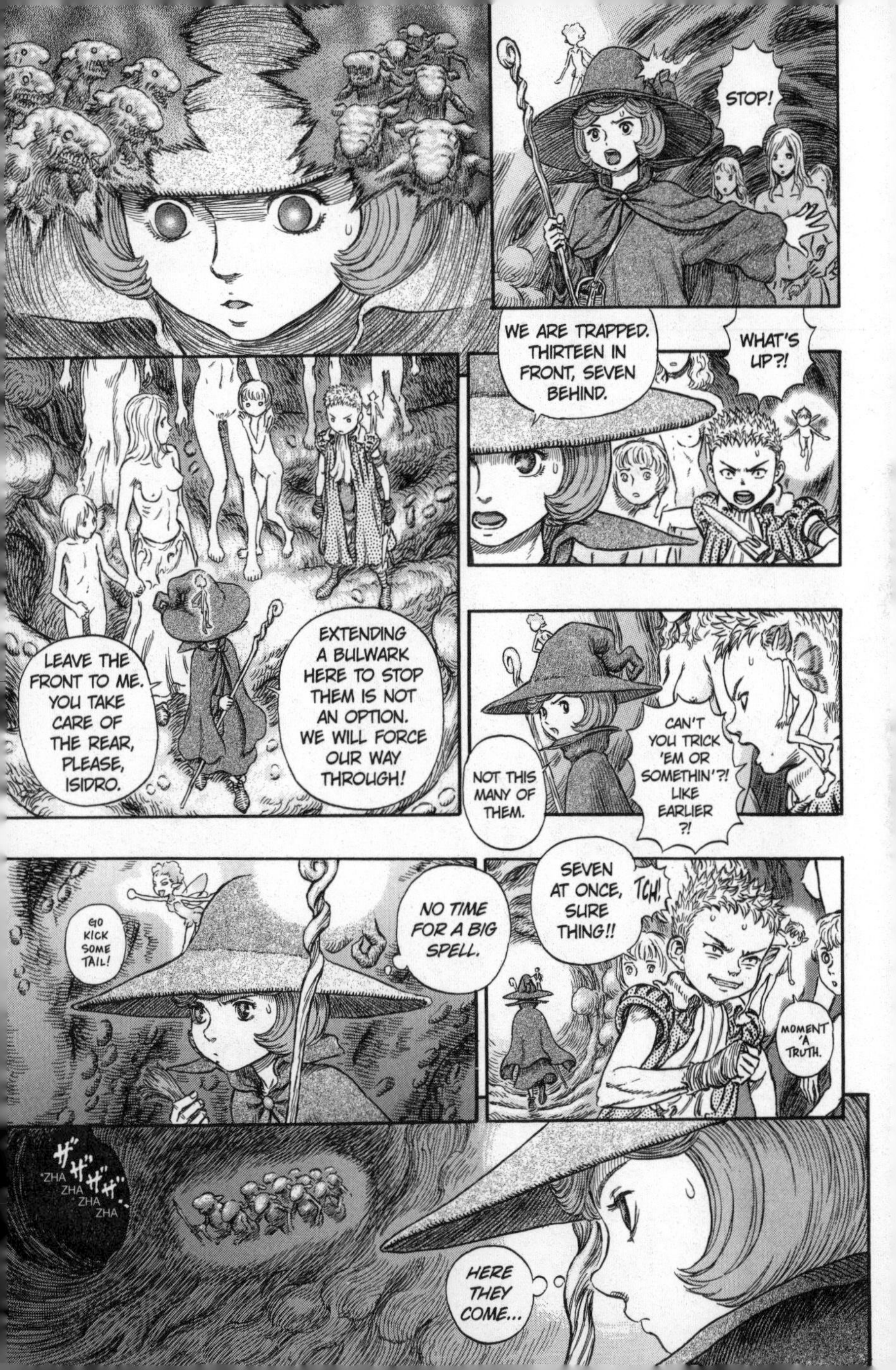
STOP!
WHAT'S UP?!
WE ARE TRAPPED. THIRTEEN IN FRONT, SEVEN BEHIND.
EXTENDING A BULWARK HERE TO STOP THEM IS NOT AN OPTION. WE WILL FORCE OUR WAY THROUGH!
LEAVE THE FRONT TO ME. YOU TAKE CARE OF THE REAR, PLEASE, ISIDRO.
CAN'T YOU TRICK 'EM OR SOMETHIN'?! LIKE EARLIER ?!
NOT THIS MANY OF THEM.
SEVEN AT ONCE, SURE THING!!
TCH!
MOMENT 'A TRUTH.
NO TIME FOR A BIG SPELL.
GO KICK SOME TAIL!
HERE THEY COME...
ザザザザ…
*ZHA ZHA ZHA ZHA

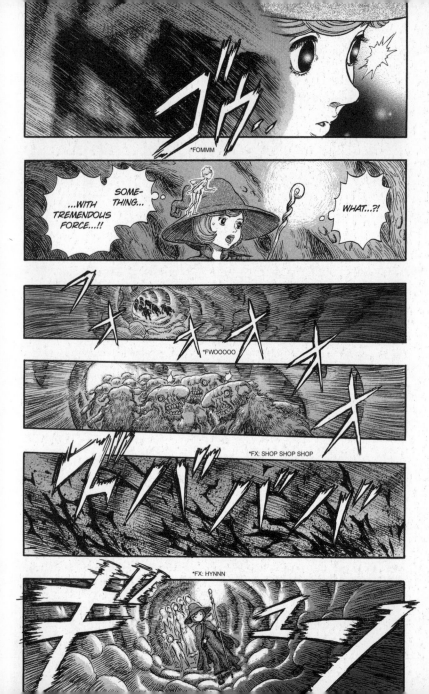

*FOMMM

...WITH TREMENDOUS FORCE...!!

SOME- THING...

WHAT...?!

*FWOOOOO

*FX: SHOP SHOP SHOP

*FX: HYNNN

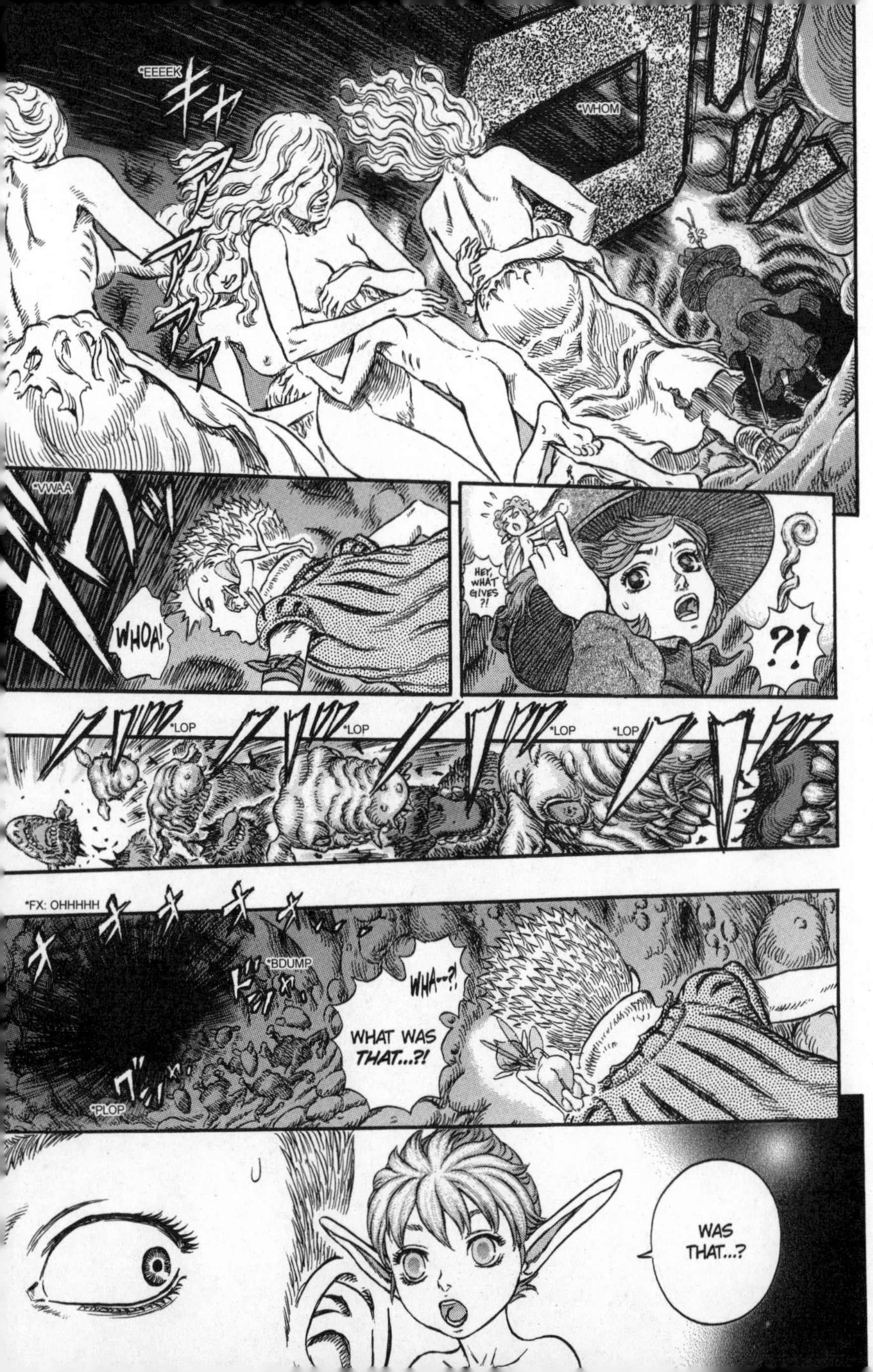
*WHOM
*EEEEK
?!
HEY, WHAT GIVES?!
*VWAA
WHOA!
*LOP
*LOP
*LOP
*LOP
WHA--?!
WHAT WAS THAT...?!
*FX: OHHHHH
*BDUMP
*PLOP
WAS THAT...?

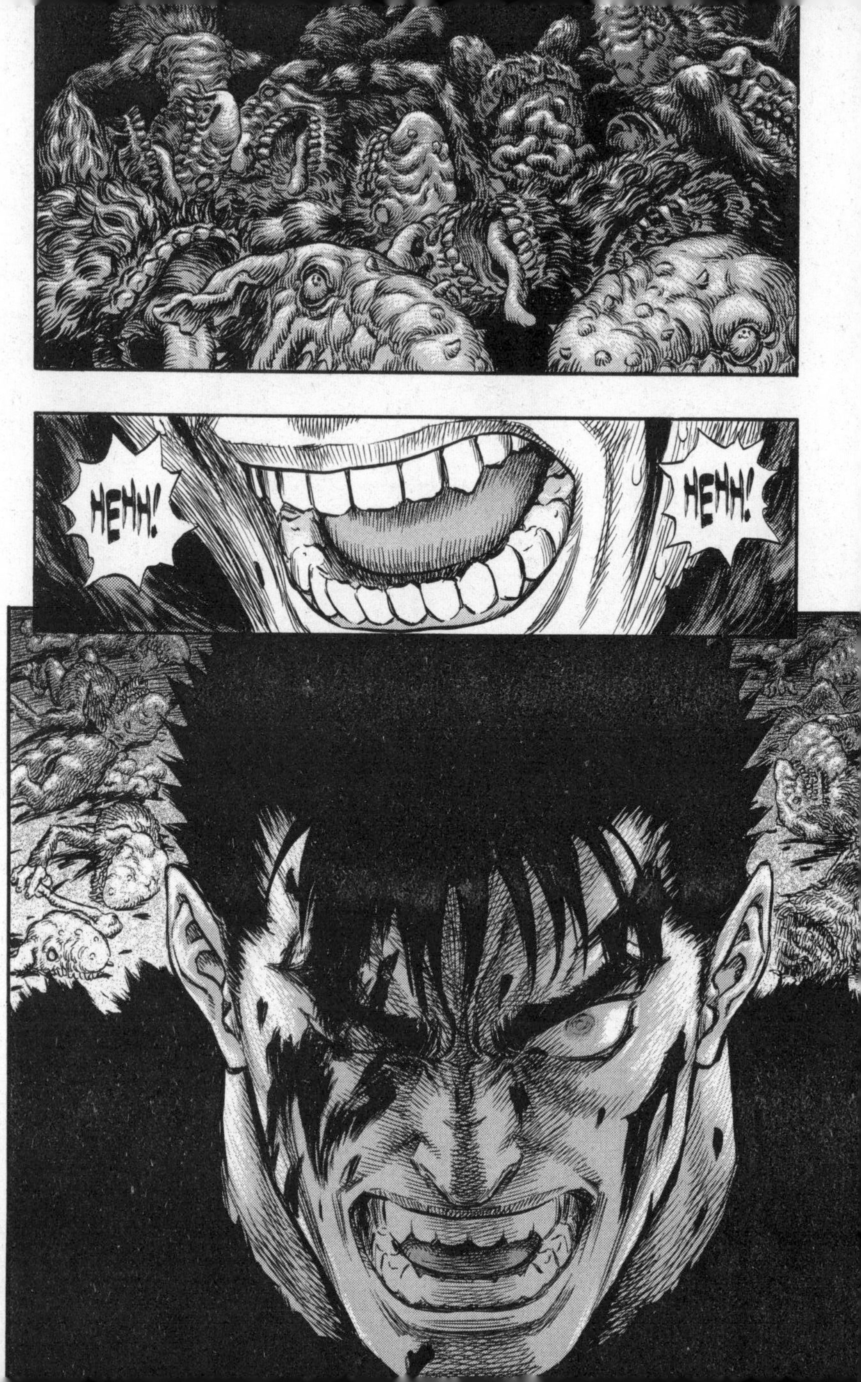
HEHH!
HEHH!

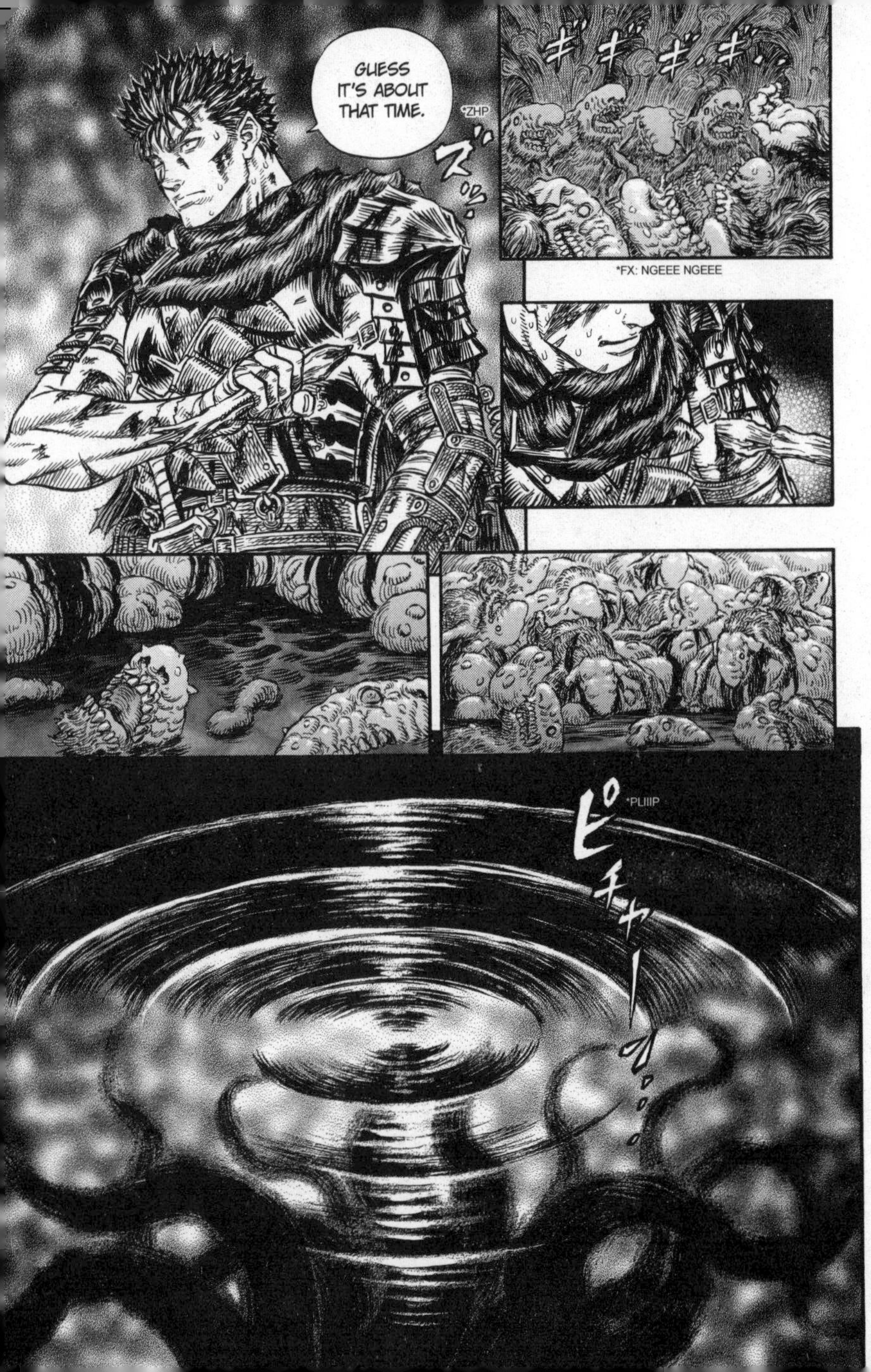
*FX: NGEEE NGEEE
GUESS IT'S ABOUT THAT TIME.
*ZHP
*PLIIIP

VICINITY OF THE
NETHERWORLD
黄泉のほとり

BERSERK

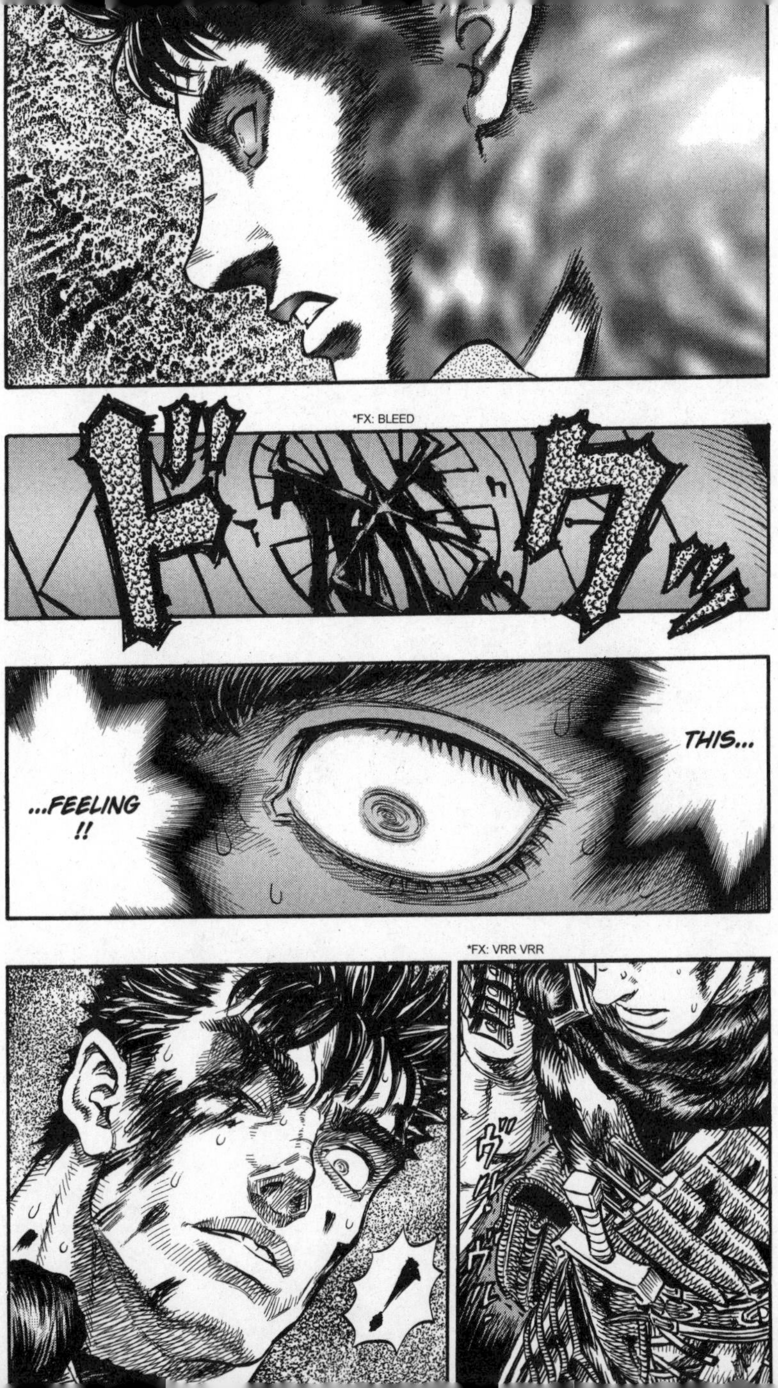
*FX: BLEED
THIS...
...FEELING !!
*FX: VRR VRR
!

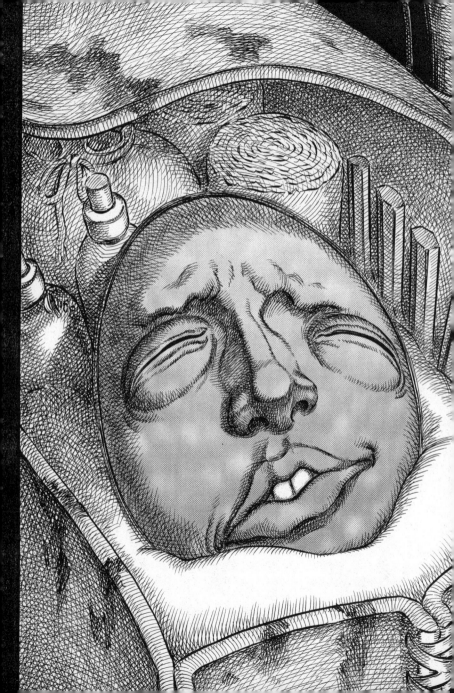

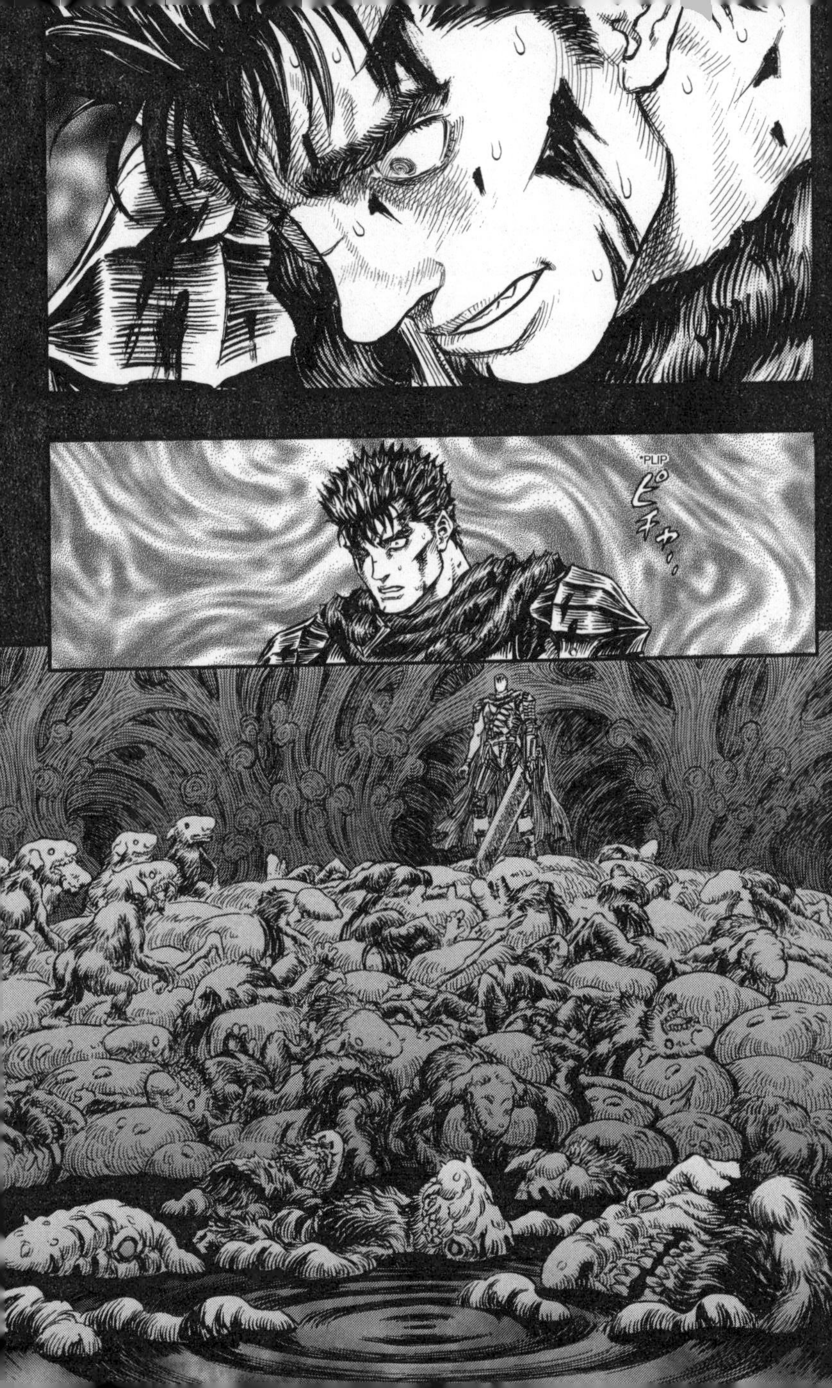
*PLIP
ピチャ

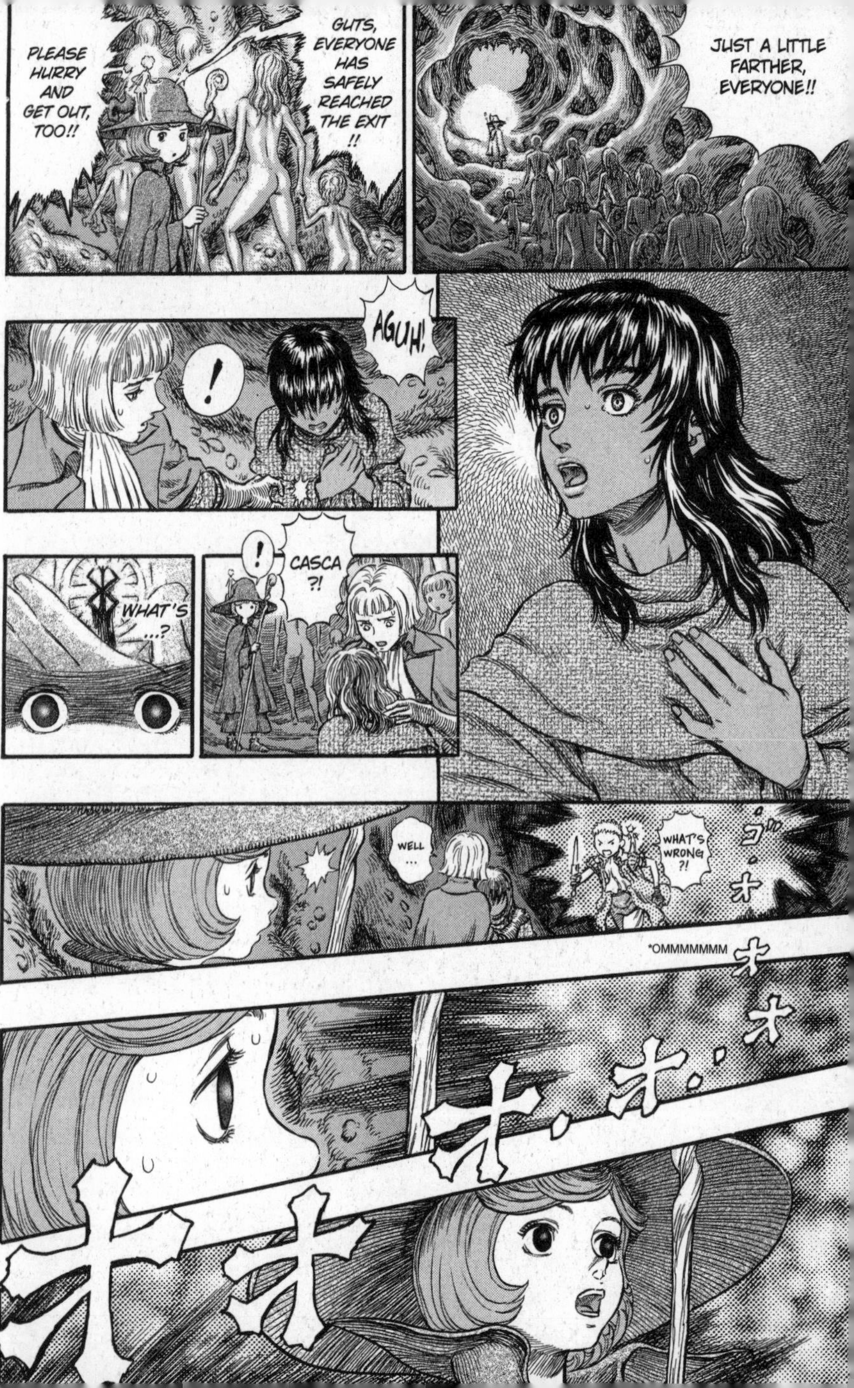
JUST A LITTLE FARTHER, EVERYONE!!
GUTS, EVERYONE HAS SAFELY REACHED THE EXIT!!
PLEASE HURRY AND GET OUT, TOO!!
AGUH!
!
!
CASCA?!
WHAT'S ...?
WHAT'S WRONG?!
WELL ...
*OMMMMMMM

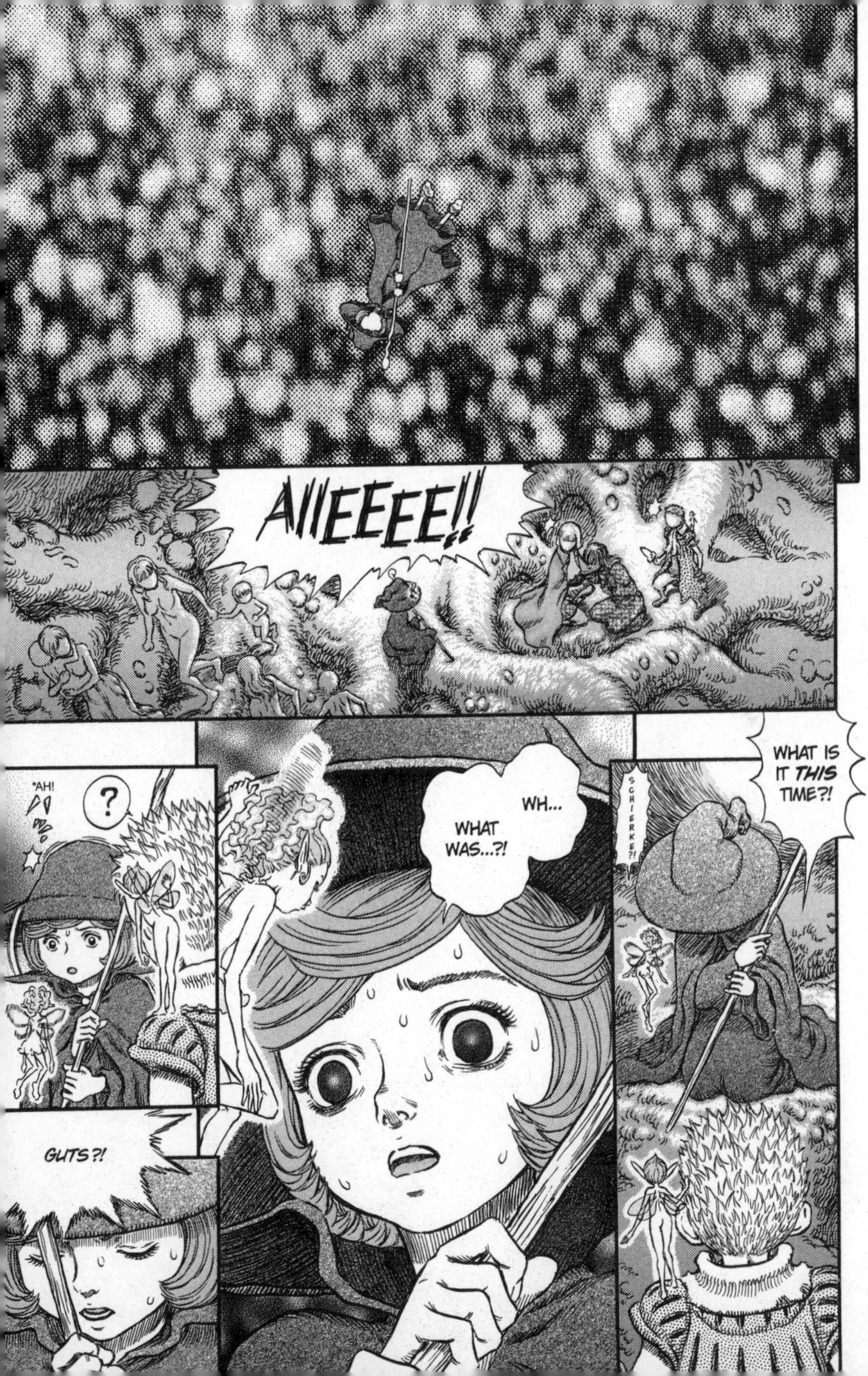
AIIEEEE!!
SCHIERKE?!
WHAT IS IT THIS TIME?!
WH... WHAT WAS...?!
*AH!
?
GUTS?!

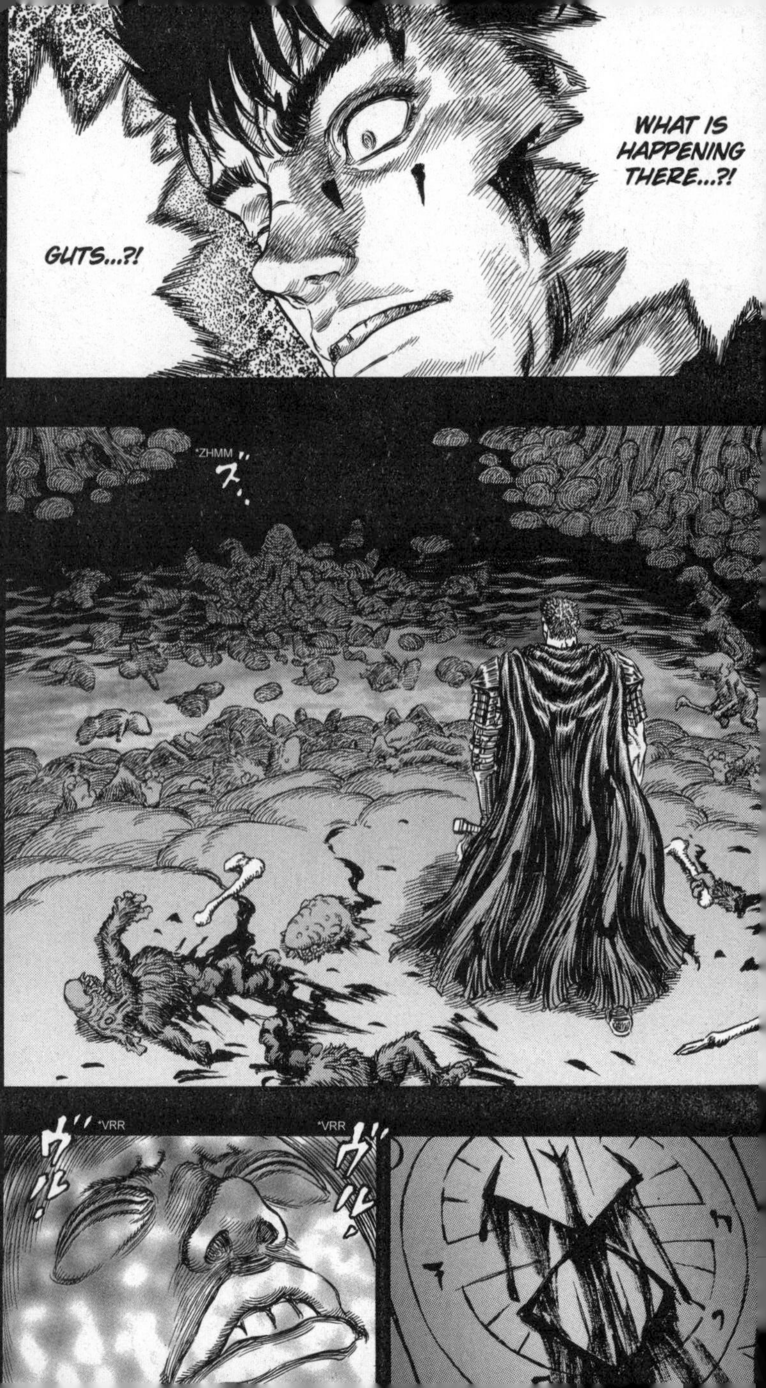
WHAT IS HAPPENING THERE...?!
GUTS...?!
*ZHMM
ズ
*VRR
*VRR

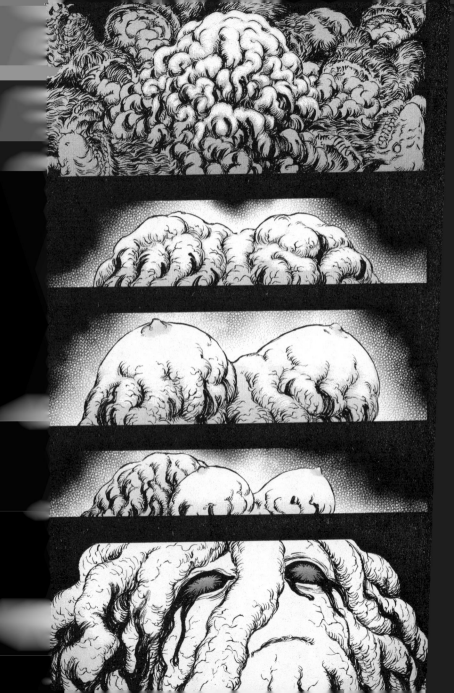

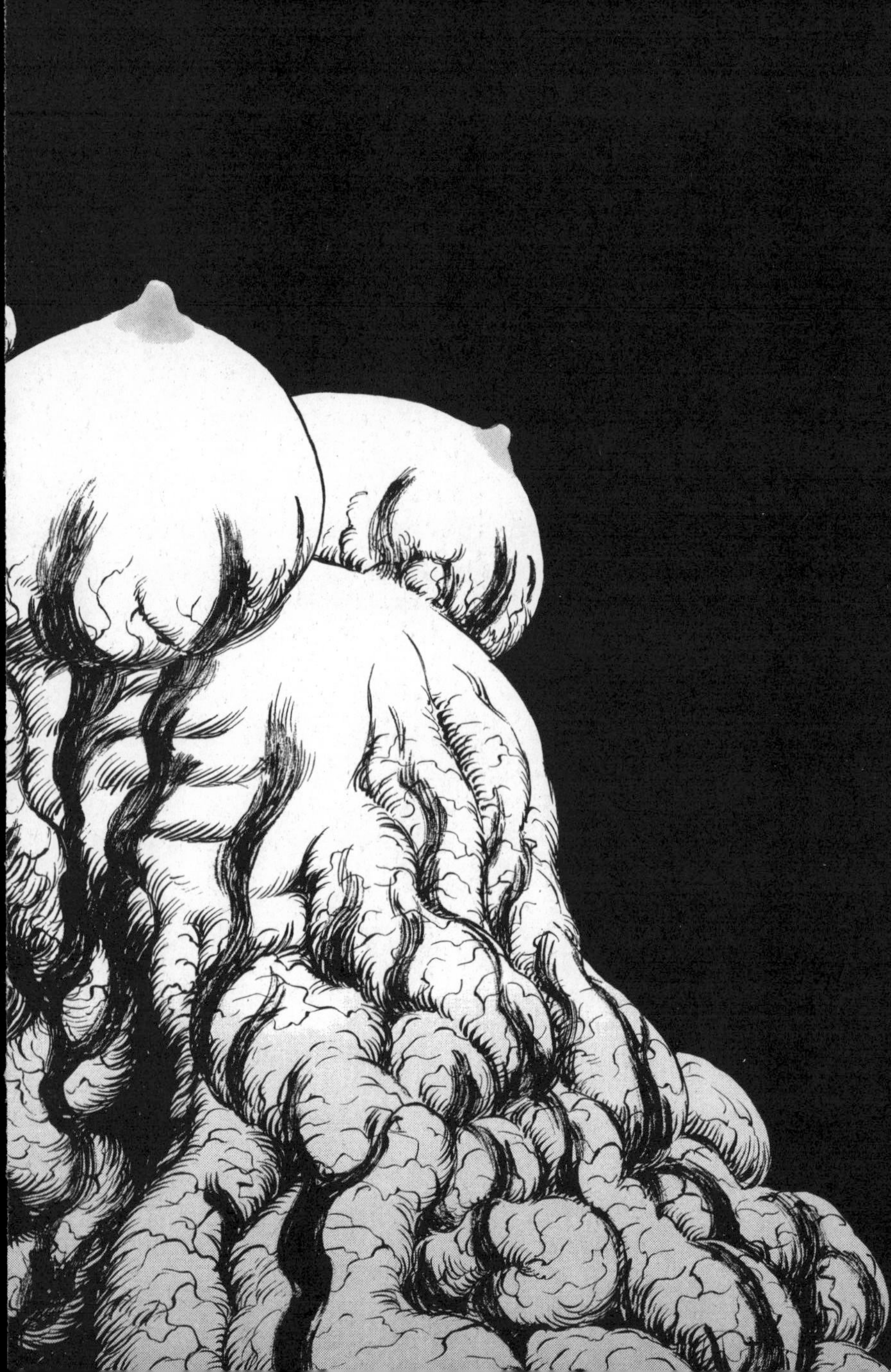

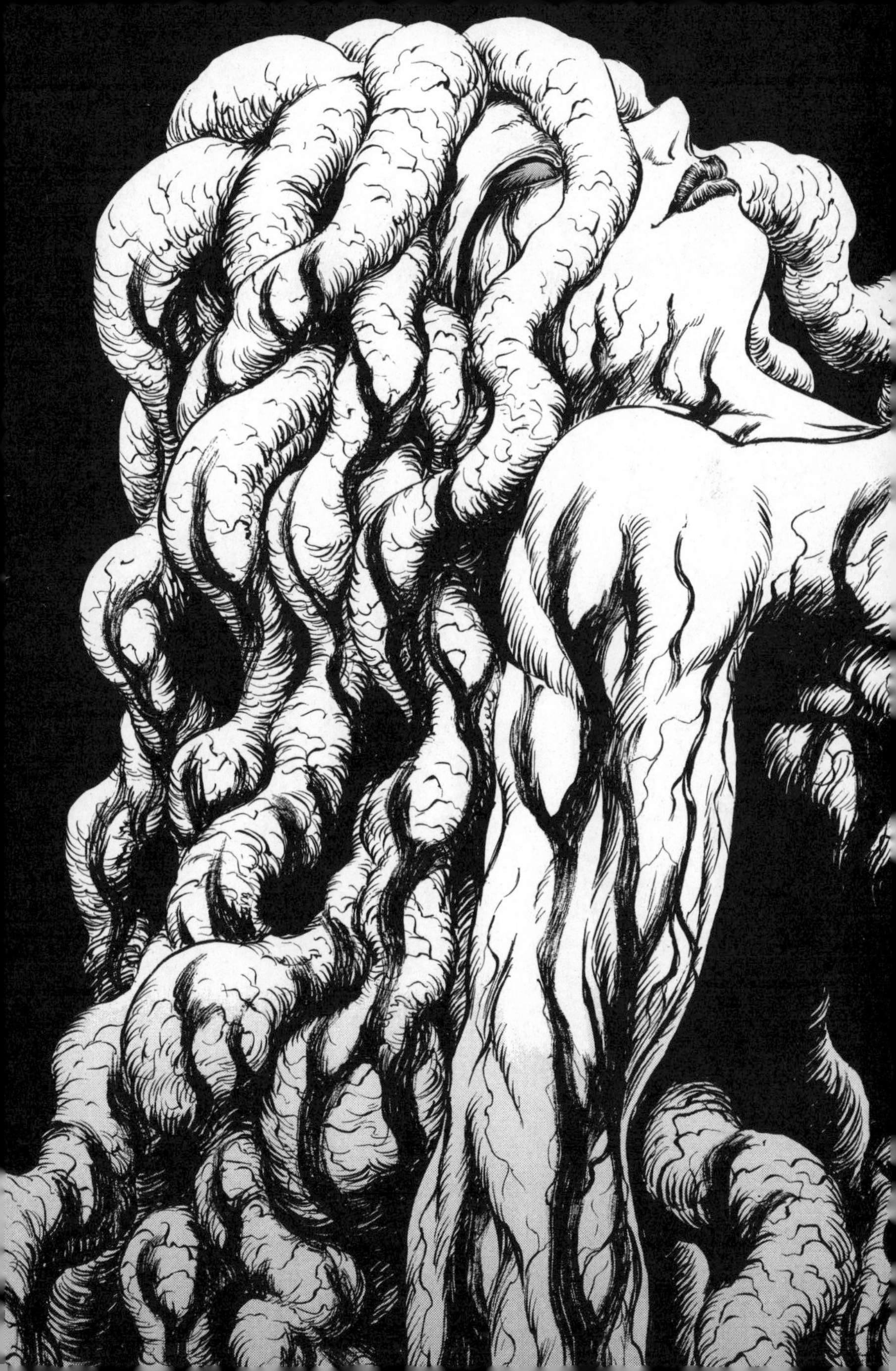

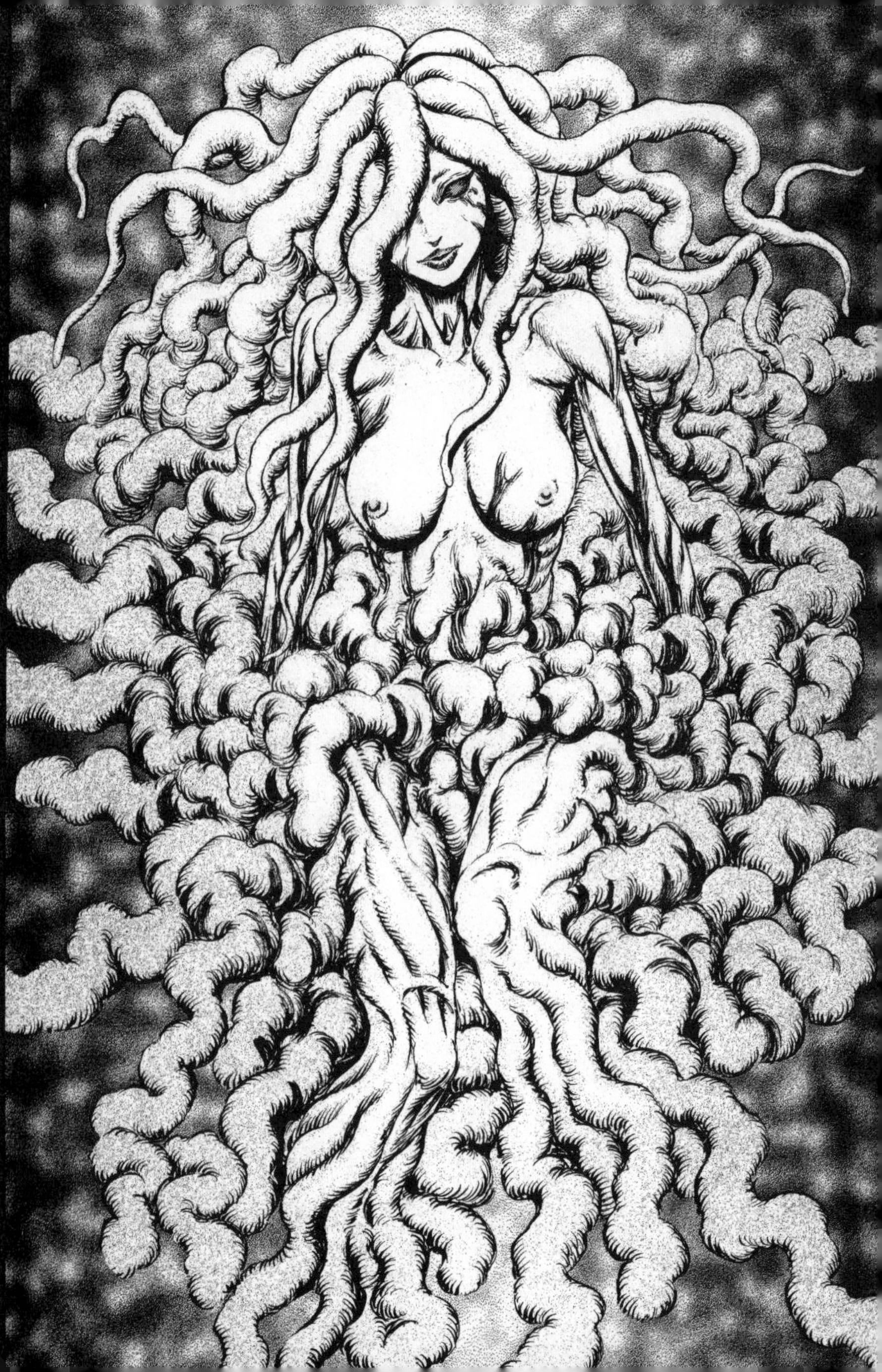

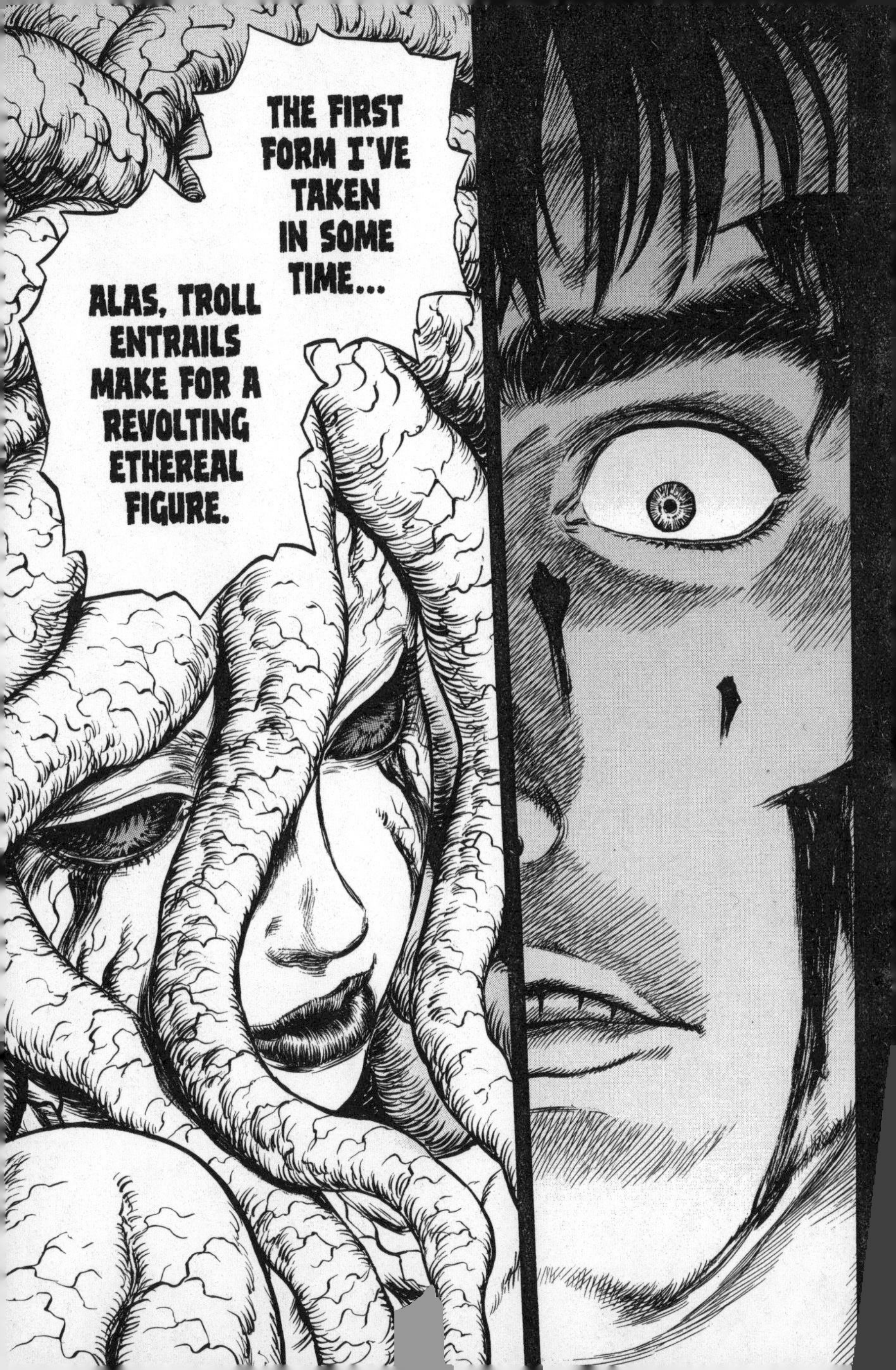
THE FIRST FORM I'VE TAKEN IN SOME TIME...
ALAS, TROLL ENTRAILS MAKE FOR A REVOLTING ETHEREAL FIGURE.

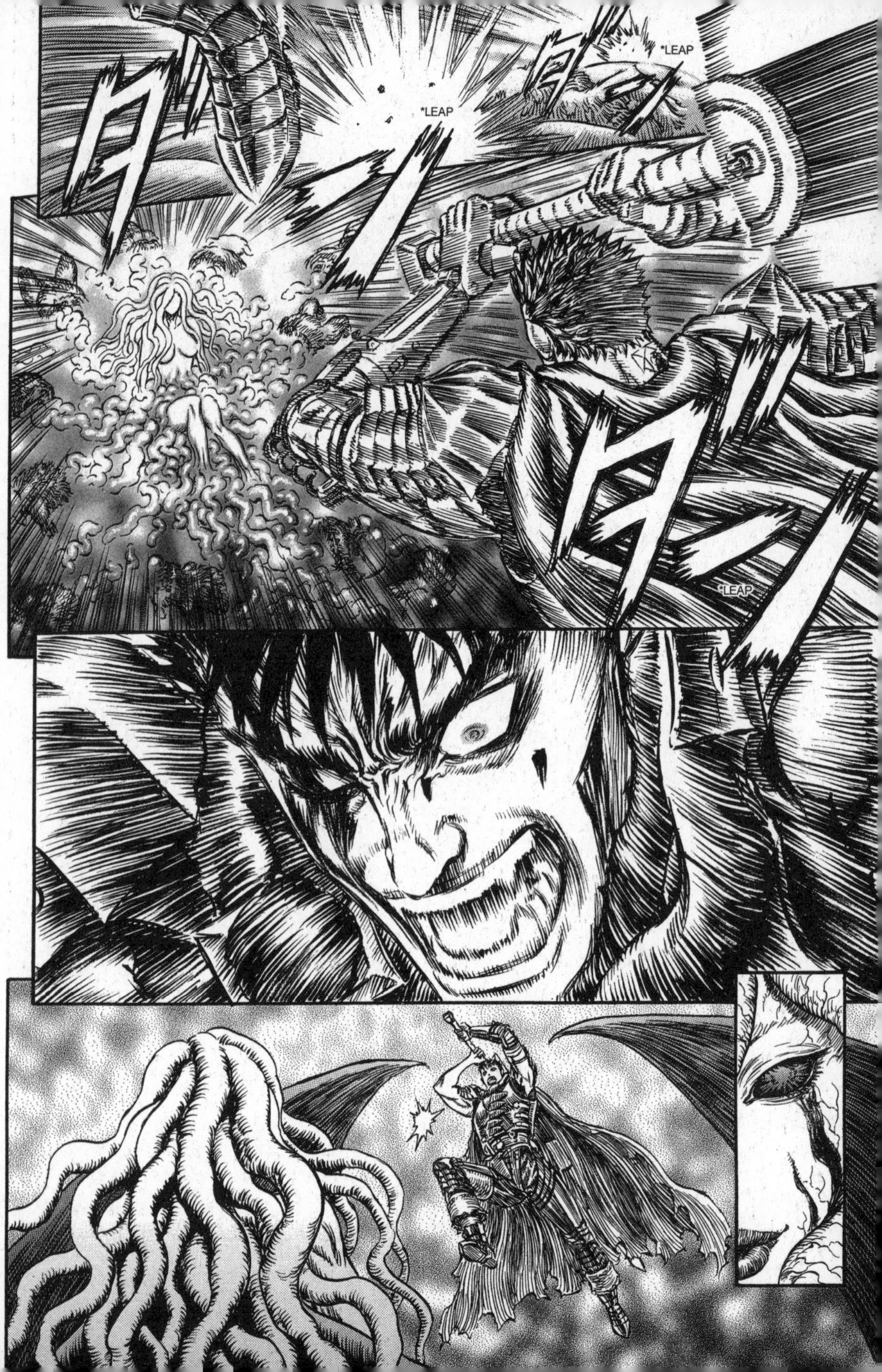
*LEAP
*LEAP
*LEAP

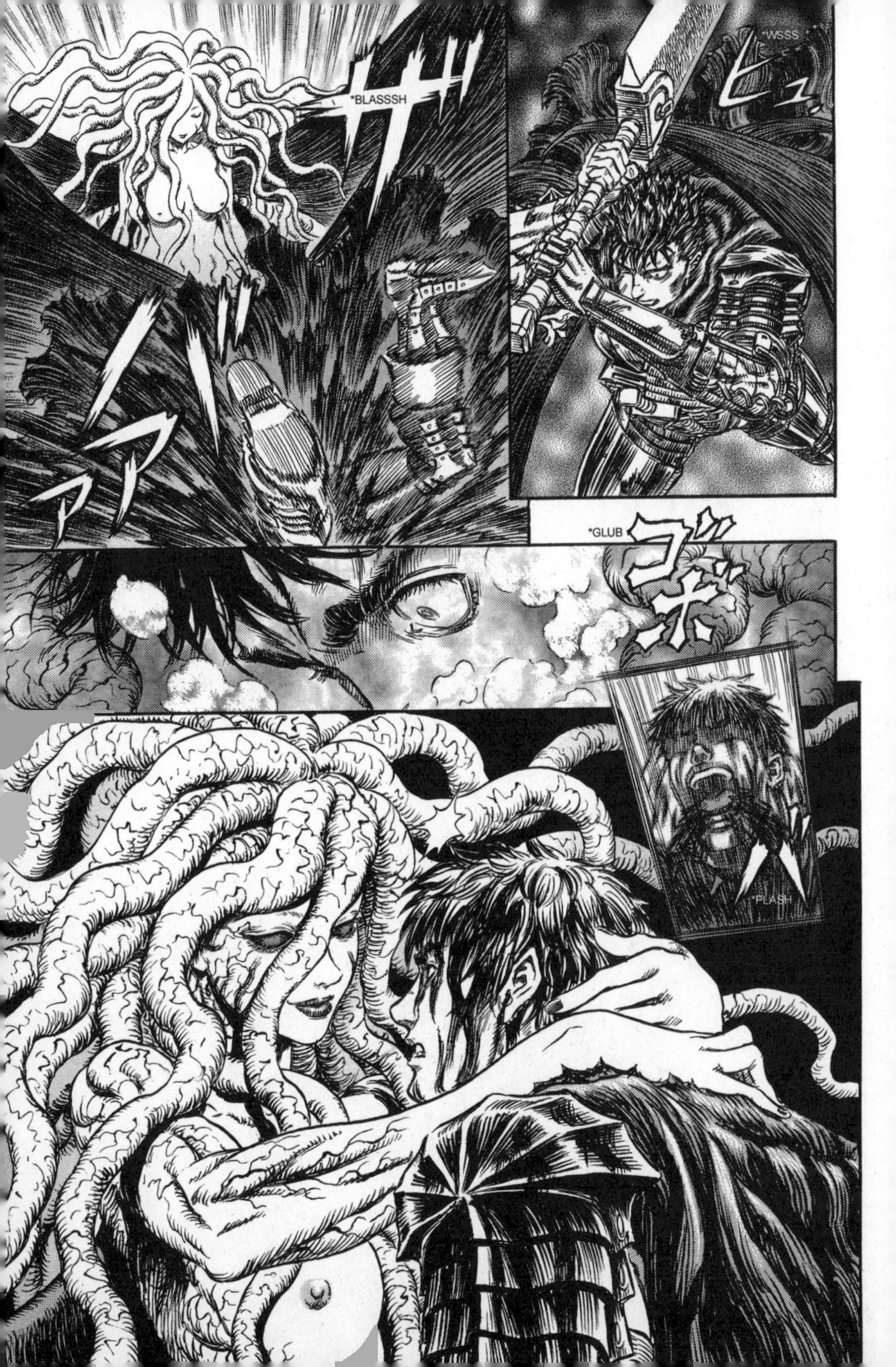
*WSS
*BLASSSH
*GLUB
*PLASH

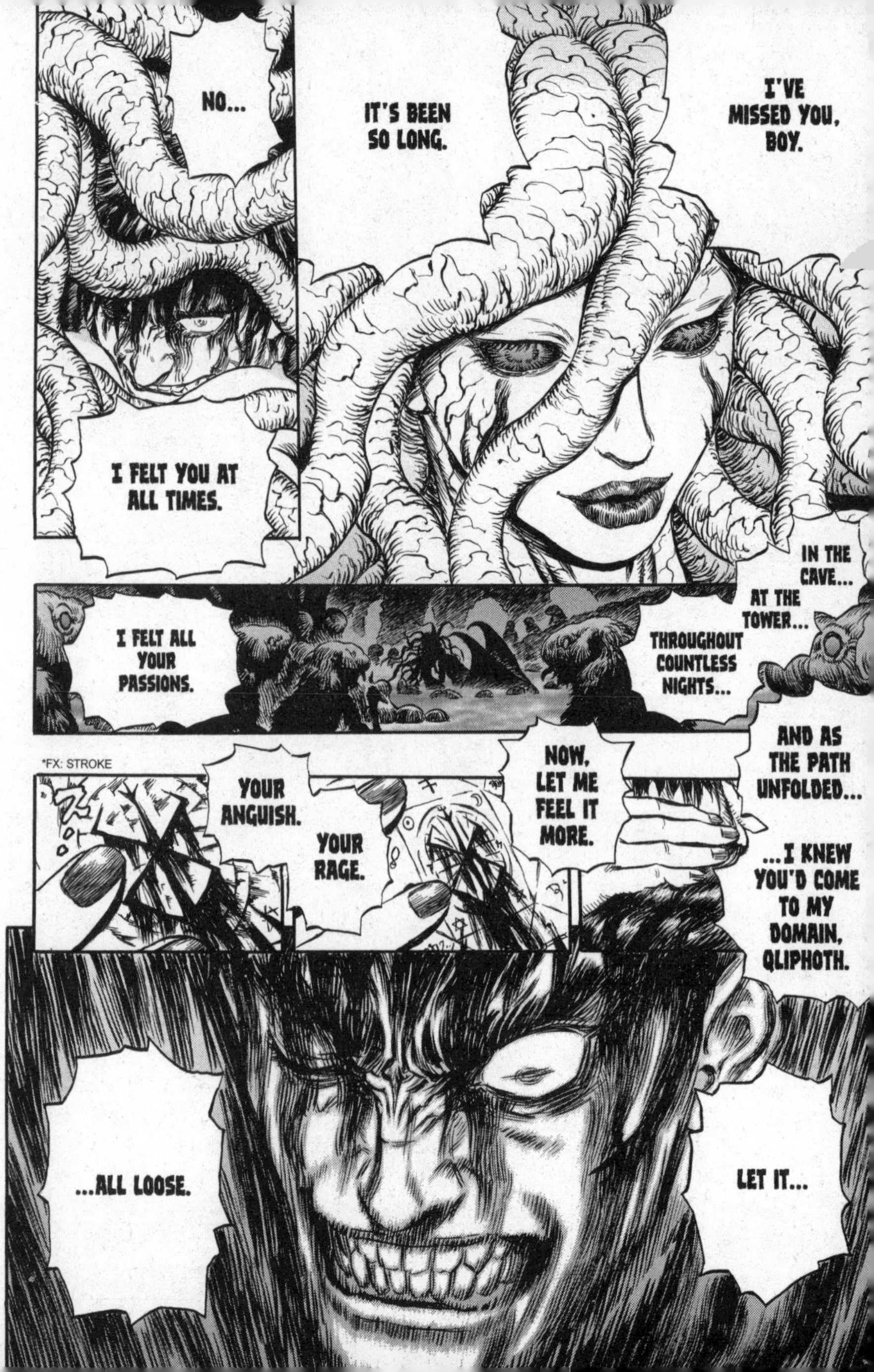
I'VE MISSED YOU, BOY.
IT'S BEEN SO LONG.
NO...
I FELT YOU AT ALL TIMES.
IN THE CAVE...
AT THE TOWER...
THROUGHOUT COUNTLESS NIGHTS...
I FELT ALL YOUR PASSIONS.
AND AS THE PATH UNFOLDED...
...I KNEW YOU'D COME TO MY DOMAIN, QLIPHOTH.
NOW, LET ME FEEL IT MORE.
YOUR RAGE.
YOUR ANGUISH.
*FX: STROKE
LET IT...
...ALL LOOSE.

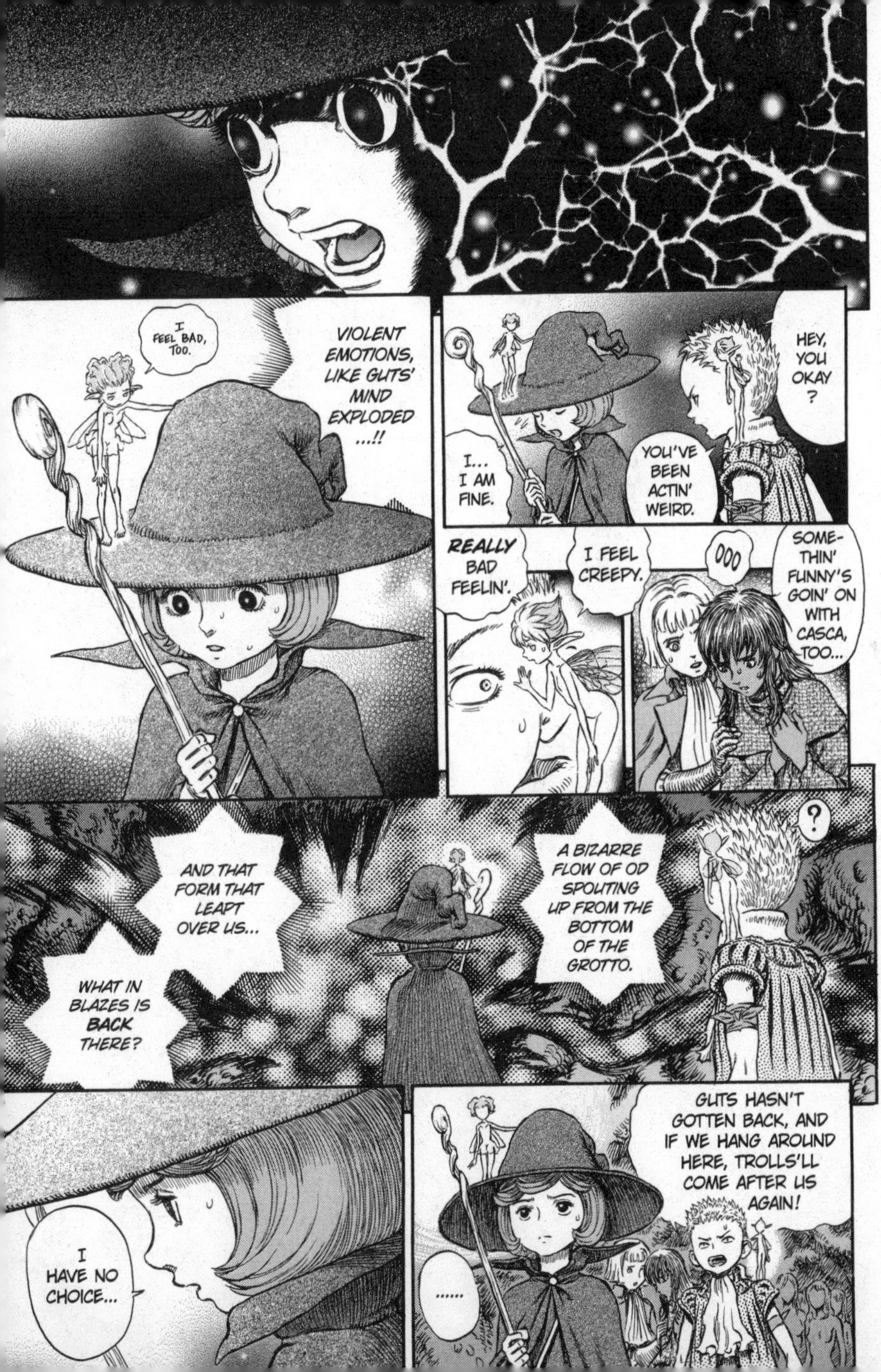
HEY, YOU OKAY?
YOU'VE BEEN ACTIN' WEIRD.
I... I AM FINE.
SOMETHIN' FUNNY'S GOIN' ON WITH CASCA, TOO...
OOO
I FEEL CREEPY.
REALLY BAD FEELIN'.
VIOLENT EMOTIONS, LIKE GUTS' MIND EXPLODED ...!!
I FEEL BAD, TOO.
?
A BIZARRE FLOW OF OD SPOUTING UP FROM THE BOTTOM OF THE GROTTO.
AND THAT FORM THAT LEAPT OVER US...
WHAT IN BLAZES IS **BACK** THERE?
GUTS HASN'T GOTTEN BACK, AND IF WE HANG AROUND HERE, TROLLS'LL COME AFTER US AGAIN!
......
I HAVE NO CHOICE...

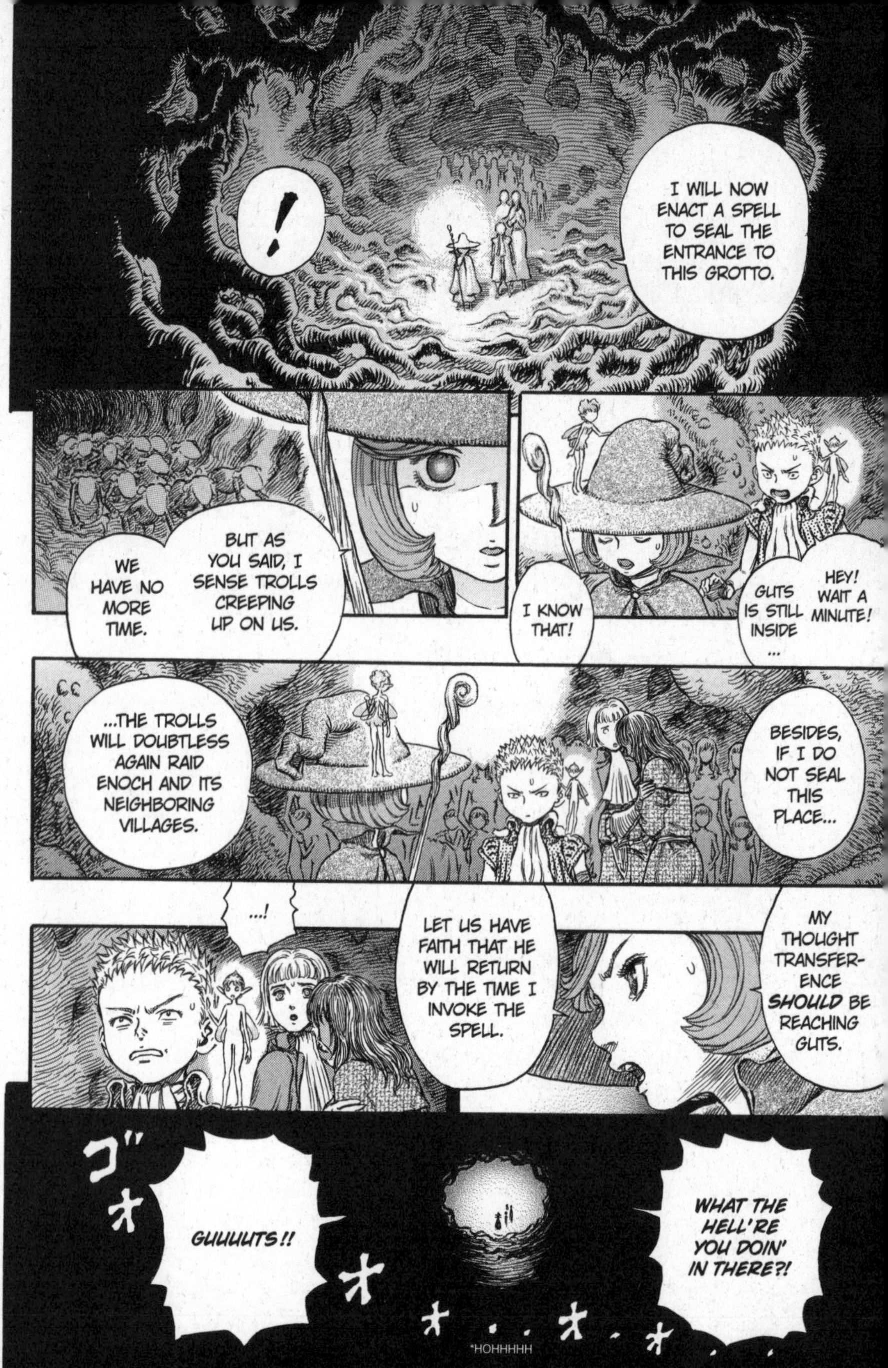

I WILL NOW ENACT A SPELL TO SEAL THE ENTRANCE TO THIS GROTTO.
!
HEY! WAIT A MINUTE!
GUTS IS STILL INSIDE ...
I KNOW THAT!
BUT AS YOU SAID, I SENSE TROLLS CREEPING UP ON US.
WE HAVE NO MORE TIME.
BESIDES, IF I DO NOT SEAL THIS PLACE...
...THE TROLLS WILL DOUBTLESS AGAIN RAID ENOCH AND ITS NEIGHBORING VILLAGES.
MY THOUGHT TRANSFERENCE *SHOULD* BE REACHING GUTS.
LET US HAVE FAITH THAT HE WILL RETURN BY THE TIME I INVOKE THE SPELL.
...!
WHAT THE HELL'RE YOU DOIN' IN THERE?!
GUUUUTS!!
ゴオ
オ・・オ・・オ・・
*HOHHHHH

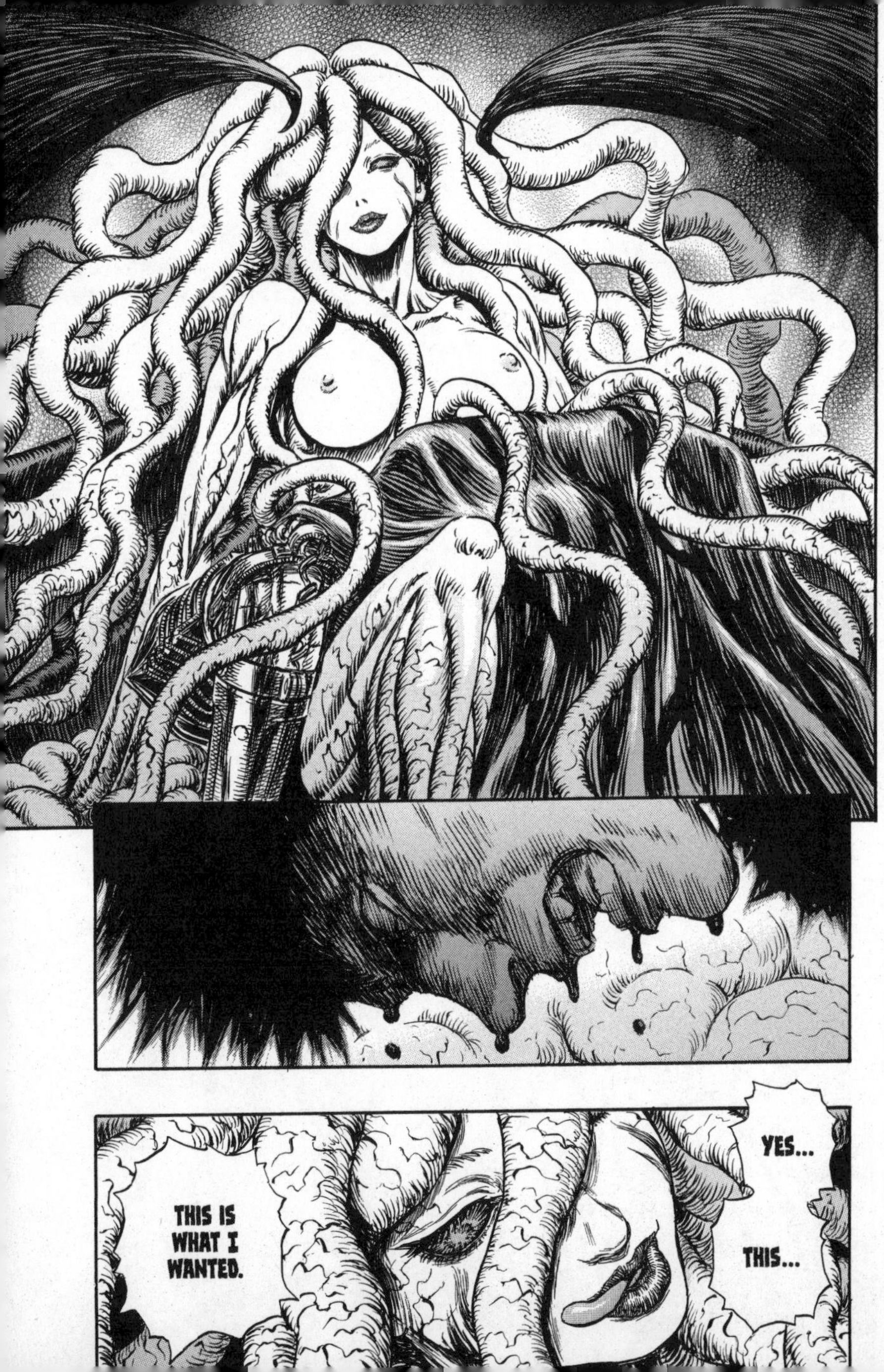
YES...
THIS...
THIS IS WHAT I WANTED.

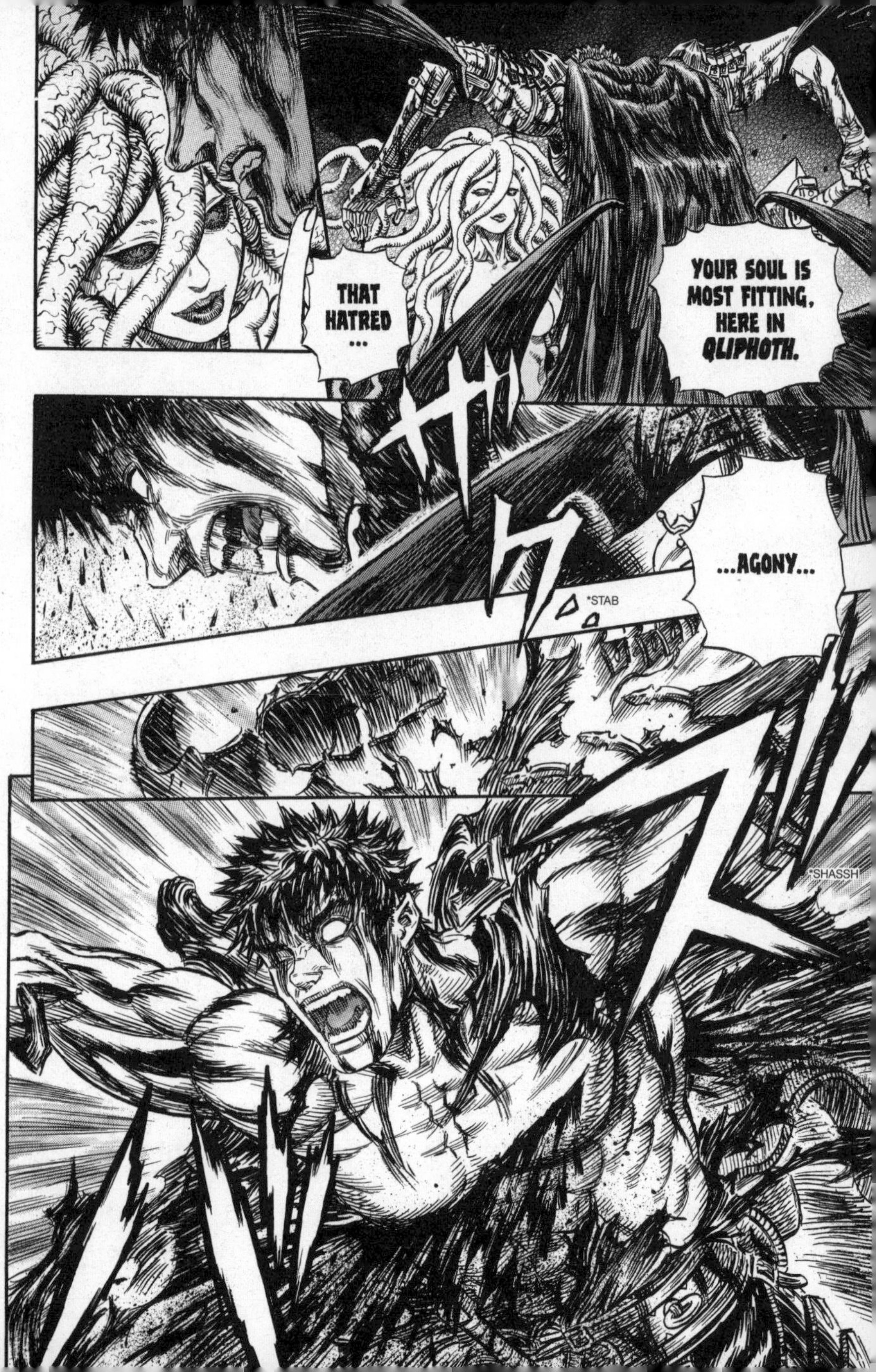
YOUR SOUL IS MOST FITTING, HERE IN QLIPHOTH.
THAT HATRED ...
...AGONY...
*STAB
*SHASSH

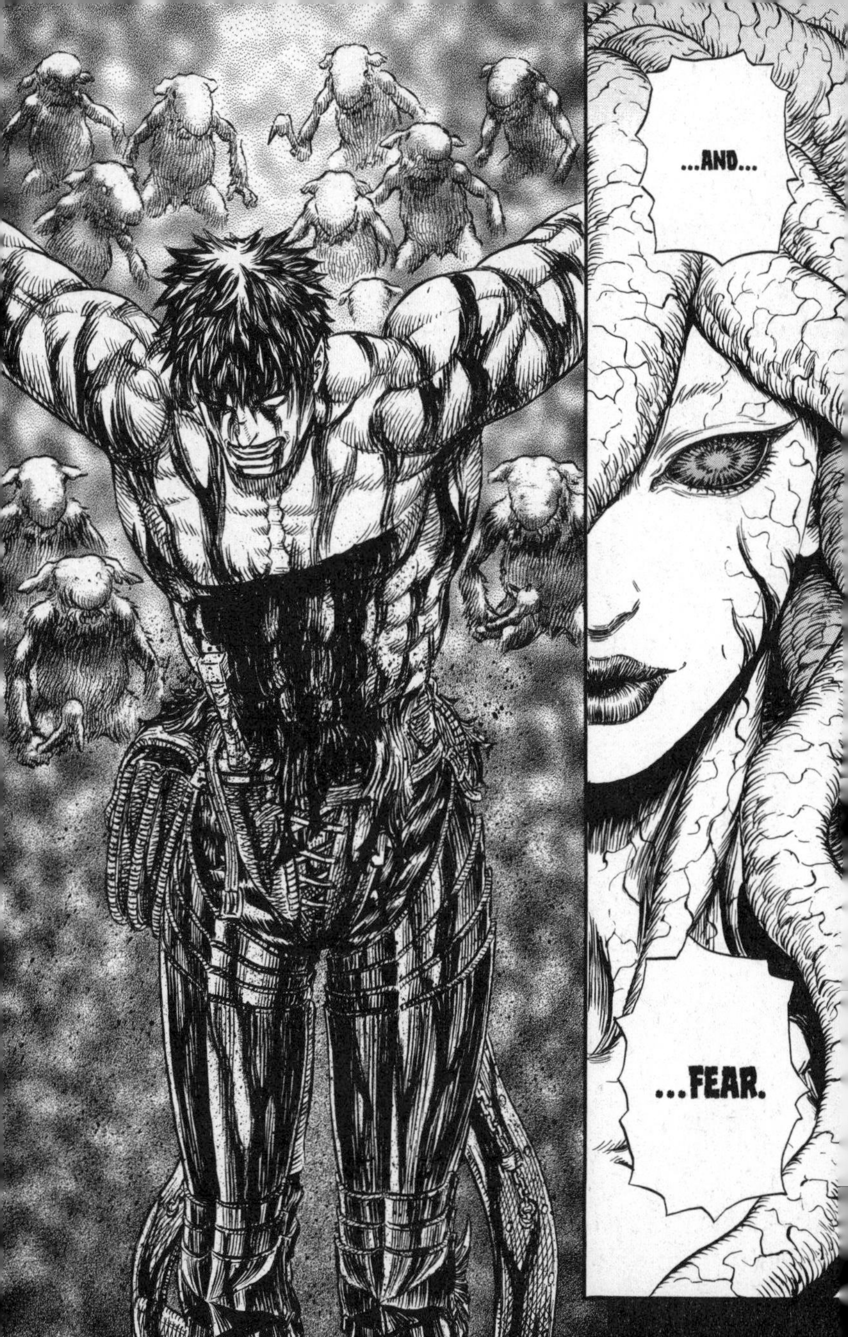
...AND...
...FEAR.

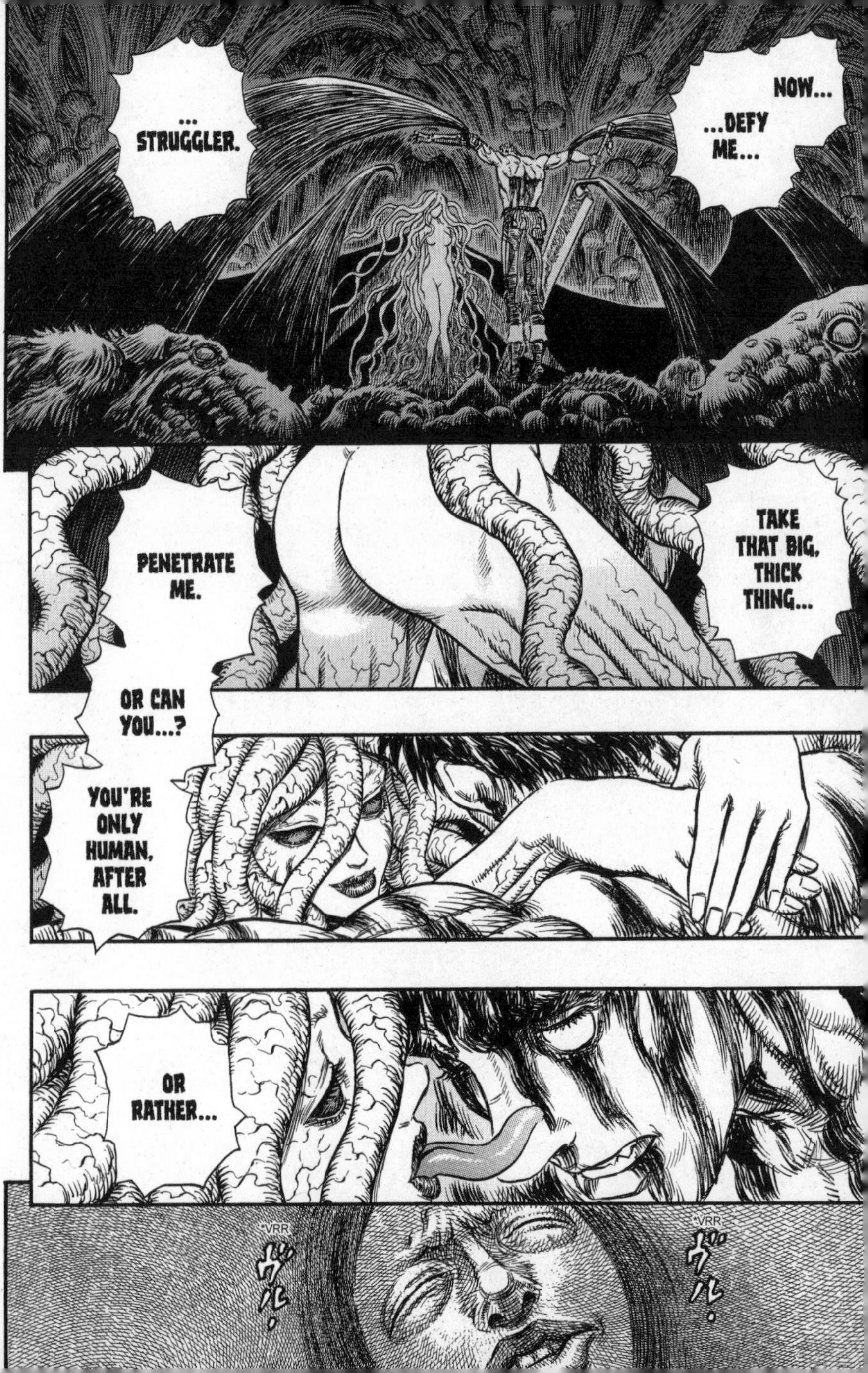
NOW...
...DEFY ME...
... STRUGGLER.
TAKE THAT BIG, THICK THING...
PENETRATE ME.
OR CAN YOU...?
YOU'RE ONLY HUMAN, AFTER ALL.
OR RATHER...
*VRR
*VRR

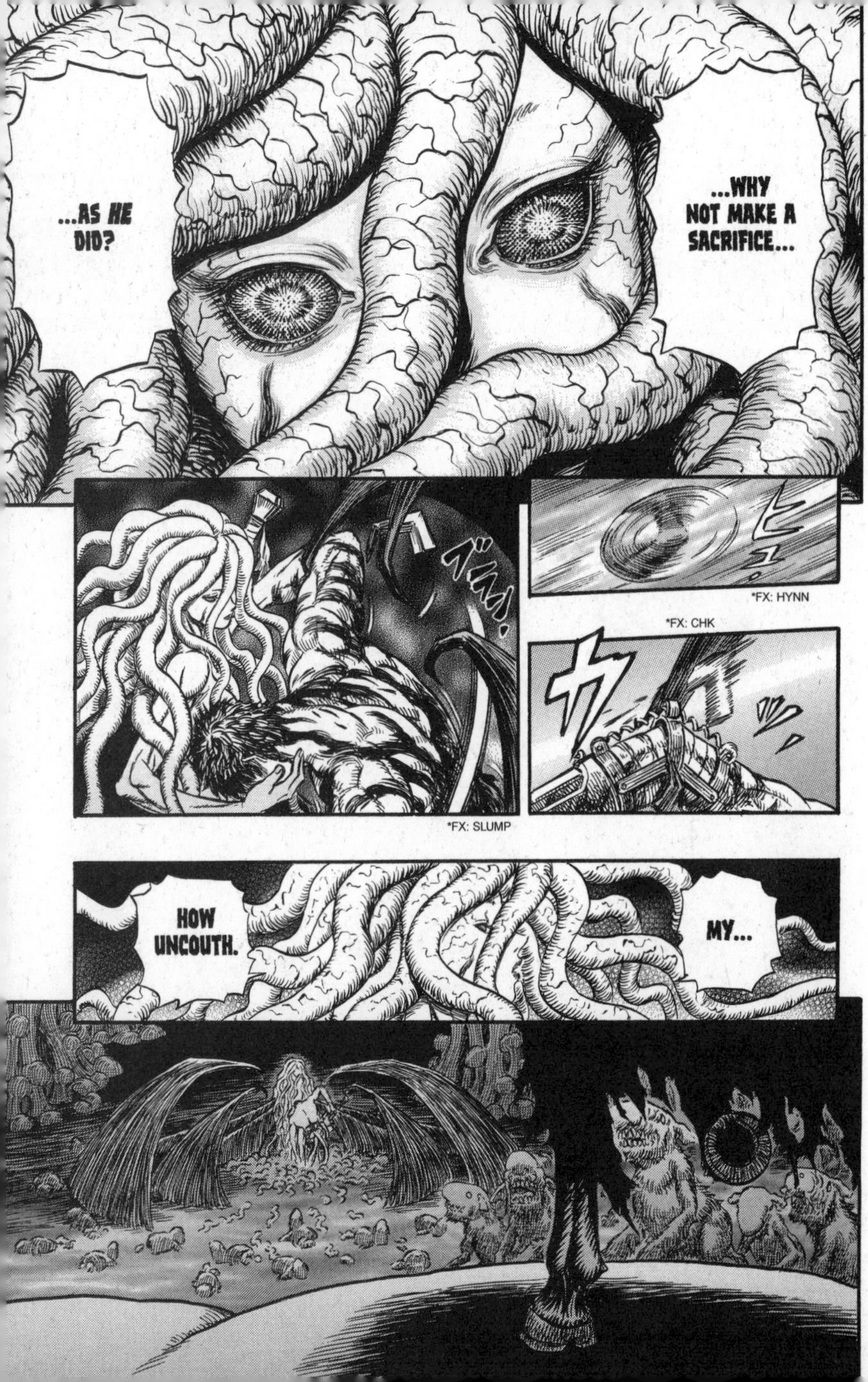
...WHY NOT MAKE A SACRIFICE...
...AS HE DID?
*FX: HYNN
*FX: CHK
*FX: SLUMP
MY...
HOW UNCOUTH.

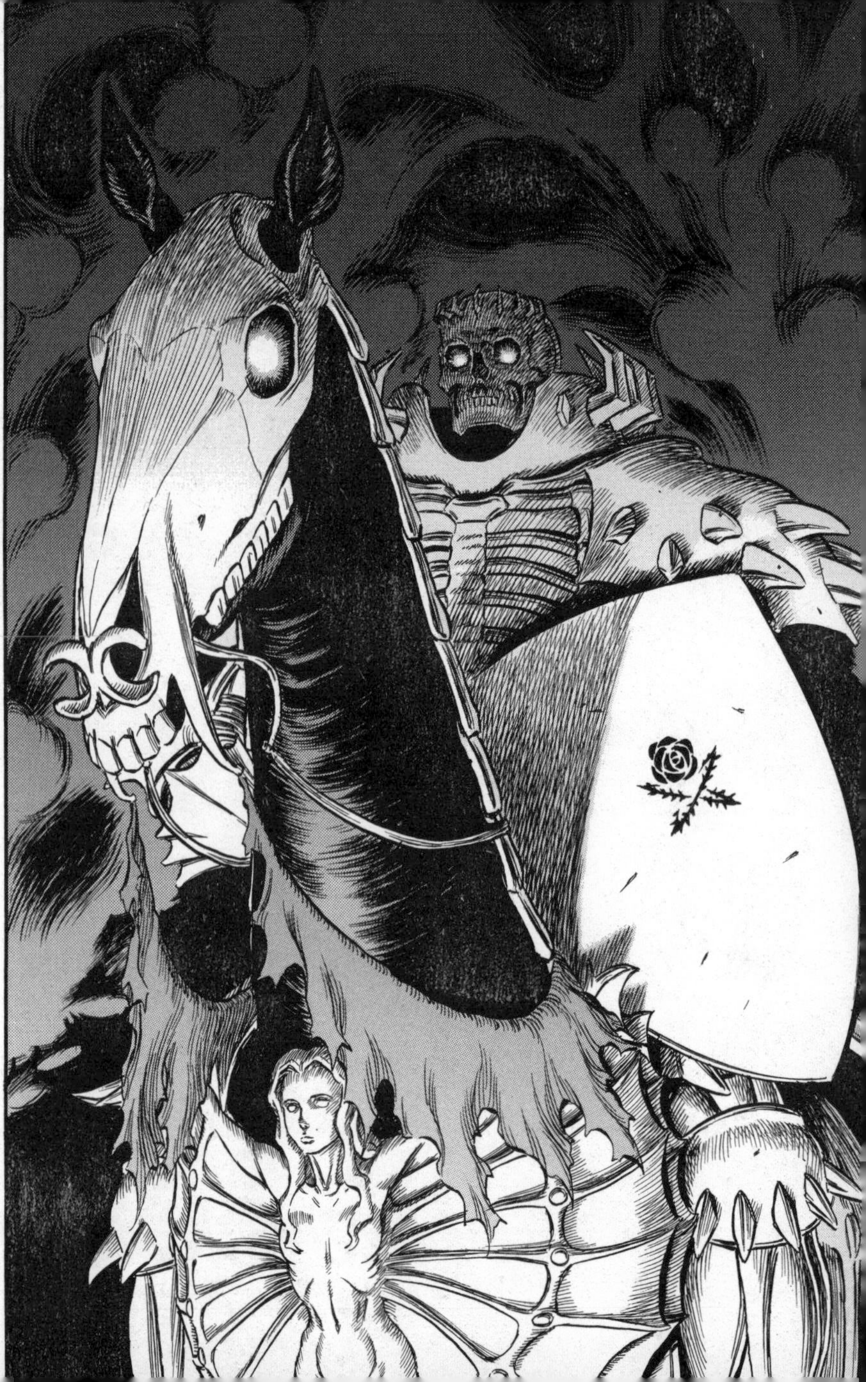

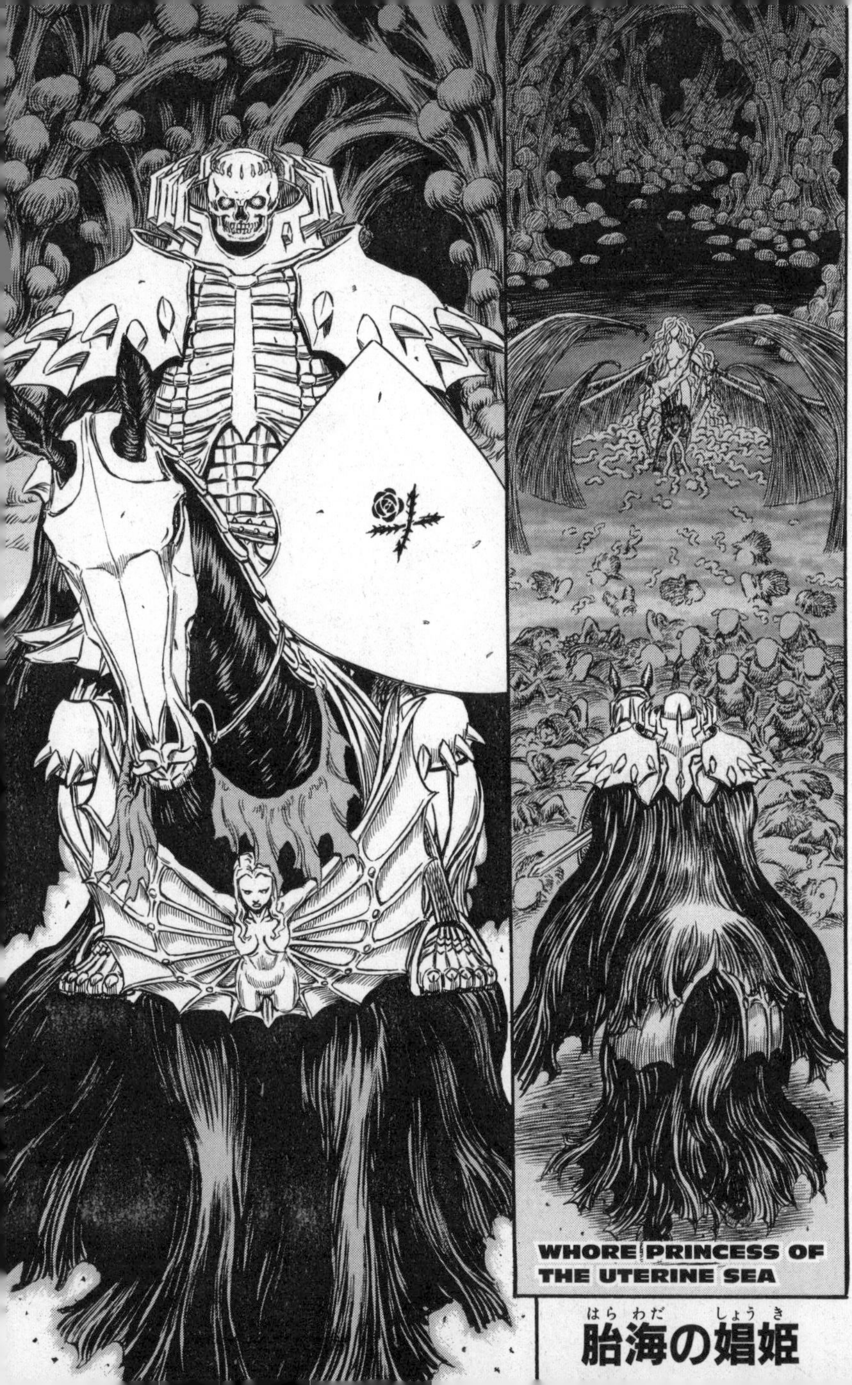

WHORE PRINCESS OF THE UTERINE SEA

胎海の娼姫

ONE SHOULD
NOT MEDDLE
IN THE
CLANDESTINE
AFFAIRS OF
MEN AND
WOMEN.

OR ARE
YOU
JOINING
US...

...YOUR
MAJESTY
?!

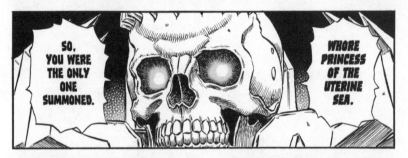

WHORE
PRINCESS
OF THE
UTERINE
SEA.

SO,
YOU WERE
THE ONLY
ONE
SUMMONED.

SUM-
MONED,
YOU SAY
?

I CAME
HERE ON
MY OWN.

I WISHED
TO SEE
THIS BOY.

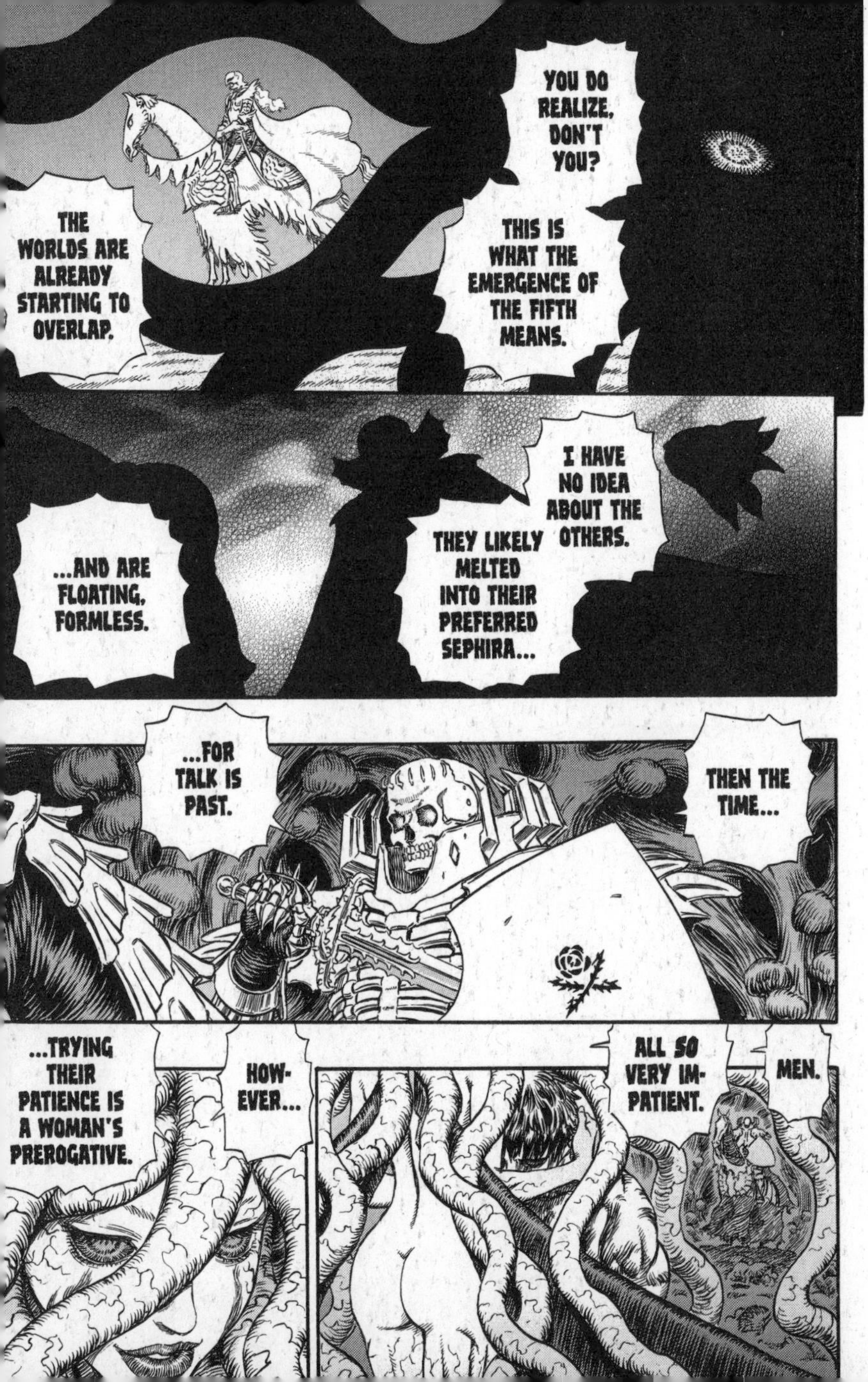
YOU DO REALIZE, DON'T YOU?
THIS IS WHAT THE EMERGENCE OF THE FIFTH MEANS.
THE WORLDS ARE ALREADY STARTING TO OVERLAP.
I HAVE NO IDEA ABOUT THE OTHERS.
THEY LIKELY MELTED INTO THEIR PREFERRED SEPHIRA...
...AND ARE FLOATING, FORMLESS.
THEN THE TIME...
...FOR TALK IS PAST.
MEN.
ALL SO VERY IM-PATIENT.
HOW-EVER...
...TRYING THEIR PATIENCE IS A WOMAN'S PREROGATIVE.

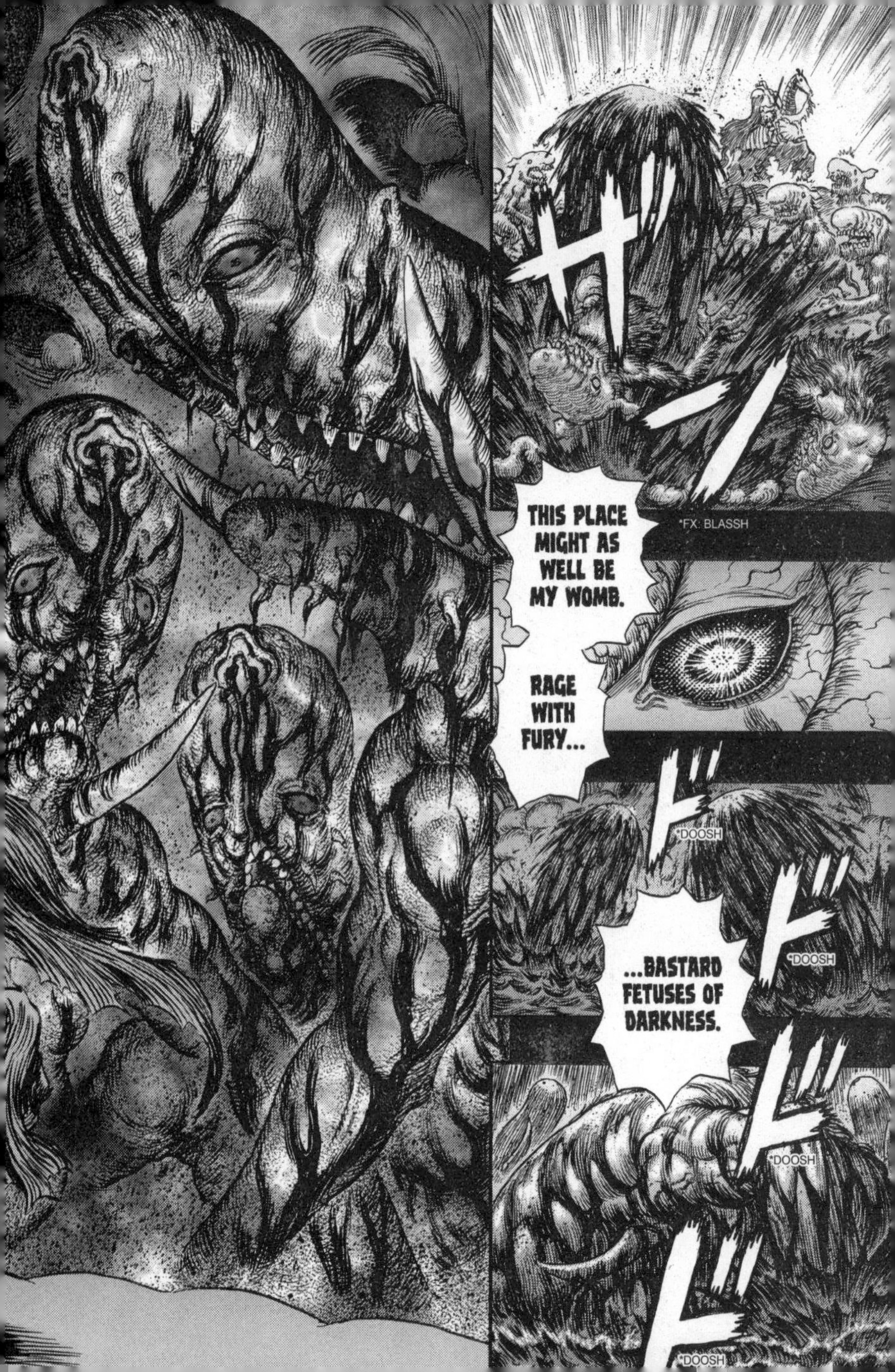
*FX: BLASSH
THIS PLACE MIGHT AS WELL BE MY WOMB.
RAGE WITH FURY...
*DOOSH
...BASTARD FETUSES OF DARKNESS.
*DOOSH
*DOOSH
*DOOSH

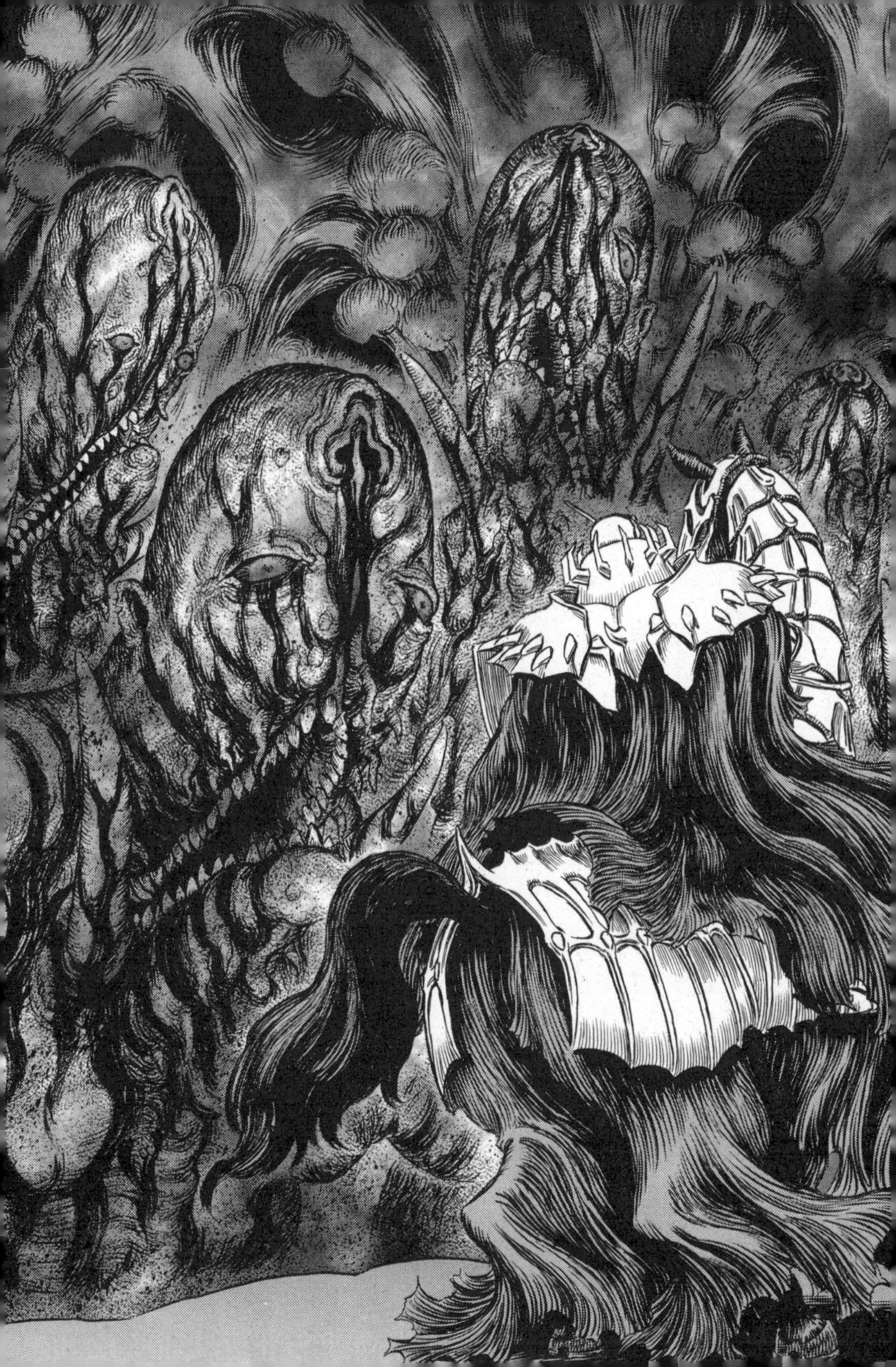

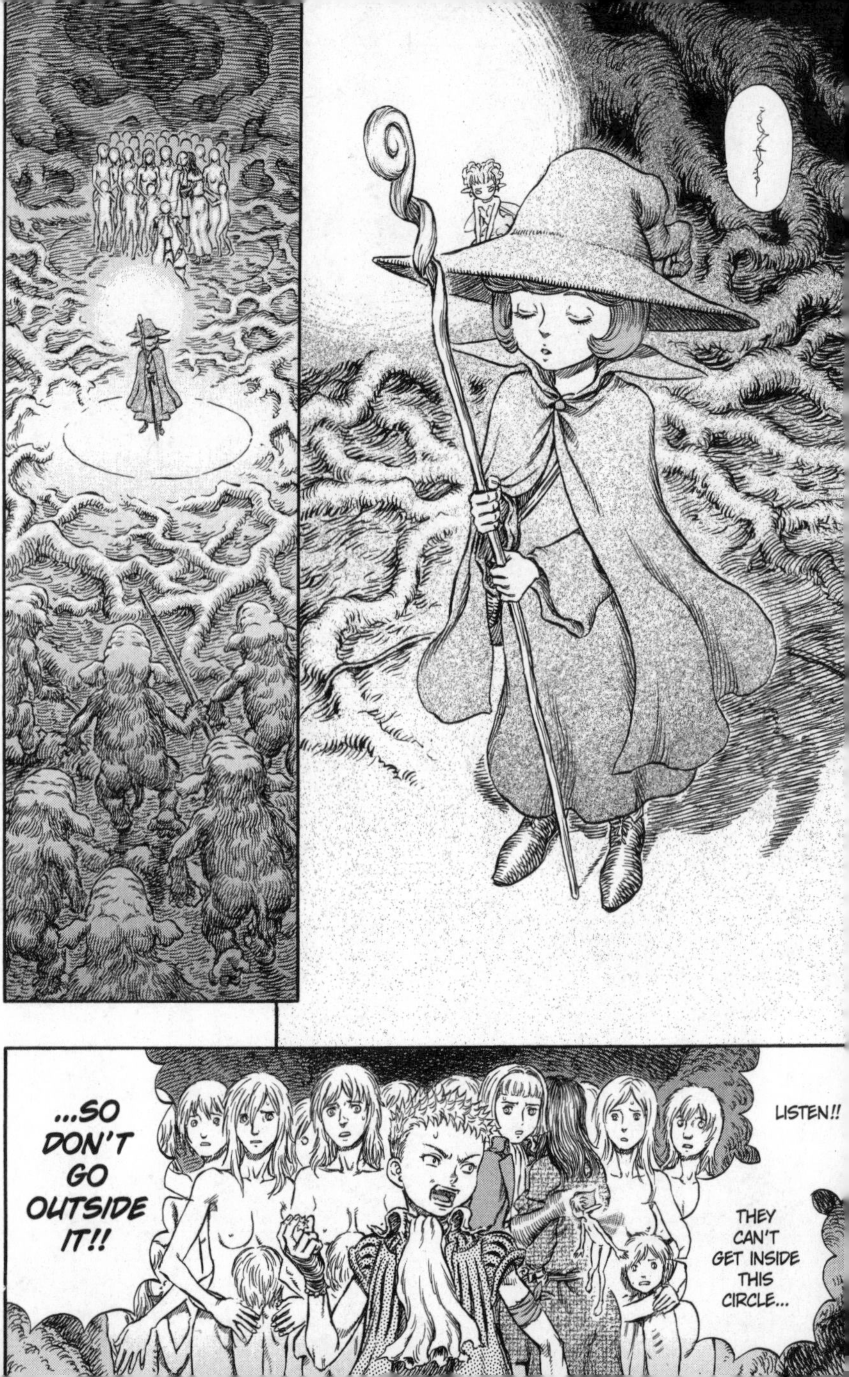
LISTEN!!
THEY CAN'T GET INSIDE THIS CIRCLE...
...SO DON'T GO OUTSIDE IT!!

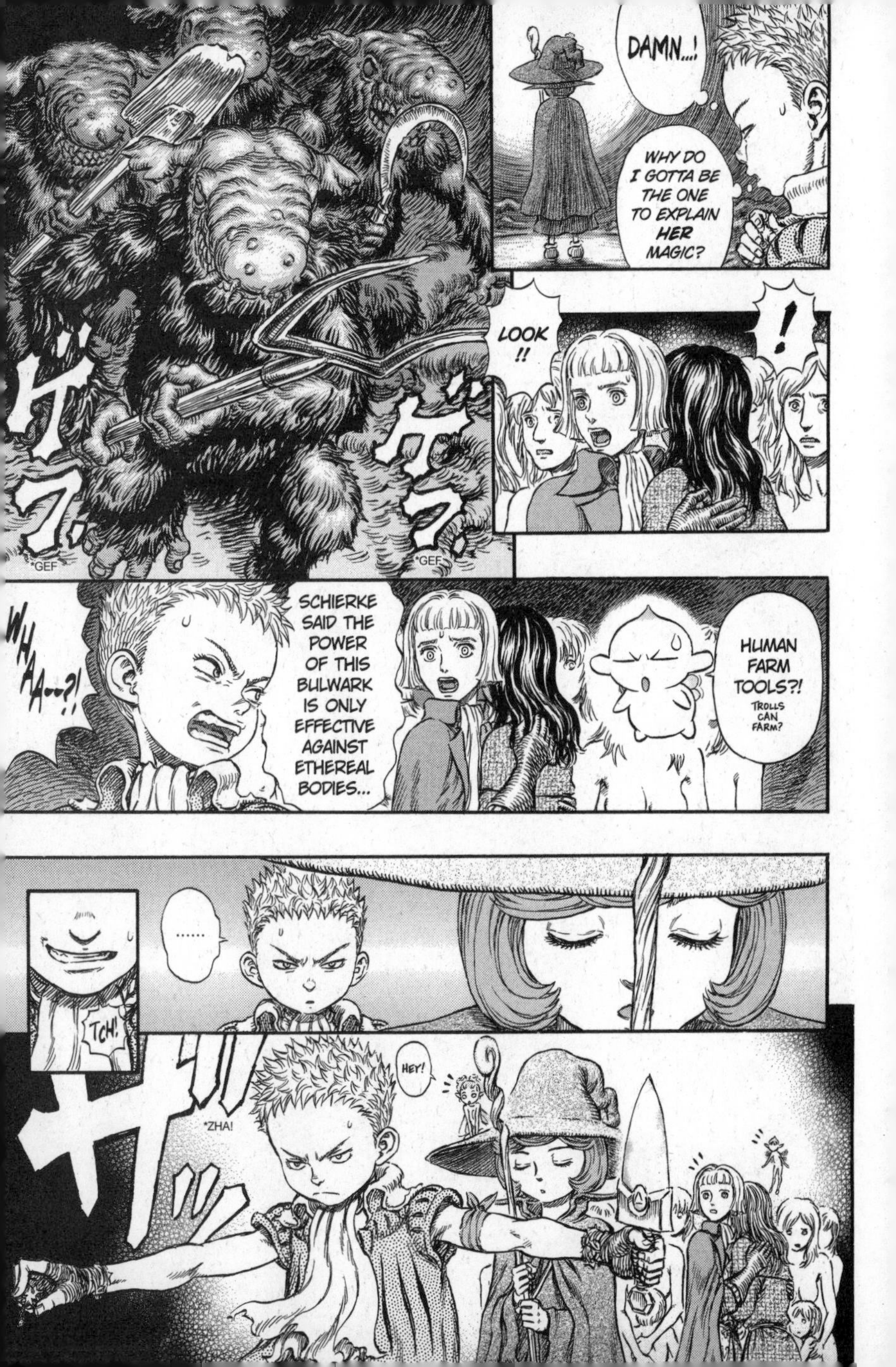
DAMN...!
WHY DO I GOTTA BE THE ONE TO EXPLAIN HER MAGIC?
!
LOOK !!
*GEF
*GEF
HUMAN FARM TOOLS?!
TROLLS CAN FARM?
SCHIERKE SAID THE POWER OF THIS BULWARK IS ONLY EFFECTIVE AGAINST ETHEREAL BODIES...
WHAAA--?!
......
TCH!
HEY!
*ZHA!

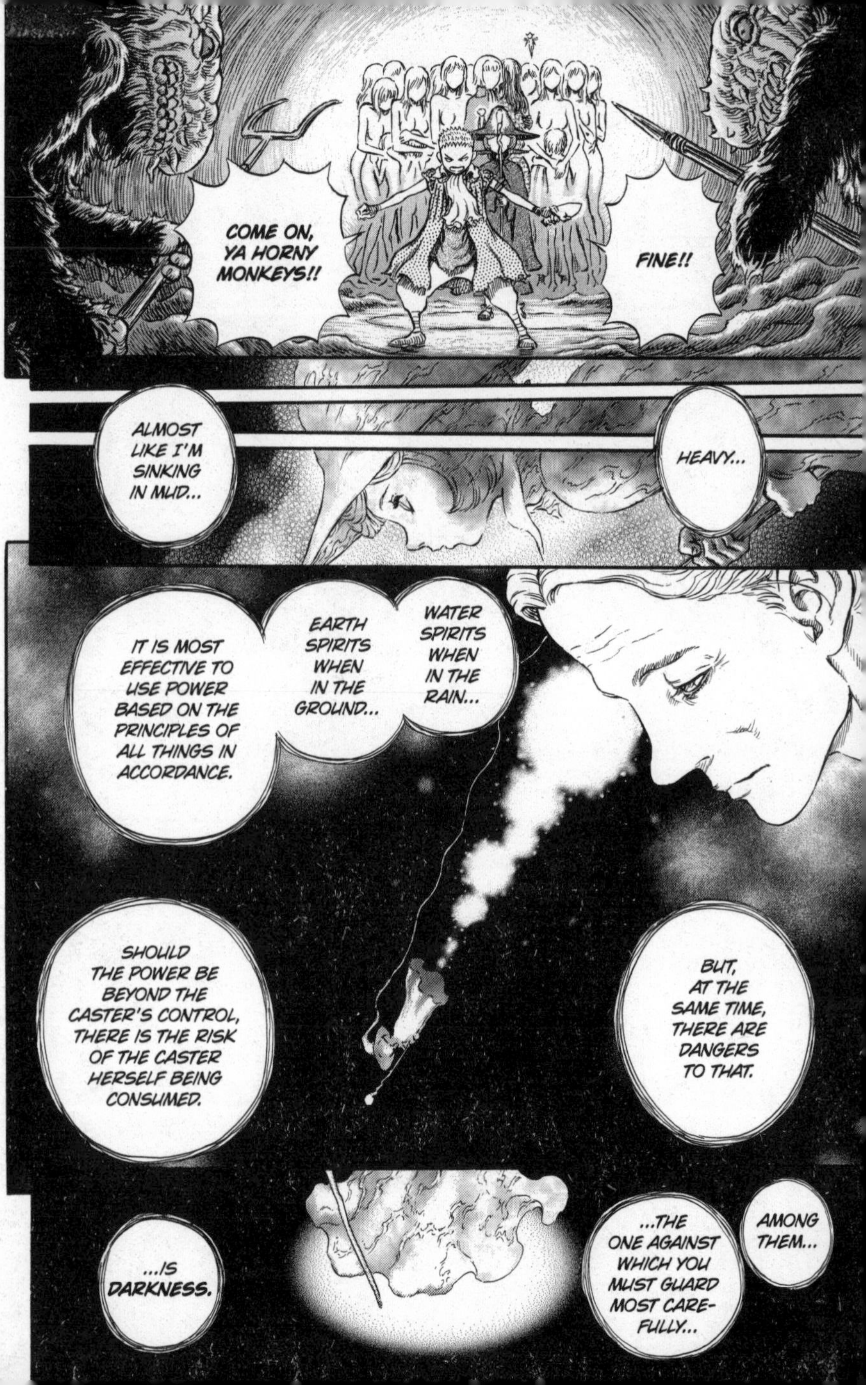
FINE!!
COME ON, YA HORNY MONKEYS!!
HEAVY...
ALMOST LIKE I'M SINKING IN MUD...
WATER SPIRITS WHEN IN THE RAIN...
EARTH SPIRITS WHEN IN THE GROUND...
IT IS MOST EFFECTIVE TO USE POWER BASED ON THE PRINCIPLES OF ALL THINGS IN ACCORDANCE.
BUT, AT THE SAME TIME, THERE ARE DANGERS TO THAT.
SHOULD THE POWER BE BEYOND THE CASTER'S CONTROL, THERE IS THE RISK OF THE CASTER HERSELF BEING CONSUMED.
AMONG THEM...
...THE ONE AGAINST WHICH YOU MUST GUARD MOST CARE-FULLY...
...IS DARKNESS.

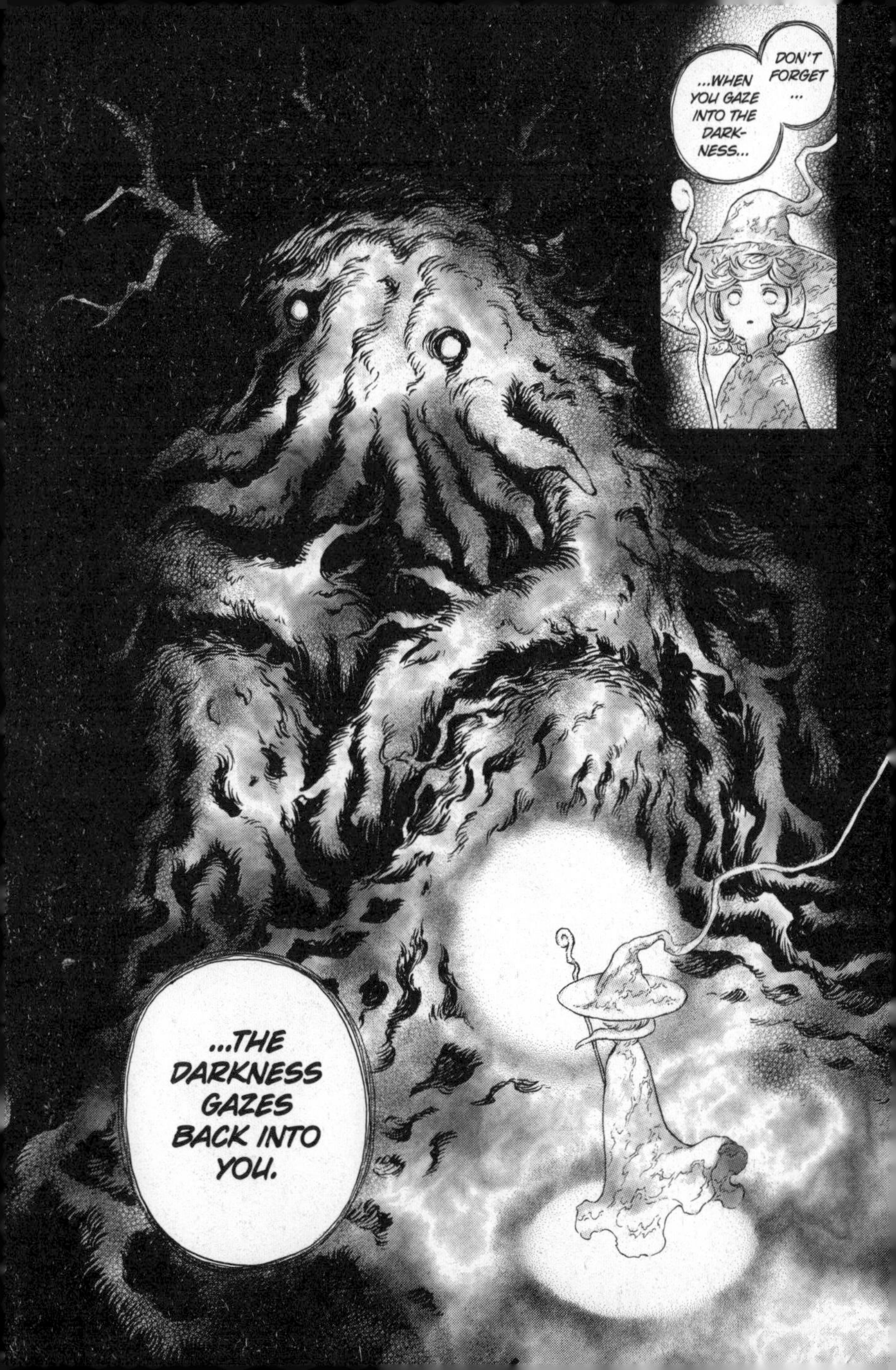
DON'T FORGET ...
...WHEN YOU GAZE INTO THE DARK-NESS...
...THE DARKNESS GAZES BACK INTO YOU.

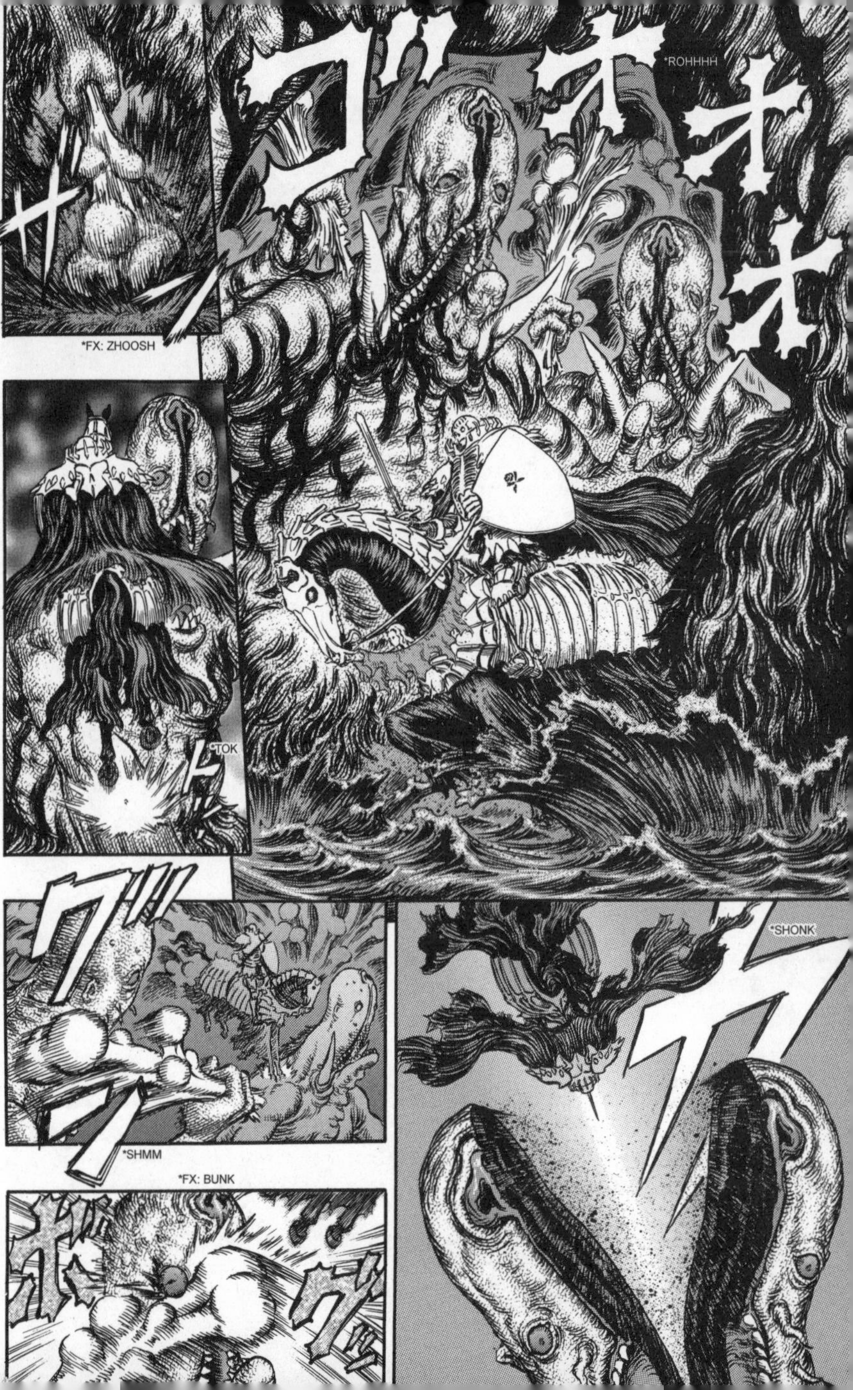
*ROHHHH
*FX: ZHOOSH
*TOK
*SHONK
*SHMM
*FX: BUNK

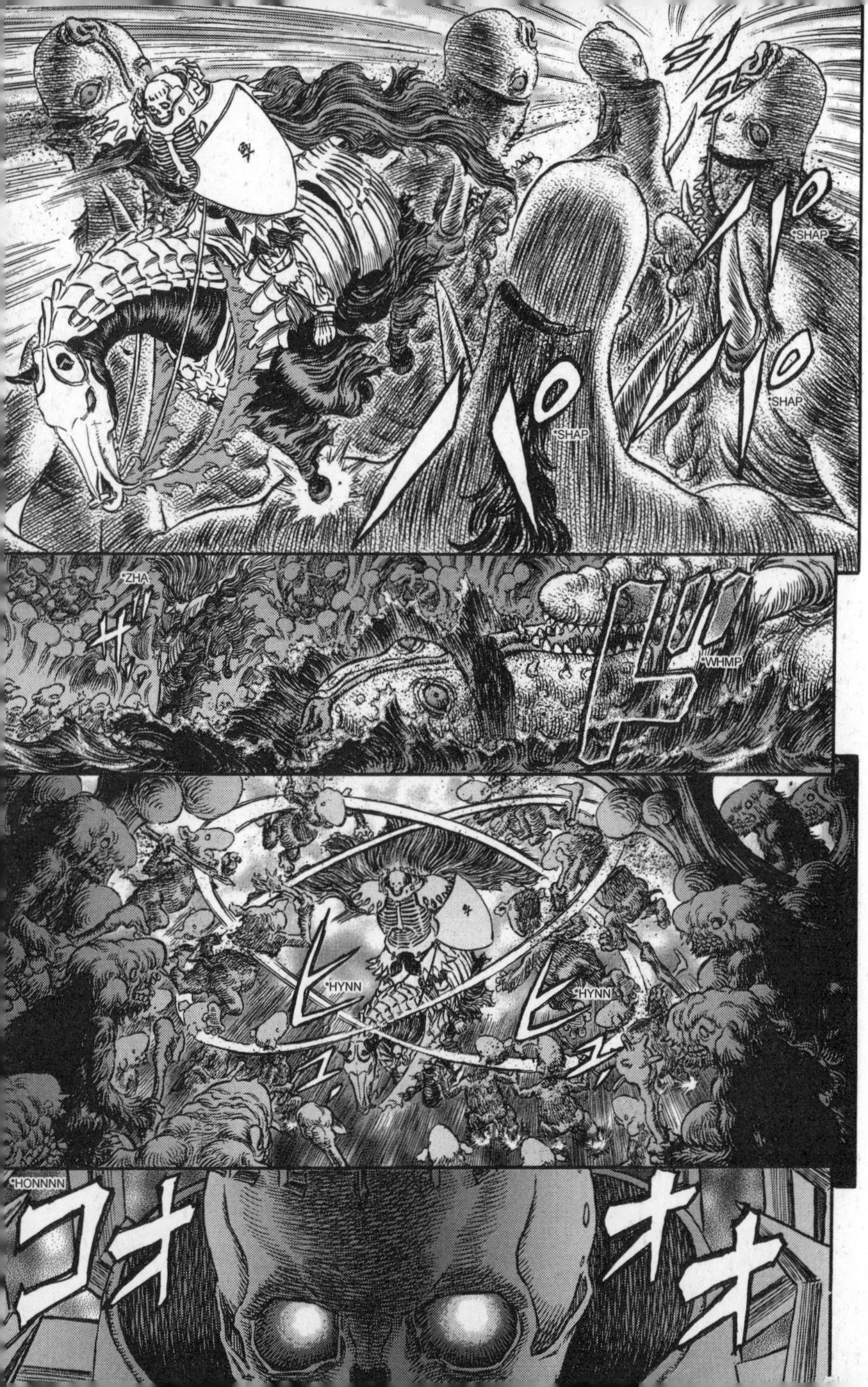
*SHAP
SHAP
*SHAP
*WHMP
*ZHA
*HYNN
*HYNN
*HONNNN

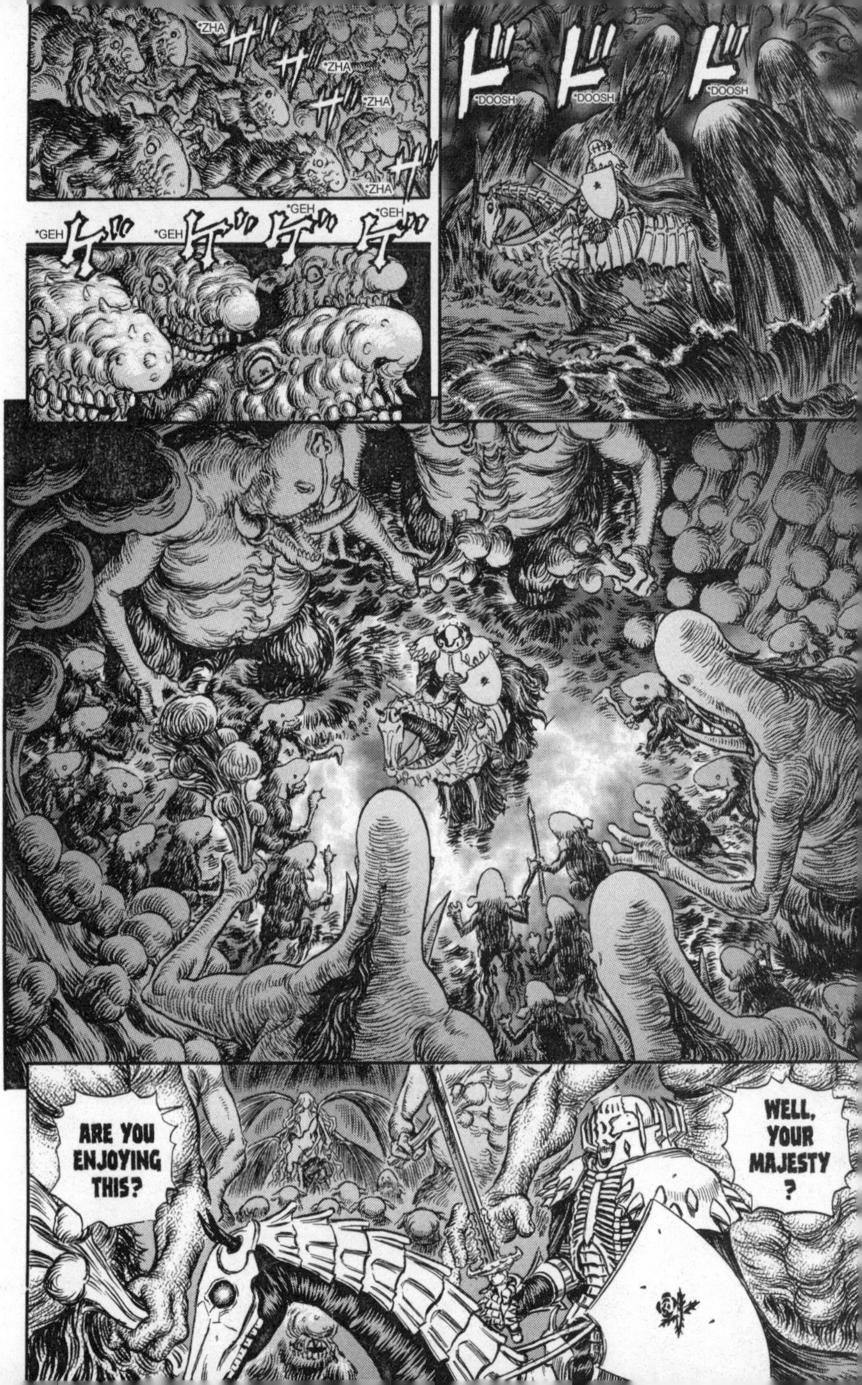

ド
*DOOSH
ド
*DOOSH
ド
*DOOSH
ザ
*ZHA
ザ
*ZHA
ザ
*ZHA
ザ
*ZHA
ゲ
*GEH
ゲ
*GEH
ゲ
*GEH
ゲ
*GEH
WELL, YOUR MAJESTY ?
ARE YOU ENJOYING THIS?

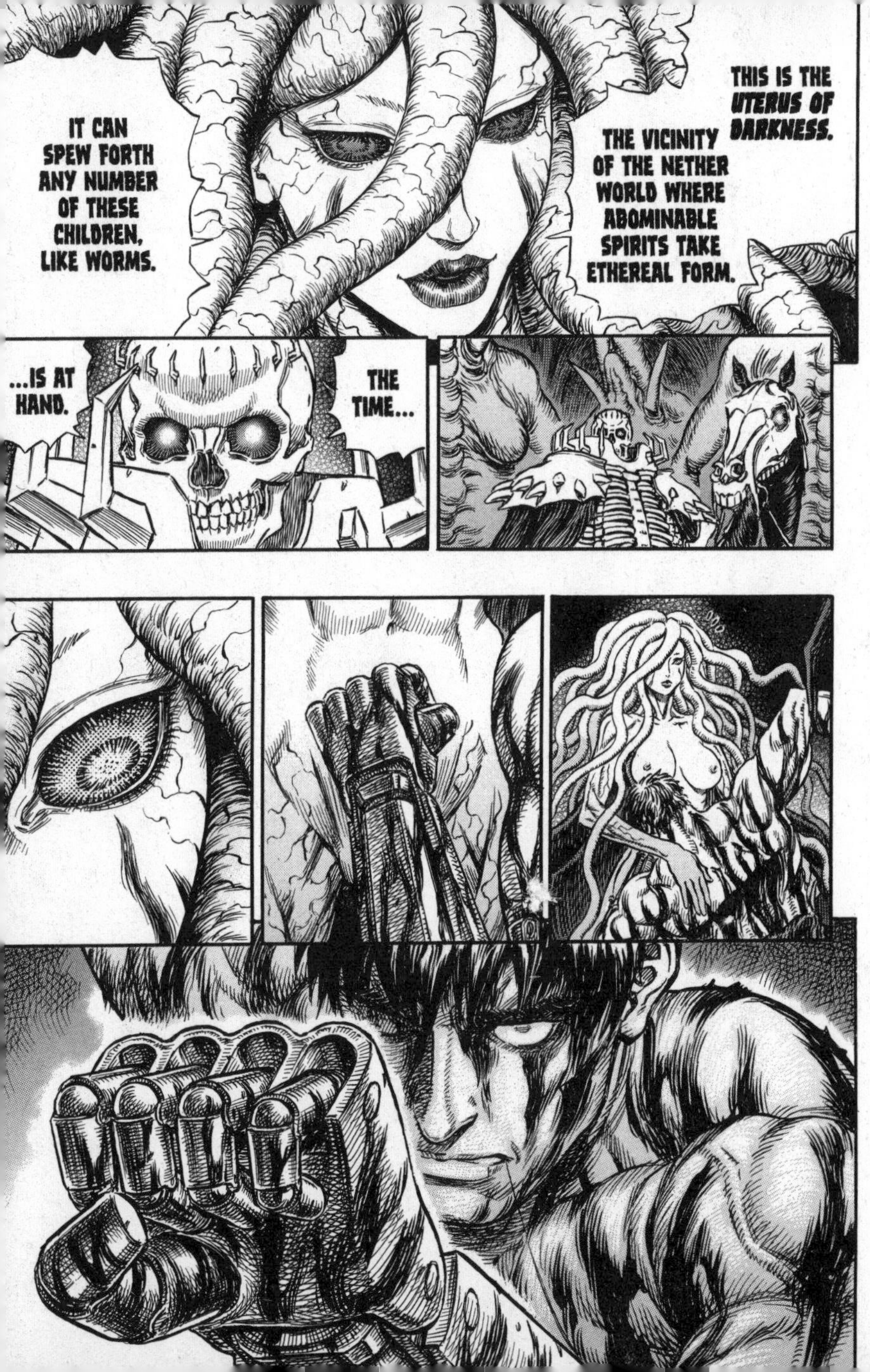
THIS IS THE *UTERUS OF DARKNESS.*
THE VICINITY OF THE NETHER WORLD WHERE ABOMINABLE SPIRITS TAKE ETHEREAL FORM.
IT CAN SPEW FORTH ANY NUMBER OF THESE CHILDREN, LIKE WORMS.
THE TIME...
...IS AT HAND.

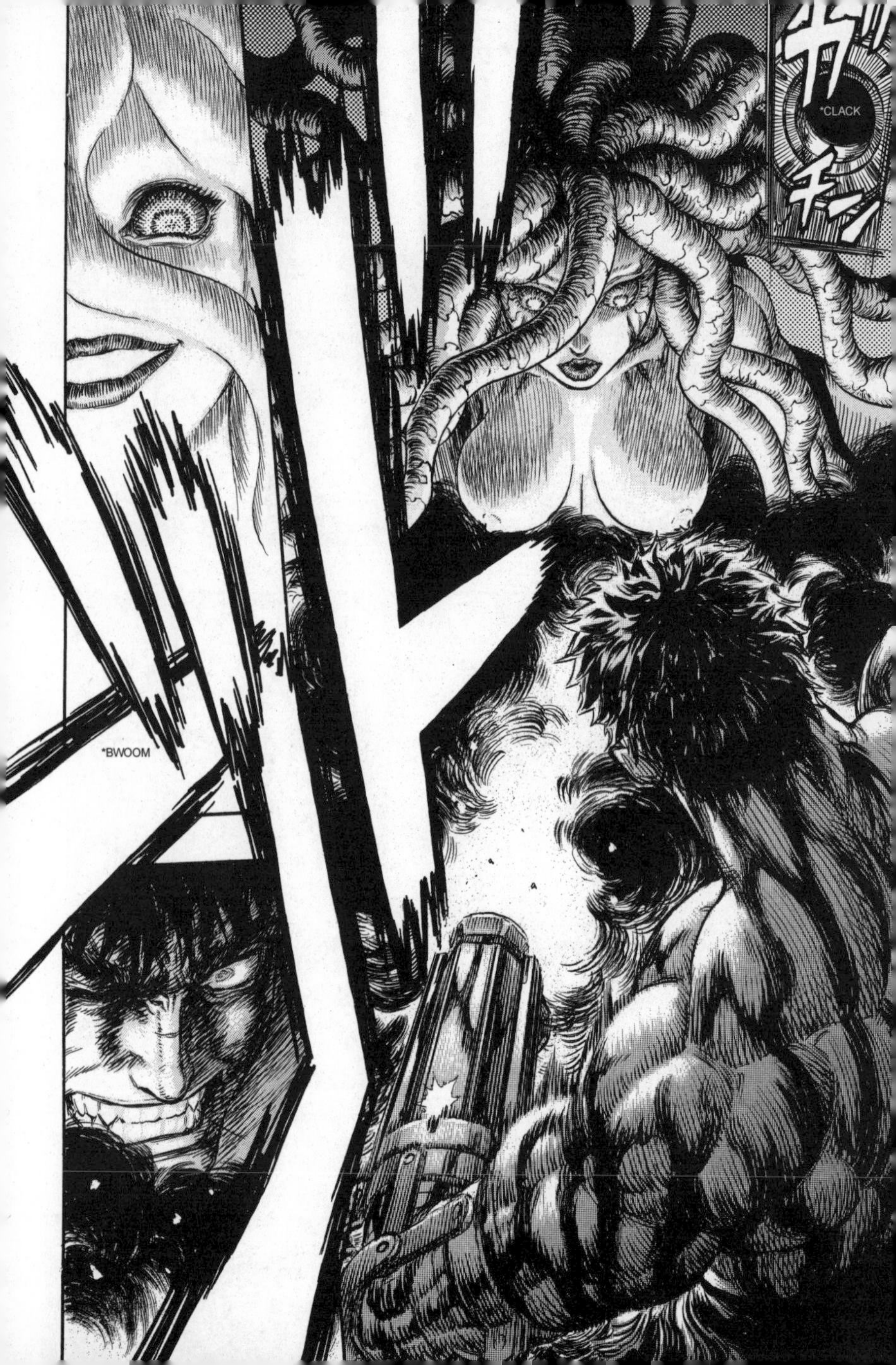
*CLACK
*BWOOM

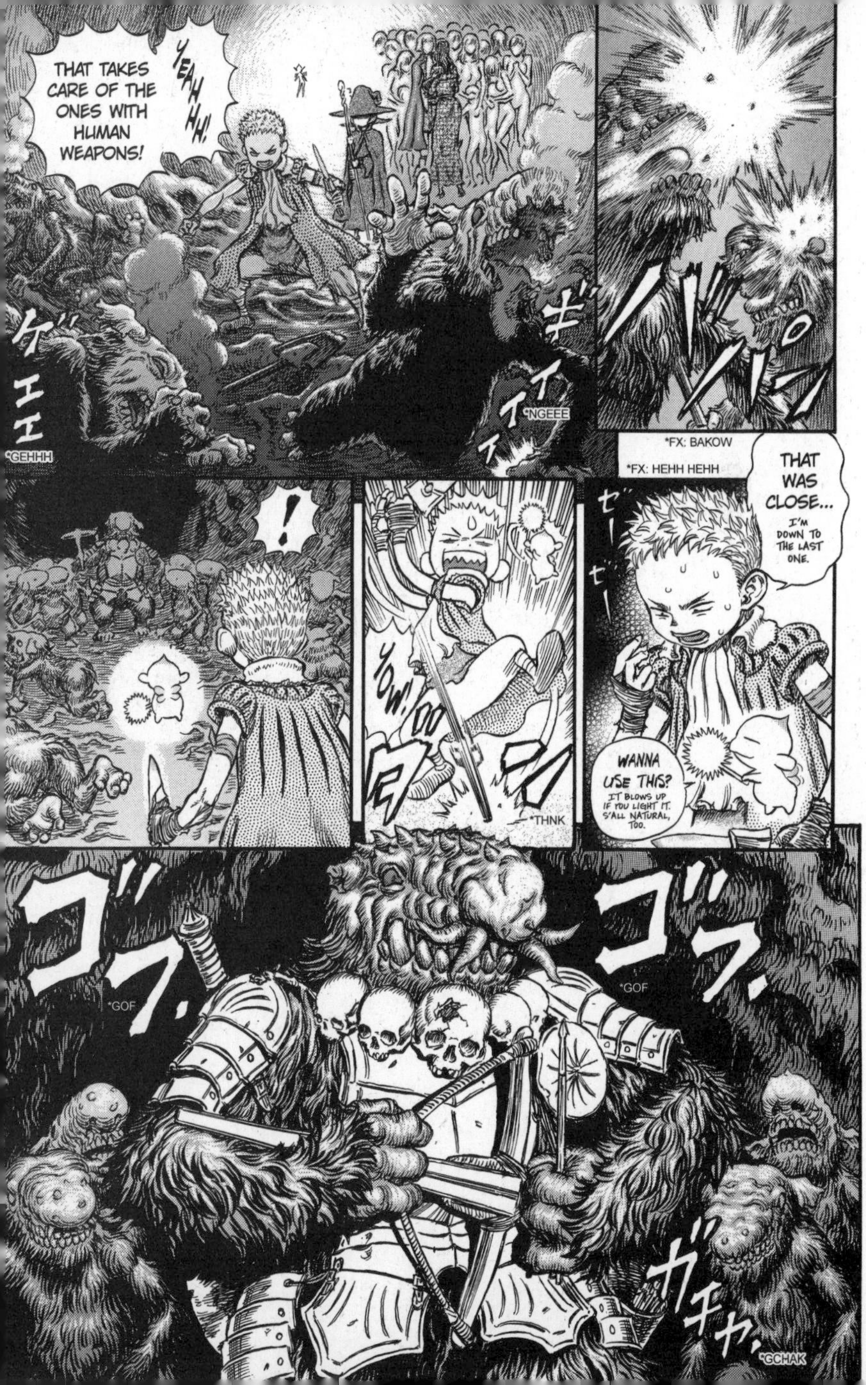
*FX: BAKOW
YEAHHHH!
THAT TAKES CARE OF THE ONES WITH HUMAN WEAPONS!
*NGEEE
*GEHHH
*FX: HEHH HEHH
THAT WAS CLOSE... I'M DOWN TO THE LAST ONE.
WANNA USE THIS? IT BLOWS UP IF YOU LIGHT IT. S'ALL NATURAL, TOO.
YOW!
*THNK
!
*GOF
*GOF
*GCHAK

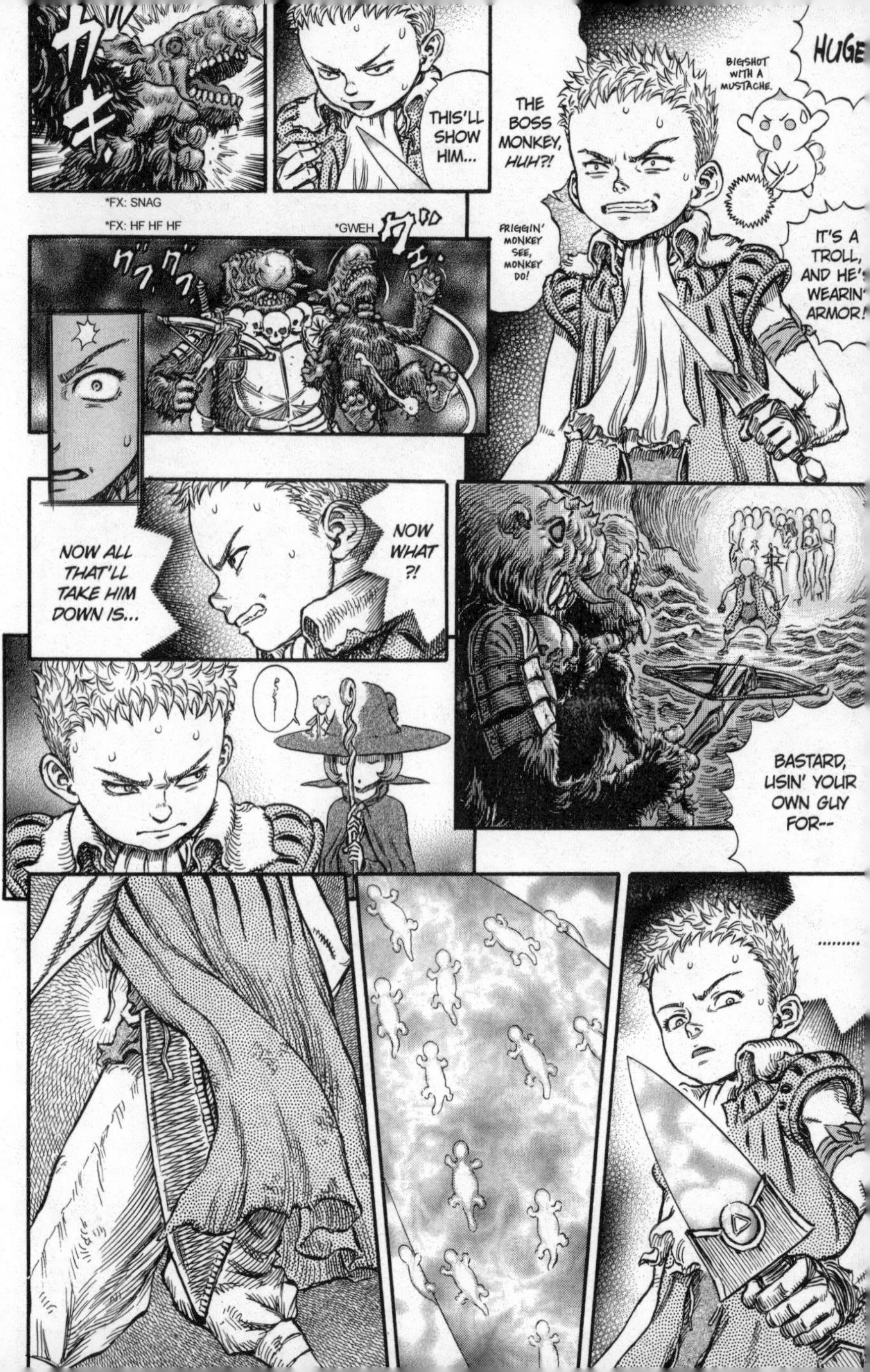
HUGE
BIGSHOT WITH A MUSTACHE.
THE BOSS MONKEY, HUH?!
FRIGGIN' MONKEY SEE, MONKEY DO!
IT'S A TROLL, AND HE'S WEARIN' ARMOR!
THIS'LL SHOW HIM...
*FX: SNAG
*FX: HF HF HF
*GWEH
BASTARD, USIN' YOUR OWN GUY FOR--
NOW WHAT ?!
NOW ALL THAT'LL TAKE HIM DOWN IS...
....

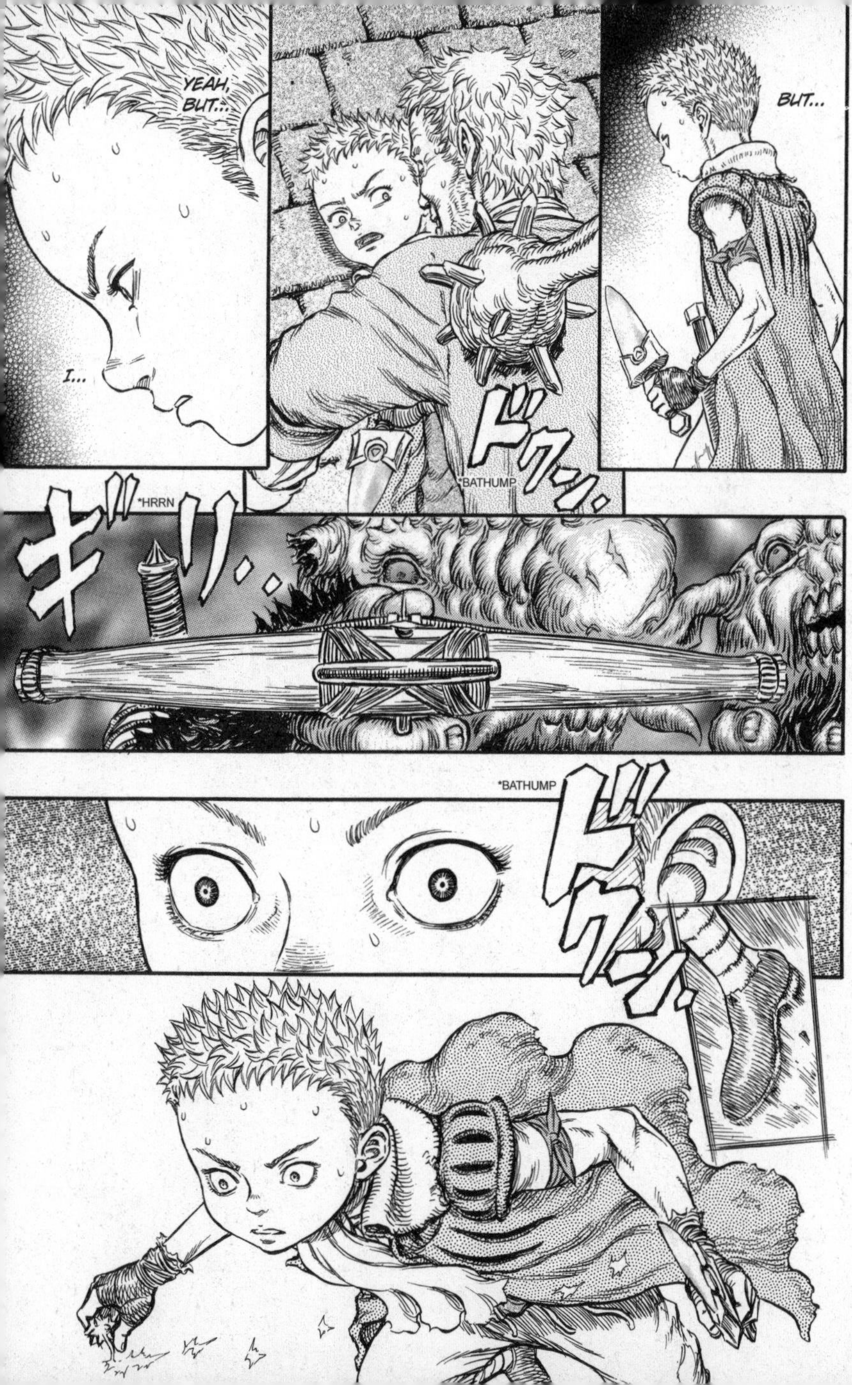

BUT...
ドクン
*BATHUMP
YEAH, BUT...
I...
ギリ
*HRRN
ドクン
*BATHUMP

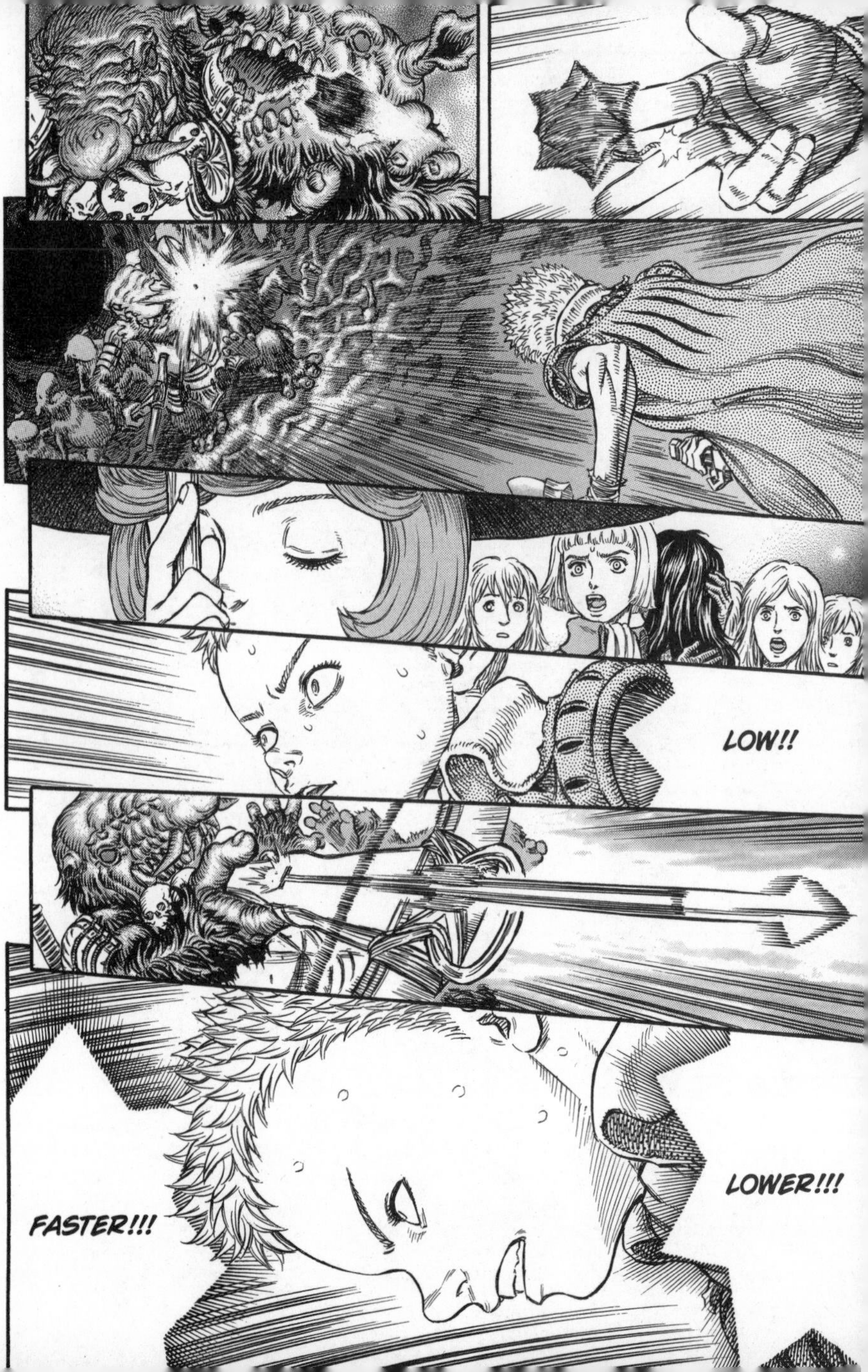
LOW!!
LOWER!!!
FASTER!!!

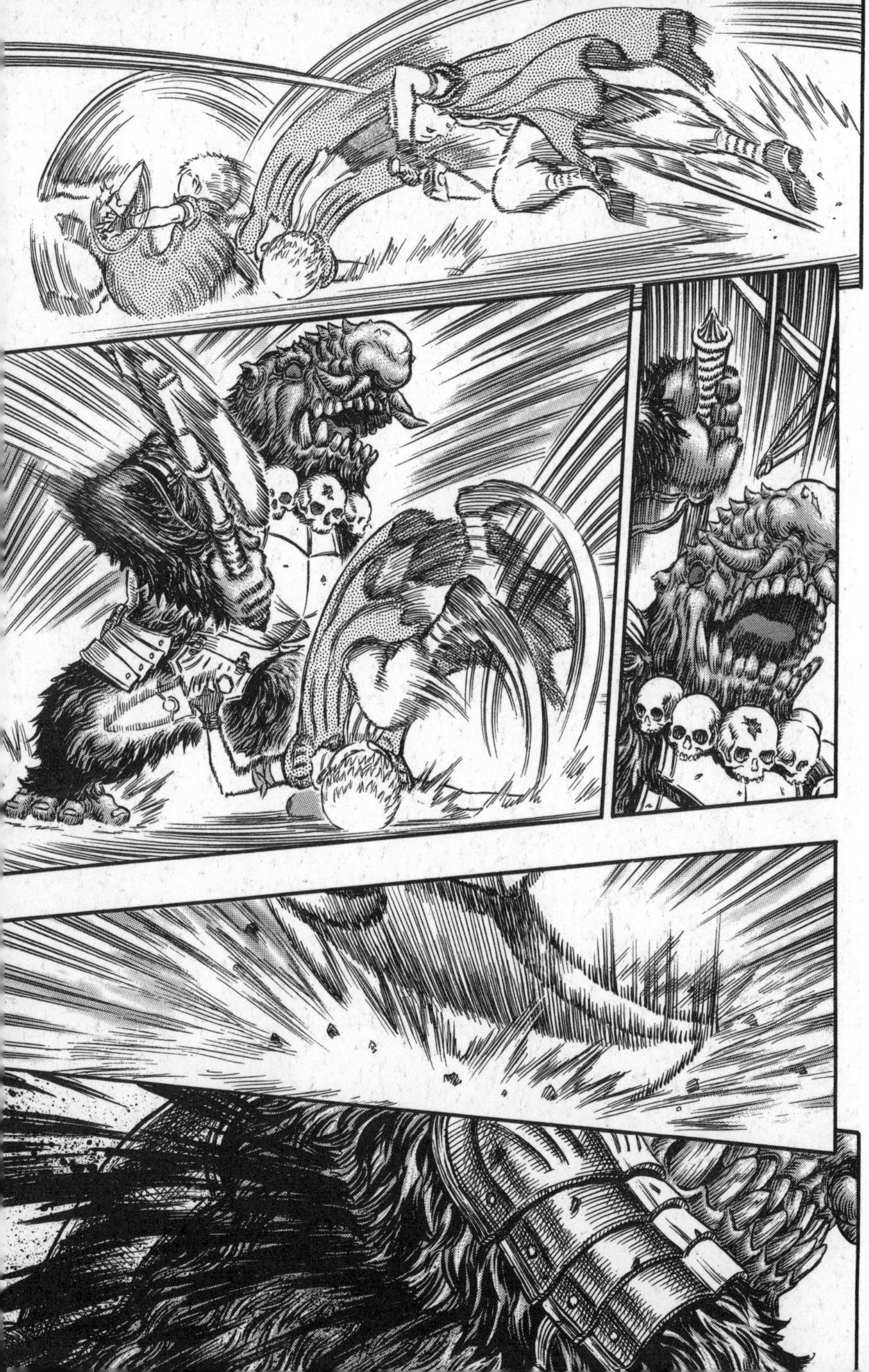

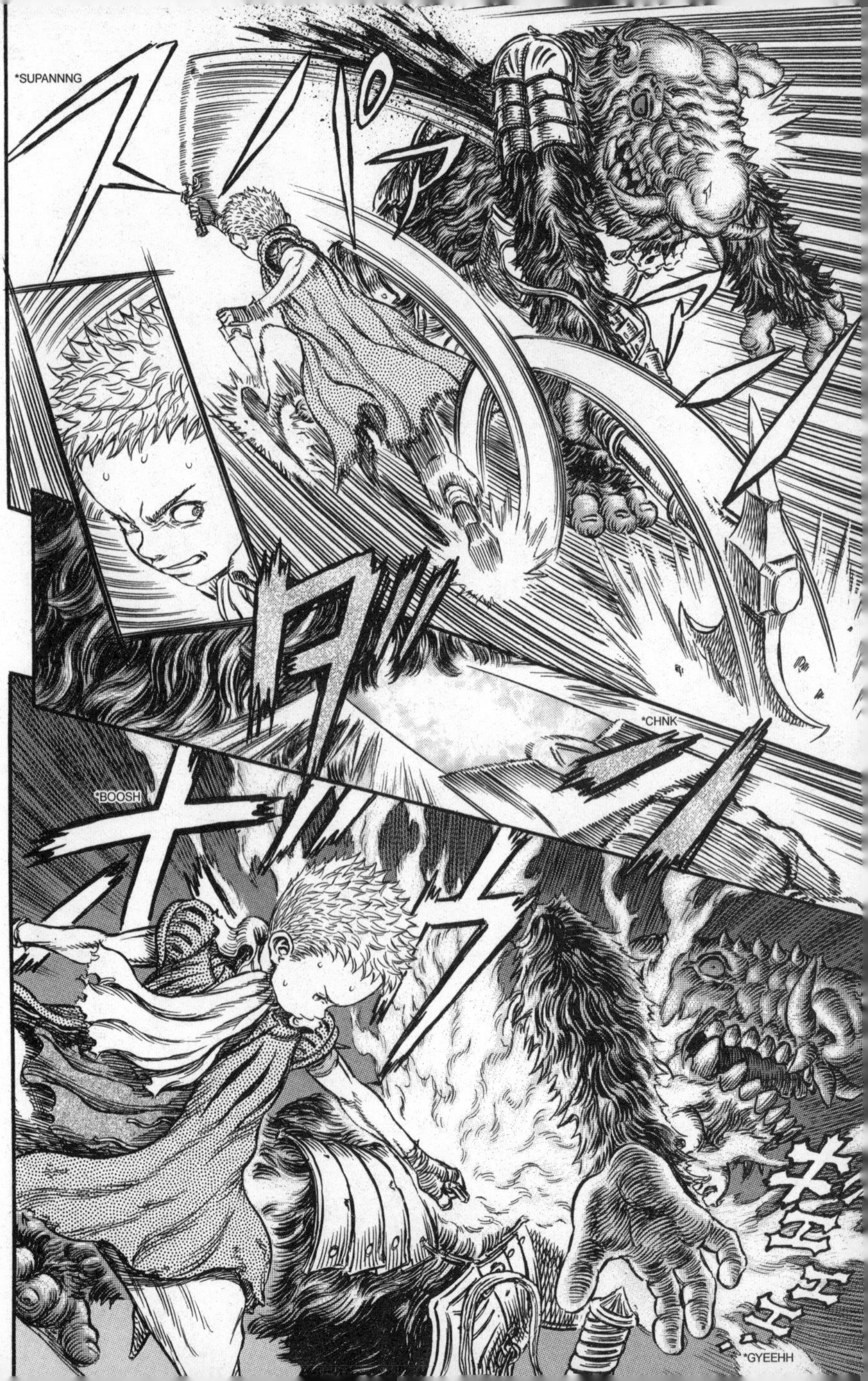
*SUPANNNG
*CHNK
*BOOSH
*GYEEHH

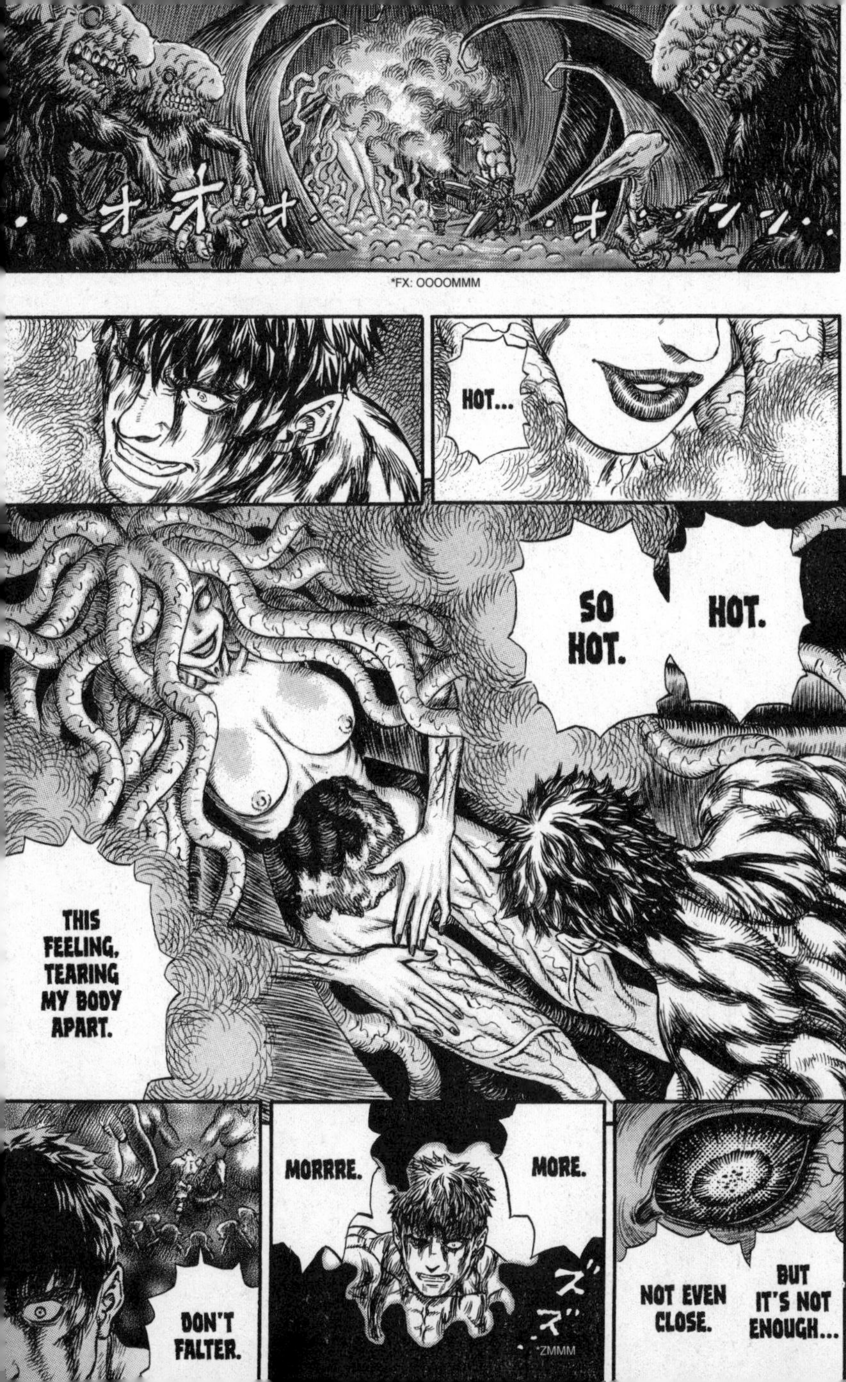
*FX: OOOOMMM
HOT...
HOT.
SO HOT.
THIS FEELING, TEARING MY BODY APART.
BUT IT'S NOT ENOUGH...
NOT EVEN CLOSE.
MORE.
MORRRE.
*ZMMM
DON'T FALTER.

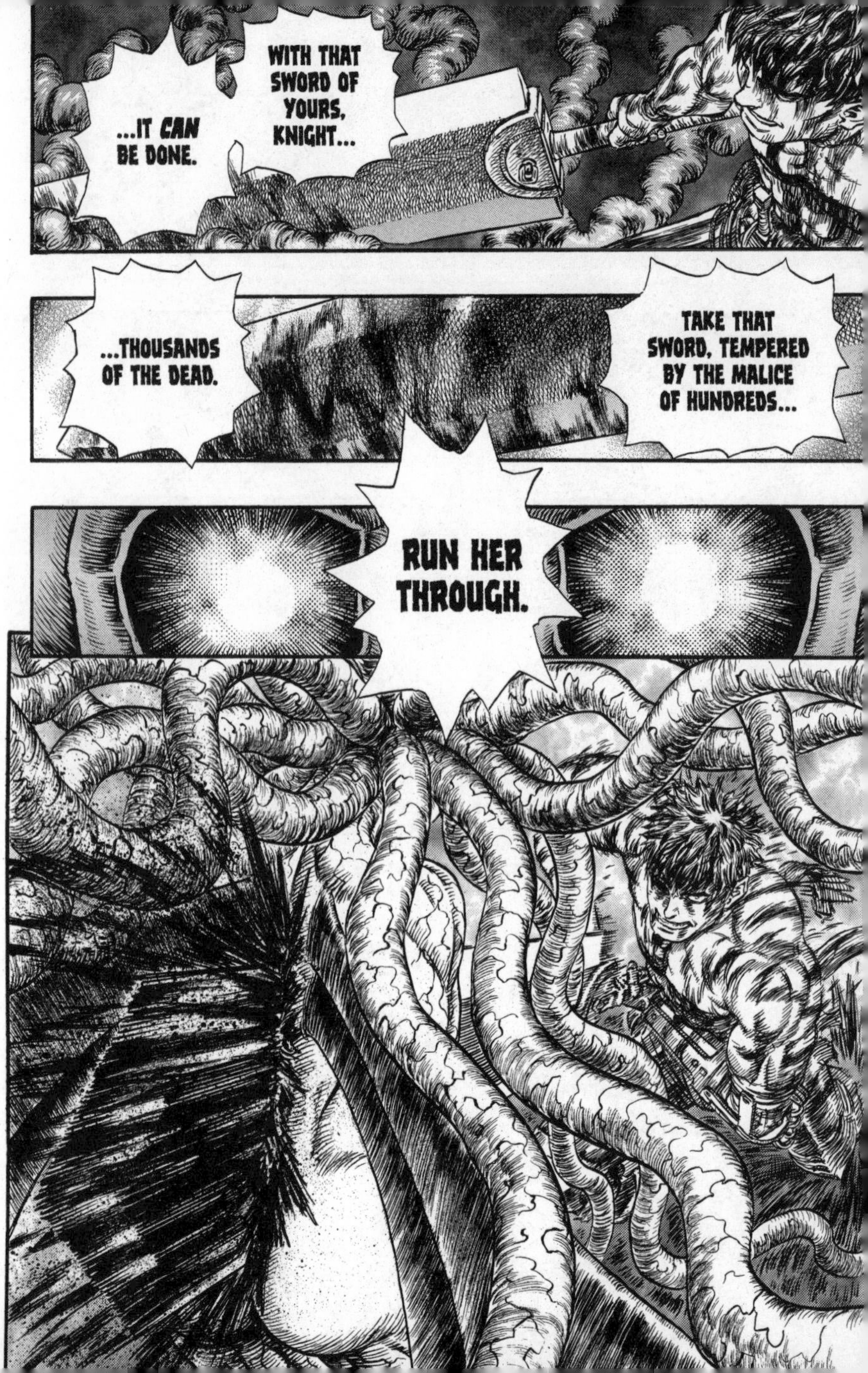
WITH THAT SWORD OF YOURS, KNIGHT...
...IT *CAN* BE DONE.
TAKE THAT SWORD, TEMPERED BY THE MALICE OF HUNDREDS...
...THOUSANDS OF THE DEAD.
RUN HER THROUGH.

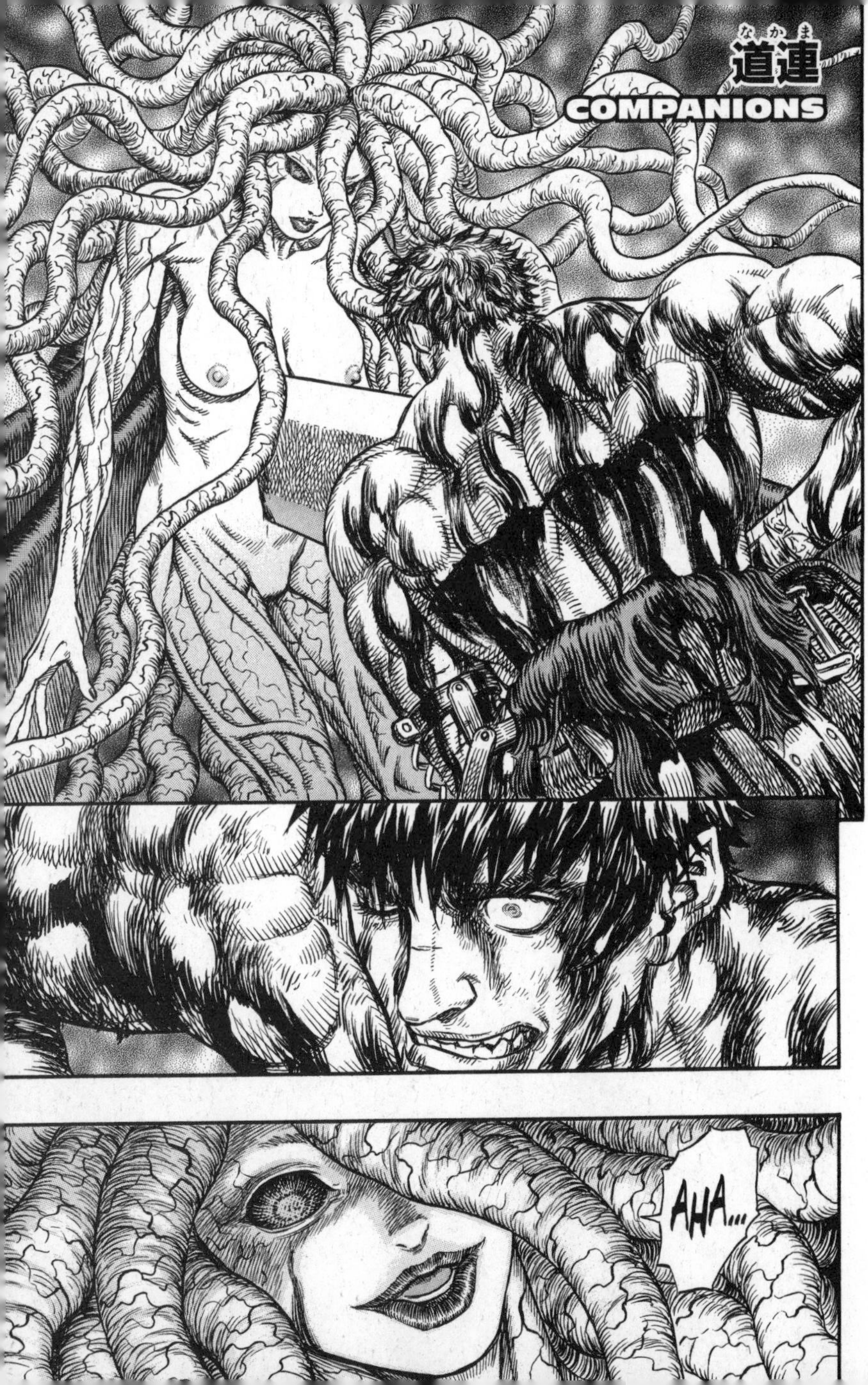
道連
COMPANIONS
AHA...

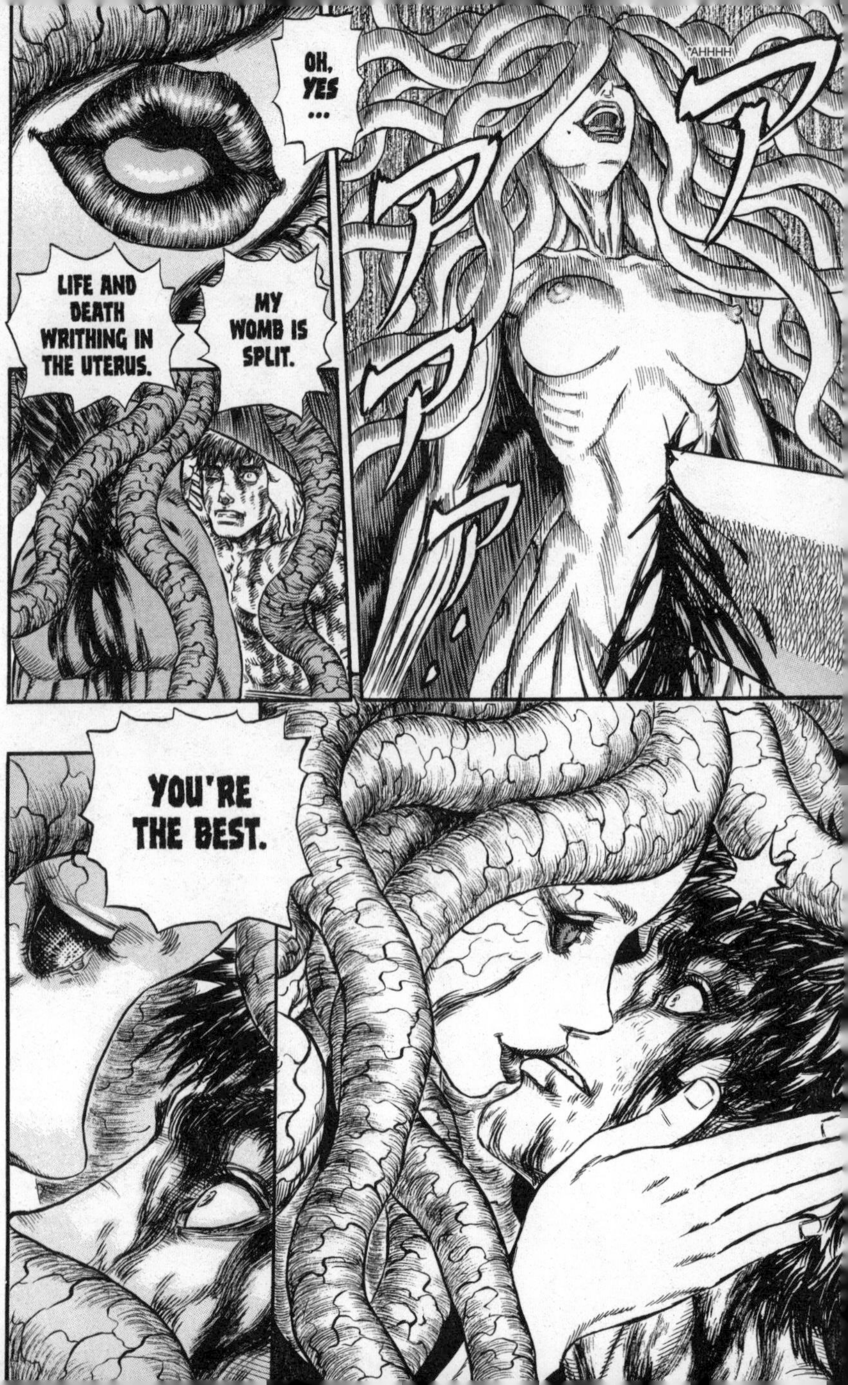
*AHHHH
OH, YES ...
MY WOMB IS SPLIT.
LIFE AND DEATH WRITHING IN THE UTERUS.
YOU'RE THE BEST.

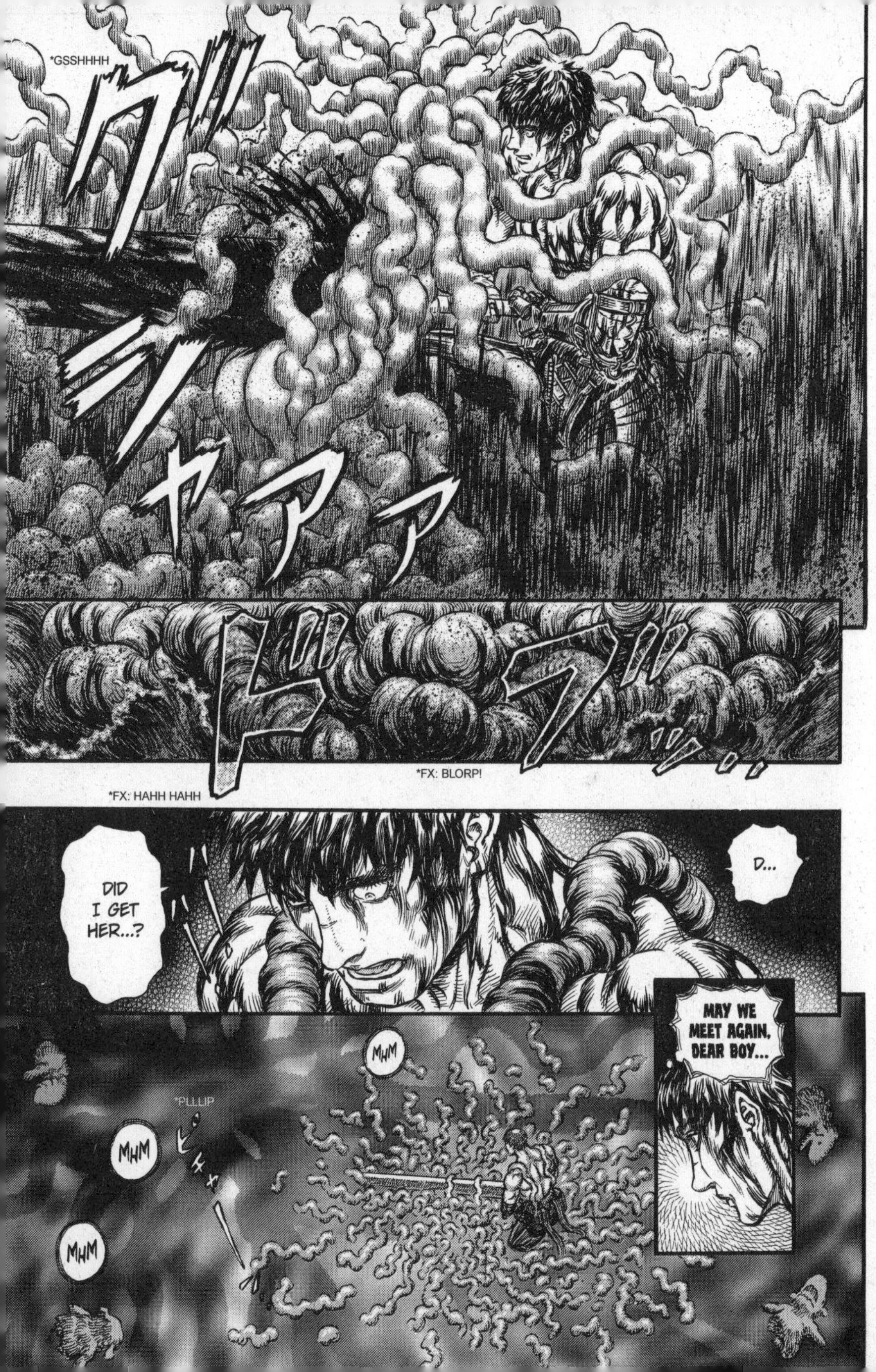
*GSSHHHH
*FX: BLORP!
*FX: HAHH HAHH
D...
DID I GET HER...?
MAY WE MEET AGAIN, DEAR BOY...
MHM
*PLLLIP
MHM
MHM

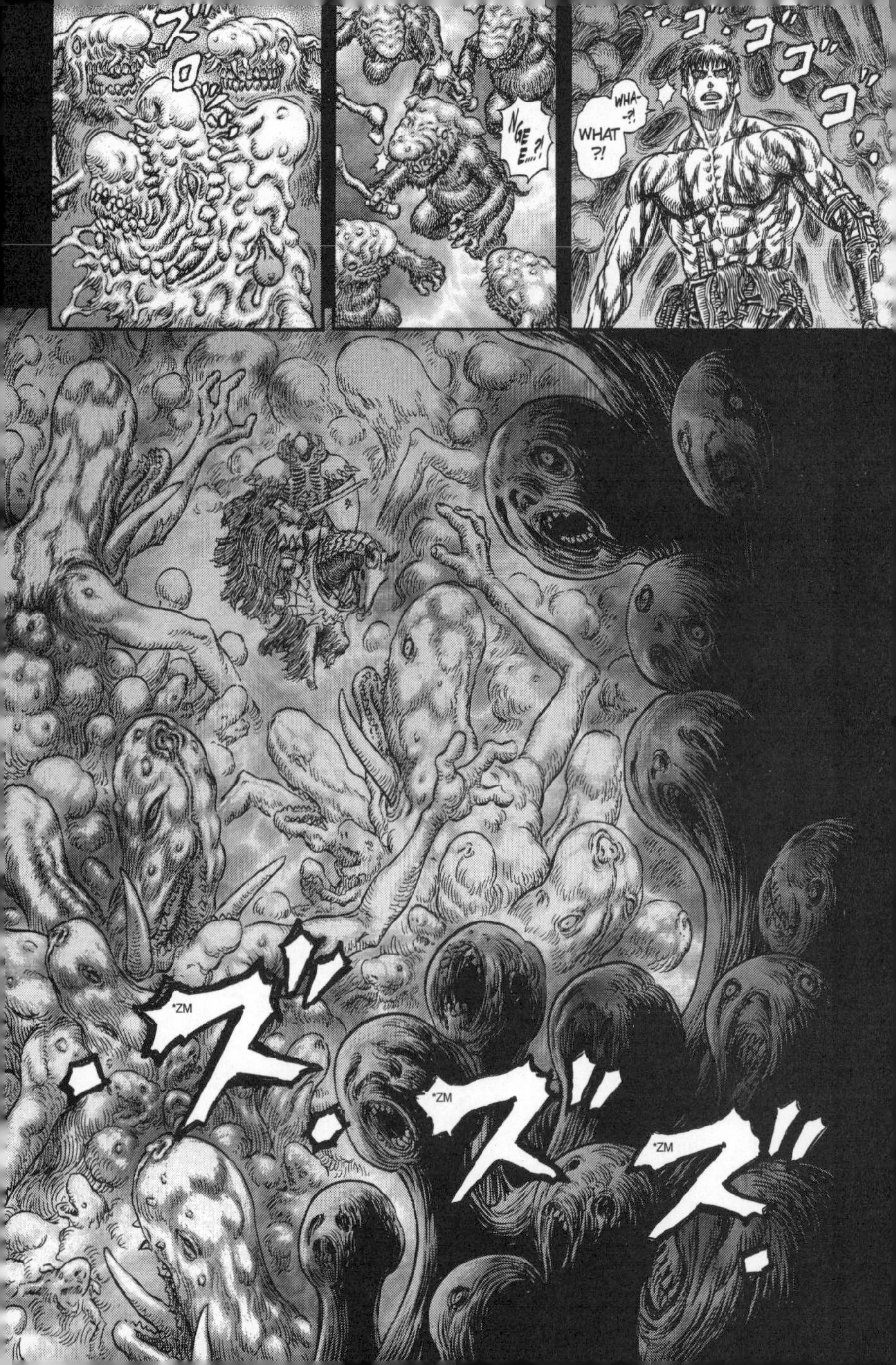
WHA--?!
WHAT?!
NGEE...?!
*ZM
*ZM
*ZM

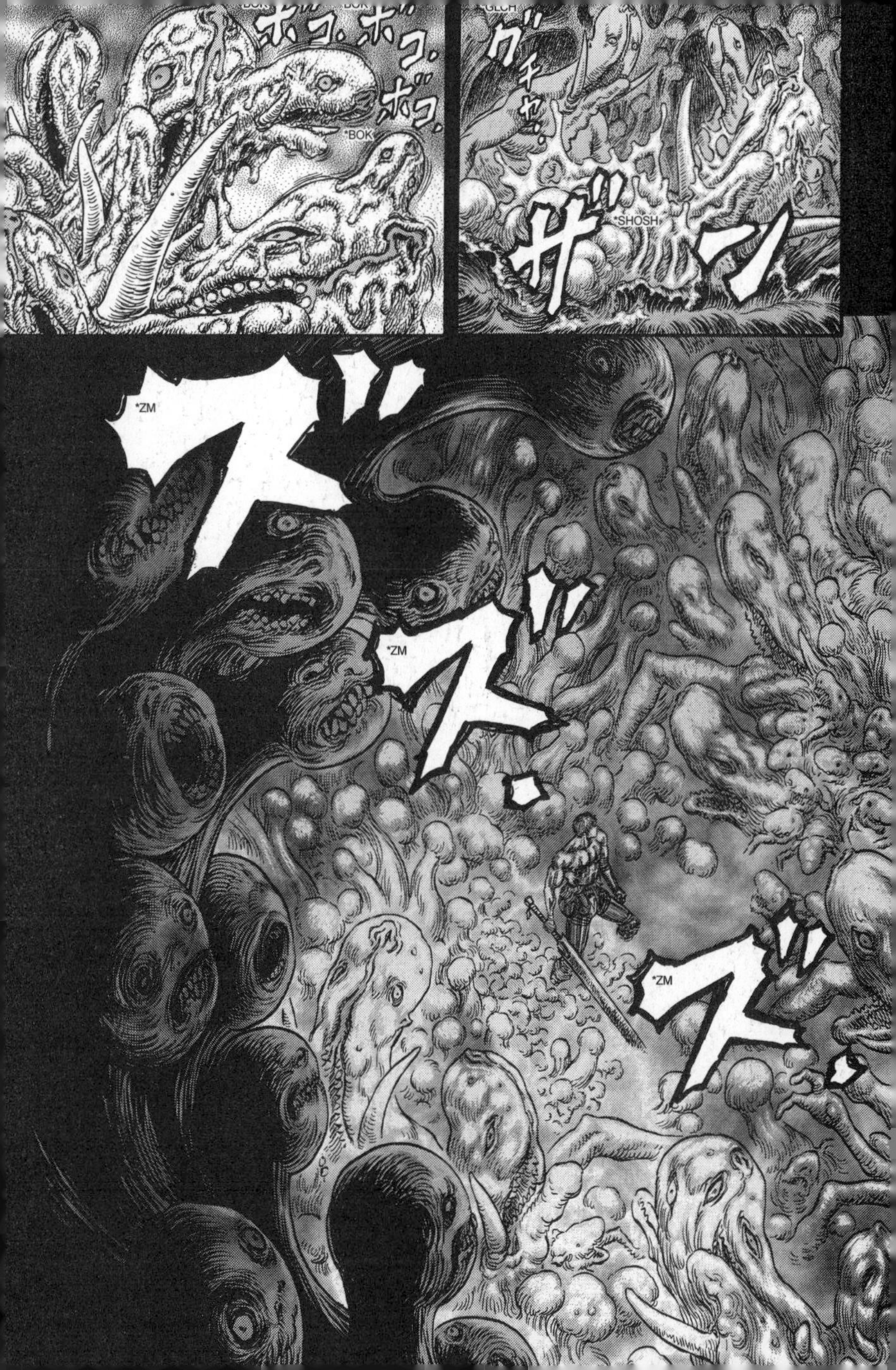
GLCH
グチャ。
*SHOSH
ボコ。ボコ。ボコ。
*BOK
*ZM
*ZM
*ZM

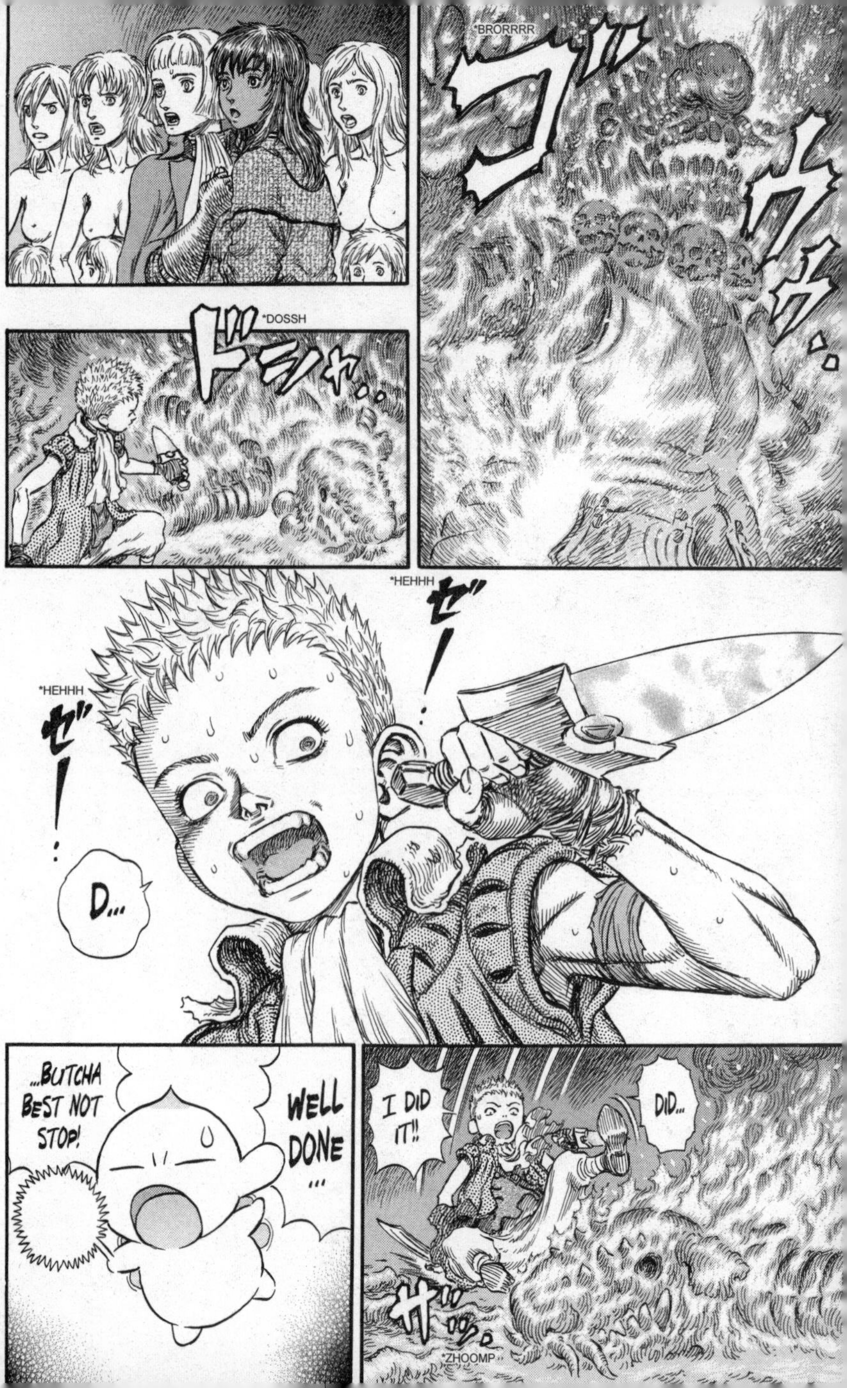
*BRORRRR
*DOSSH
*HEHHH
*HEHHH
D...
DID...
I DID IT!!
*ZHOOMP
WELL DONE ...
...BUTCHA BEST NOT STOP!

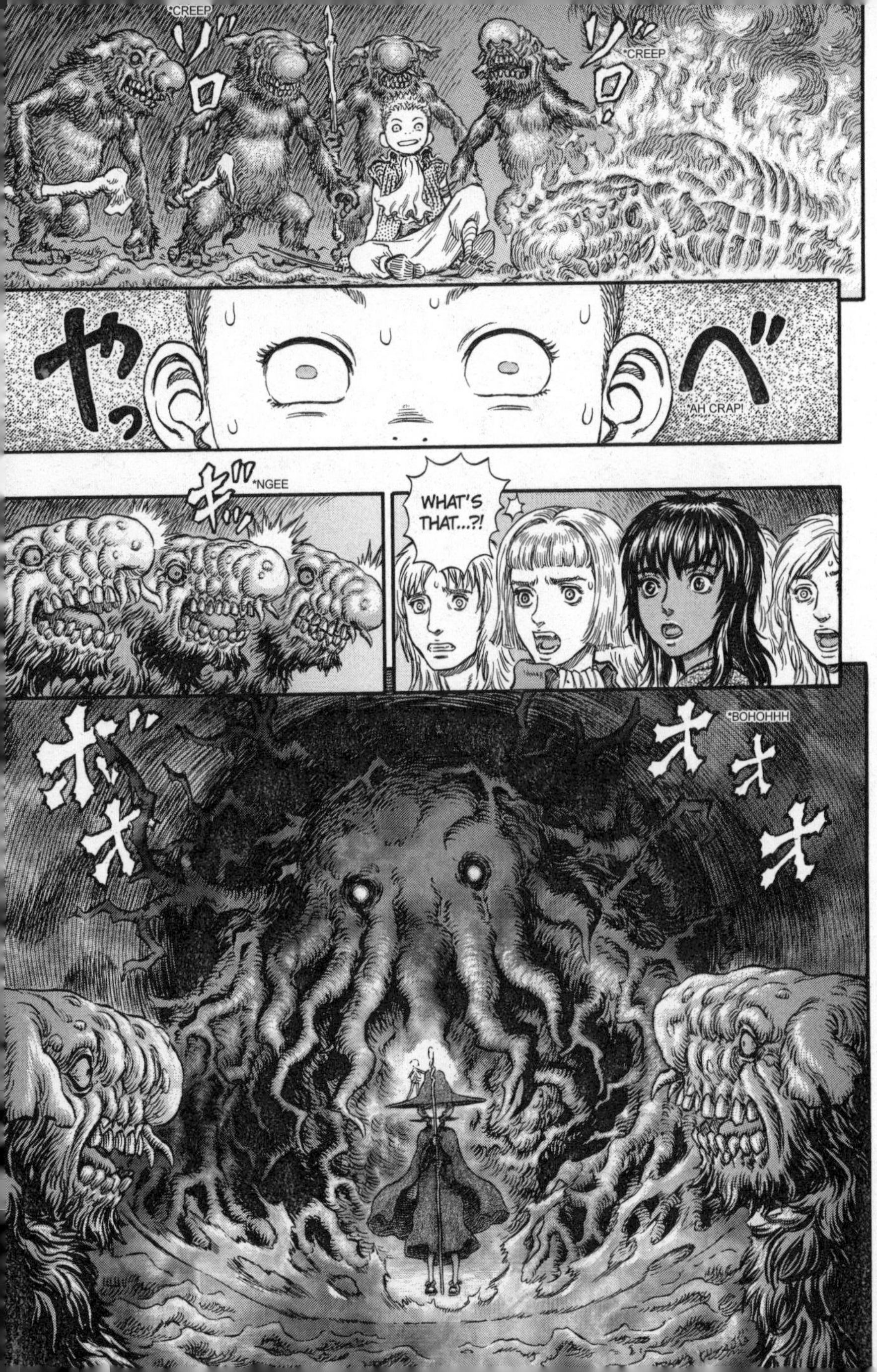
ゾロ
*CREEP
ゾロ
*CREEP
やっべ
*AH CRAP!
WHAT'S THAT...?!
ギッ
*NGEE
ボォ
オォォ
*BOHOHHH

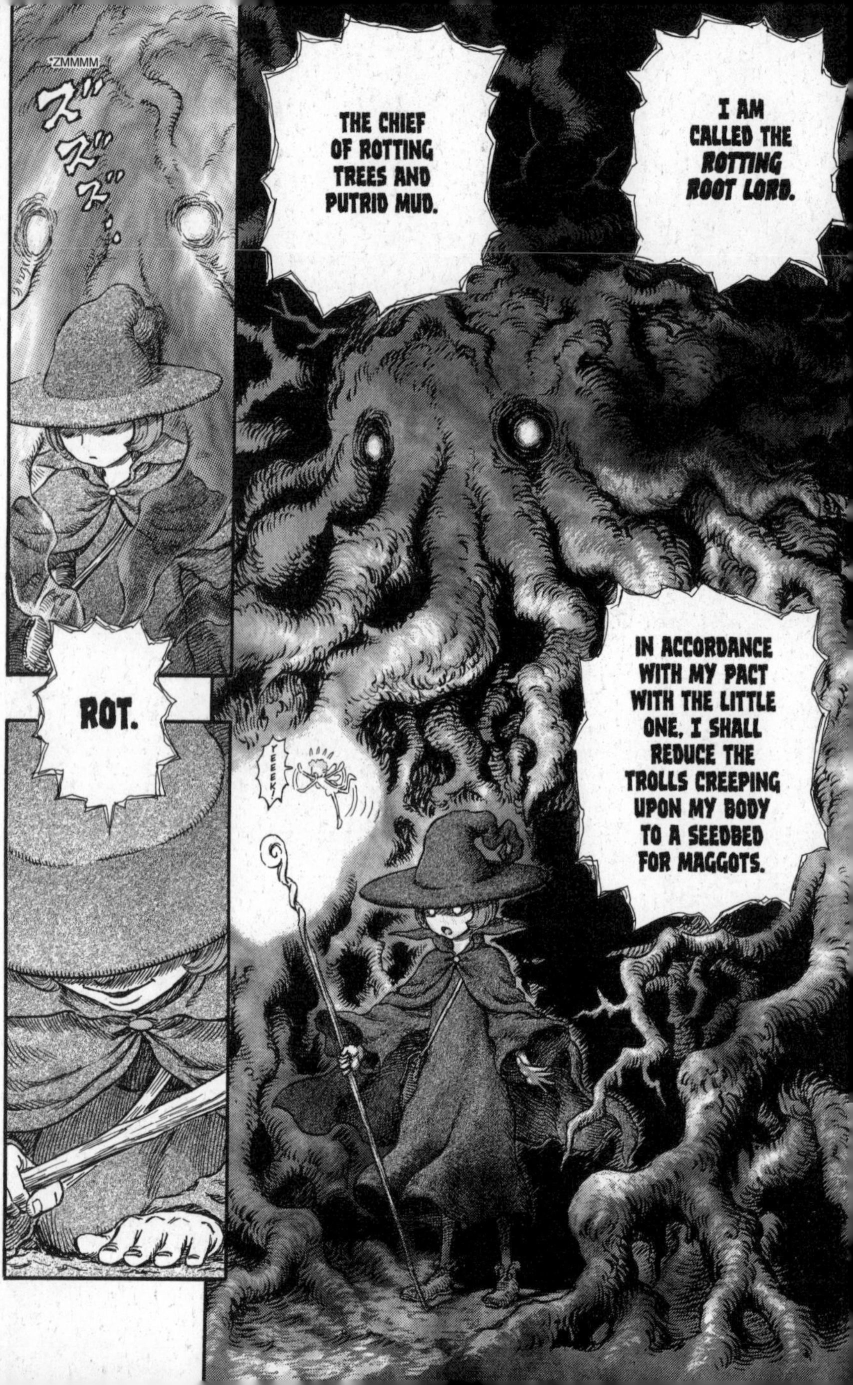
I AM CALLED THE ROTTING ROOT LORD.
THE CHIEF OF ROTTING TREES AND PUTRID MUD.
IN ACCORDANCE WITH MY PACT WITH THE LITTLE ONE, I SHALL REDUCE THE TROLLS CREEPING UPON MY BODY TO A SEEDBED FOR MAGGOTS.
YEEEK!
*ZMMMM
ズズズ
ROT.

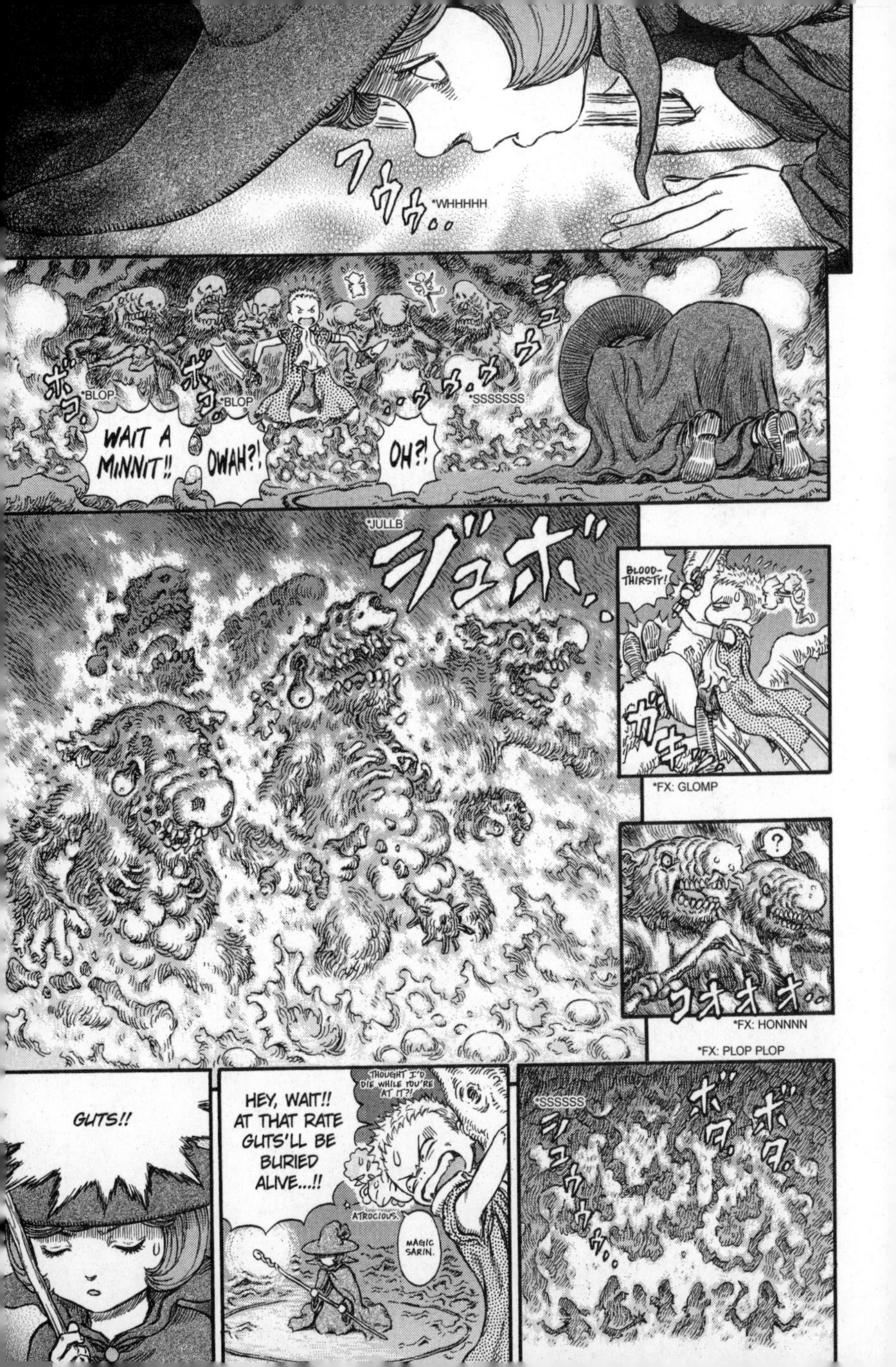
*WHHHHH
*SSSSSS
OH?!
*BLOP
OWAH?!
*BLOP
WAIT A MINNIT!!
BLOOD-THIRSTY!
*FX: GLOMP
?
*FX: HONNNN
*JULLB
*FX: PLOP PLOP
*SSSSSS
THOUGHT I'D DIE WHILE YOU'RE AT IT.
HEY, WAIT!! AT THAT RATE GUTS'LL BE BURIED ALIVE...!!
ATROCIOUS.
MAGIC SARIN.
GUTS!!

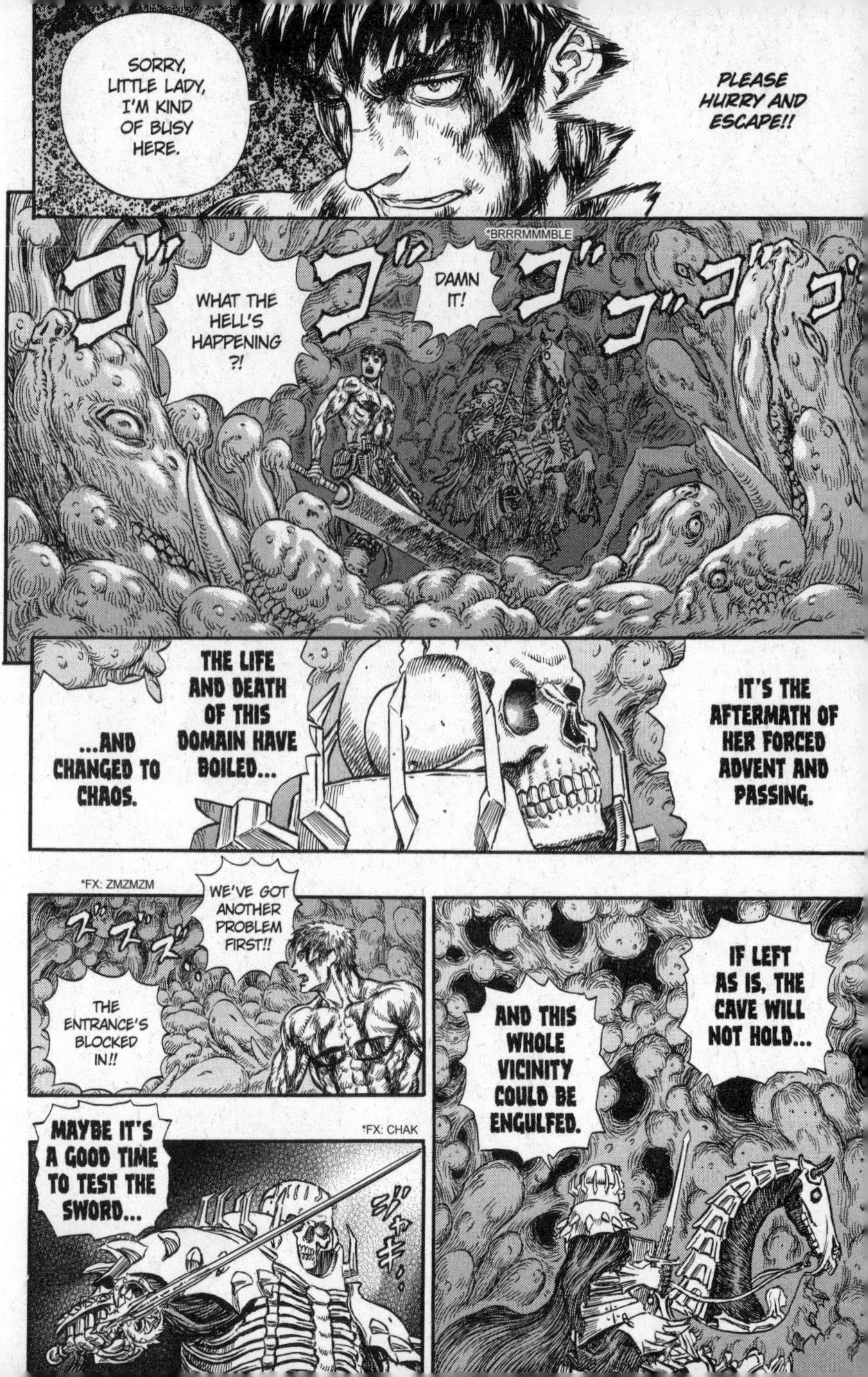
PLEASE HURRY AND ESCAPE!!
SORRY, LITTLE LADY, I'M KIND OF BUSY HERE.
*BRRRMMMBLE
DAMN IT!
WHAT THE HELL'S HAPPENING ?!
IT'S THE AFTERMATH OF HER FORCED ADVENT AND PASSING.
THE LIFE AND DEATH OF THIS DOMAIN HAVE BOILED...
...AND CHANGED TO CHAOS.
IF LEFT AS IS, THE CAVE WILL NOT HOLD...
AND THIS WHOLE VICINITY COULD BE ENGULFED.
*FX: ZMZMZM
WE'VE GOT ANOTHER PROBLEM FIRST!!
THE ENTRANCE'S BLOCKED IN!!
*FX: CHAK
MAYBE IT'S A GOOD TIME TO TEST THE SWORD...

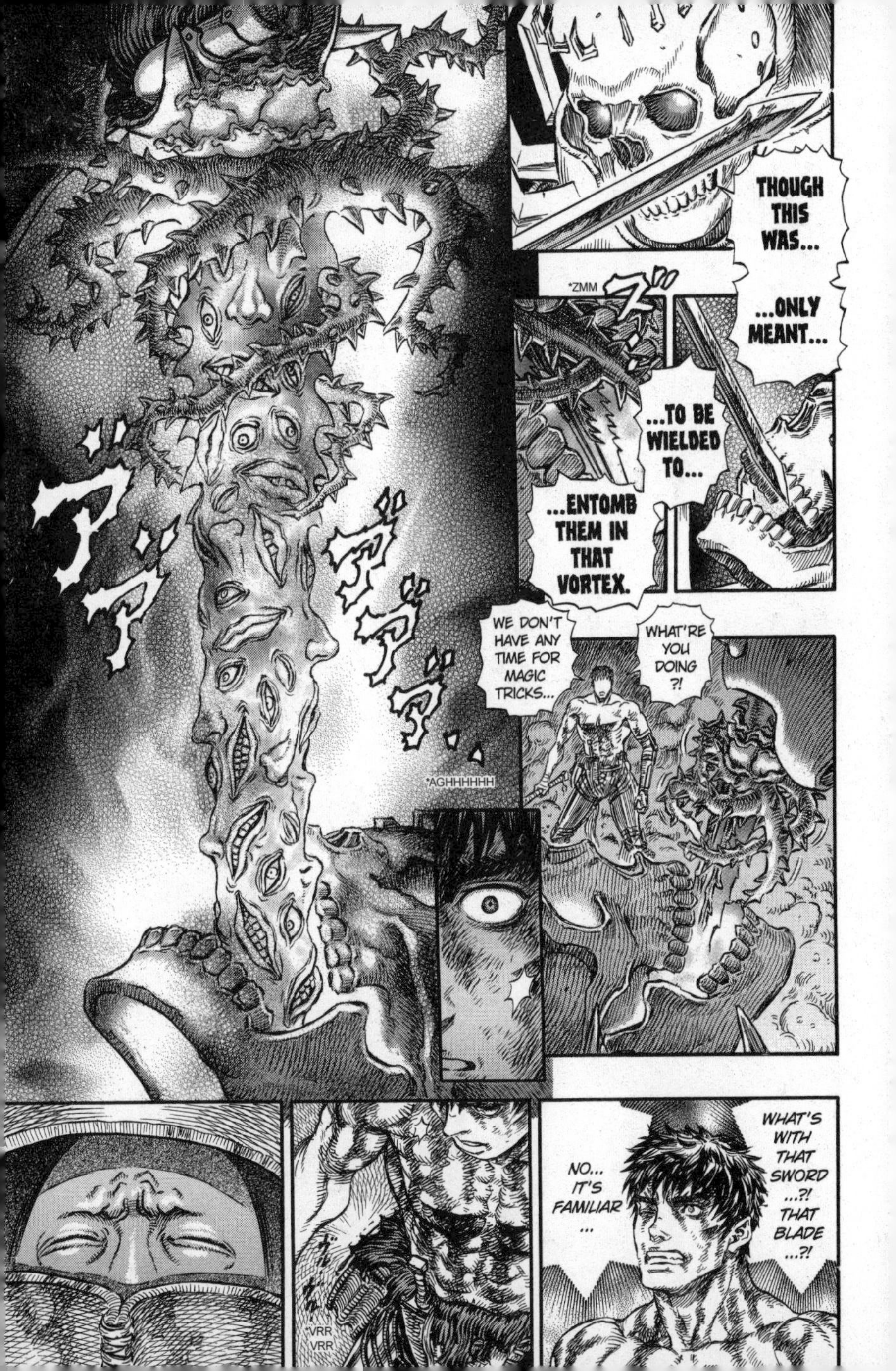
THOUGH THIS WAS...
...ONLY MEANT...
*ZMM
...TO BE WIELDED TO...
...ENTOMB THEM IN THAT VORTEX.
WHAT'RE YOU DOING ?!
WE DON'T HAVE ANY TIME FOR MAGIC TRICKS...
*AGHHHHHH
WHAT'S WITH THAT SWORD ...?! THAT BLADE ...?!
NO... IT'S FAMILIAR ...
*VRR VRR

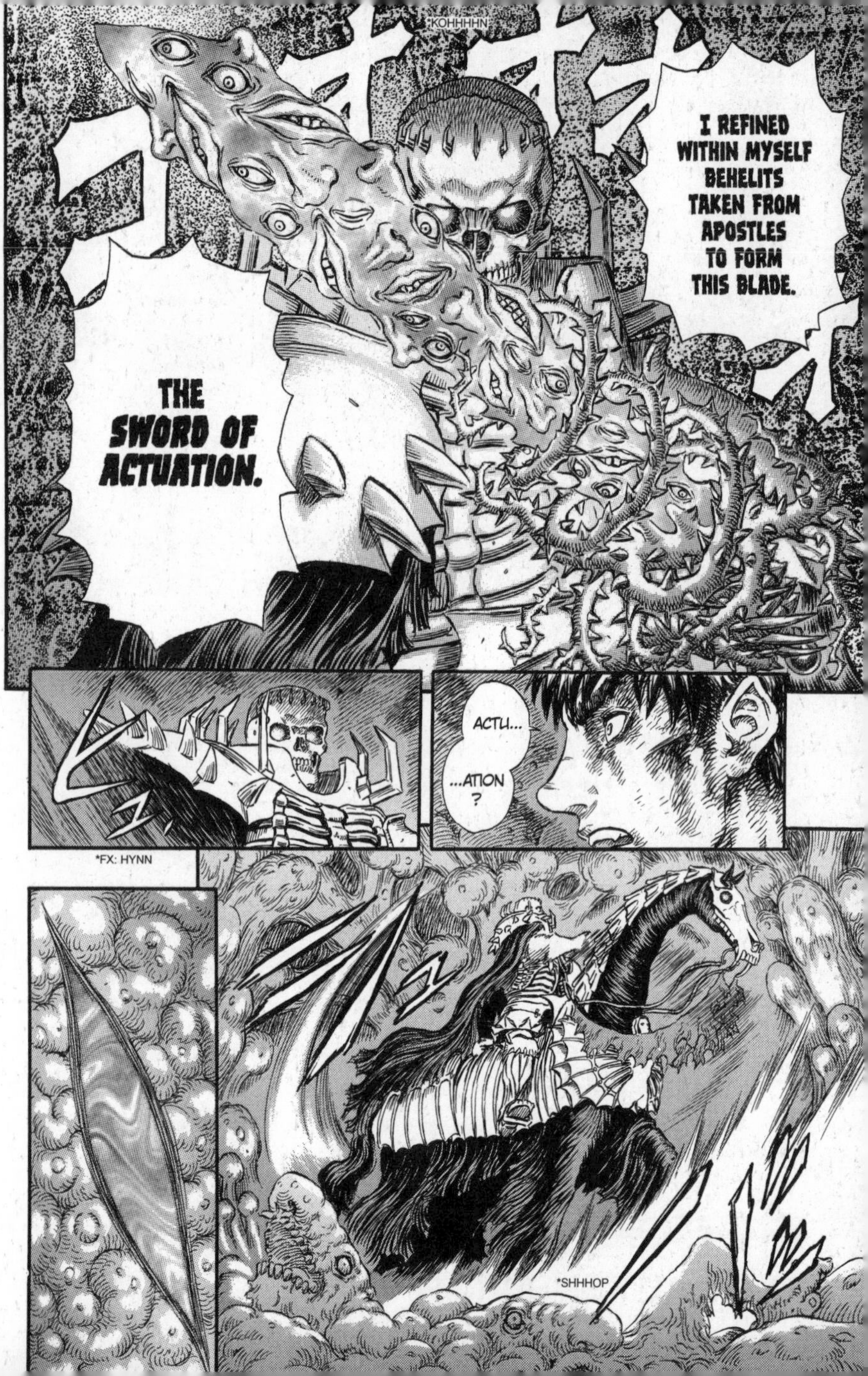
*KOHHHHN
I REFINED WITHIN MYSELF BEHELITS TAKEN FROM APOSTLES TO FORM THIS BLADE.
THE SWORD OF ACTUATION.
ACTU...
...ATION ?
*FX: HYNN
*SHHHOP

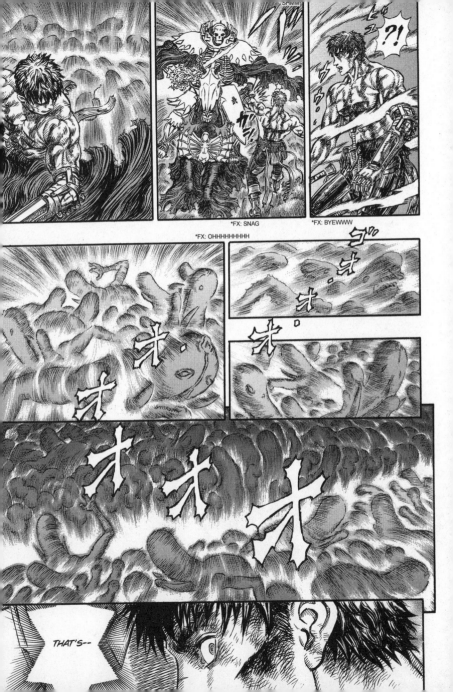

*FX: SNAG

*FX: OHHHHHHHHH

*FX: BYEWWW

THAT'S--

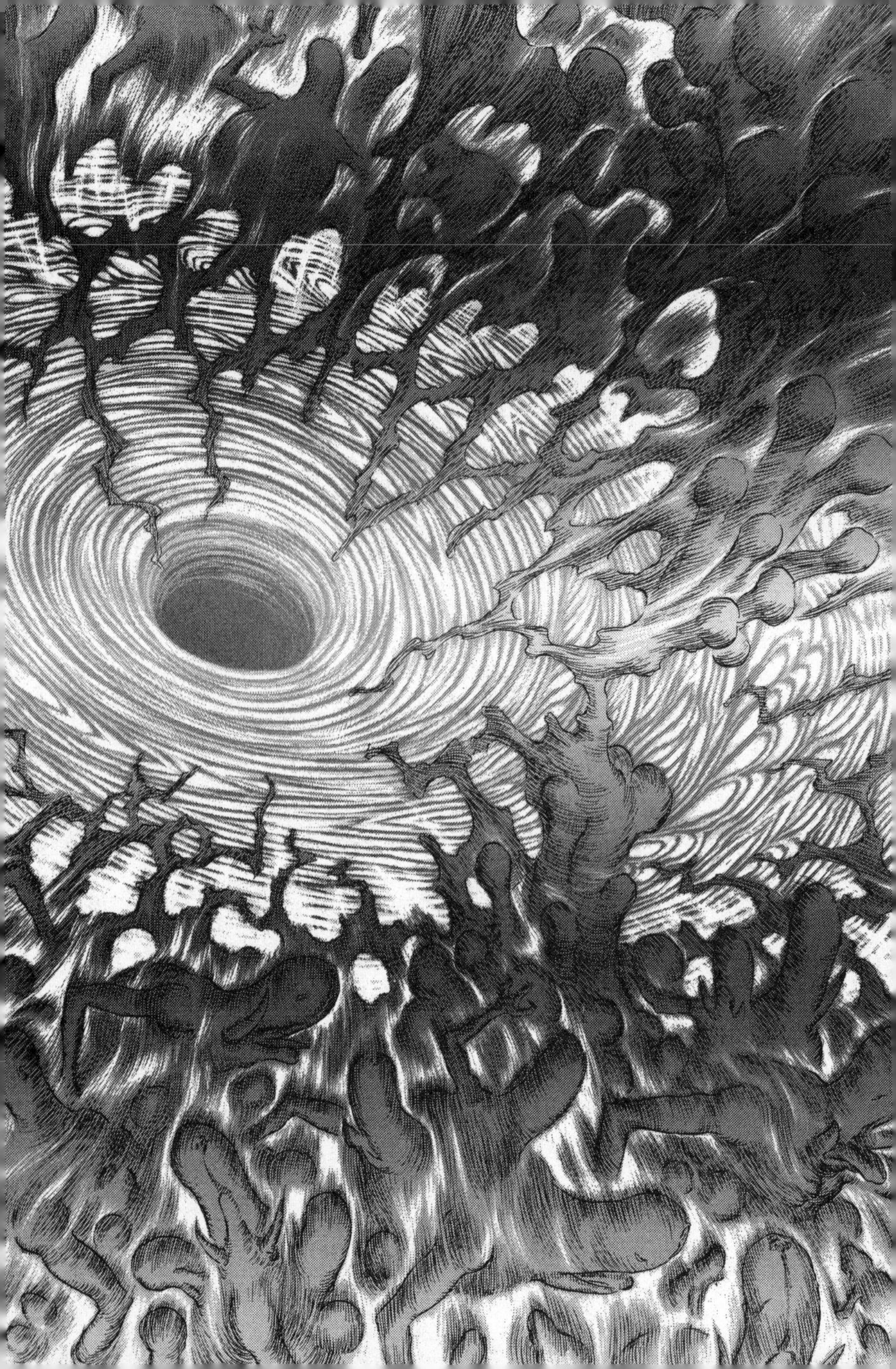

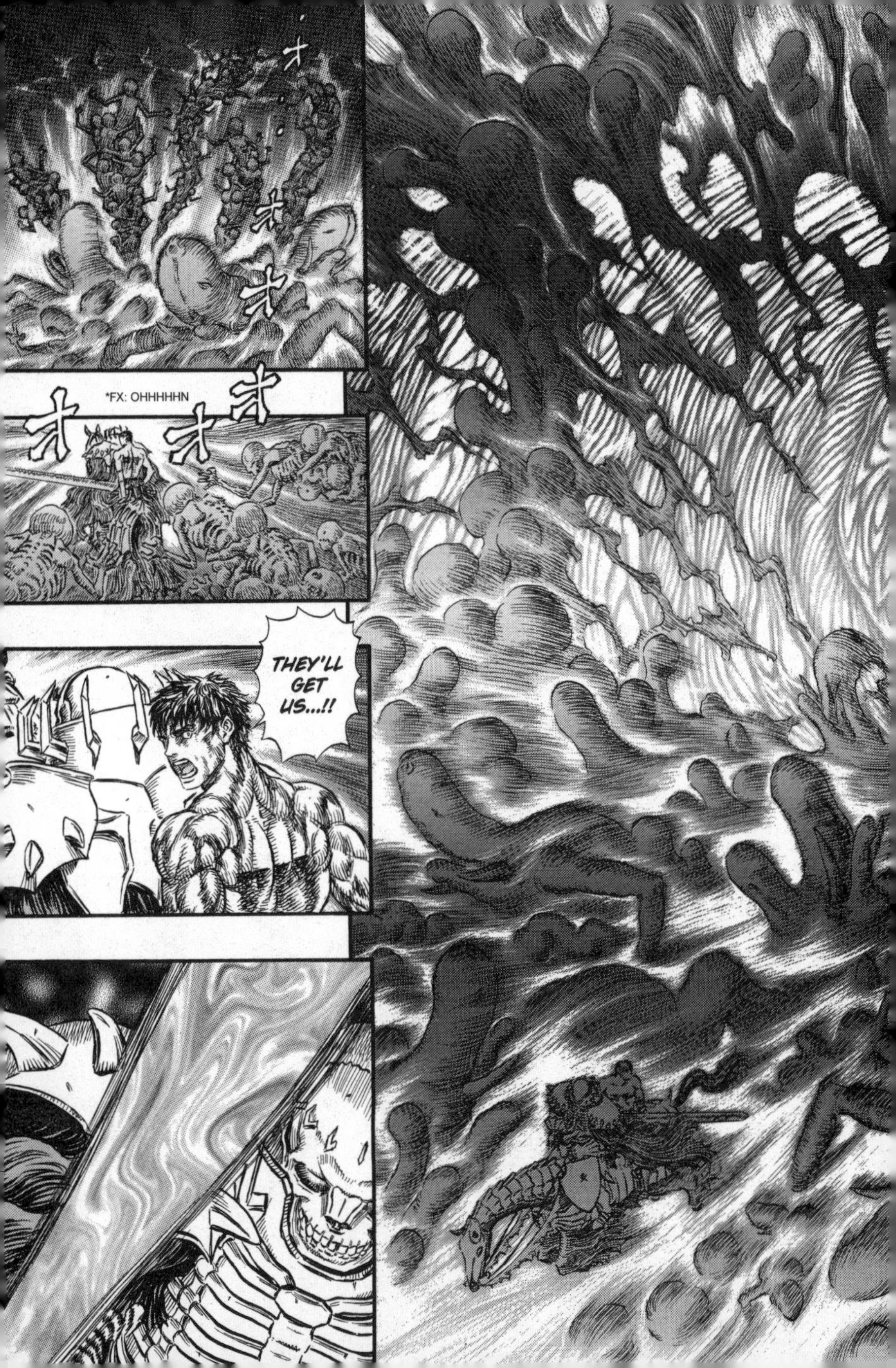
*FX: OHHHHHN
THEY'LL GET US...!!

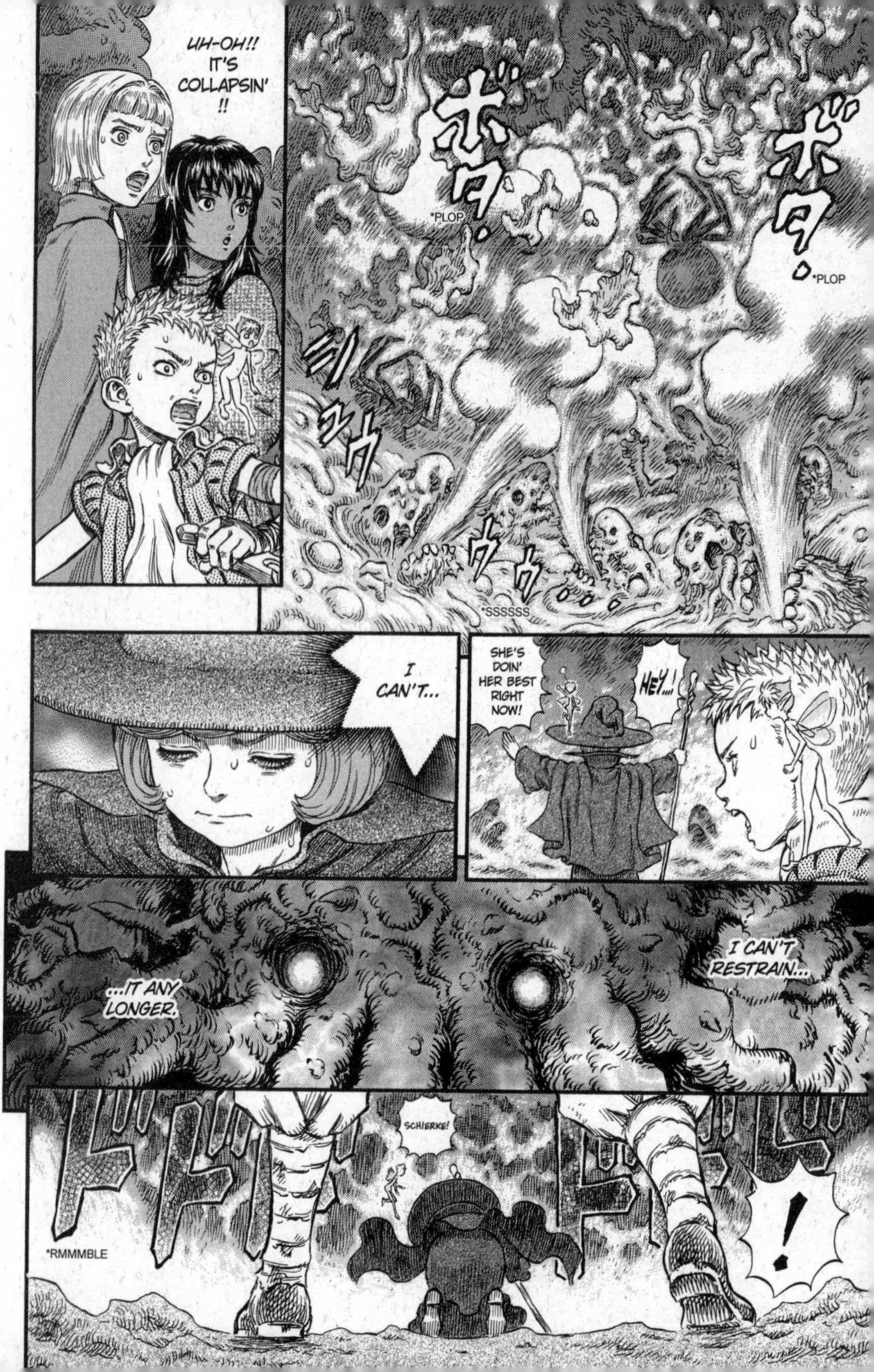
ボタ。
*PLOP
ボタ。
*PLOP
*SSSSSS
UH-OH!! IT'S COLLAPSIN' !!
HEY...!
SHE'S DOIN' HER BEST RIGHT NOW!
I CAN'T...
I CAN'T RESTRAIN...
...IT ANY LONGER.
!
SCHIERKE!
*RMMMBLE

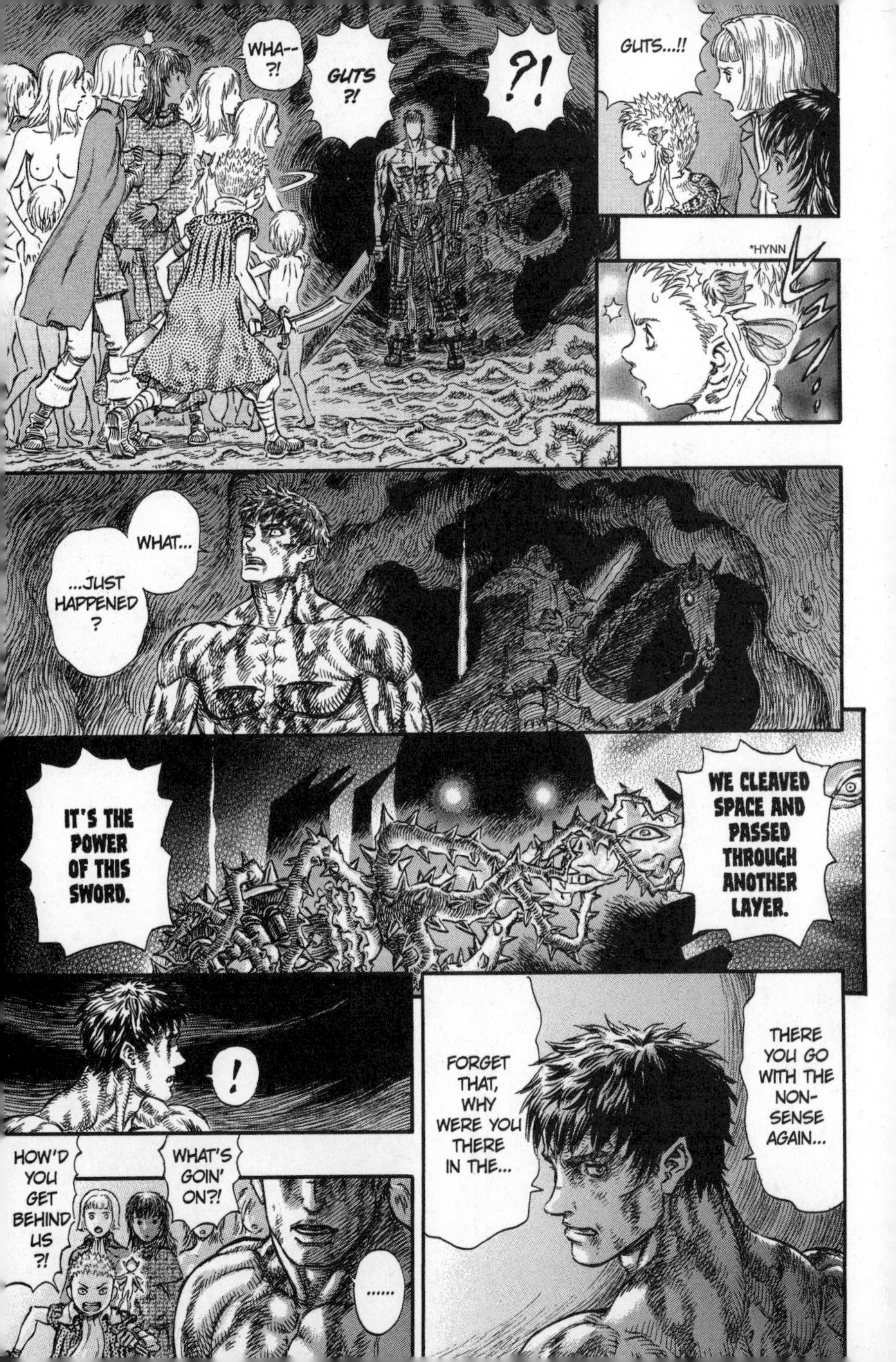
GUTS...!!
*HYNN
?!
GUTS ?!
WHA-- ?!
WHAT...
...JUST HAPPENED ?
WE CLEAVED SPACE AND PASSED THROUGH ANOTHER LAYER.
IT'S THE POWER OF THIS SWORD.
THERE YOU GO WITH THE NON-SENSE AGAIN...
FORGET THAT, WHY WERE YOU THERE IN THE...
!
WHAT'S GOIN' ON?!
HOW'D YOU GET BEHIND US ?!
......

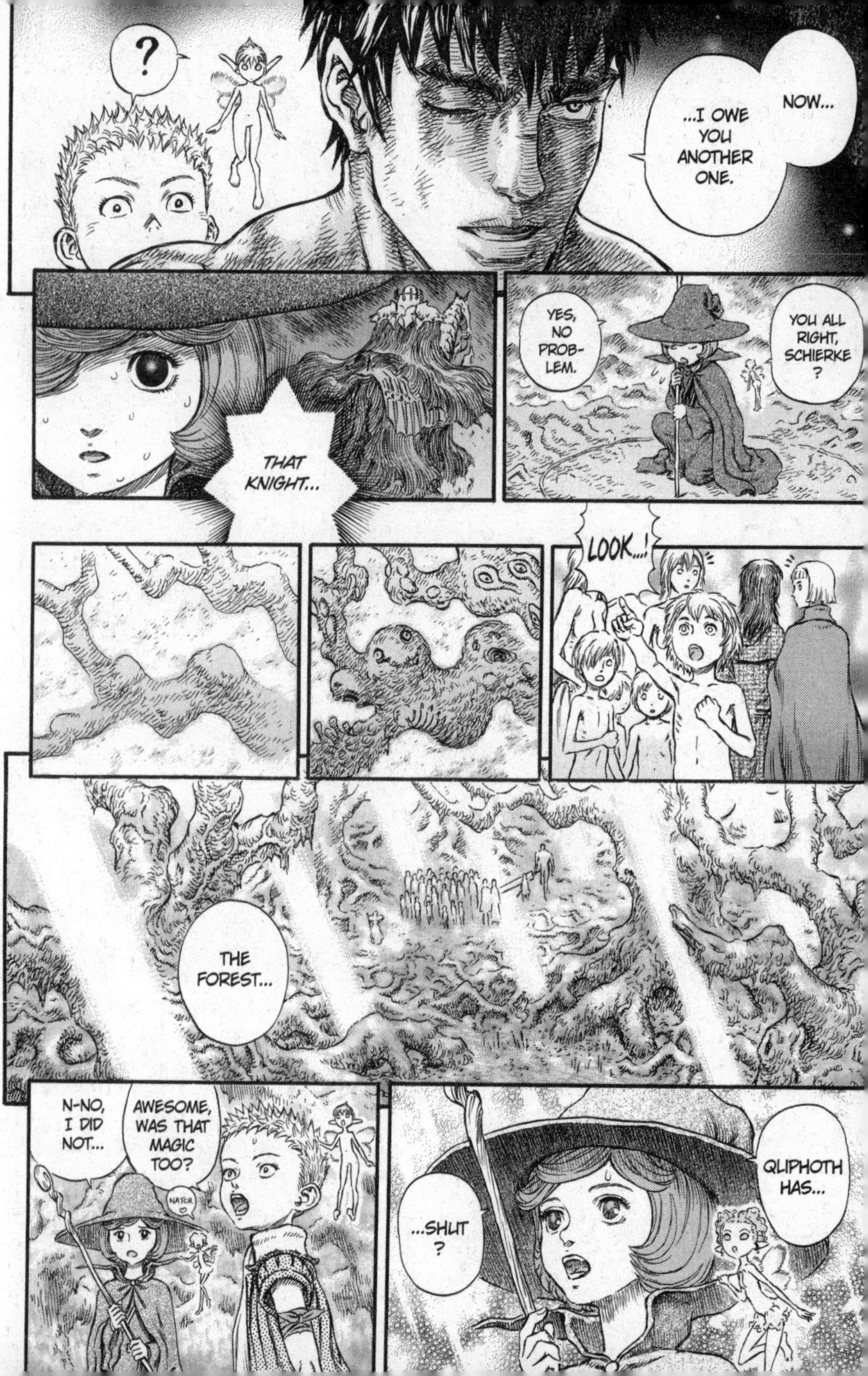
NOW...
...I OWE YOU ANOTHER ONE.
?
YOU ALL RIGHT, SCHIERKE?
YES, NO PROB-LEM.
THAT KNIGHT...
LOOK...!
THE FOREST...
QLIPHOTH HAS...
...SHUT?
AWESOME, WAS THAT MAGIC TOO?
N-NO, I DID NOT...
NATCH.

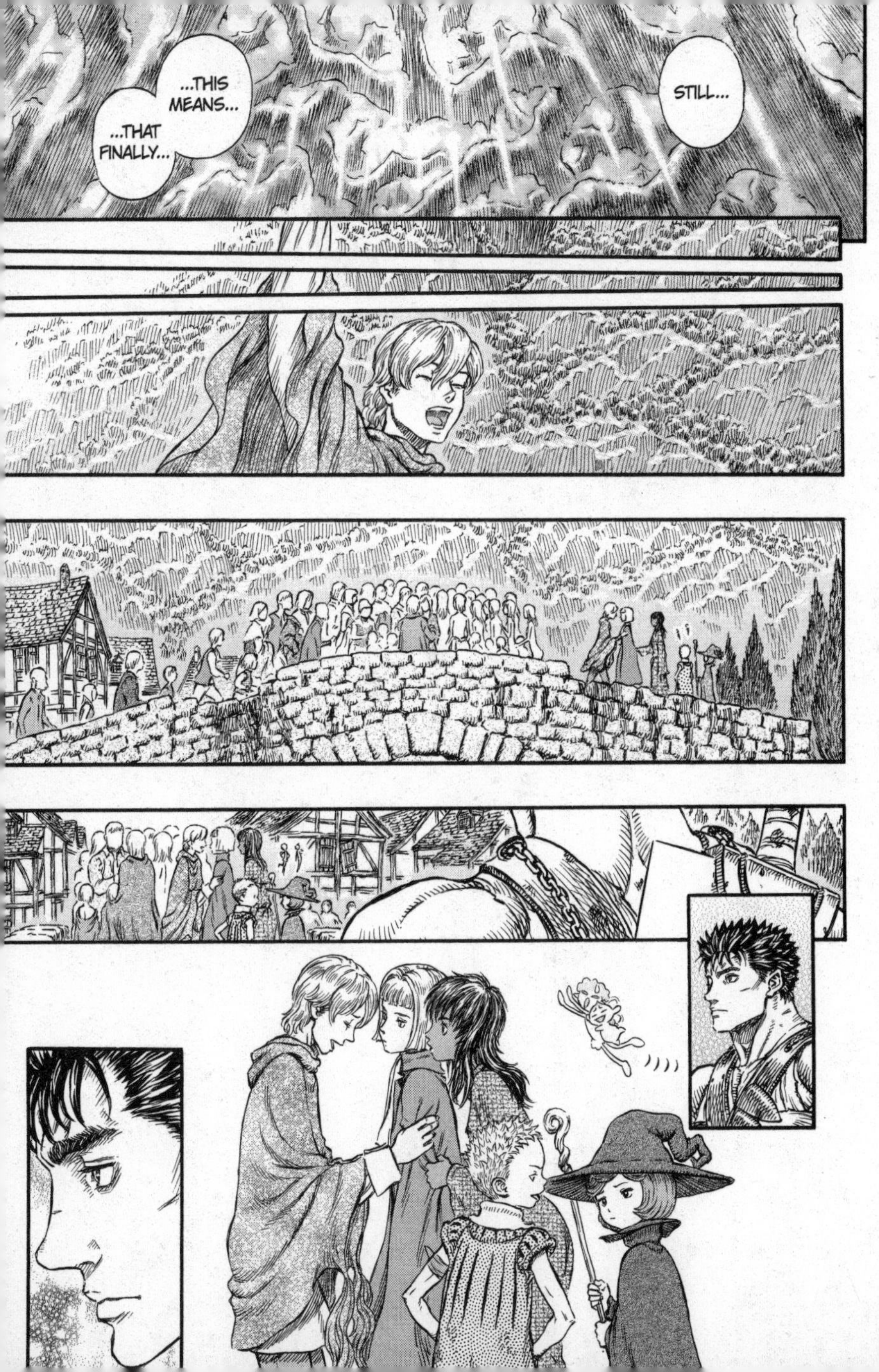
STILL...
...THIS MEANS...
...THAT FINALLY...

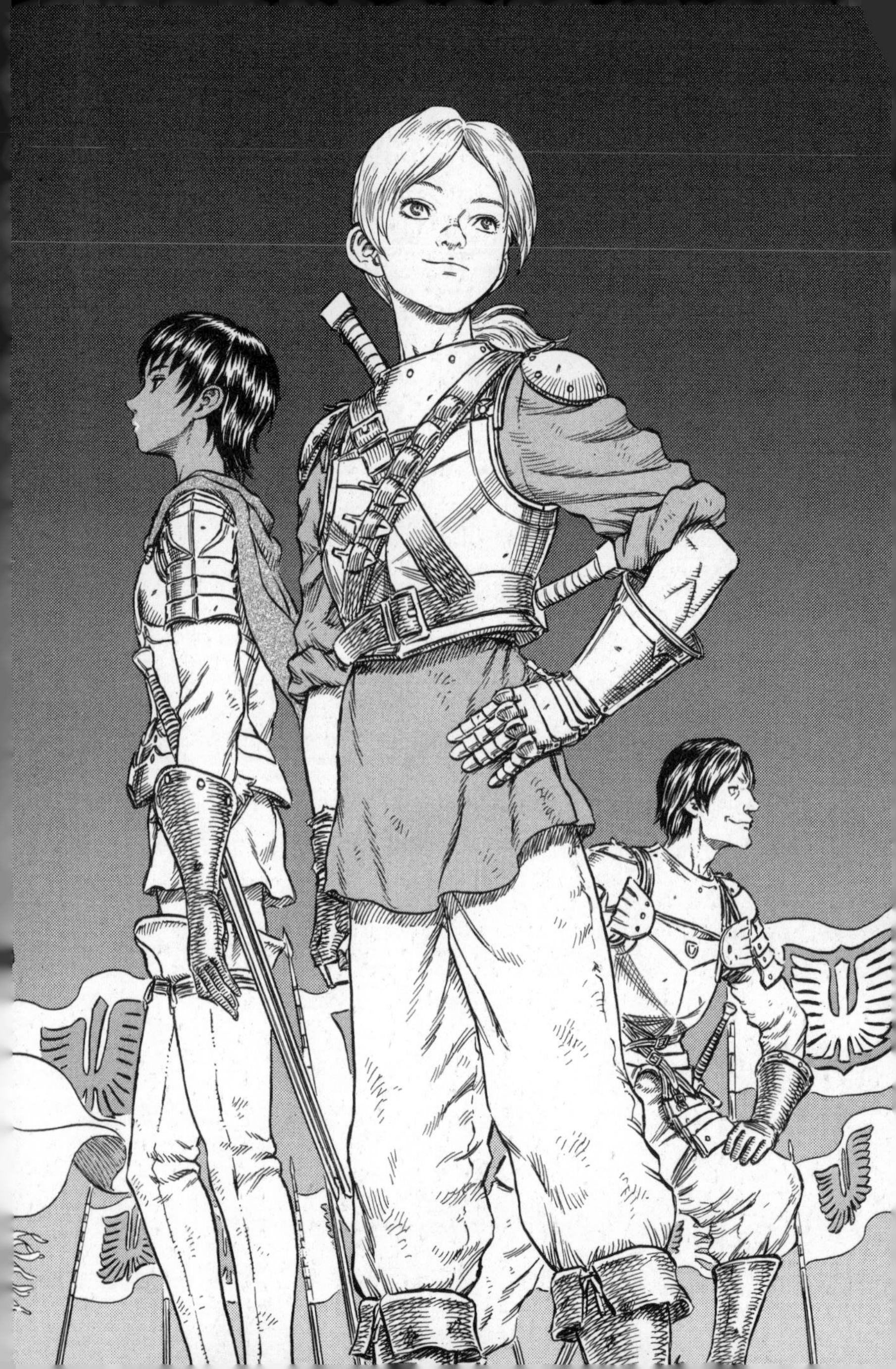

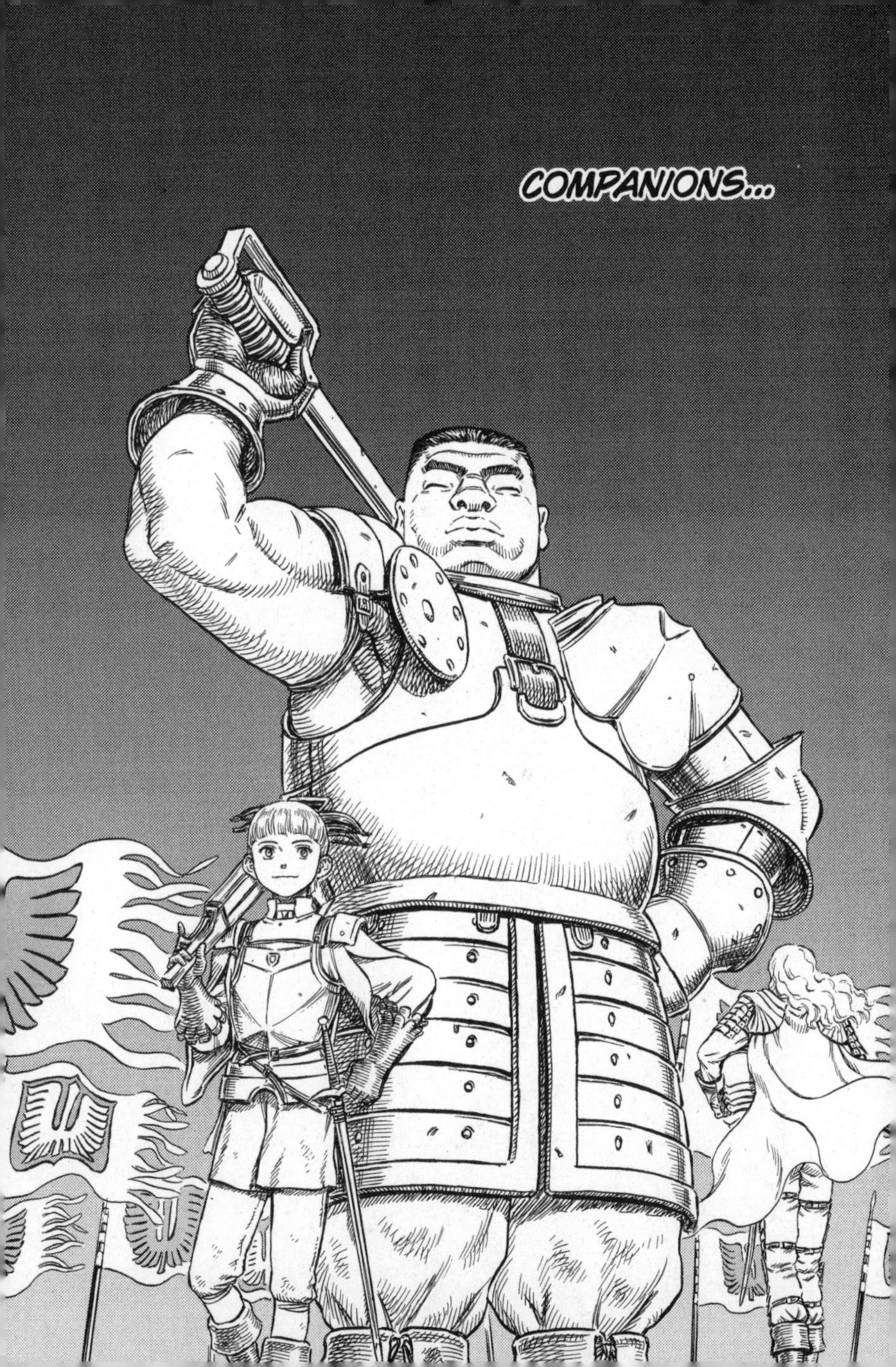
COMPANIONS...

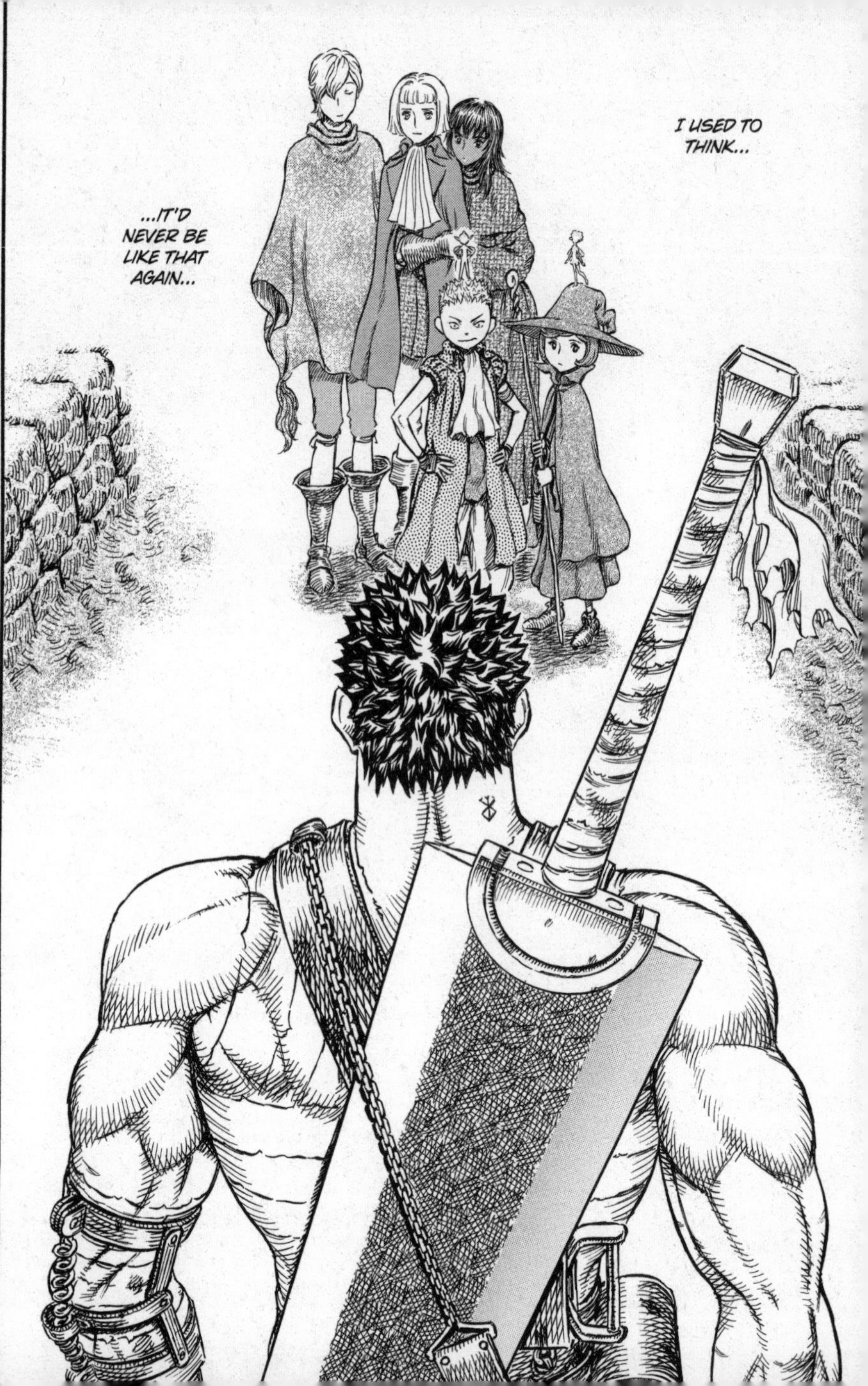
I USED TO THINK...
...IT'D NEVER BE LIKE THAT AGAIN...

BERSERK

CLAW MARKS

爪痕

BERSERK

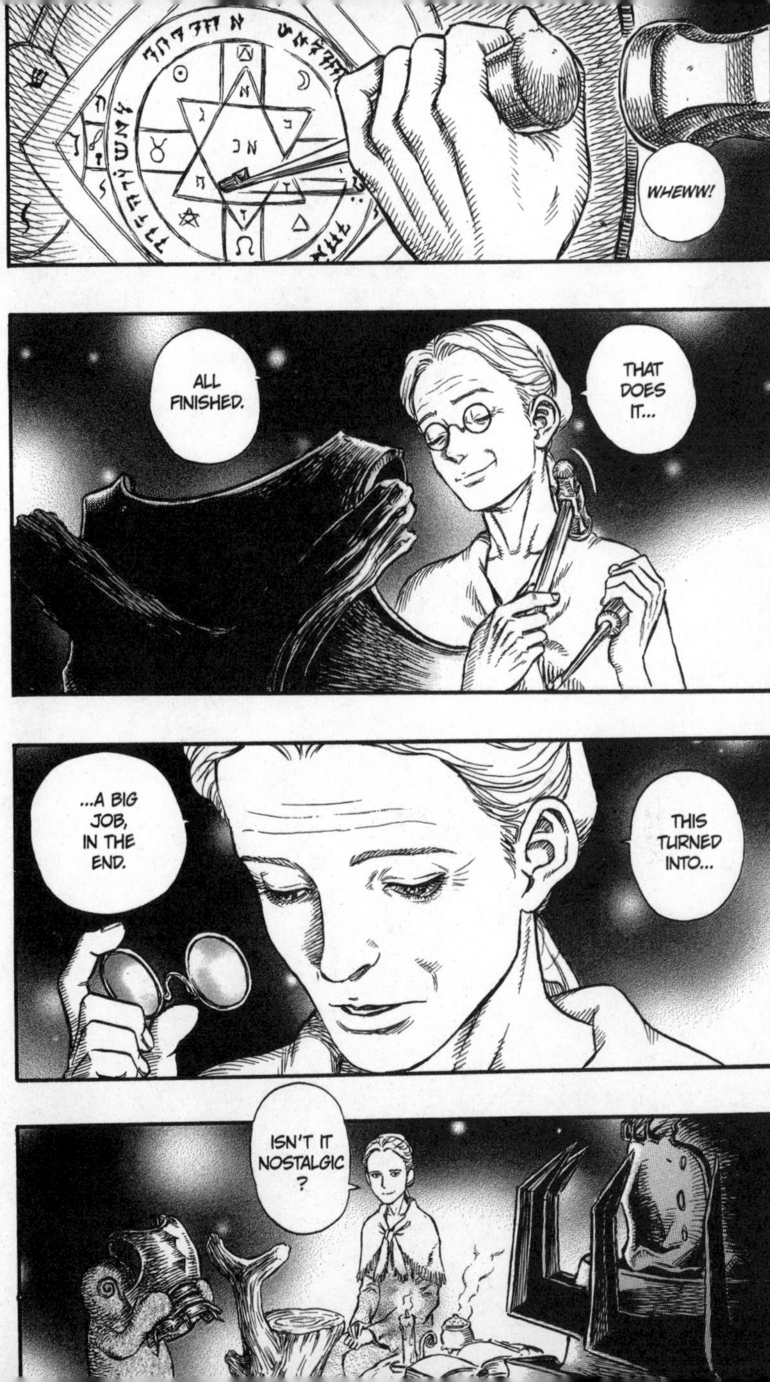
WHEWW!
THAT DOES IT...
ALL FINISHED.
THIS TURNED INTO...
...A BIG JOB, IN THE END.
ISN'T IT NOSTALGIC?

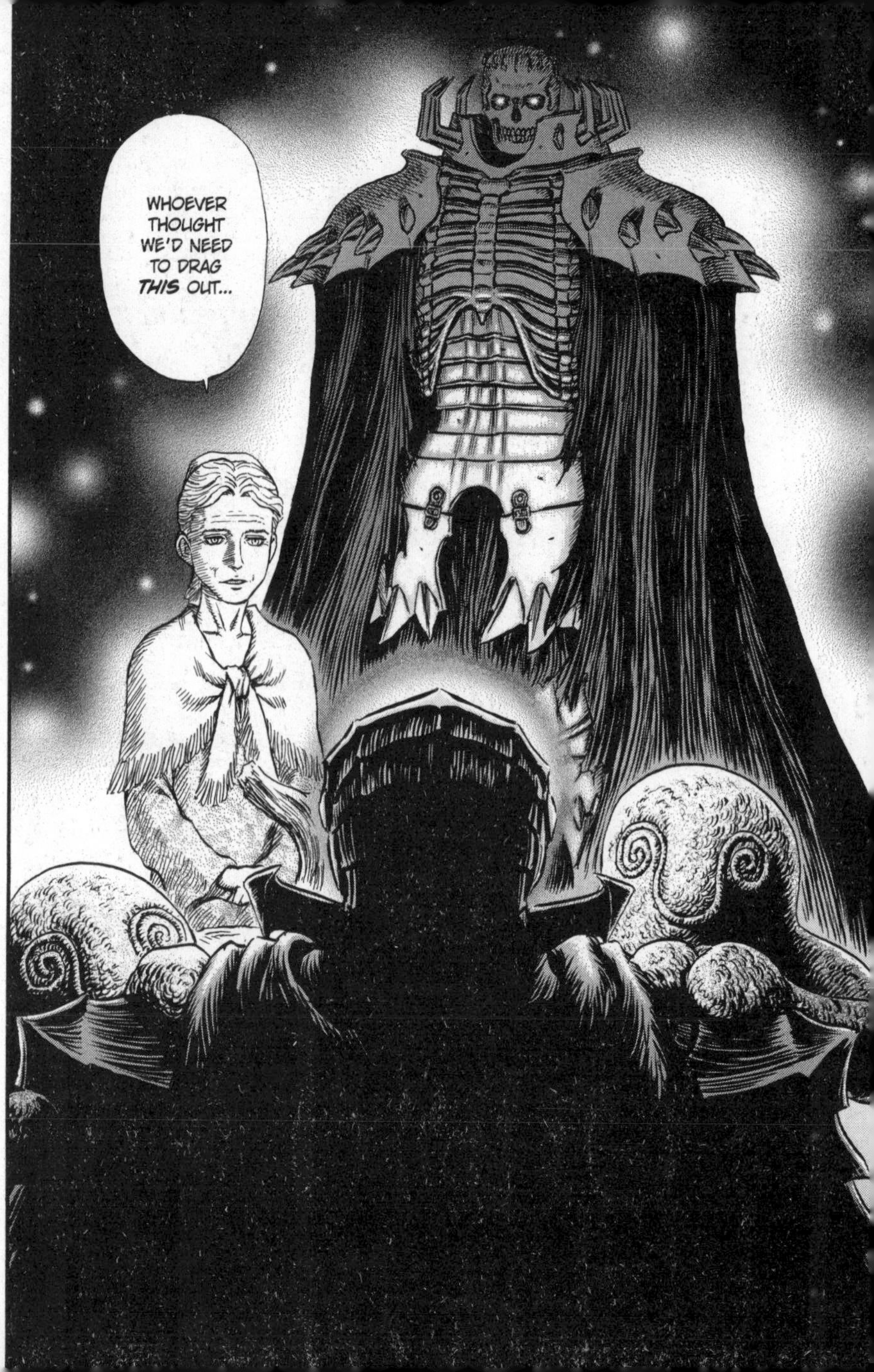
WHOEVER THOUGHT WE'D NEED TO DRAG *THIS* OUT...

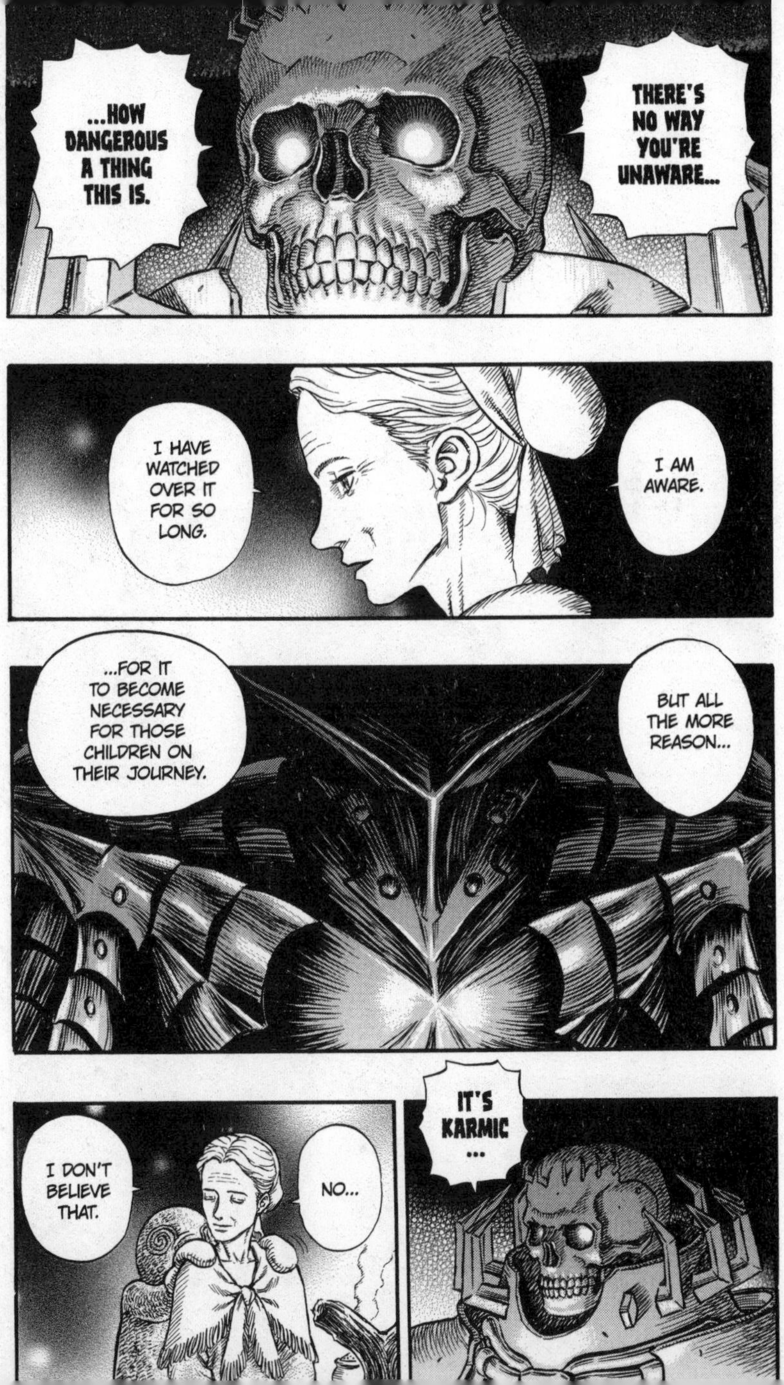
THERE'S NO WAY YOU'RE UNAWARE...
...HOW DANGEROUS A THING THIS IS.
I AM AWARE.
I HAVE WATCHED OVER IT FOR SO LONG.
BUT ALL THE MORE REASON...
...FOR IT TO BECOME NECESSARY FOR THOSE CHILDREN ON THEIR JOURNEY.
IT'S KARMIC...
NO...
I DON'T BELIEVE THAT.

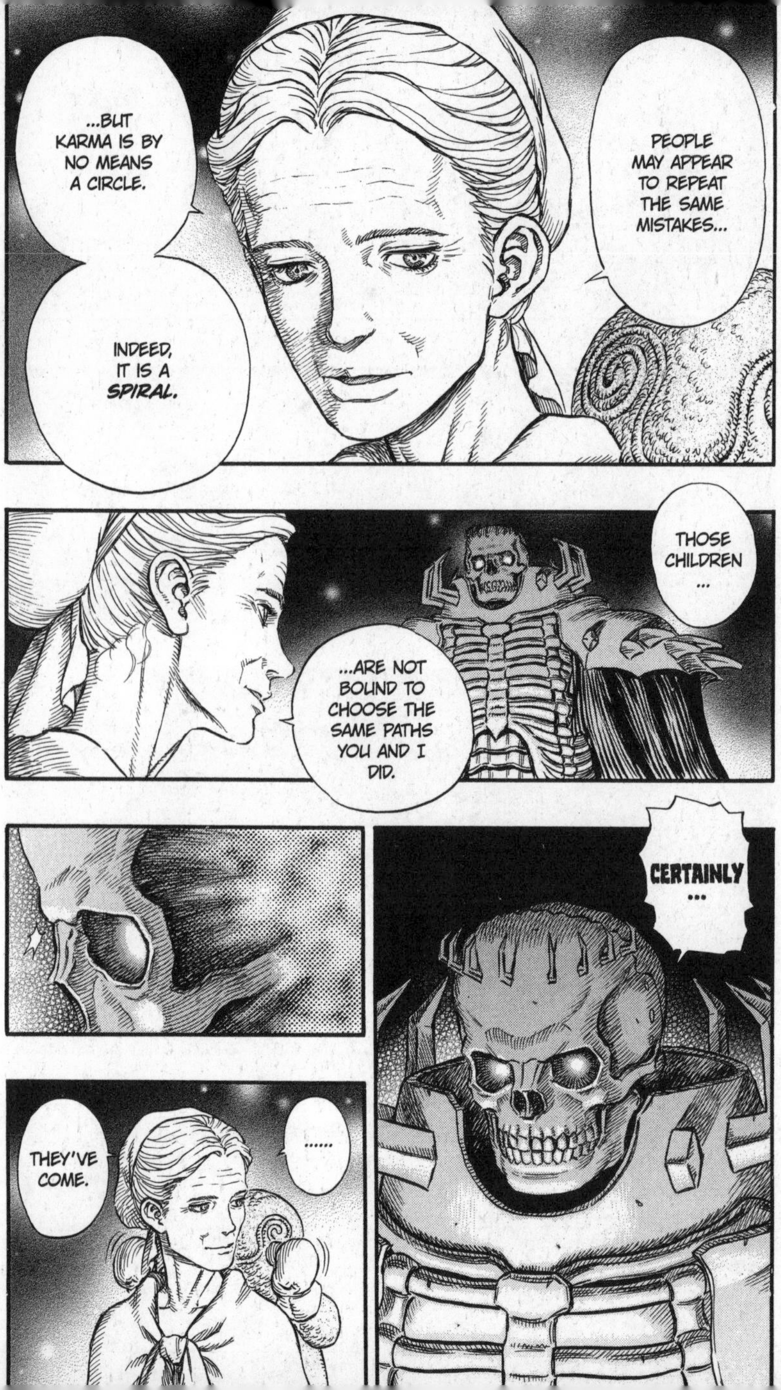
PEOPLE MAY APPEAR TO REPEAT THE SAME MISTAKES...
...BUT KARMA IS BY NO MEANS A CIRCLE.
INDEED, IT IS A *SPIRAL.*
THOSE CHILDREN ...
...ARE NOT BOUND TO CHOOSE THE SAME PATHS YOU AND I DID.
CERTAINLY ...
......
THEY'VE COME.

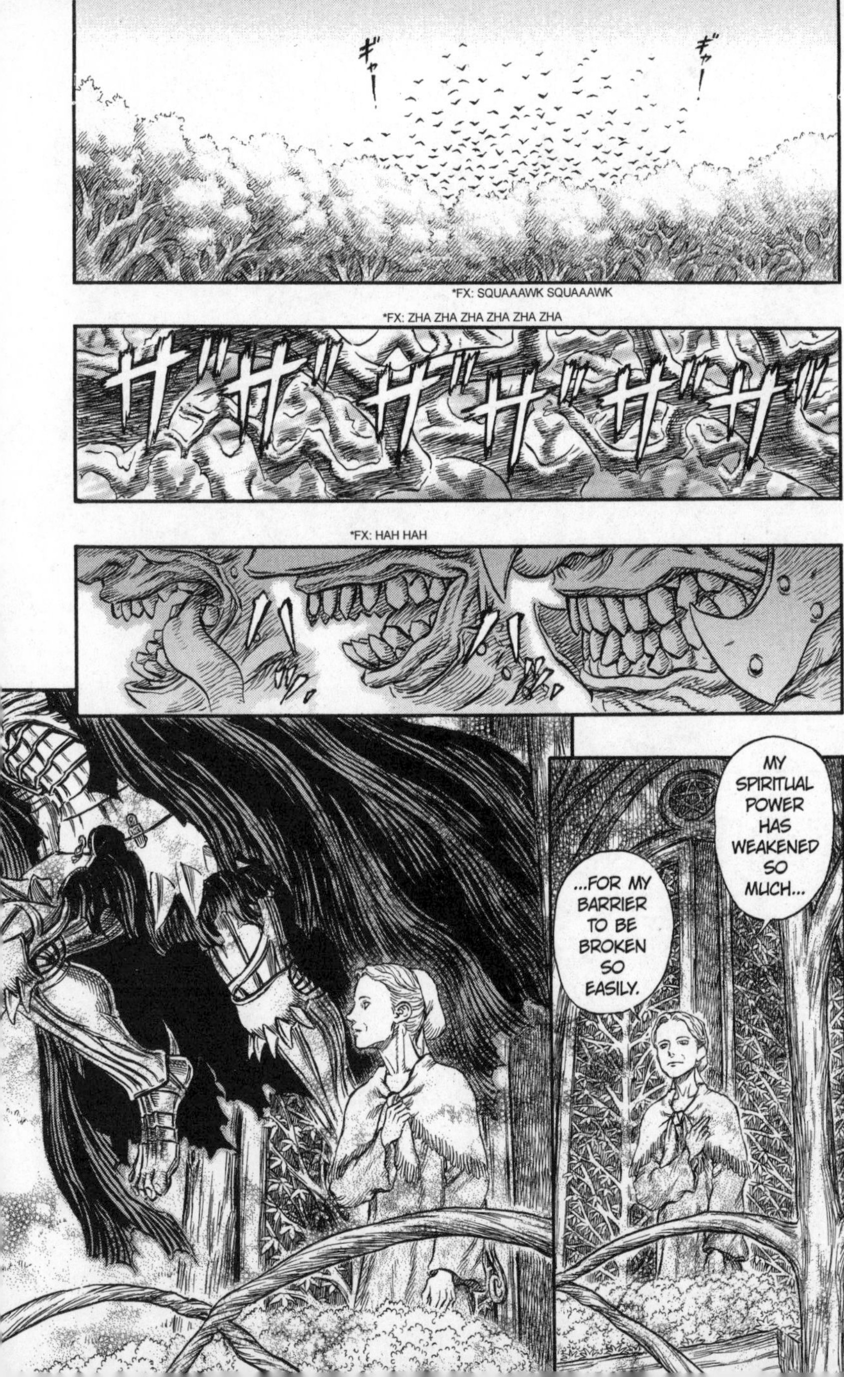
ギャー!
ギャー!
*FX: SQUAAAWK SQUAAAWK
*FX: ZHA ZHA ZHA ZHA ZHA ZHA
*FX: HAH HAH
MY SPIRITUAL POWER HAS WEAKENED SO MUCH...
...FOR MY BARRIER TO BE BROKEN SO EASILY.

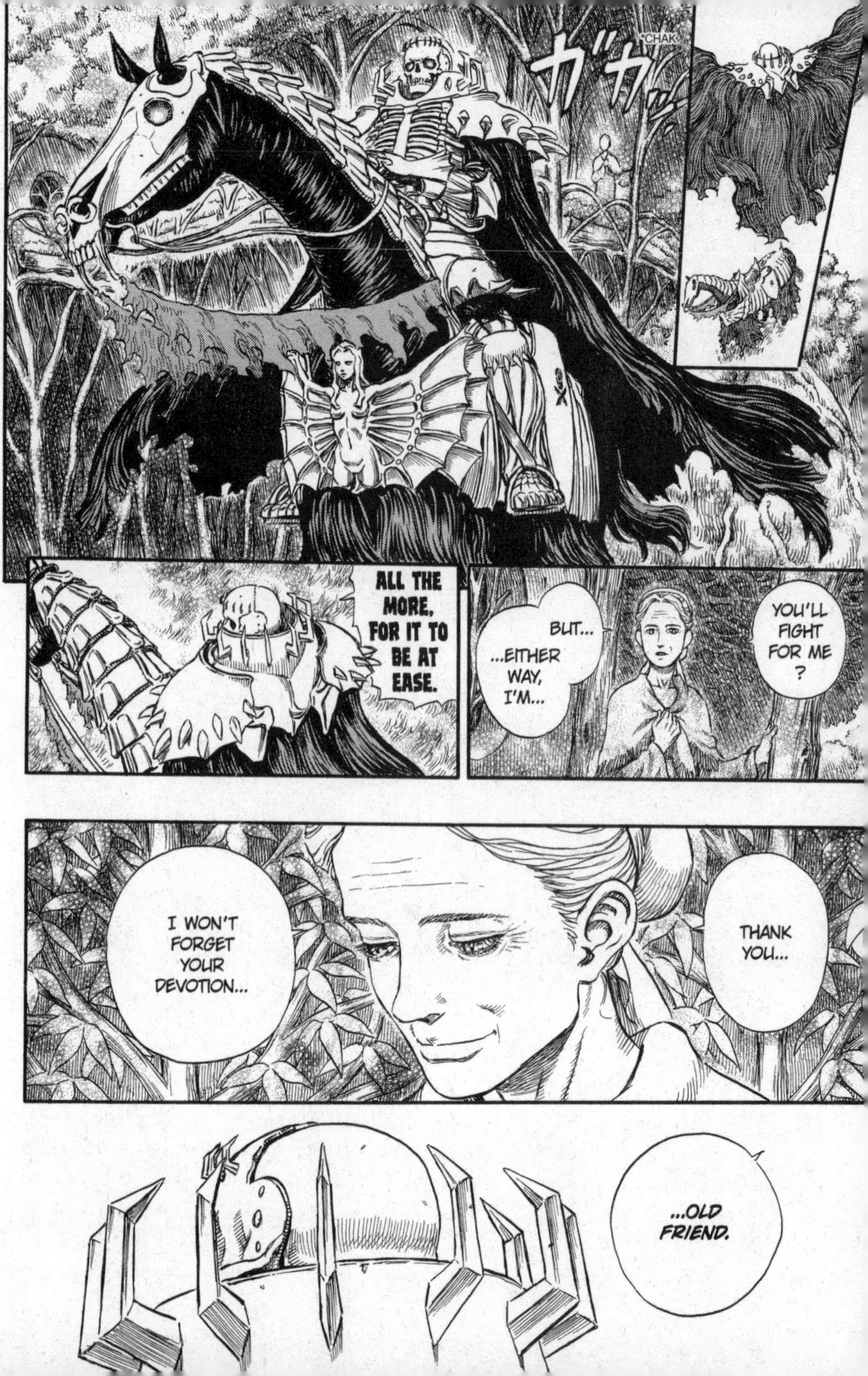
ガガッ
CHAK
YOU'LL FIGHT FOR ME ?
BUT...
...EITHER WAY, I'M...
ALL THE MORE, FOR IT TO BE AT EASE.
THANK YOU...
I WON'T FORGET YOUR DEVOTION...
...OLD FRIEND.

*FX: ZMMM

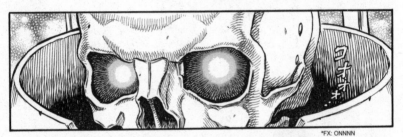

*FX: ONNNN

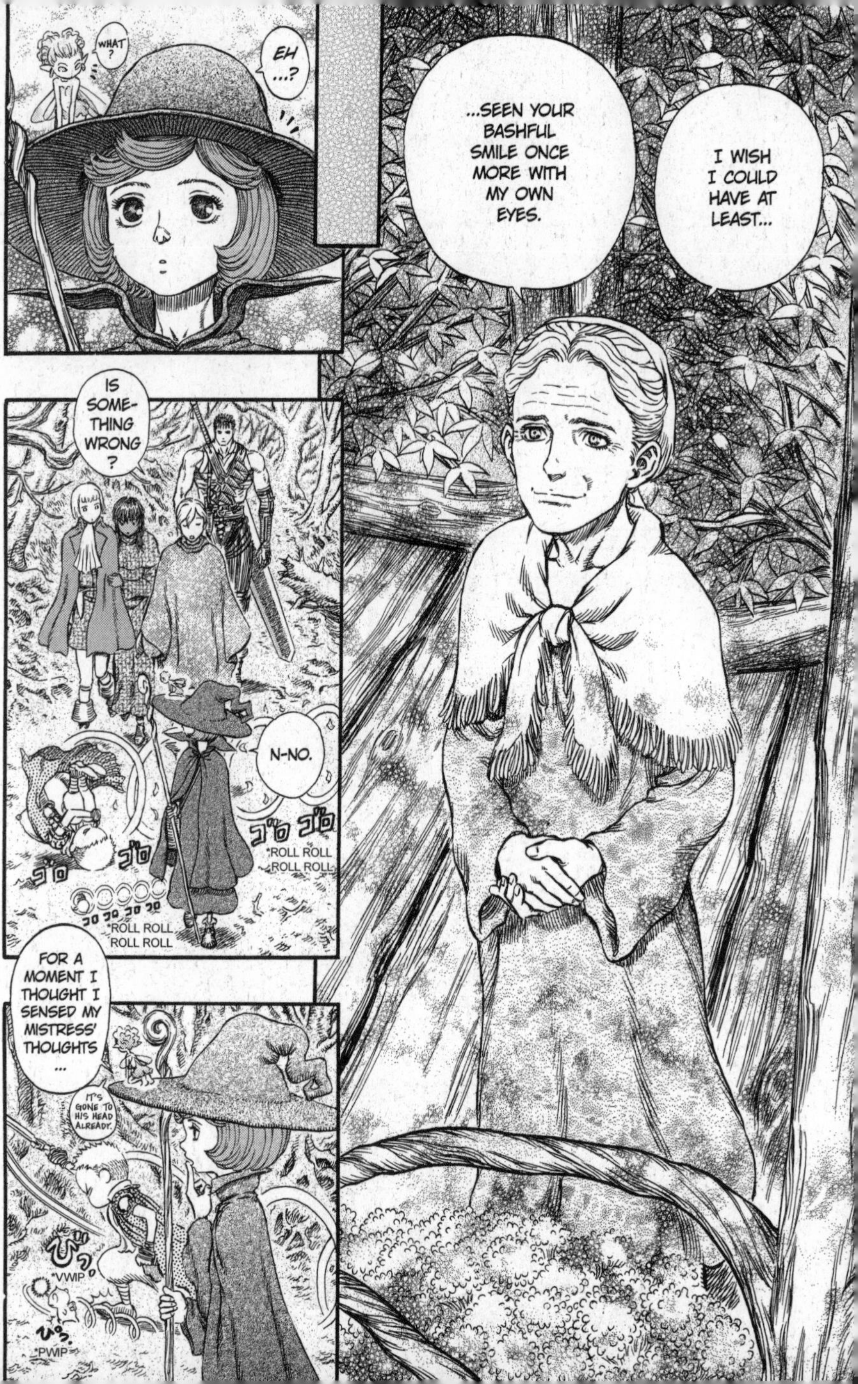
I WISH I COULD HAVE AT LEAST...
...SEEN YOUR BASHFUL SMILE ONCE MORE WITH MY OWN EYES.
EH ...?
WHAT?
IS SOMETHING WRONG?
N-NO.
*ROLL ROLL ROLL ROLL
*ROLL ROLL ROLL ROLL
FOR A MOMENT I THOUGHT I SENSED MY MISTRESS' THOUGHTS ...
IT'S GONE TO HIS HEAD ALREADY.
*VWIP
*PWIP

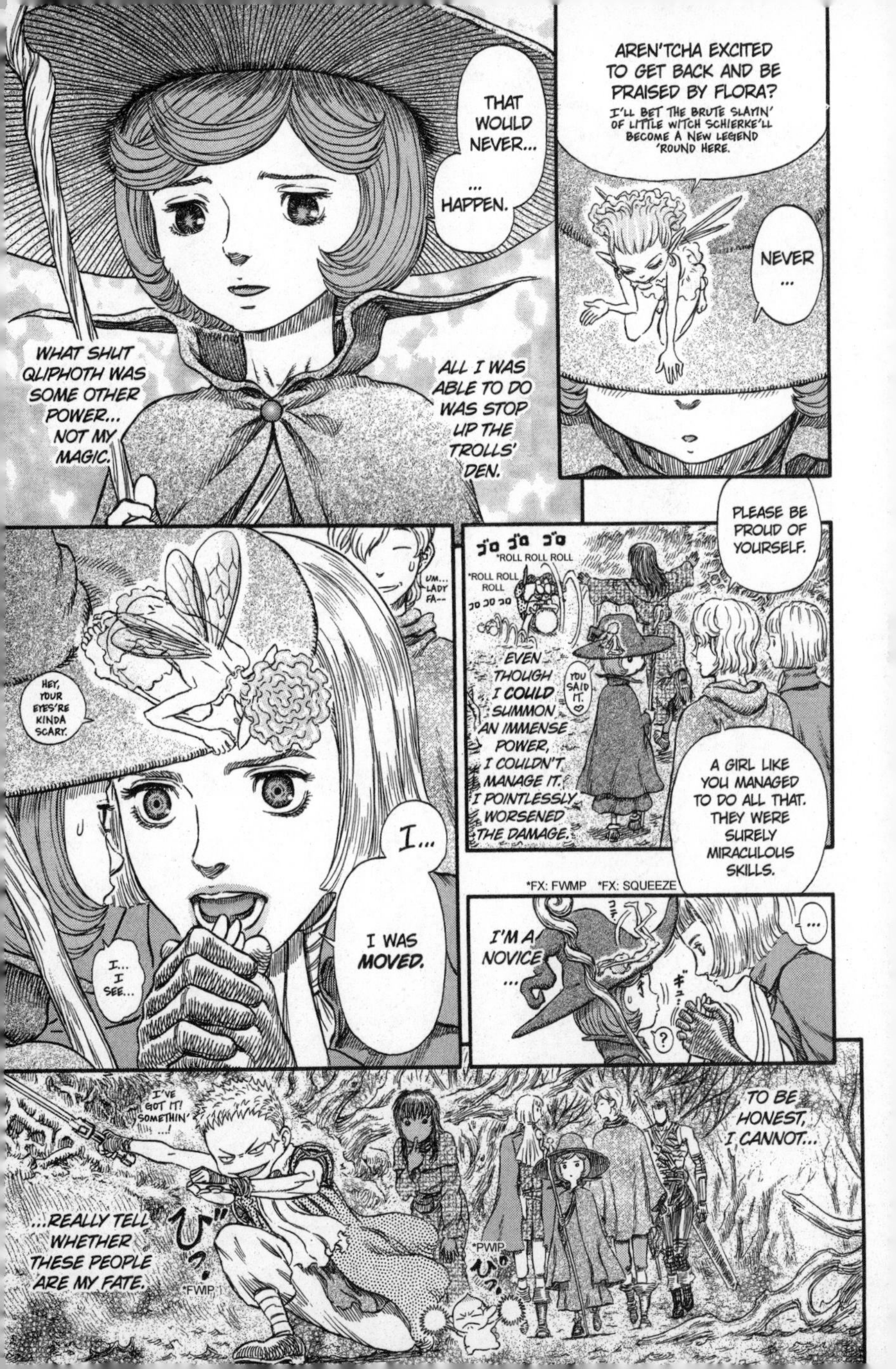
AREN'TCHA EXCITED TO GET BACK AND BE PRAISED BY FLORA?
I'LL BET THE BRUTE SLAYIN' OF LITTLE WITCH SCHIERKE'LL BECOME A NEW LEGEND 'ROUND HERE.
NEVER ...
THAT WOULD NEVER...
... HAPPEN.
ALL I WAS ABLE TO DO WAS STOP UP THE TROLLS' DEN.
WHAT SHUT QLIPHOTH WAS SOME OTHER POWER... NOT MY MAGIC.
PLEASE BE PROUD OF YOURSELF.
ゴロゴロ ゴロ
*ROLL ROLL ROLL
*ROLL ROLL ROLL
コロコロコロ
EVEN THOUGH I COULD SUMMON AN IMMENSE POWER, I COULDN'T MANAGE IT. I POINTLESSLY WORSENED THE DAMAGE.
YOU SAID IT. ♡
A GIRL LIKE YOU MANAGED TO DO ALL THAT. THEY WERE SURELY MIRACULOUS SKILLS.
*FX: FWMP *FX: SQUEEZE
...
I'M A NOVICE ...
?
UM... LADY FA--
HEY, YOUR EYES'RE KINDA SCARY.
I...
I WAS MOVED.
I... I SEE...
TO BE HONEST, I CANNOT...
I'VE GOT IT! SOMETHIN' ...!
...REALLY TELL WHETHER THESE PEOPLE ARE MY FATE.
*PWIP
*FWIP

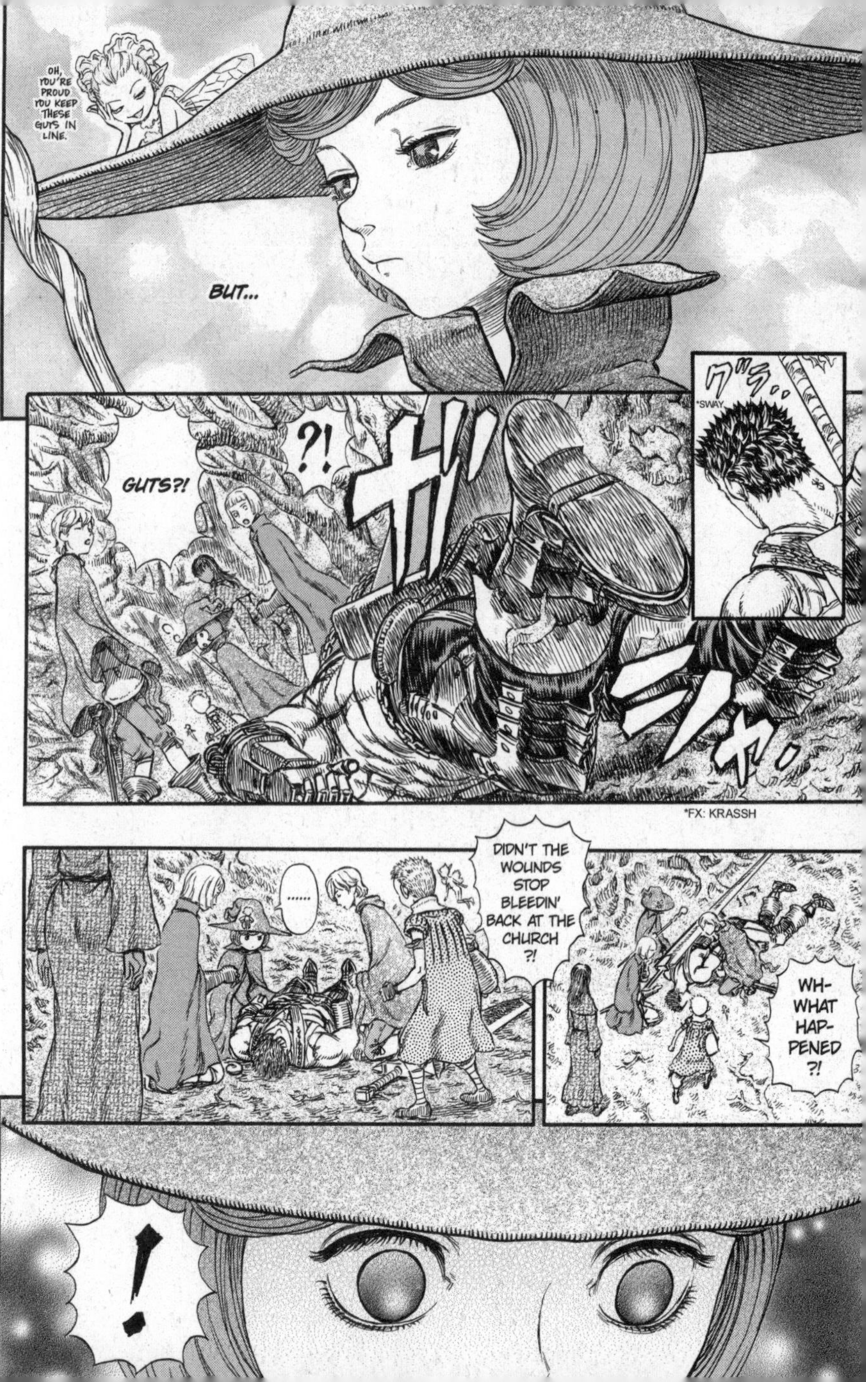
OH, YOU'RE PROUD YOU KEEP THESE GUTS IN LINE.
BUT...
グラ..
*SWAY
?!
GUTS?!
*FX: KRASSH
WH-WHAT HAP-PENED?!
DIDN'T THE WOUNDS STOP BLEEDIN' BACK AT THE CHURCH?!
......
!

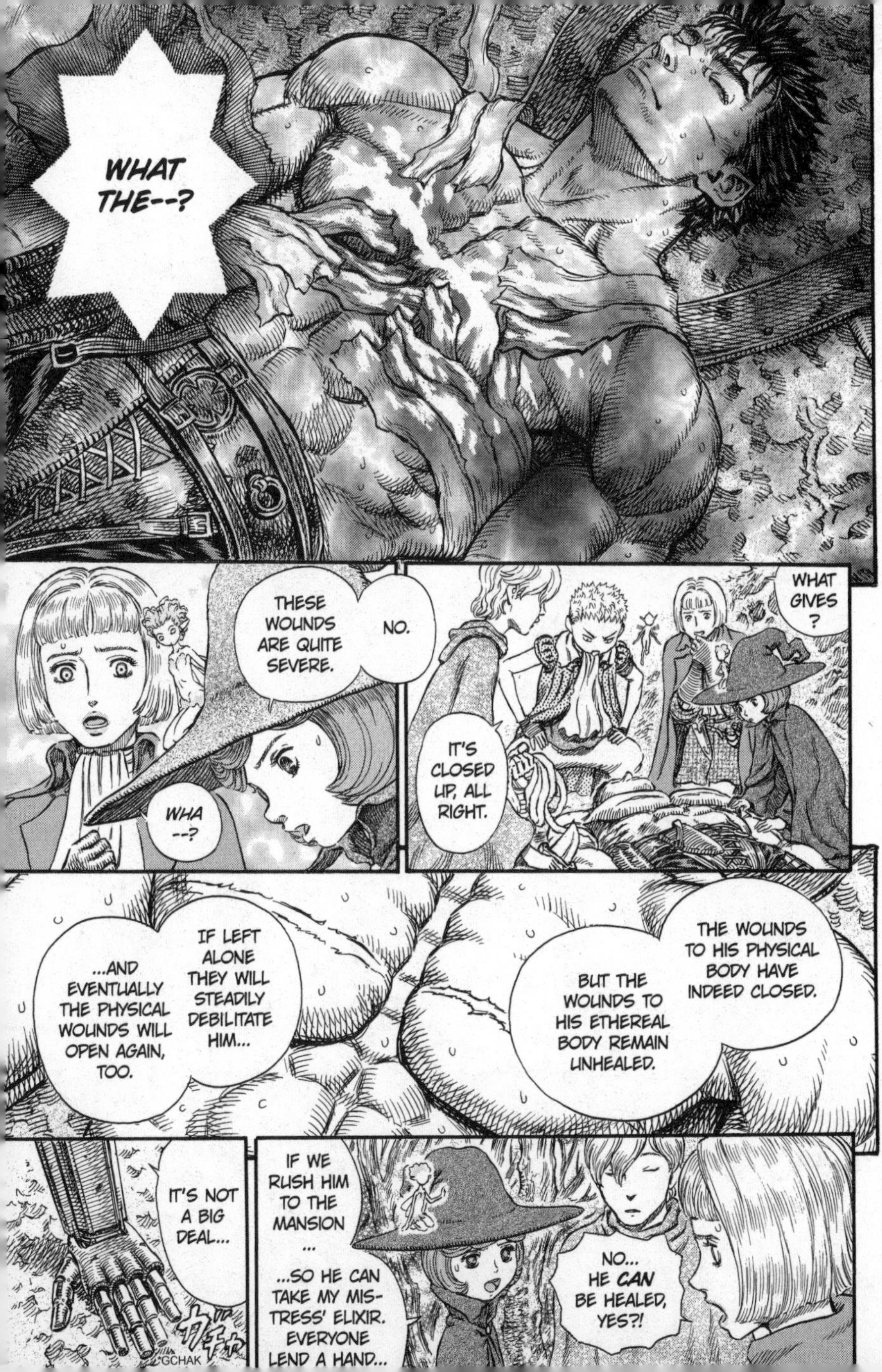
WHAT THE--?
WHAT GIVES ?
IT'S CLOSED UP, ALL RIGHT.
NO.
THESE WOUNDS ARE QUITE SEVERE.
WHA --?
THE WOUNDS TO HIS PHYSICAL BODY HAVE INDEED CLOSED.
BUT THE WOUNDS TO HIS ETHEREAL BODY REMAIN UNHEALED.
IF LEFT ALONE THEY WILL STEADILY DEBILITATE HIM...
...AND EVENTUALLY THE PHYSICAL WOUNDS WILL OPEN AGAIN, TOO.
NO... HE *CAN* BE HEALED, YES?!
IF WE RUSH HIM TO THE MANSION ...
...SO HE CAN TAKE MY MIS-TRESS' ELIXIR. EVERYONE LEND A HAND...
IT'S NOT A BIG DEAL...
GCHAK

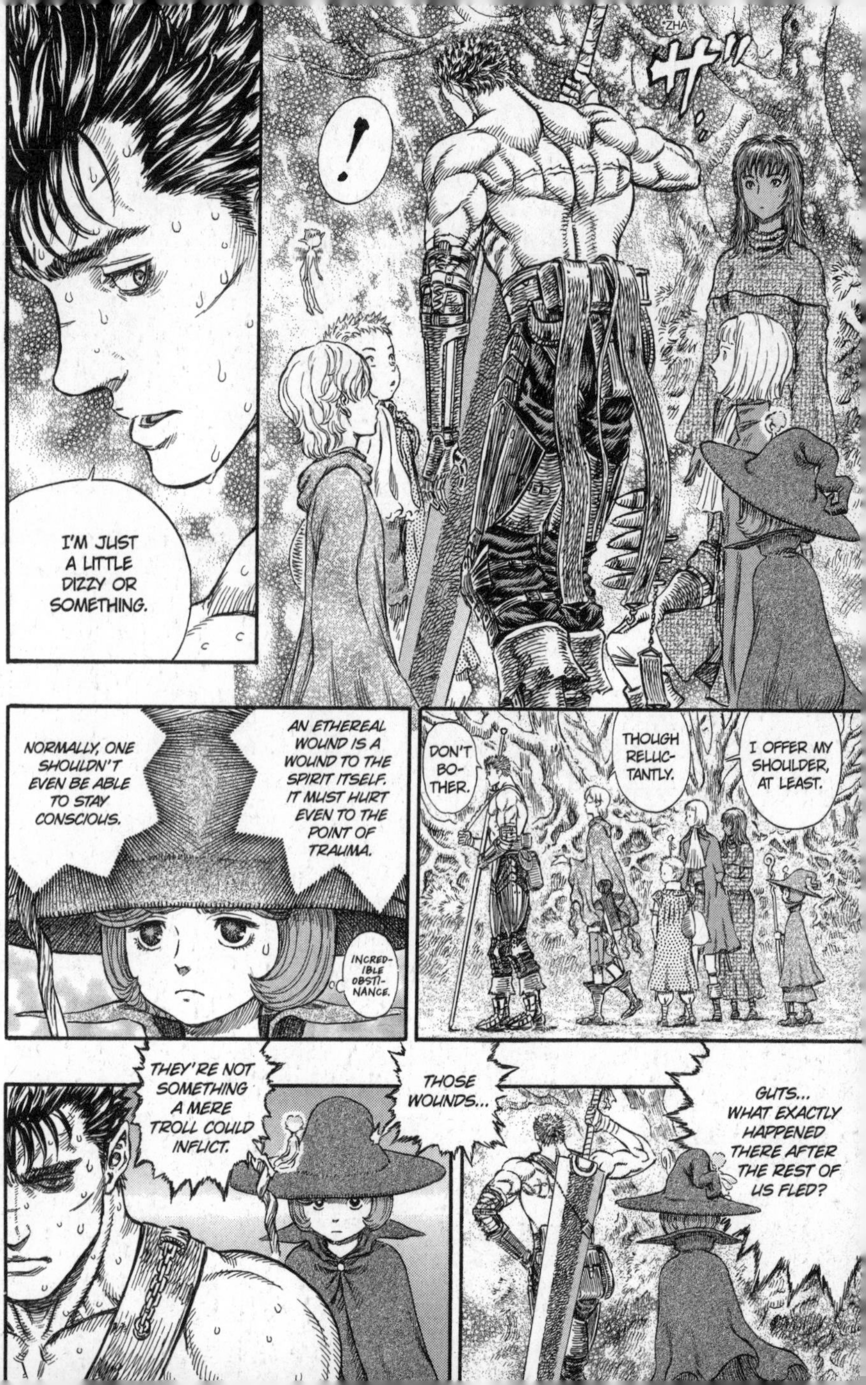
ZHA
!
I'M JUST A LITTLE DIZZY OR SOMETHING.
I OFFER MY SHOULDER, AT LEAST.
THOUGH RELUCTANTLY.
DON'T BOTHER.
AN ETHEREAL WOUND IS A WOUND TO THE SPIRIT ITSELF. IT MUST HURT EVEN TO THE POINT OF TRAUMA.
NORMALLY, ONE SHOULDN'T EVEN BE ABLE TO STAY CONSCIOUS.
INCREDIBLE OBSTINANCE.
GUTS... WHAT EXACTLY HAPPENED THERE AFTER THE REST OF US FLED?
THOSE WOUNDS...
THEY'RE NOT SOMETHING A MERE TROLL COULD INFLICT.

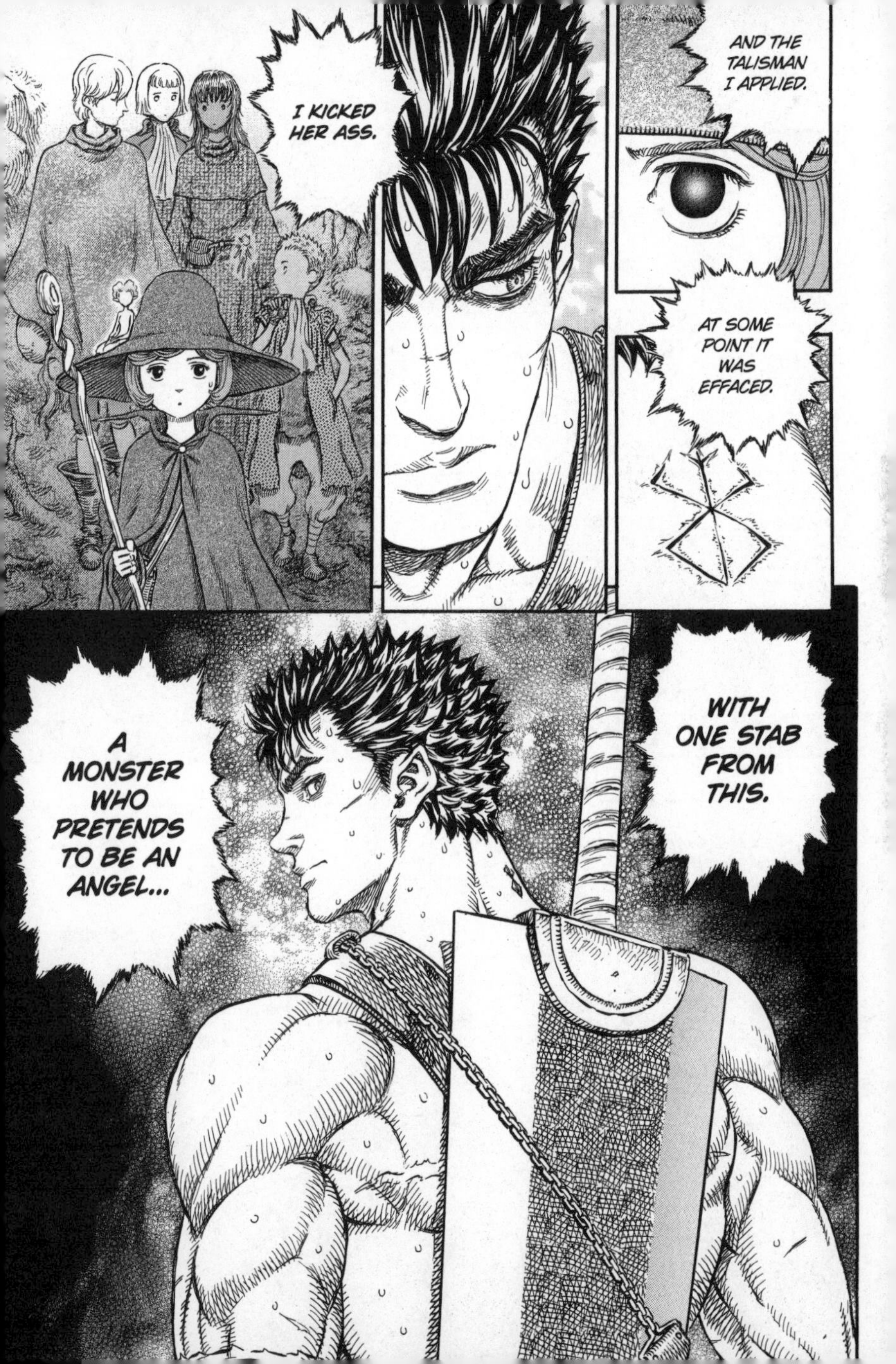
AND THE TALISMAN I APPLIED.
AT SOME POINT IT WAS EFFACED.
I KICKED HER ASS.
WITH ONE STAB FROM THIS.
A MONSTER WHO PRETENDS TO BE AN ANGEL...

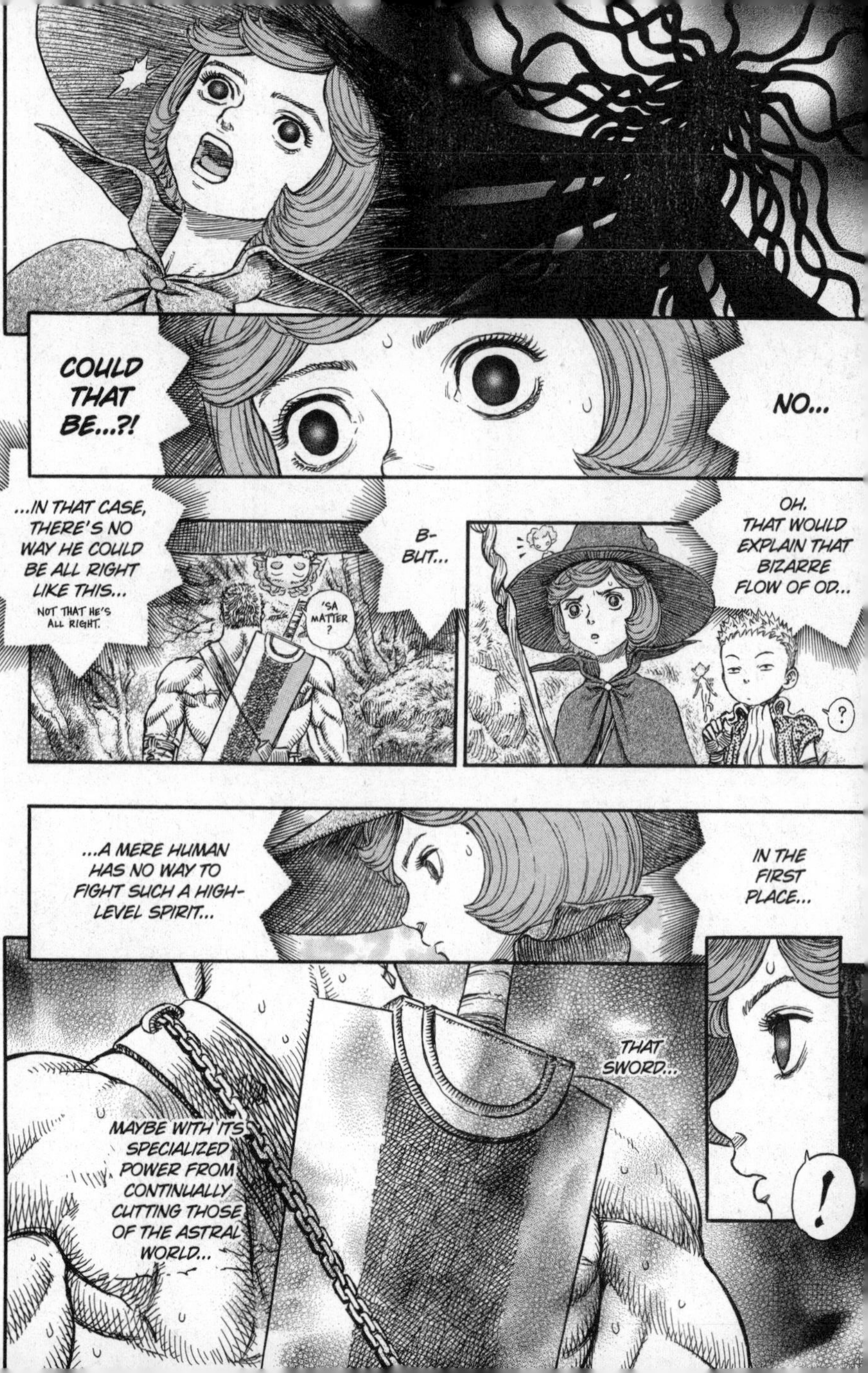
NO...
COULD THAT BE...?!
OH. THAT WOULD EXPLAIN THAT BIZARRE FLOW OF OD...
?
B-BUT...
'SA MATTER?
...IN THAT CASE, THERE'S NO WAY HE COULD BE ALL RIGHT LIKE THIS...
NOT THAT HE'S ALL RIGHT.
IN THE FIRST PLACE...
...A MERE HUMAN HAS NO WAY TO FIGHT SUCH A HIGH-LEVEL SPIRIT...
!
THAT SWORD...
MAYBE WITH ITS SPECIALIZED POWER FROM CONTINUALLY CUTTING THOSE OF THE ASTRAL WORLD...

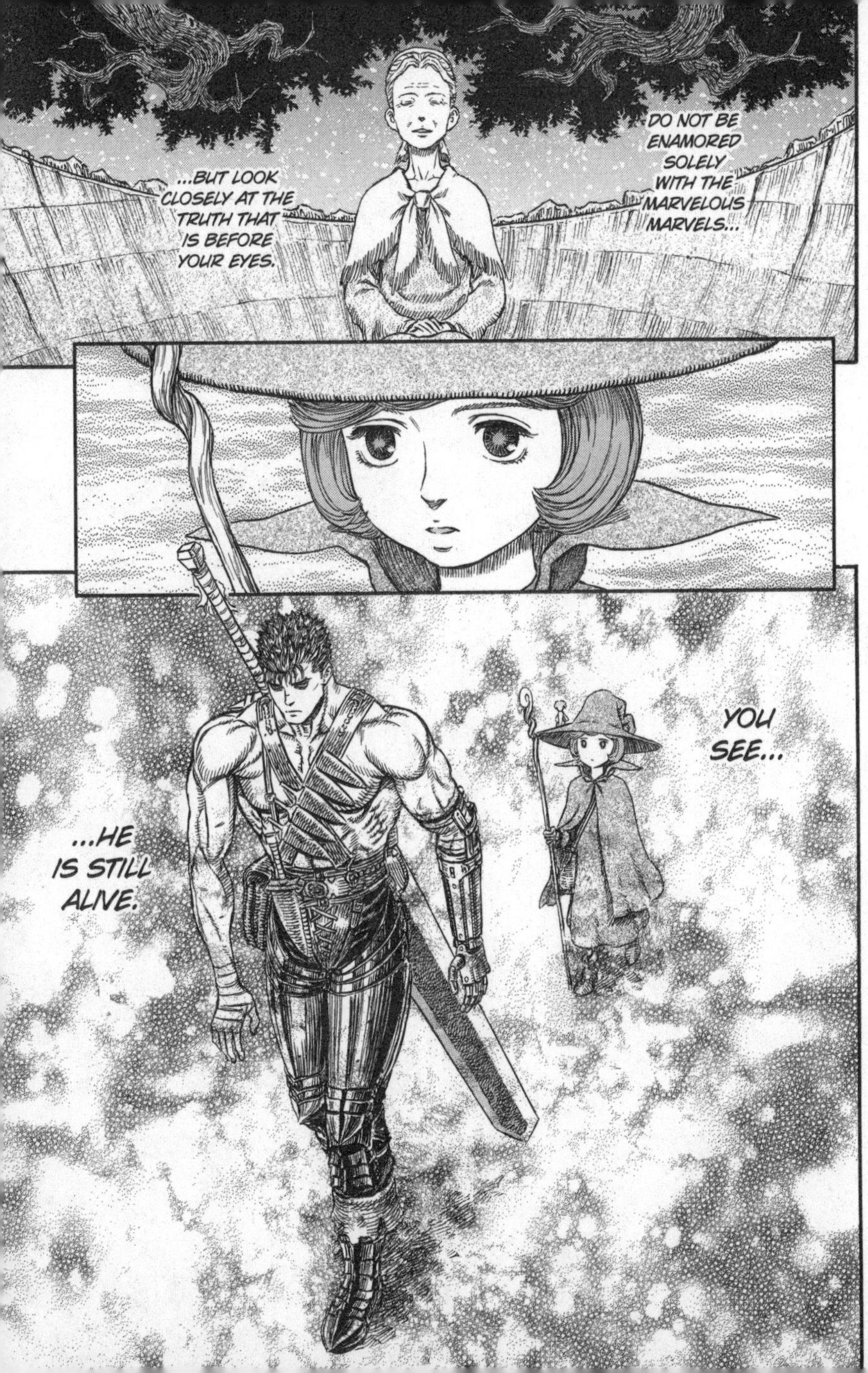
DO NOT BE ENAMORED SOLELY WITH THE MARVELOUS MARVELS...
...BUT LOOK CLOSELY AT THE TRUTH THAT IS BEFORE YOUR EYES.
YOU SEE...
...HE IS STILL ALIVE.

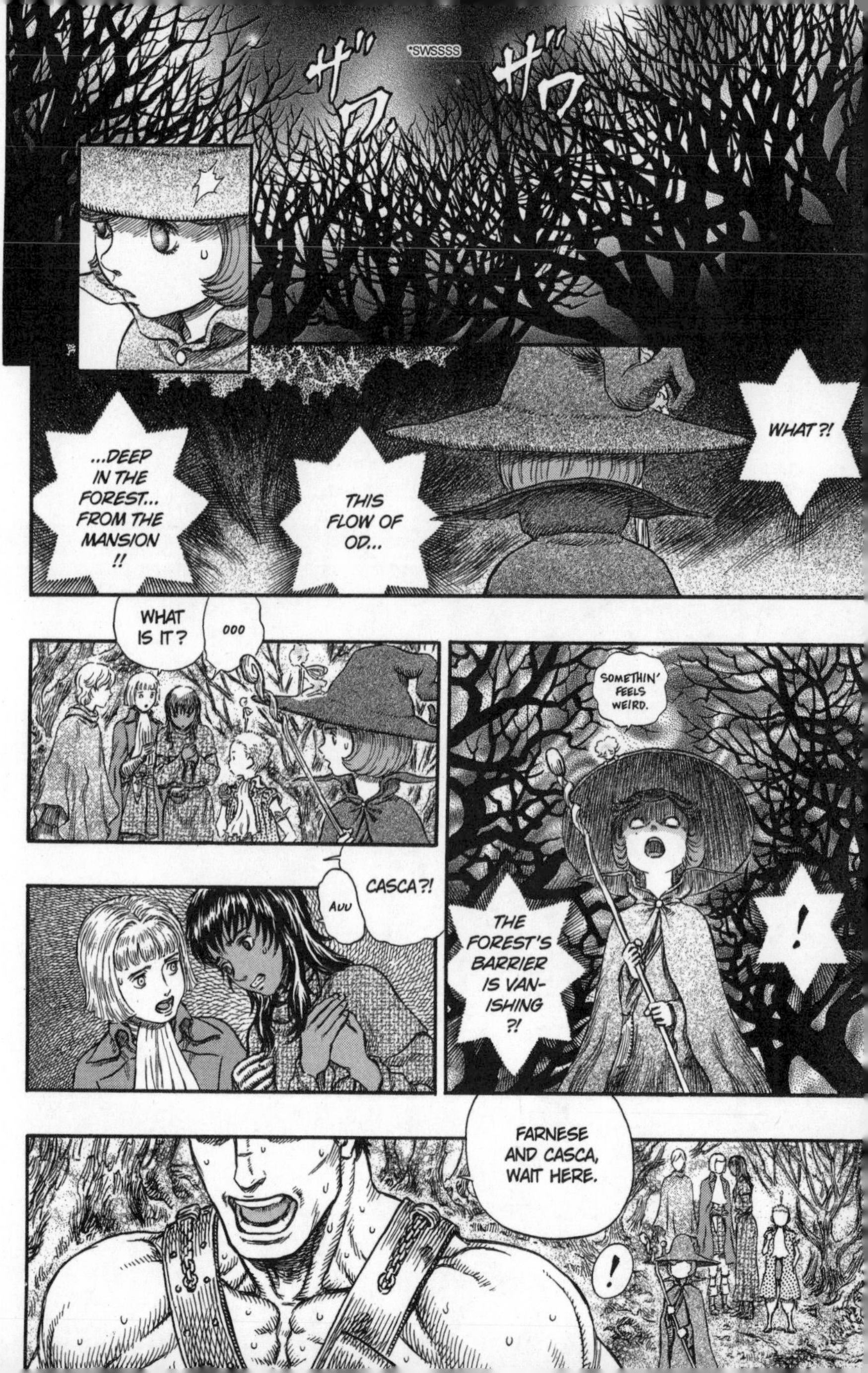
ザワ ザワ
*SWSSSS
WHAT?!
THIS FLOW OF OD...
...DEEP IN THE FOREST... FROM THE MANSION !!
SOMETHIN' FEELS WEIRD.
THE FOREST'S BARRIER IS VAN-ISHING ?!
!
WHAT IS IT?
ooo
CASCA?!
AUU
FARNESE AND CASCA, WAIT HERE.
!

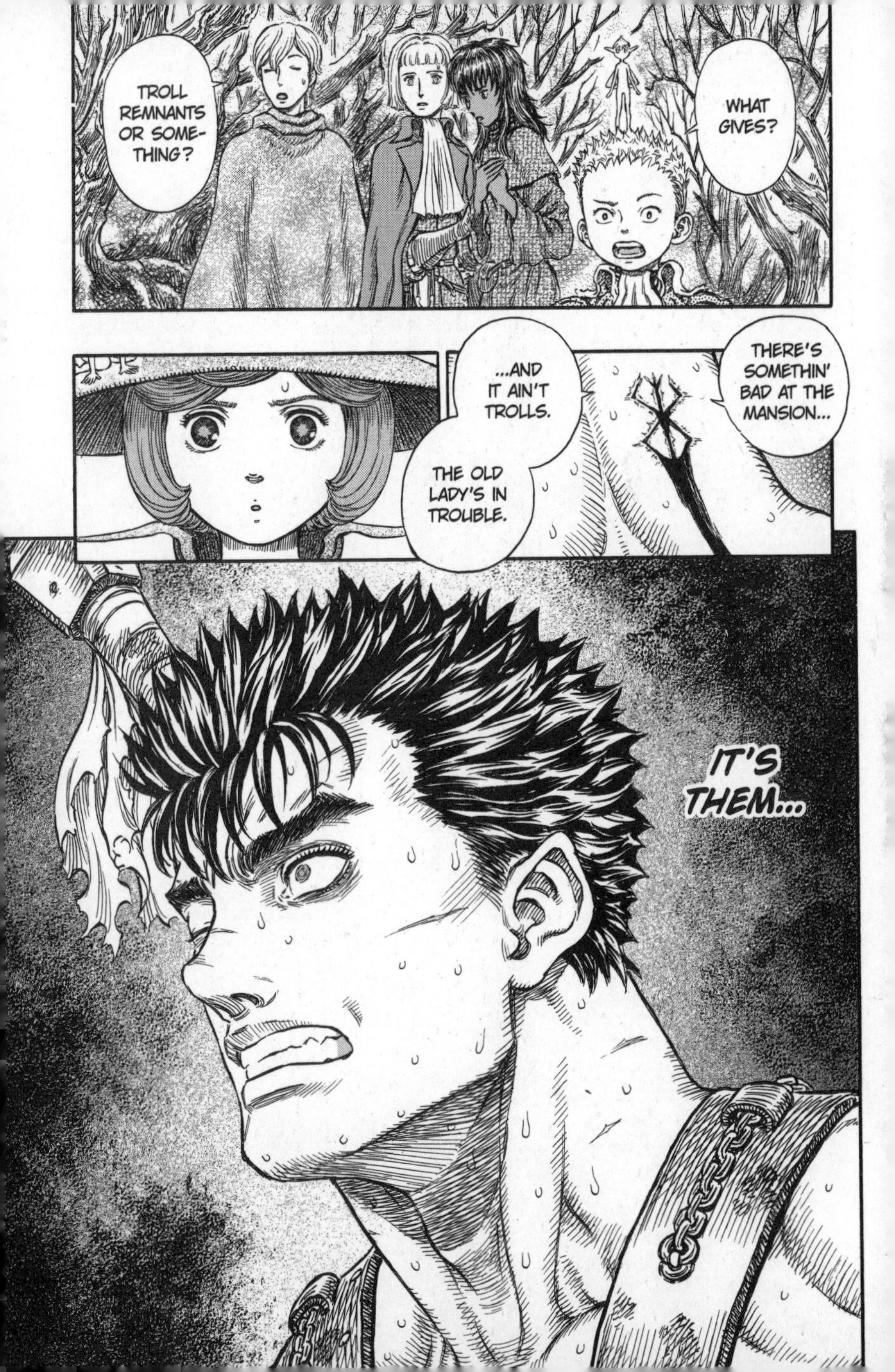
WHAT GIVES?
TROLL REMNANTS OR SOME-THING?
THERE'S SOMETHIN' BAD AT THE MANSION...
...AND IT AIN'T TROLLS.
THE OLD LADY'S IN TROUBLE.
IT'S THEM...

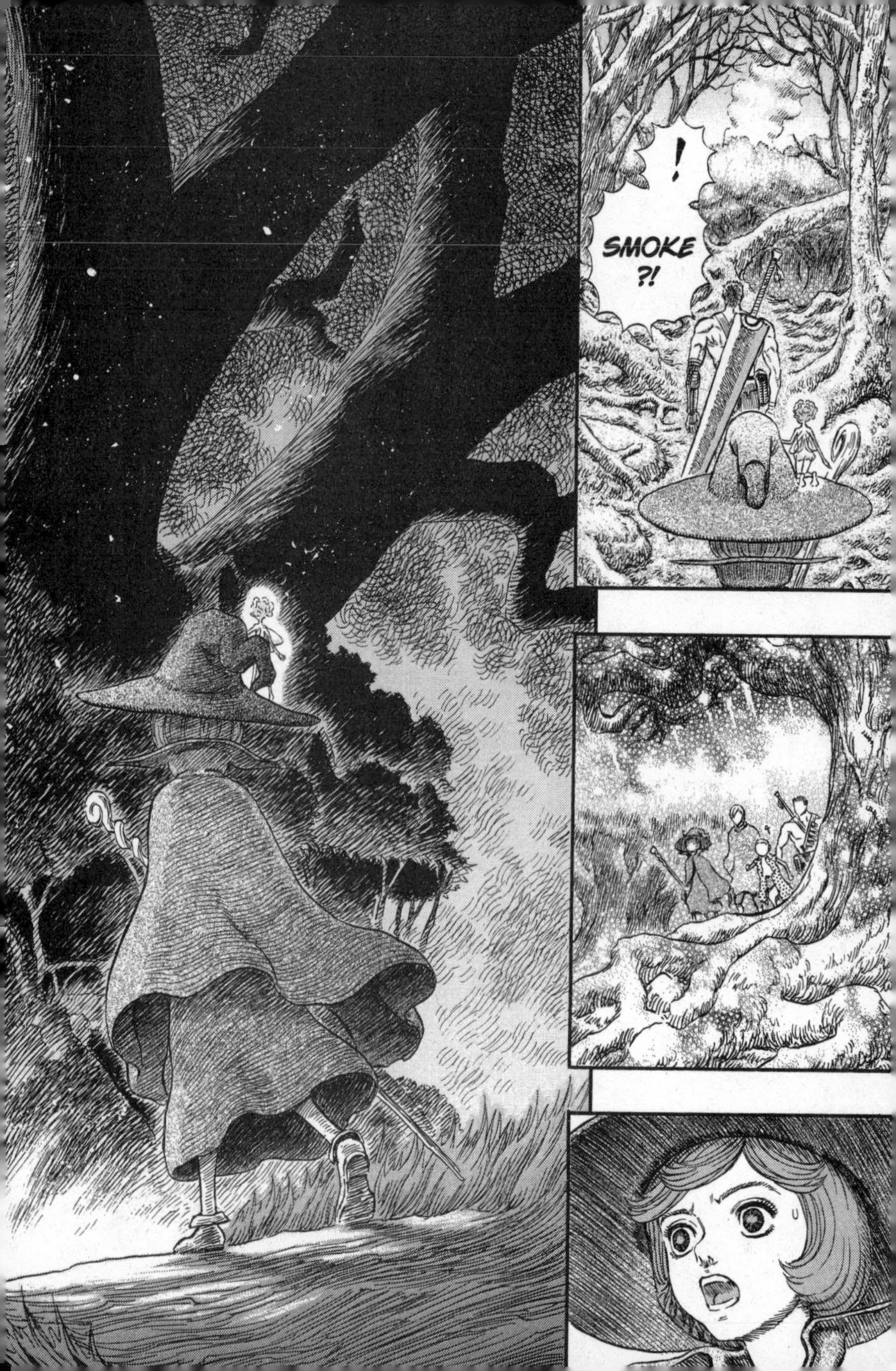
!
SMOKE ?!

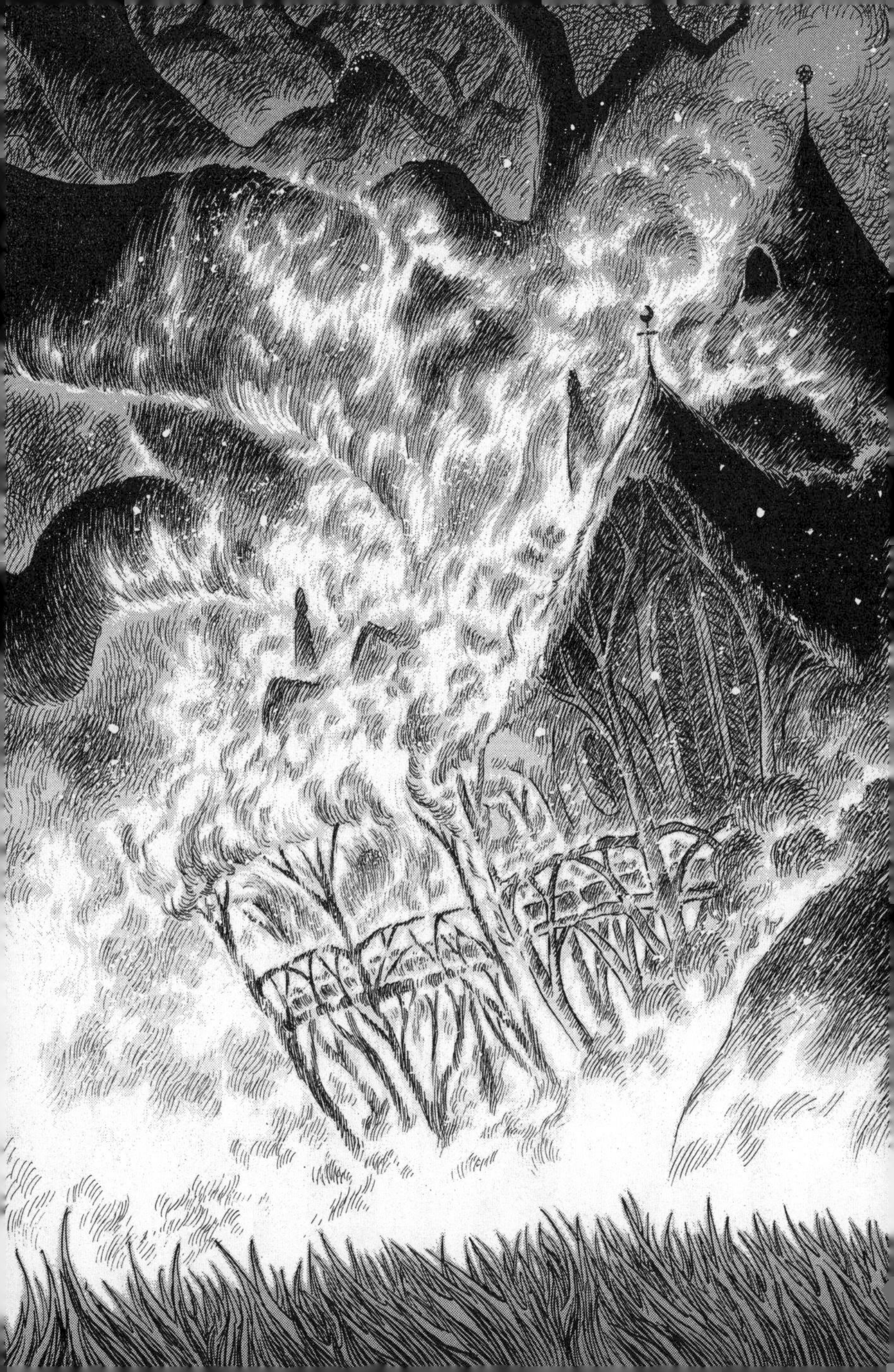

THE BLAZE, PART 1
炎上①

BERSERK

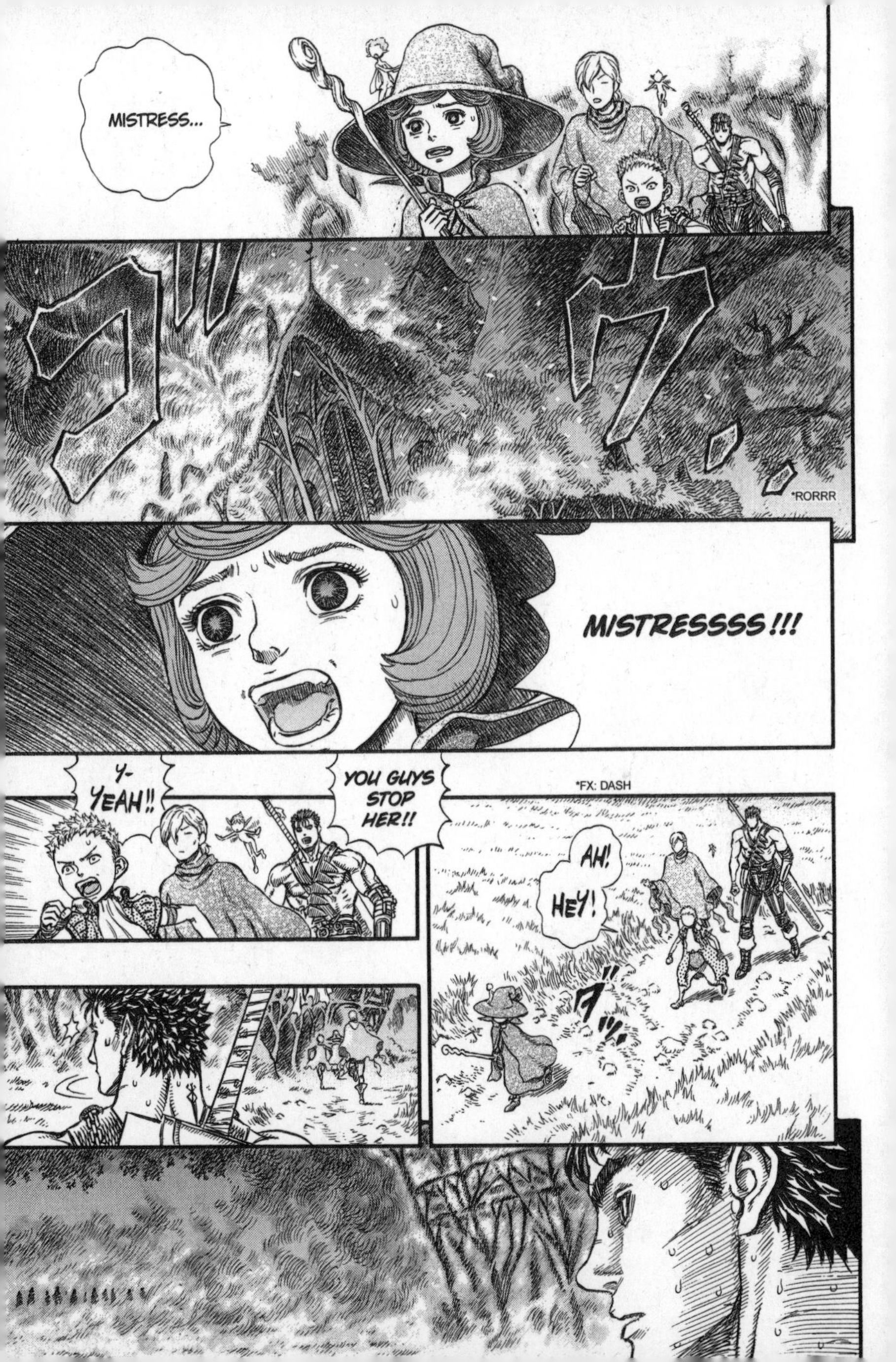
MISTRESS...
*RORRR
MISTRESSSS!!!
*FX: DASH
AH!
HEY!
YOU GUYS STOP HER!!
Y-YEAH!!

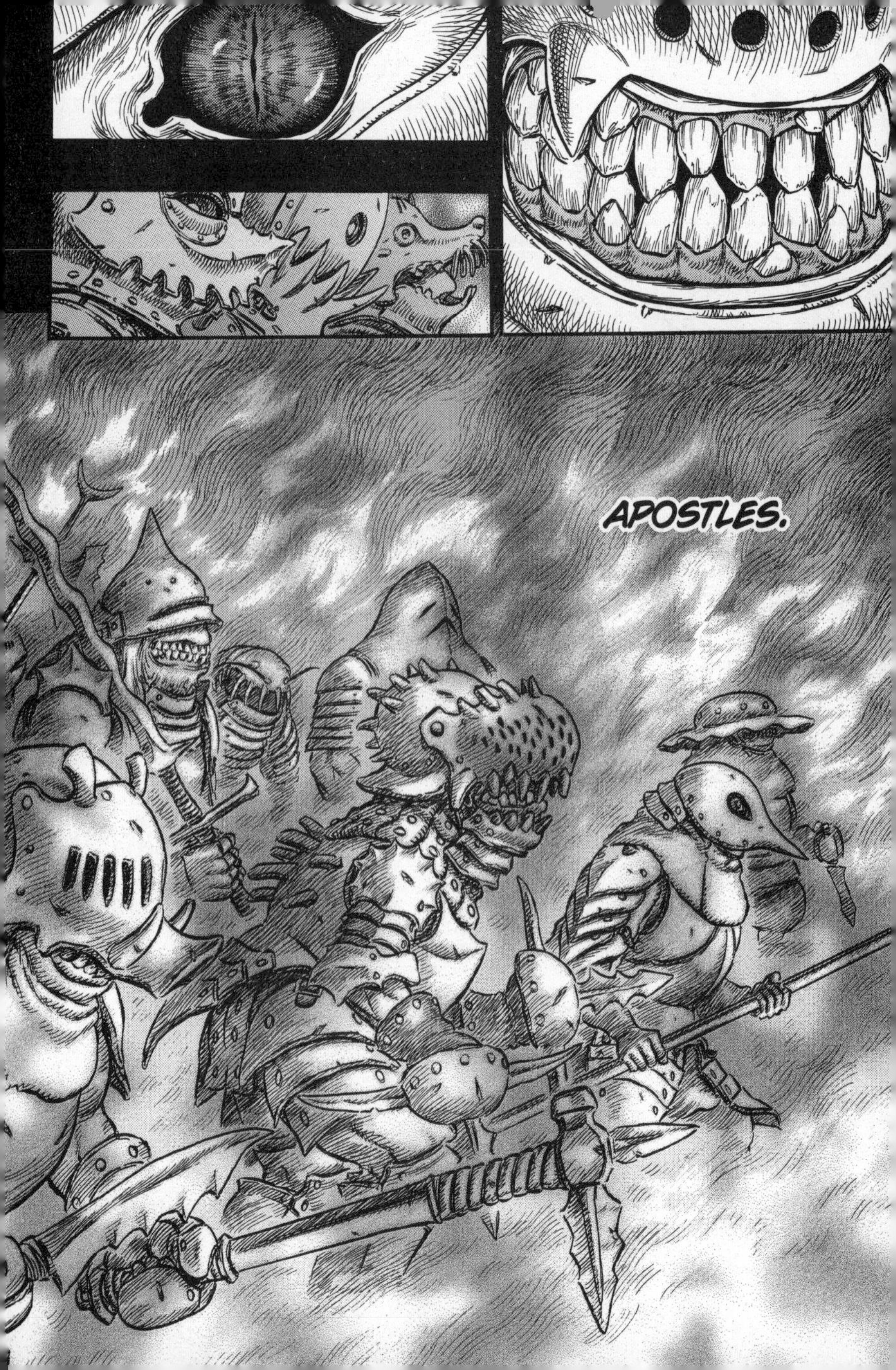
APOSTLES.

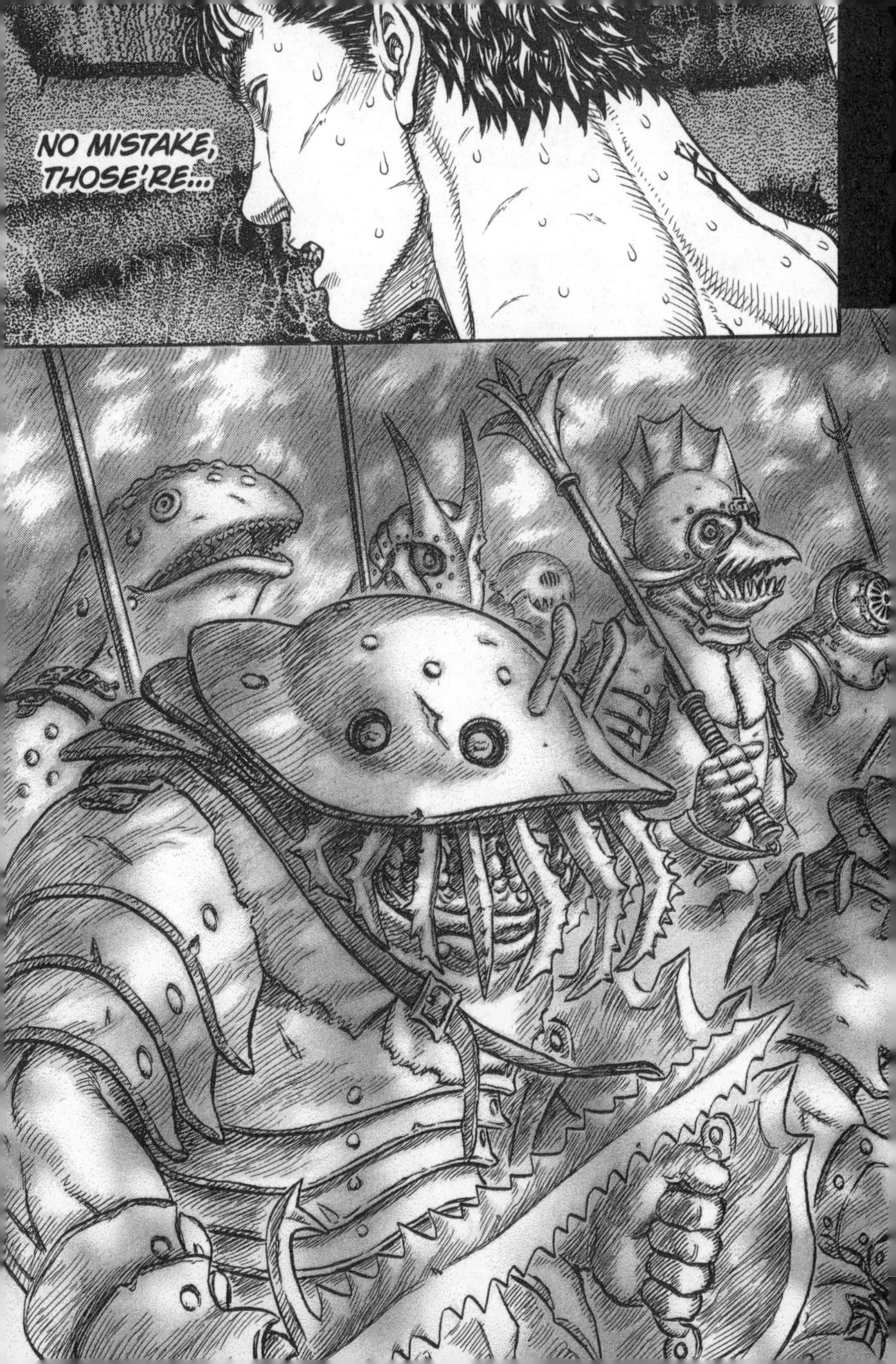
NO MISTAKE, THOSE'RE...

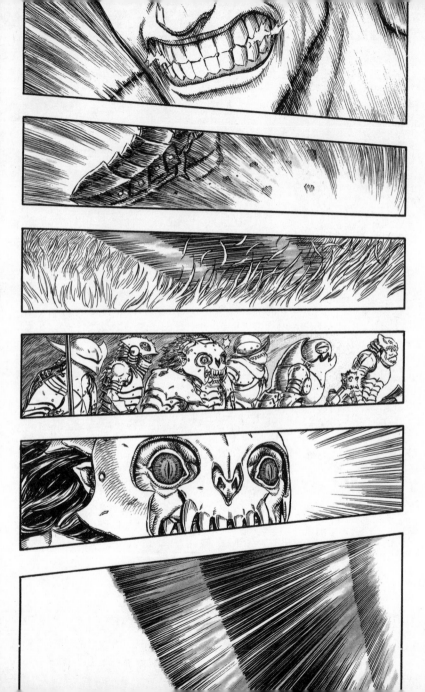

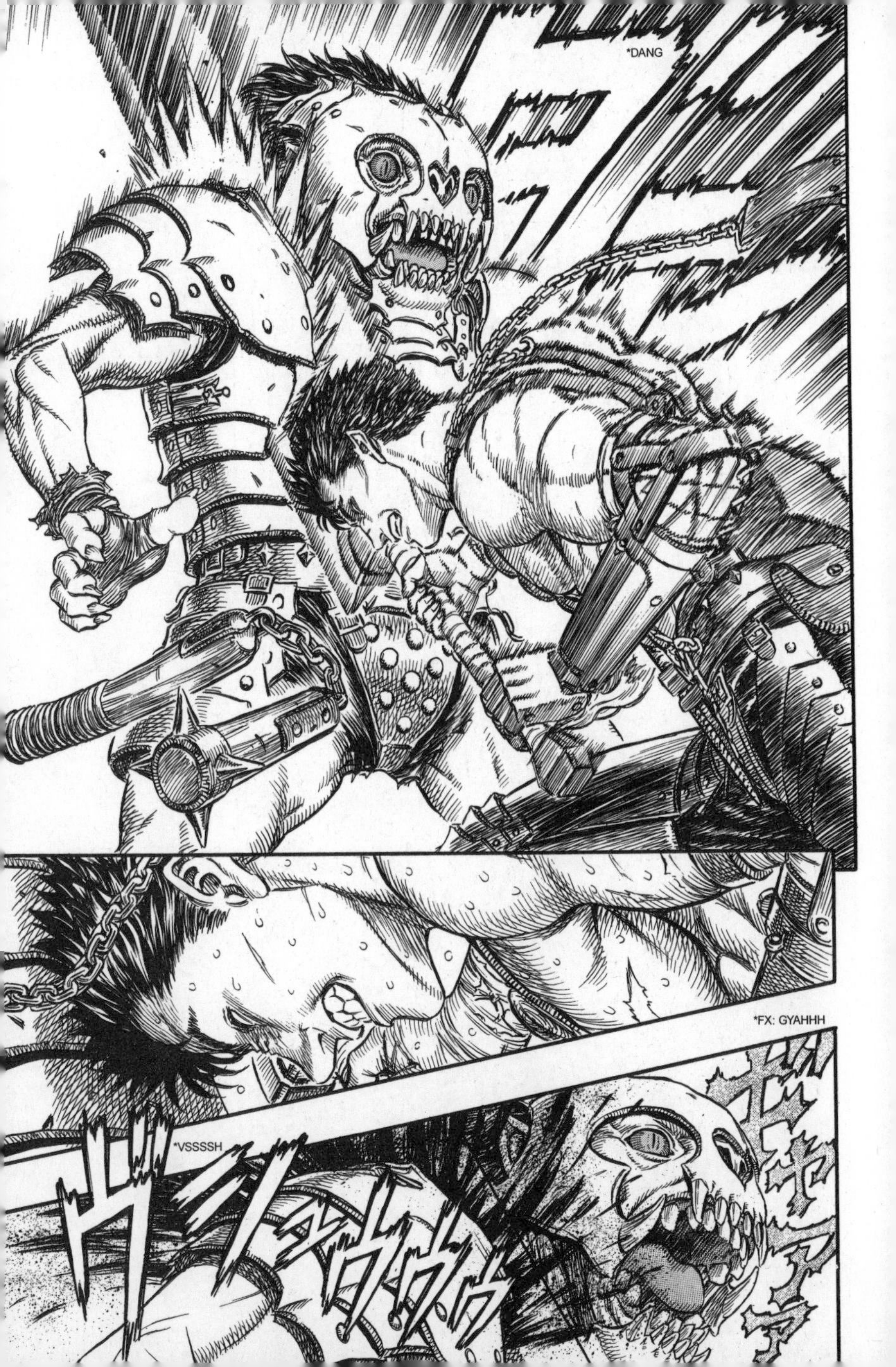
*DANG
*FX: GYAHHH
*VSSSSH

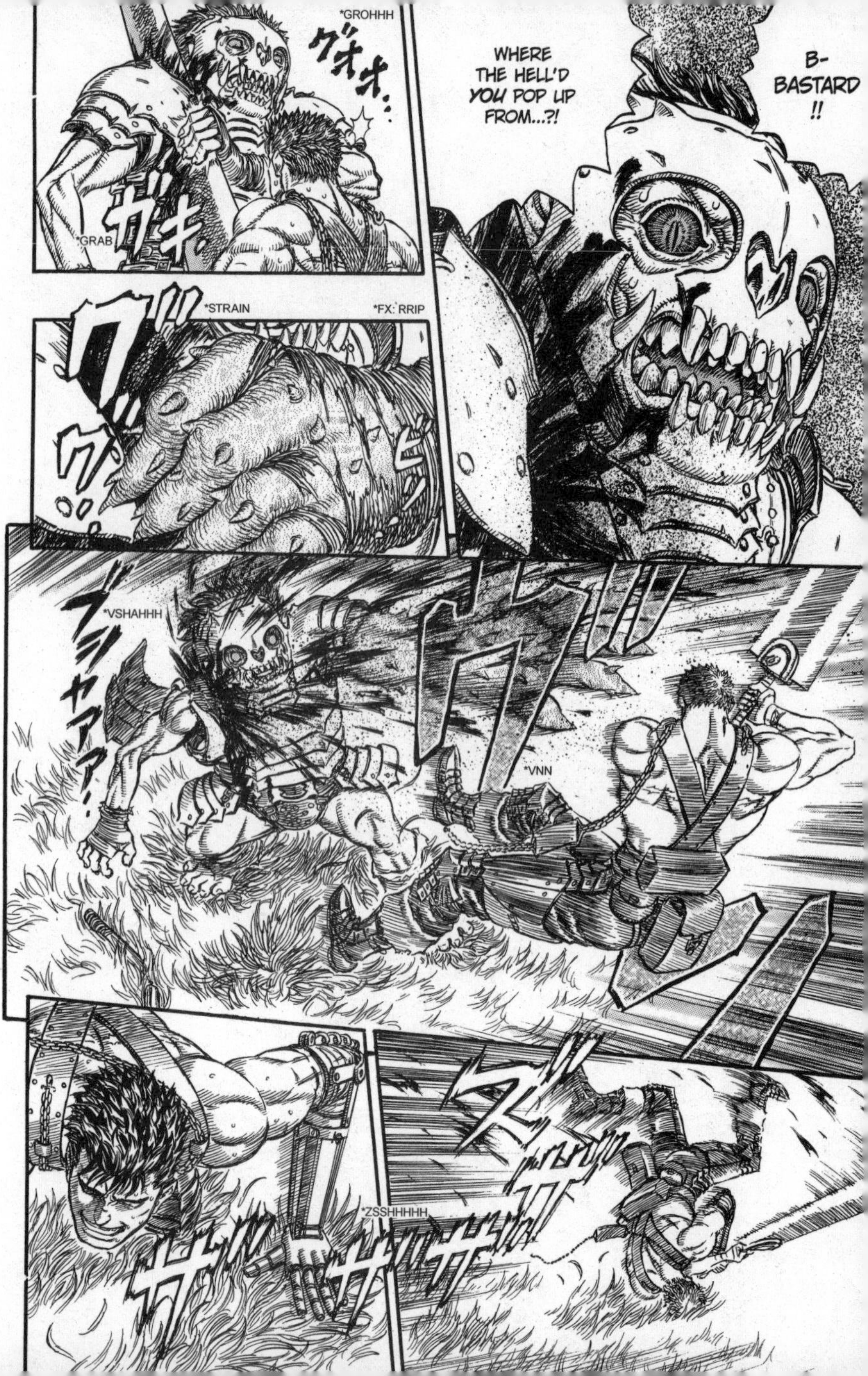
B-BASTARD !!
WHERE THE HELL'D YOU POP UP FROM...?!
*GROHHH
*GRAB
*FX: RRIP
*STRAIN
*VNN
*VSHAHHH
*ZSSHHHHH

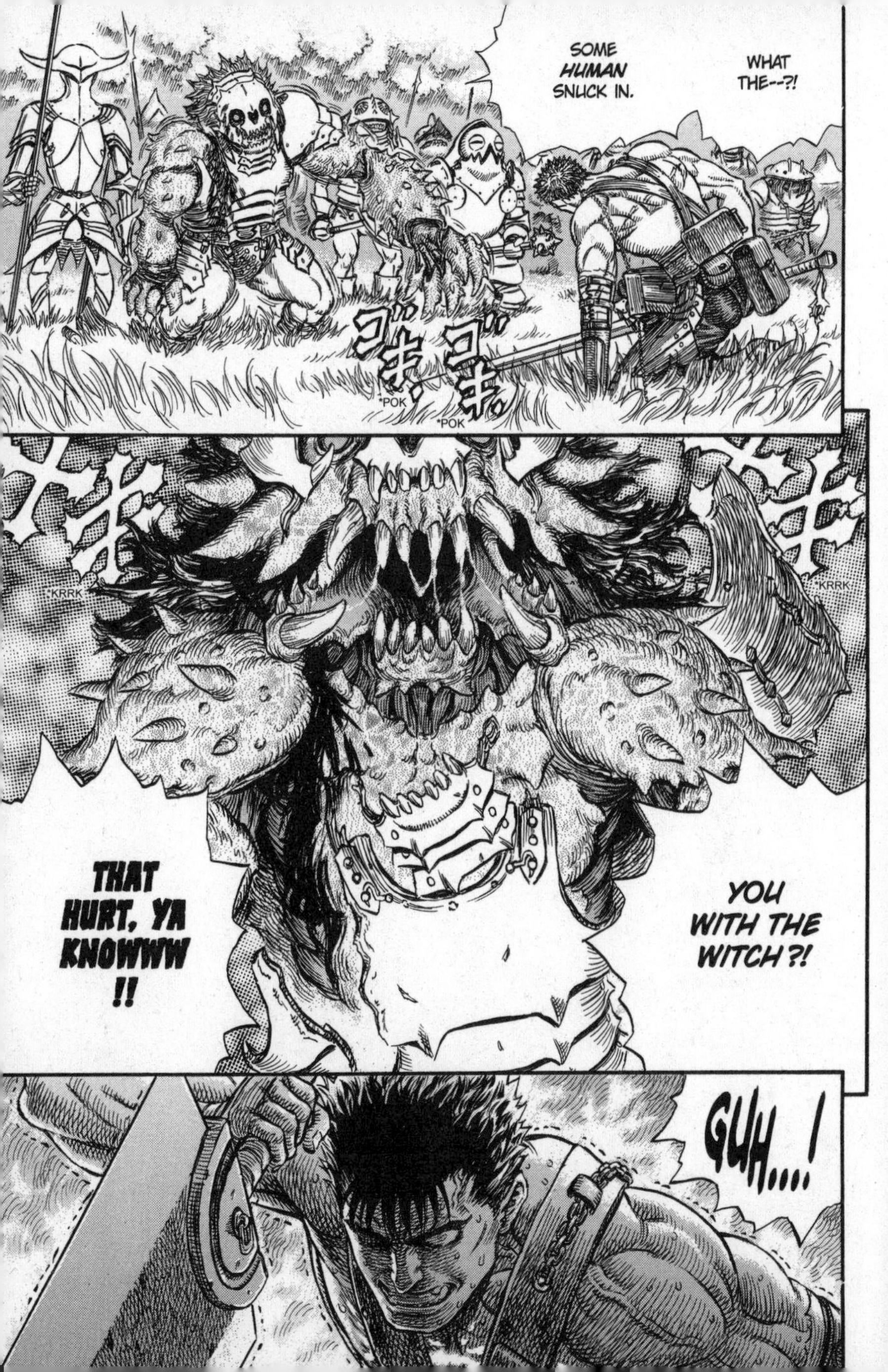
WHAT THE--?!
SOME HUMAN SNUCK IN.
*POK
*POK
*KRRK
*KRRK
YOU WITH THE WITCH?!
THAT HURT, YA KNOWWW!!
GUH...!

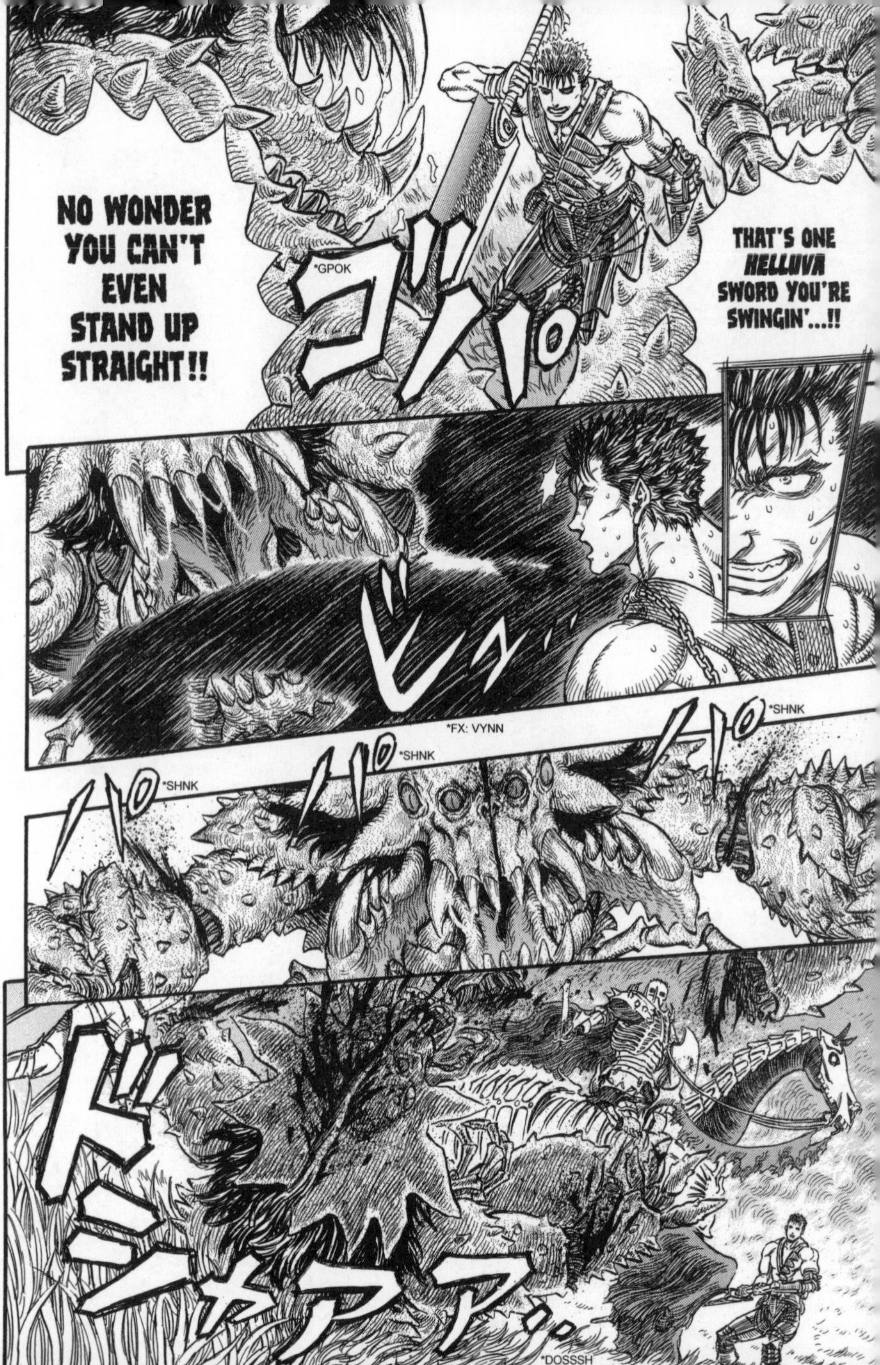
THAT'S ONE *HELLUVA* SWORD YOU'RE SWINGIN'...!!
*GPOK
NO WONDER YOU CAN'T EVEN STAND UP STRAIGHT!!
*FX: VYNN
*SHNK
*SHNK
*SHNK
*DOSSSH

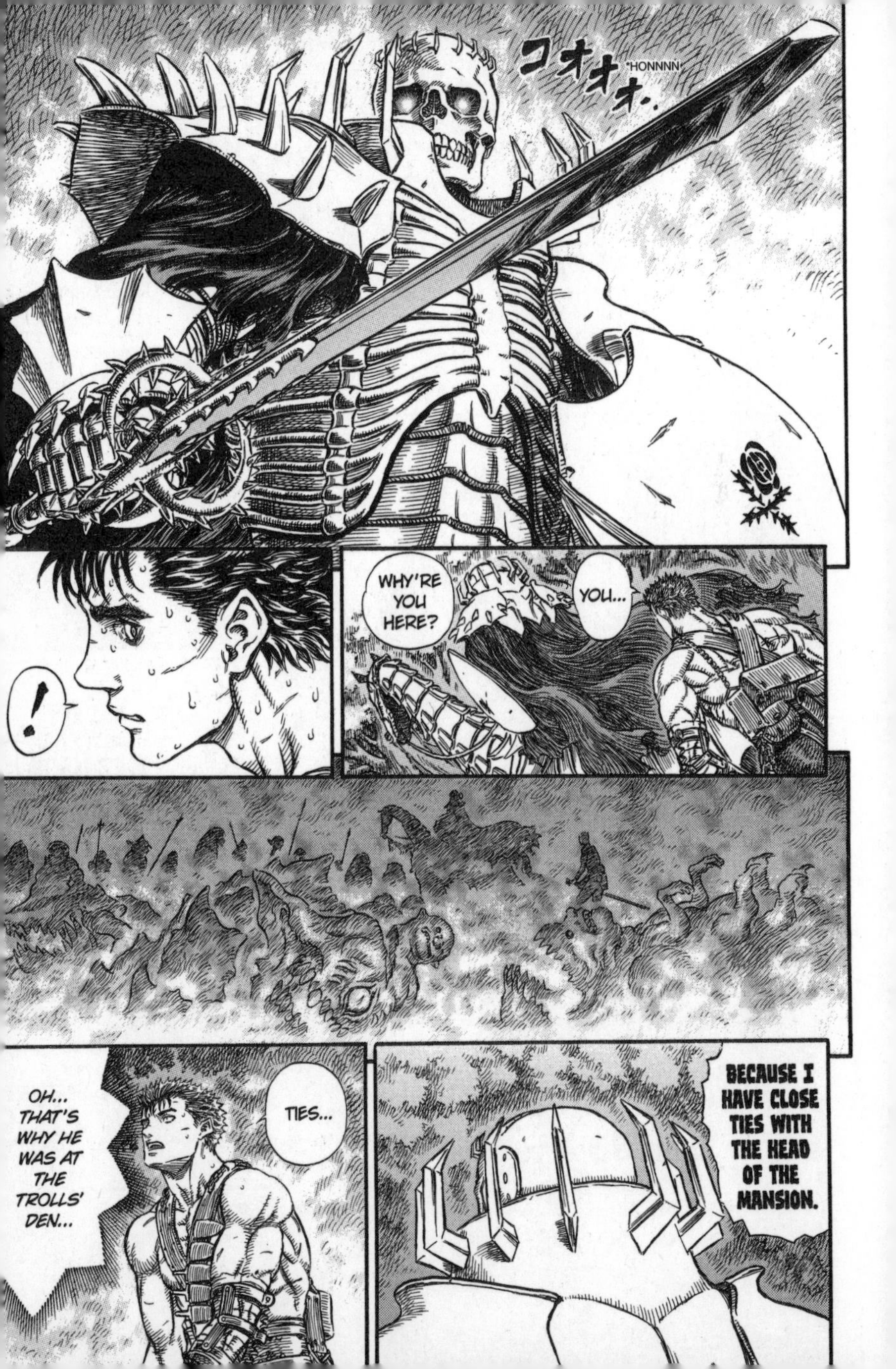
コオオオ..
*HONNNN
YOU...
WHY'RE YOU HERE?
!
BECAUSE I HAVE CLOSE TIES WITH THE HEAD OF THE MANSION.
TIES...
OH... THAT'S WHY HE WAS AT THE TROLLS' DEN...

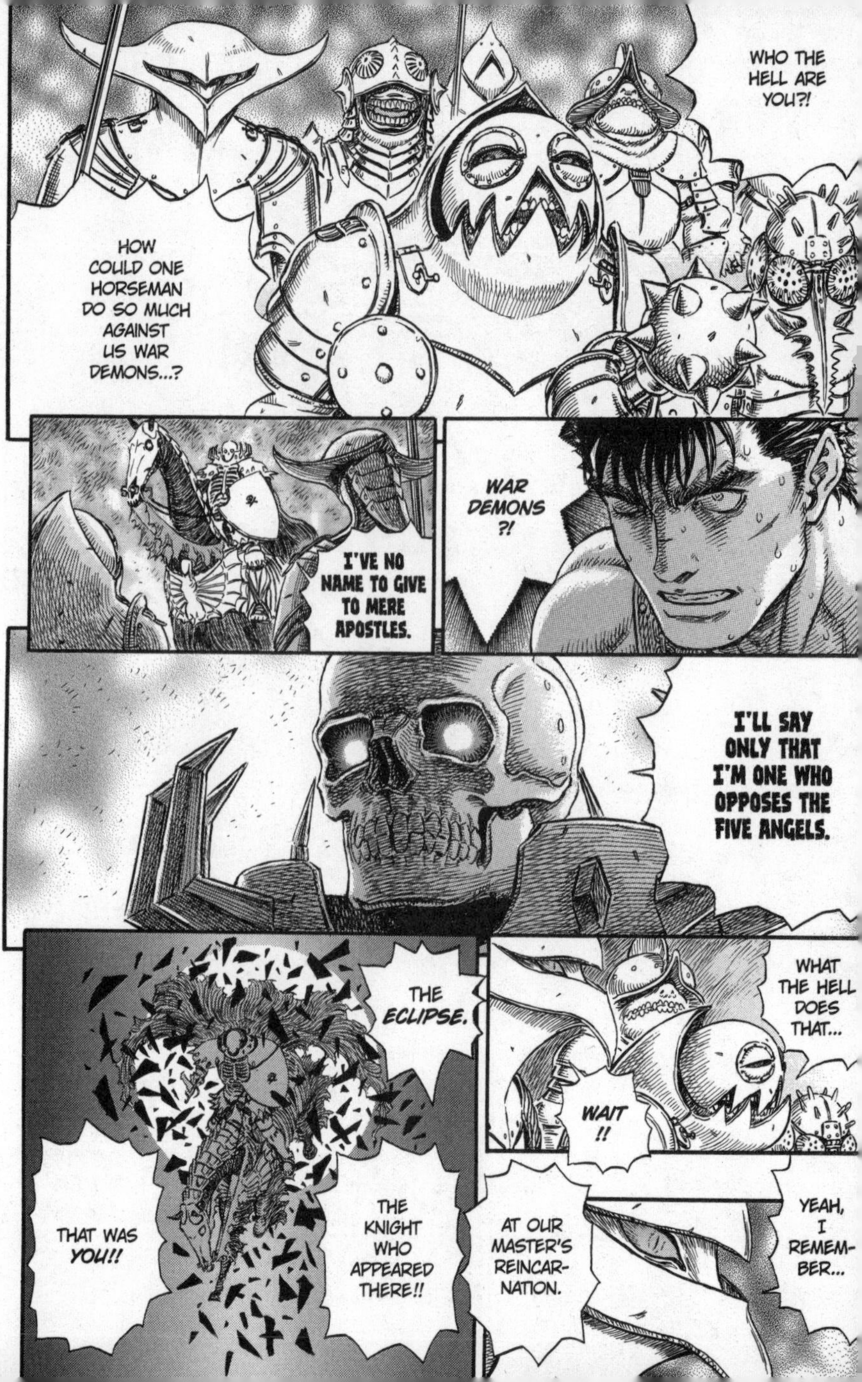
WHO THE HELL ARE YOU?!
HOW COULD ONE HORSEMAN DO SO MUCH AGAINST US WAR DEMONS...?
WAR DEMONS ?!
I'VE NO NAME TO GIVE TO MERE APOSTLES.
I'LL SAY ONLY THAT I'M ONE WHO OPPOSES THE FIVE ANGELS.
WHAT THE HELL DOES THAT...
WAIT !!
YEAH, I REMEMBER...
AT OUR MASTER'S REINCARNATION.
THE ECLIPSE.
THE KNIGHT WHO APPEARED THERE!!
THAT WAS YOU!!

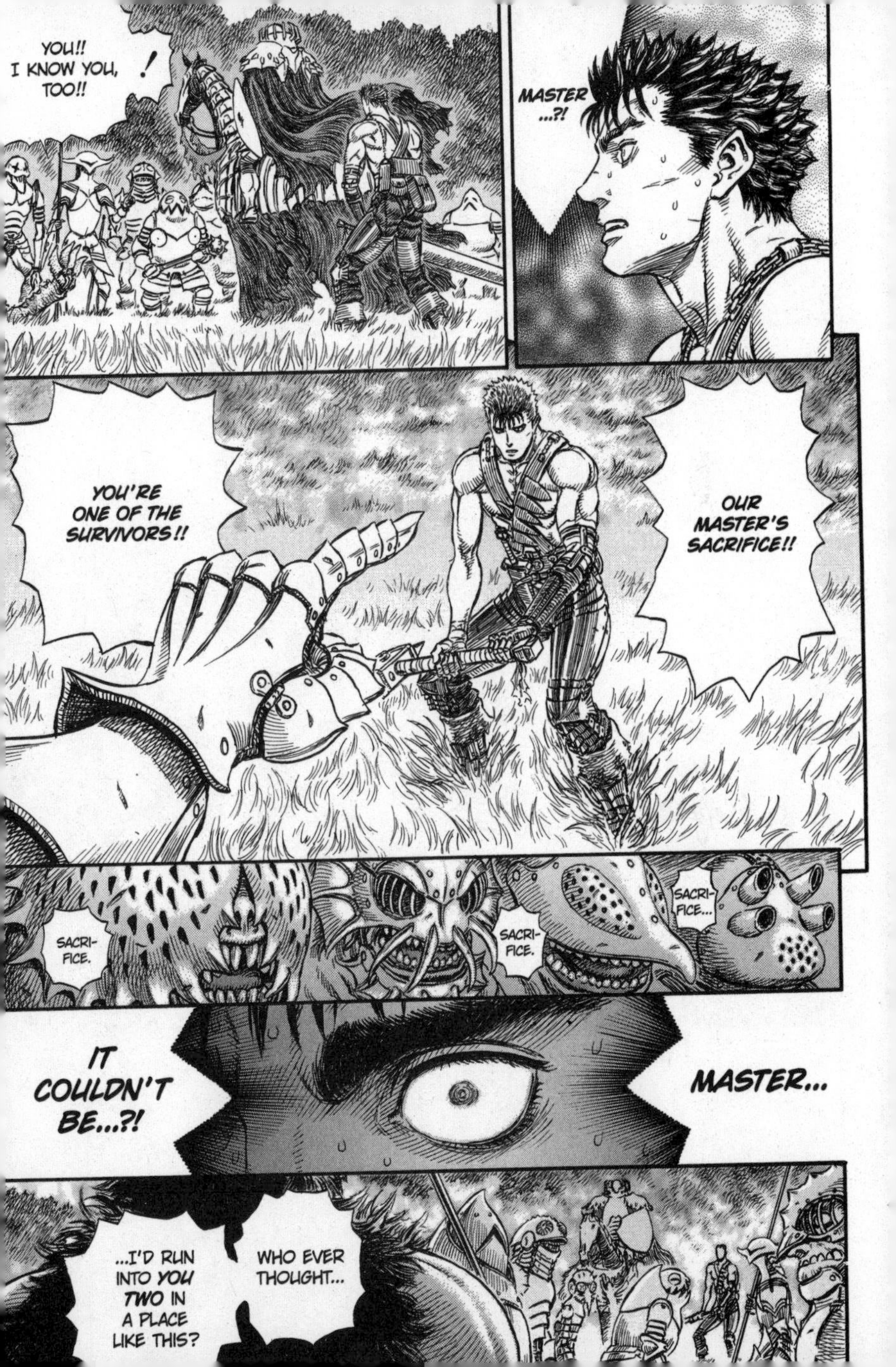
MASTER ...?!
YOU!! I KNOW YOU, TOO!!
!
OUR MASTER'S SACRIFICE!!
YOU'RE ONE OF THE SURVIVORS!!
SACRI-FICE...
SACRI-FICE.
SACRI-FICE.
MASTER...
IT COULDN'T BE...?!
WHO EVER THOUGHT...
...I'D RUN INTO YOU TWO IN A PLACE LIKE THIS?

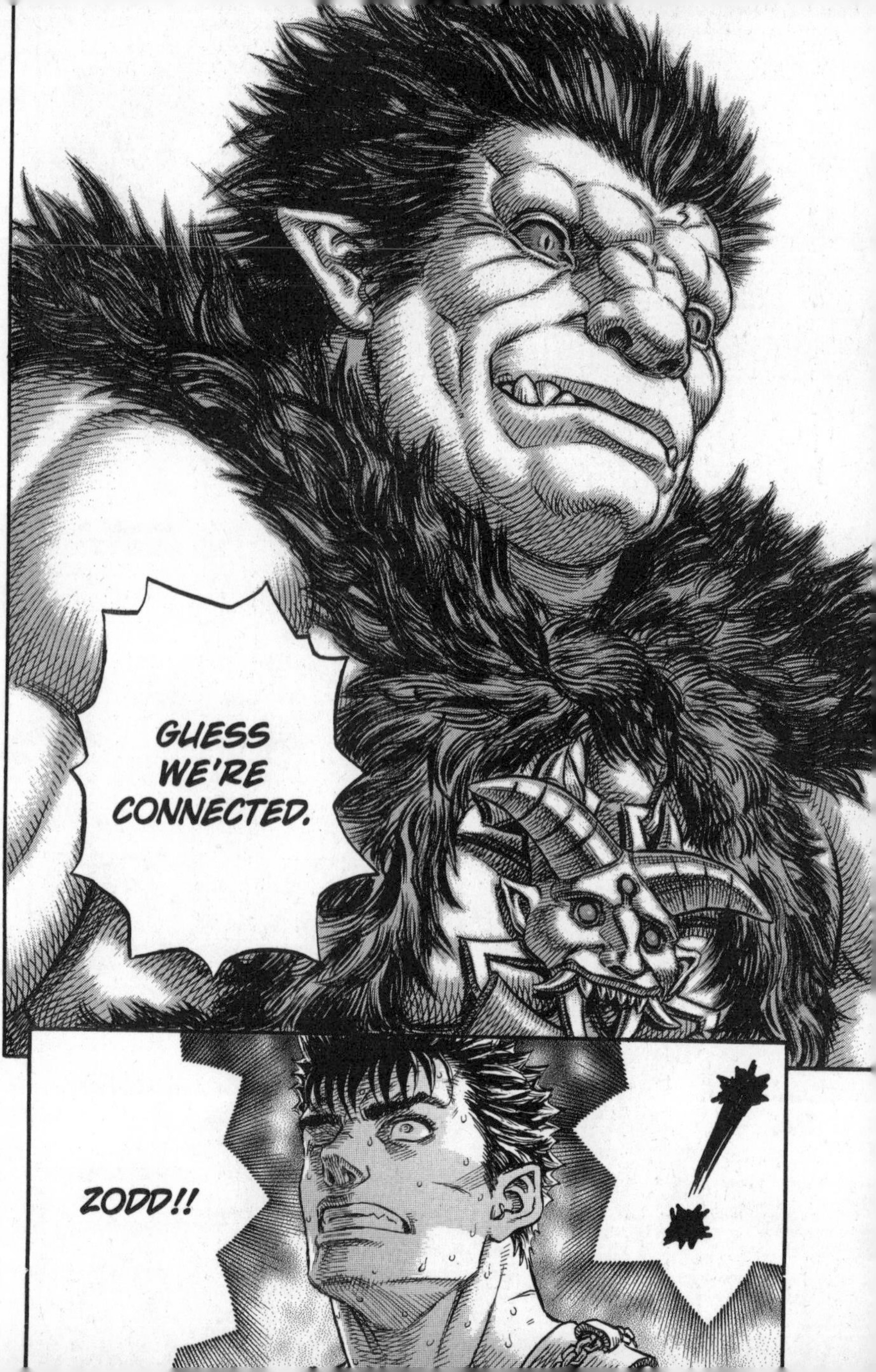
GUESS WE'RE CONNECTED.
ZODD!!

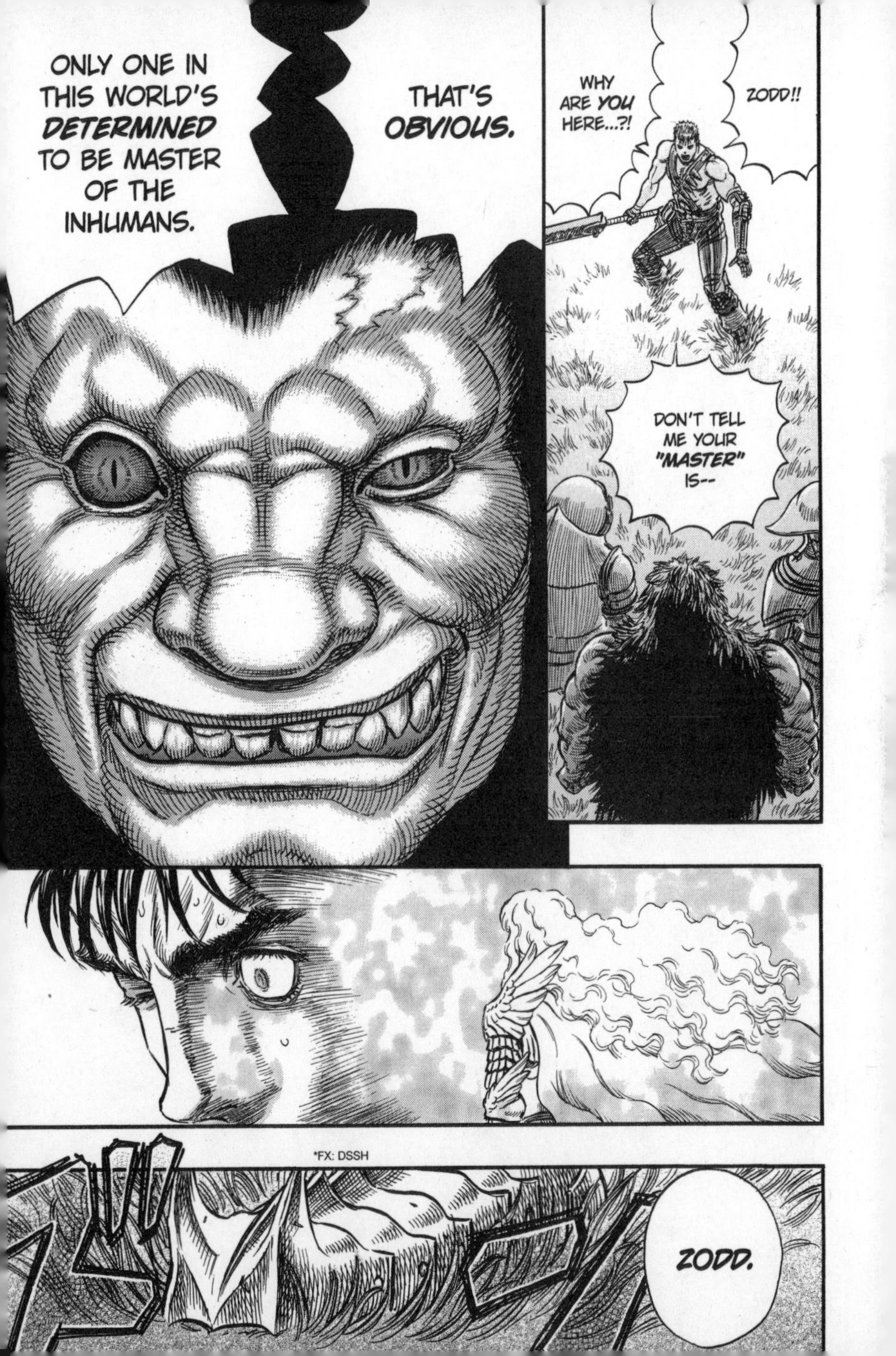
ZODD!!
WHY ARE YOU HERE...?!
DON'T TELL ME YOUR "MASTER" IS--
THAT'S OBVIOUS.
ONLY ONE IN THIS WORLD'S DETERMINED TO BE MASTER OF THE INHUMANS.
*FX: DSSH
ZODD.

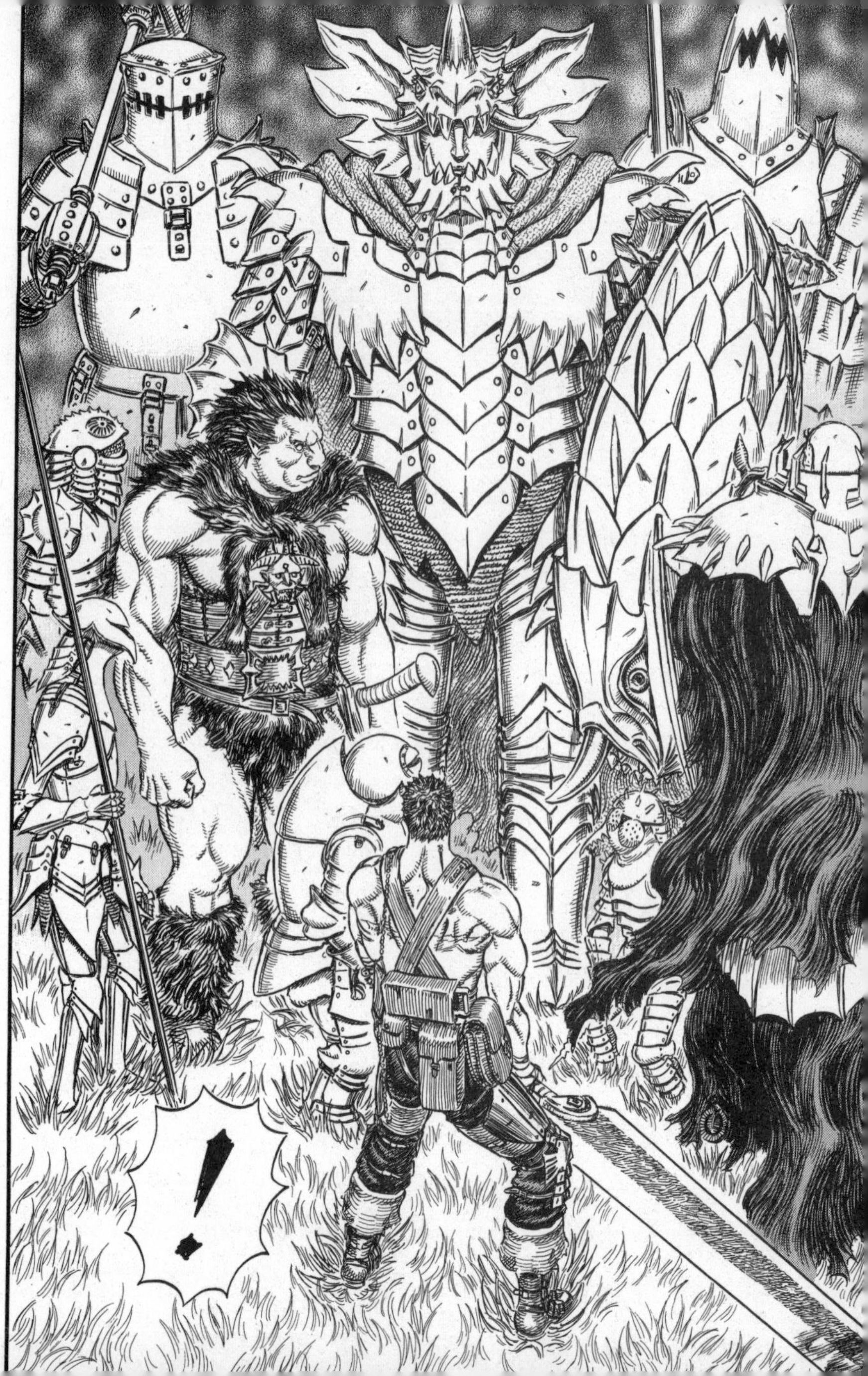
!

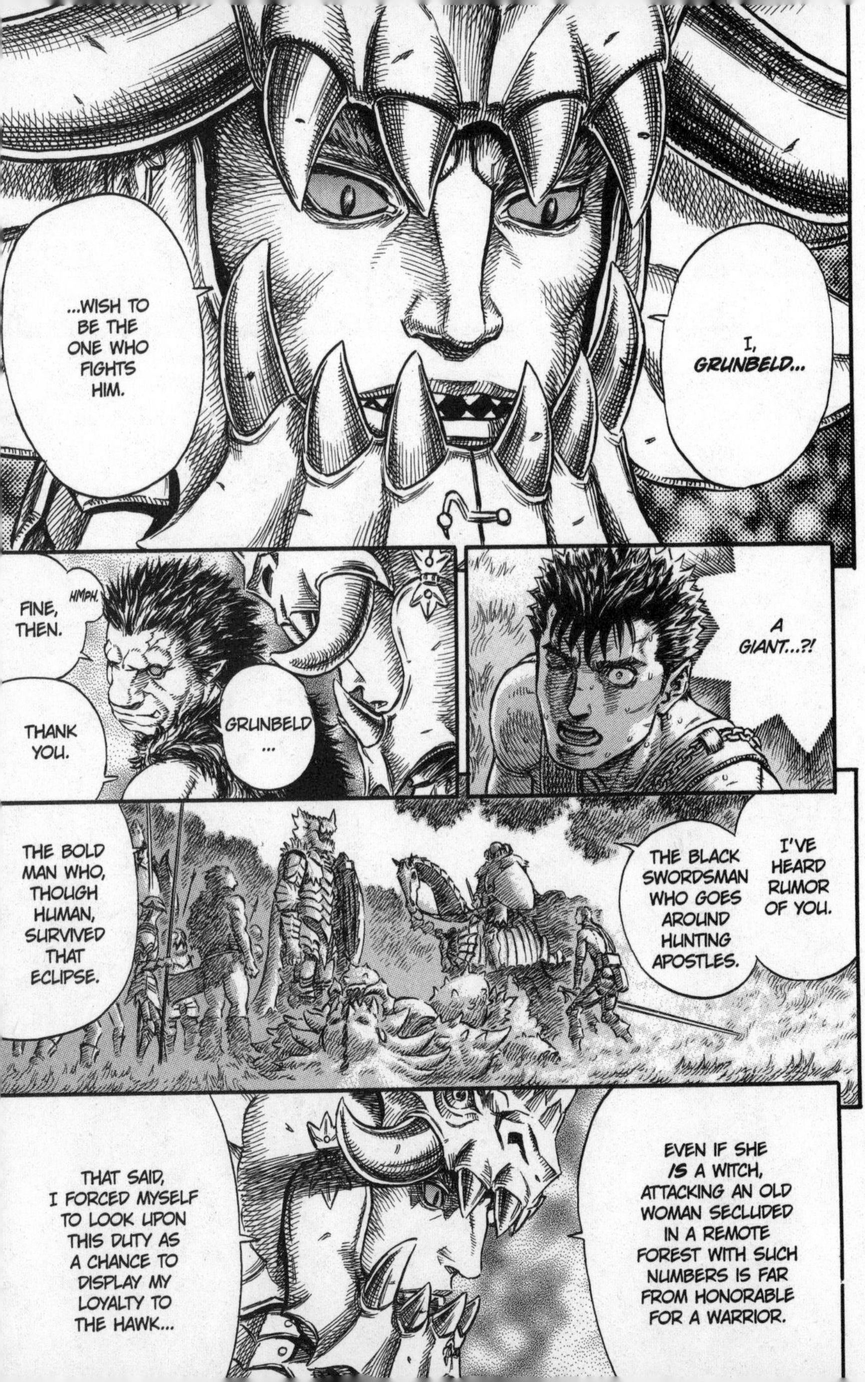
I, GRUNBELD...
...WISH TO BE THE ONE WHO FIGHTS HIM.
A GIANT...?!
HMPH.
FINE, THEN.
GRUNBELD...
THANK YOU.
I'VE HEARD RUMOR OF YOU.
THE BLACK SWORDSMAN WHO GOES AROUND HUNTING APOSTLES.
THE BOLD MAN WHO, THOUGH HUMAN, SURVIVED THAT ECLIPSE.
EVEN IF SHE IS A WITCH, ATTACKING AN OLD WOMAN SECLUDED IN A REMOTE FOREST WITH SUCH NUMBERS IS FAR FROM HONORABLE FOR A WARRIOR.
THAT SAID, I FORCED MYSELF TO LOOK UPON THIS DUTY AS A CHANCE TO DISPLAY MY LOYALTY TO THE HAWK...

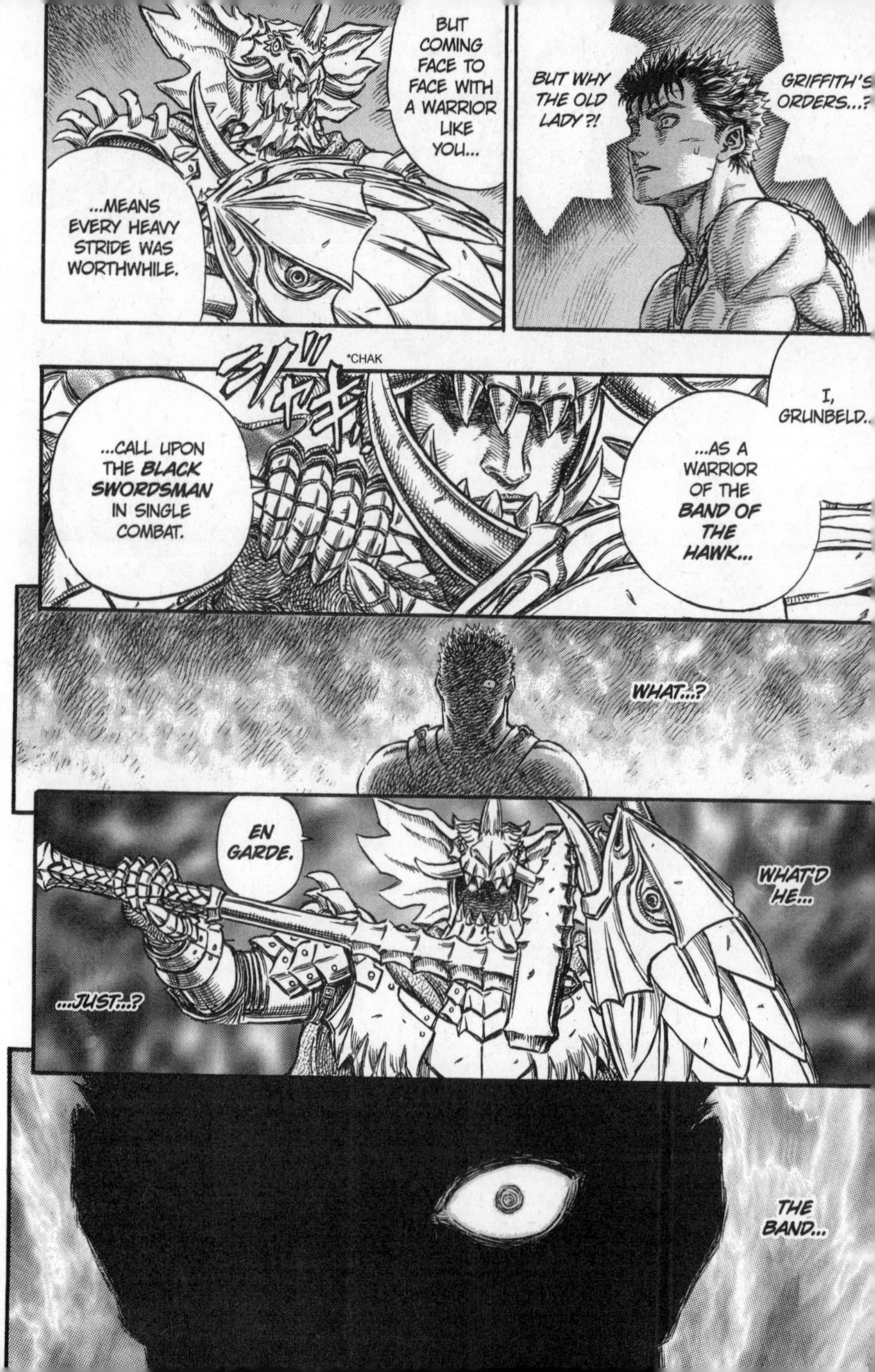
GRIFFITH'S ORDERS...?
BUT WHY THE OLD LADY?!
BUT COMING FACE TO FACE WITH A WARRIOR LIKE YOU...
...MEANS EVERY HEAVY STRIDE WAS WORTHWHILE.
I, GRUNBELD...
...AS A WARRIOR OF THE BAND OF THE HAWK...
ジャキ
*CHAK
...CALL UPON THE BLACK SWORDSMAN IN SINGLE COMBAT.
WHAT...?
EN GARDE.
WHAT'D HE...
...JUST...?
THE BAND...

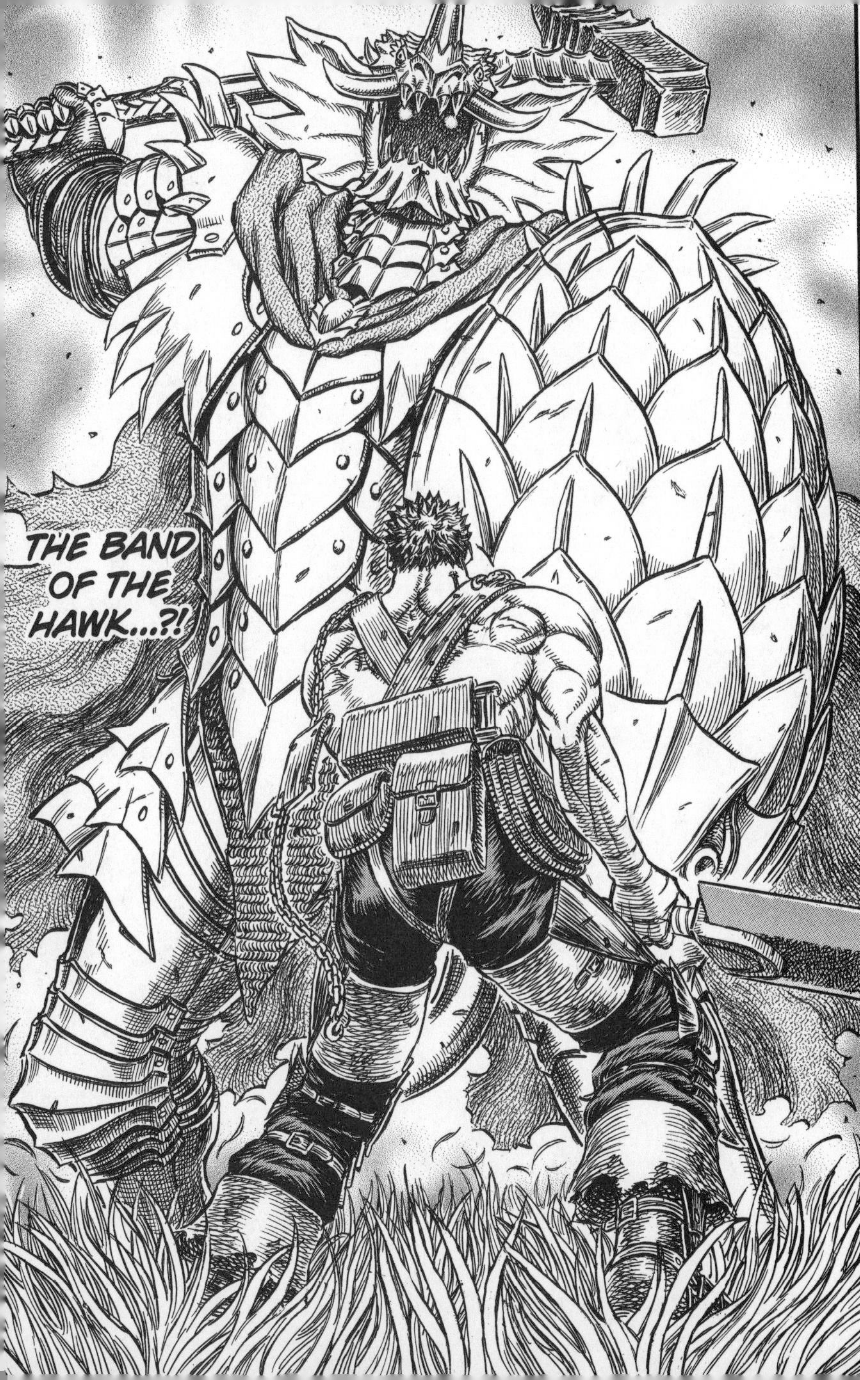
THE BAND OF THE HAWK...?!

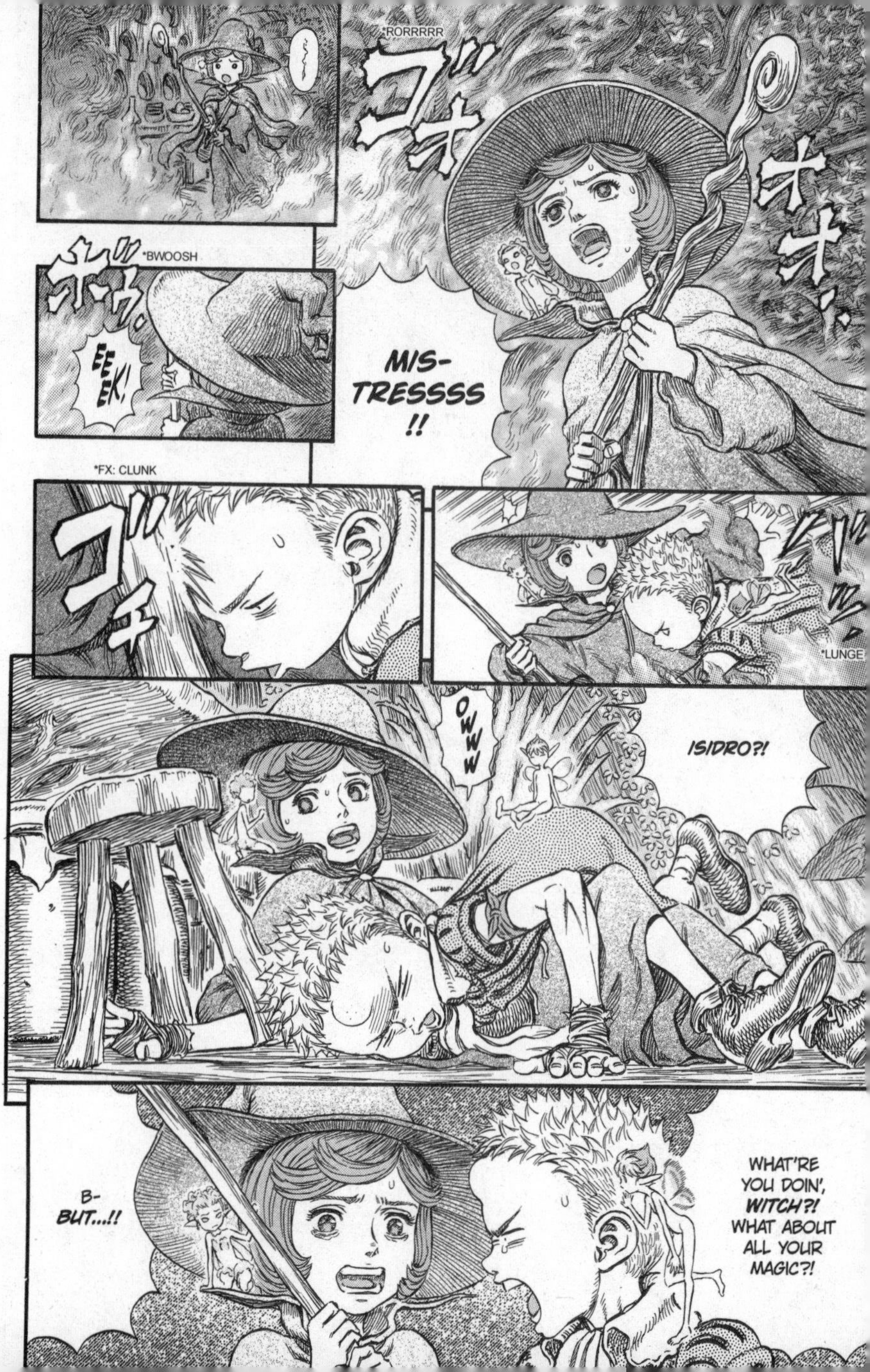
*RORRRRR
MIS-TRESSSS!!
*BWOOSH
EEEEK!
*LUNGE
*FX: CLUNK
ISIDRO?!
OWWW
WHAT'RE YOU DOIN', WITCH?! WHAT ABOUT ALL YOUR MAGIC?!
B-BUT...!!

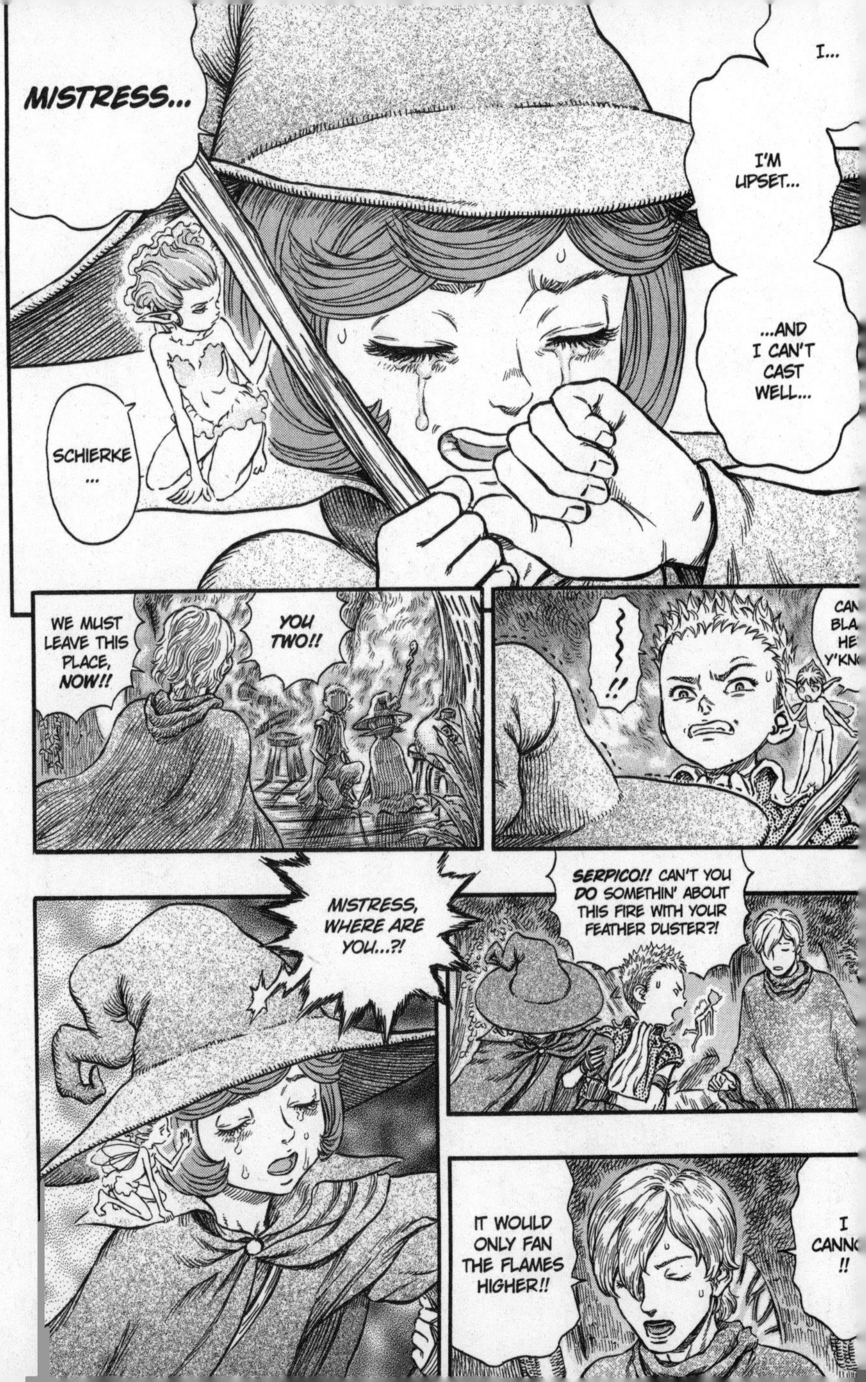
I...
I'M UPSET...
...AND I CAN'T CAST WELL...
MISTRESS...
SCHIERKE ...
CAN BLA HE Y'KNO
YOU TWO!!
WE MUST LEAVE THIS PLACE, NOW!!
SERPICO!! CAN'T YOU DO SOMETHIN' ABOUT THIS FIRE WITH YOUR FEATHER DUSTER?!
I CANN !!
IT WOULD ONLY FAN THE FLAMES HIGHER!!
MISTRESS, WHERE ARE YOU...?!

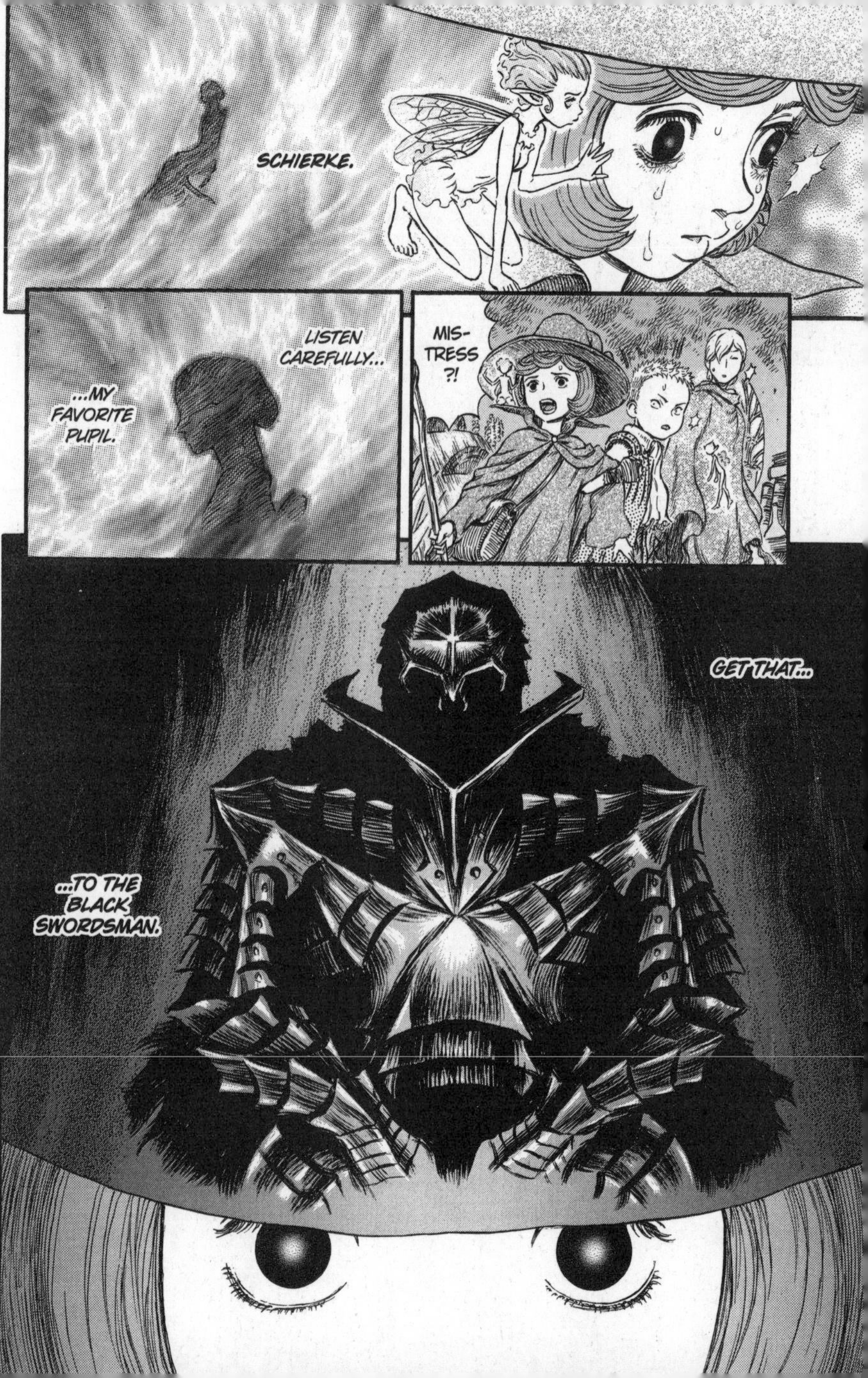
SCHIERKE.
MIS-TRESS ?!
LISTEN CAREFULLY...
...MY FAVORITE PUPIL.
GET THAT...
...TO THE BLACK SWORDSMAN.

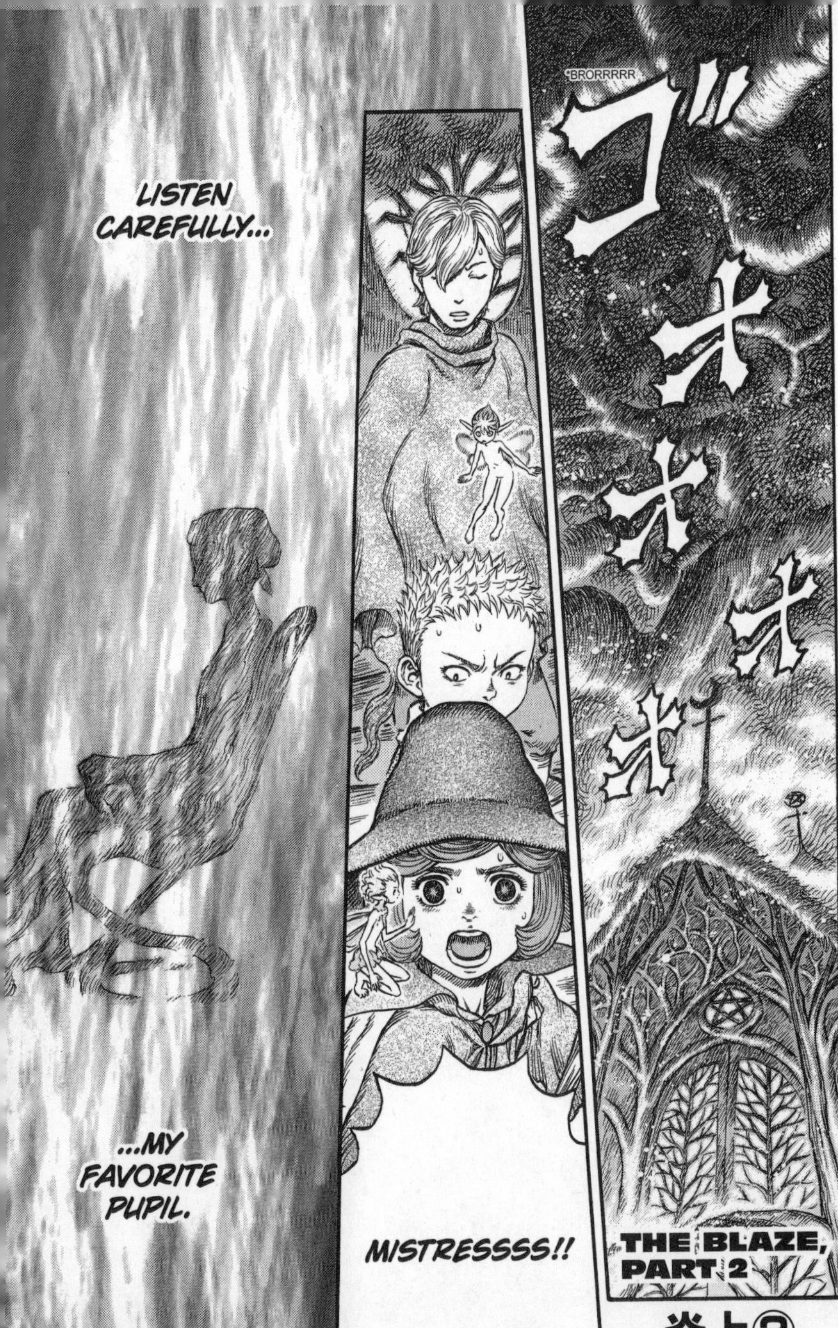
*BRORRRRR
THE BLAZE, PART 2
MISTRESSSS!!
LISTEN CAREFULLY...
...MY FAVORITE PUPIL.

炎上②

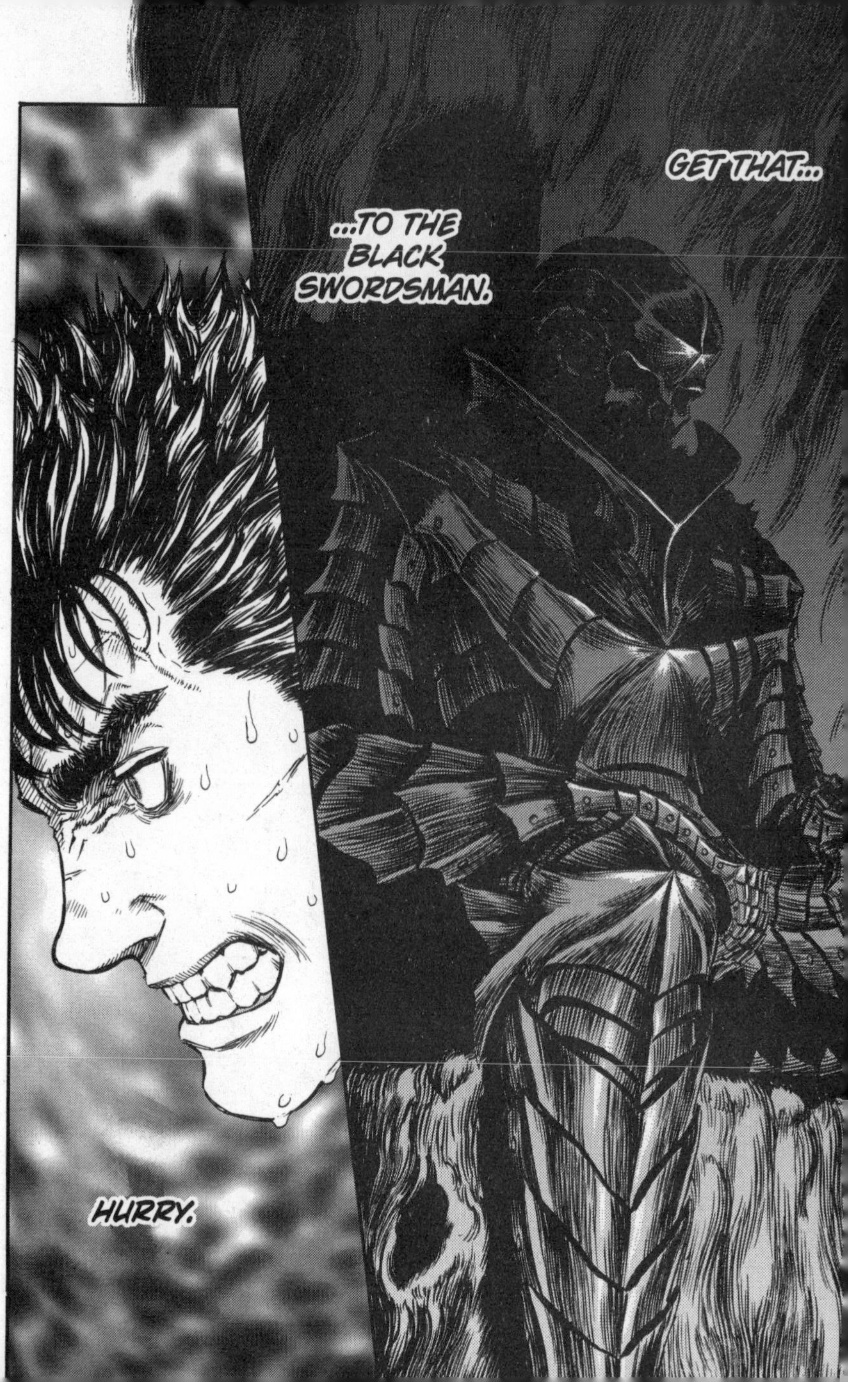
GET THAT...
...TO THE BLACK SWORDSMAN.
HURRY.

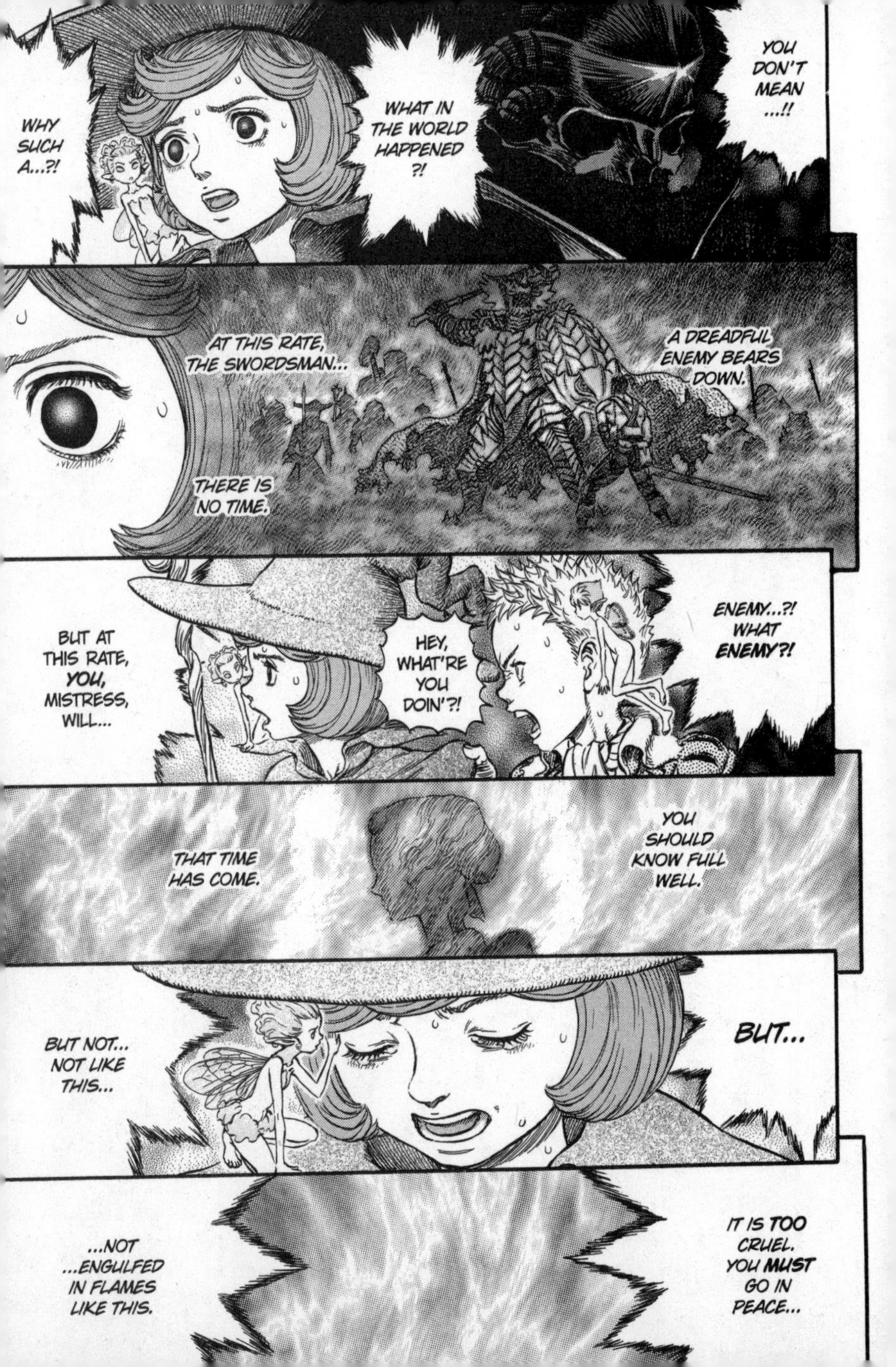
YOU DON'T MEAN ...!!
WHAT IN THE WORLD HAPPENED ?!
WHY SUCH A...?!
A DREADFUL ENEMY BEARS DOWN.
AT THIS RATE, THE SWORDSMAN...
THERE IS NO TIME.
ENEMY...?! WHAT ENEMY?!
HEY, WHAT'RE YOU DOIN'?!
BUT AT THIS RATE, YOU, MISTRESS, WILL...
YOU SHOULD KNOW FULL WELL.
THAT TIME HAS COME.
BUT...
BUT NOT... NOT LIKE THIS...
IT IS TOO CRUEL. YOU MUST GO IN PEACE...
...NOT ...ENGULFED IN FLAMES LIKE THIS.

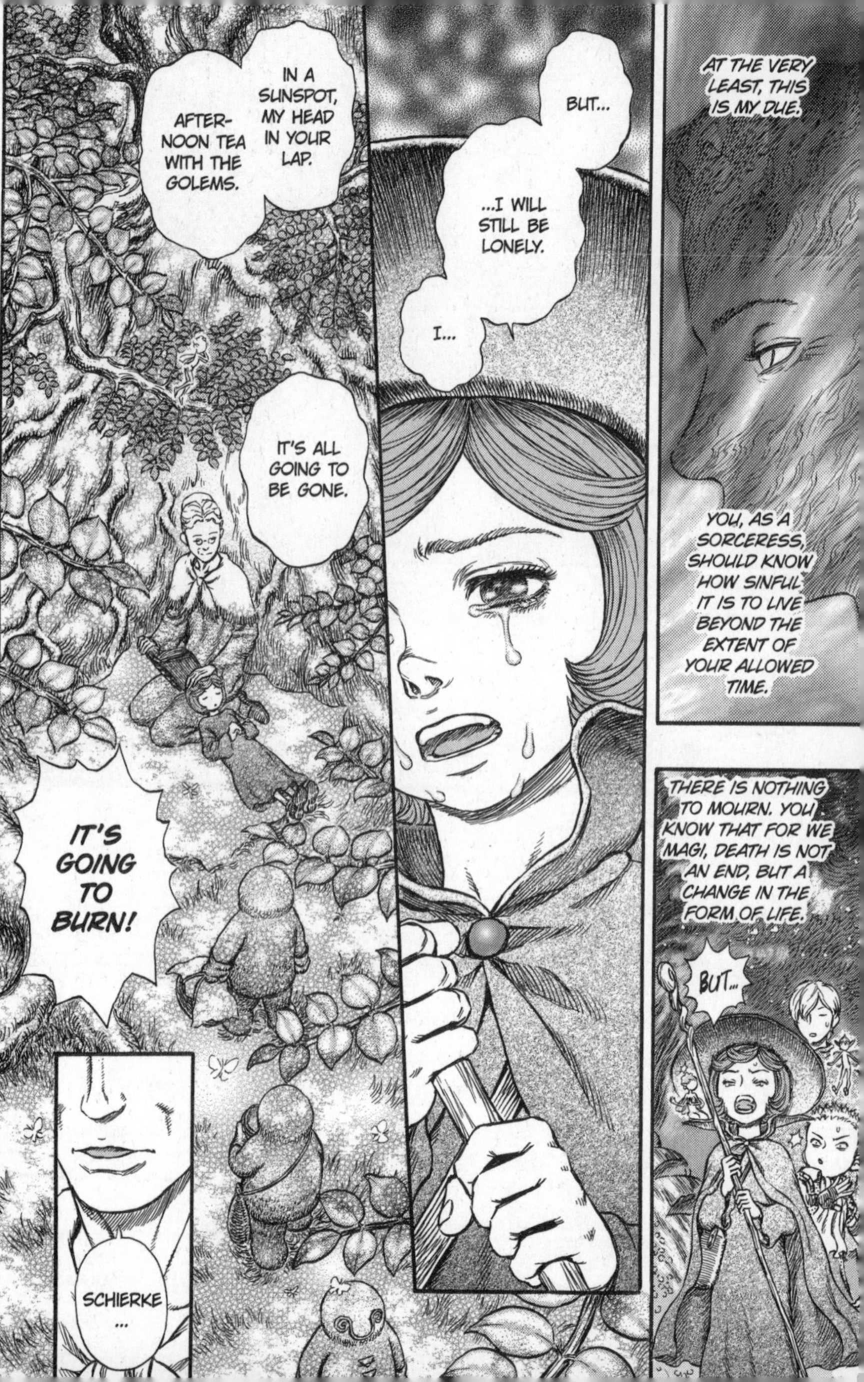
AT THE VERY LEAST, THIS IS MY DUE.
YOU, AS A SORCERESS, SHOULD KNOW HOW SINFUL IT IS TO LIVE BEYOND THE EXTENT OF YOUR ALLOWED TIME.
THERE IS NOTHING TO MOURN. YOU KNOW THAT FOR WE MAGI, DEATH IS NOT AN END, BUT A CHANGE IN THE FORM OF LIFE.
BUT...
BUT...
...I WILL STILL BE LONELY.
I...
IN A SUNSPOT, MY HEAD IN YOUR LAP.
AFTER-NOON TEA WITH THE GOLEMS.
IT'S ALL GOING TO BE GONE.
IT'S GOING TO BURN!
SCHIERKE ...

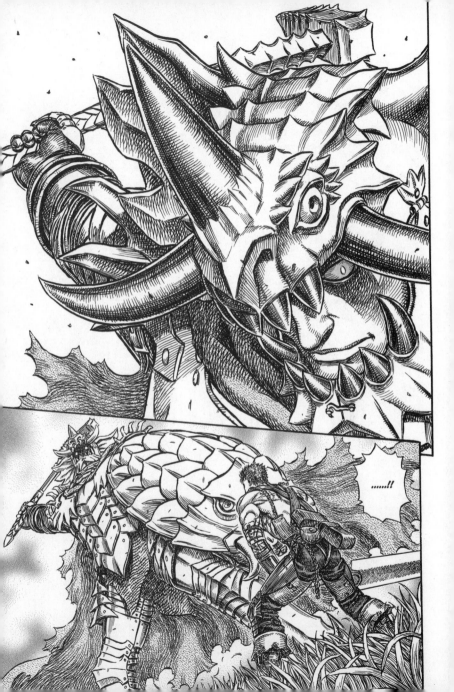

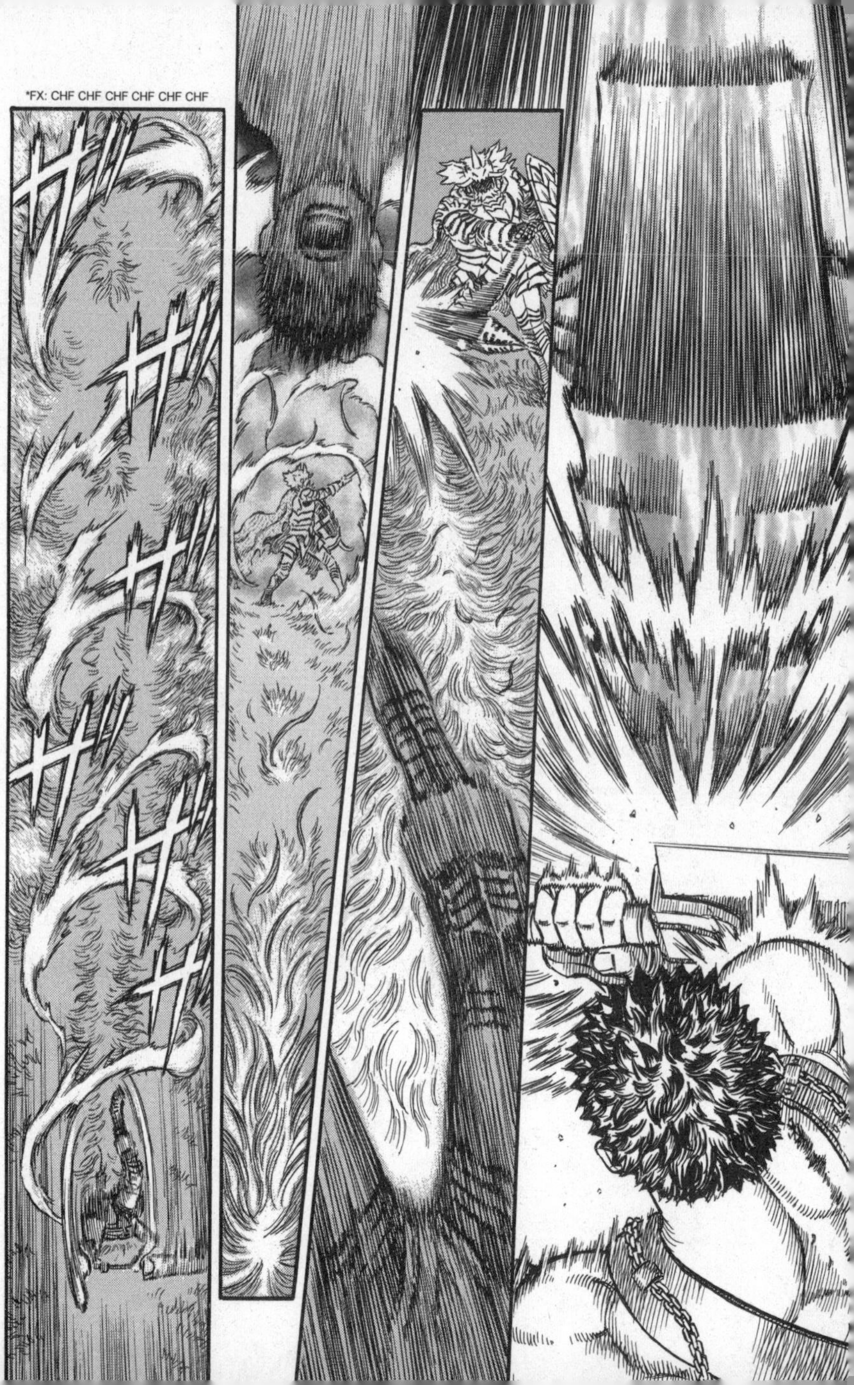
*FX: CHF CHF CHF CHF CHF CHF

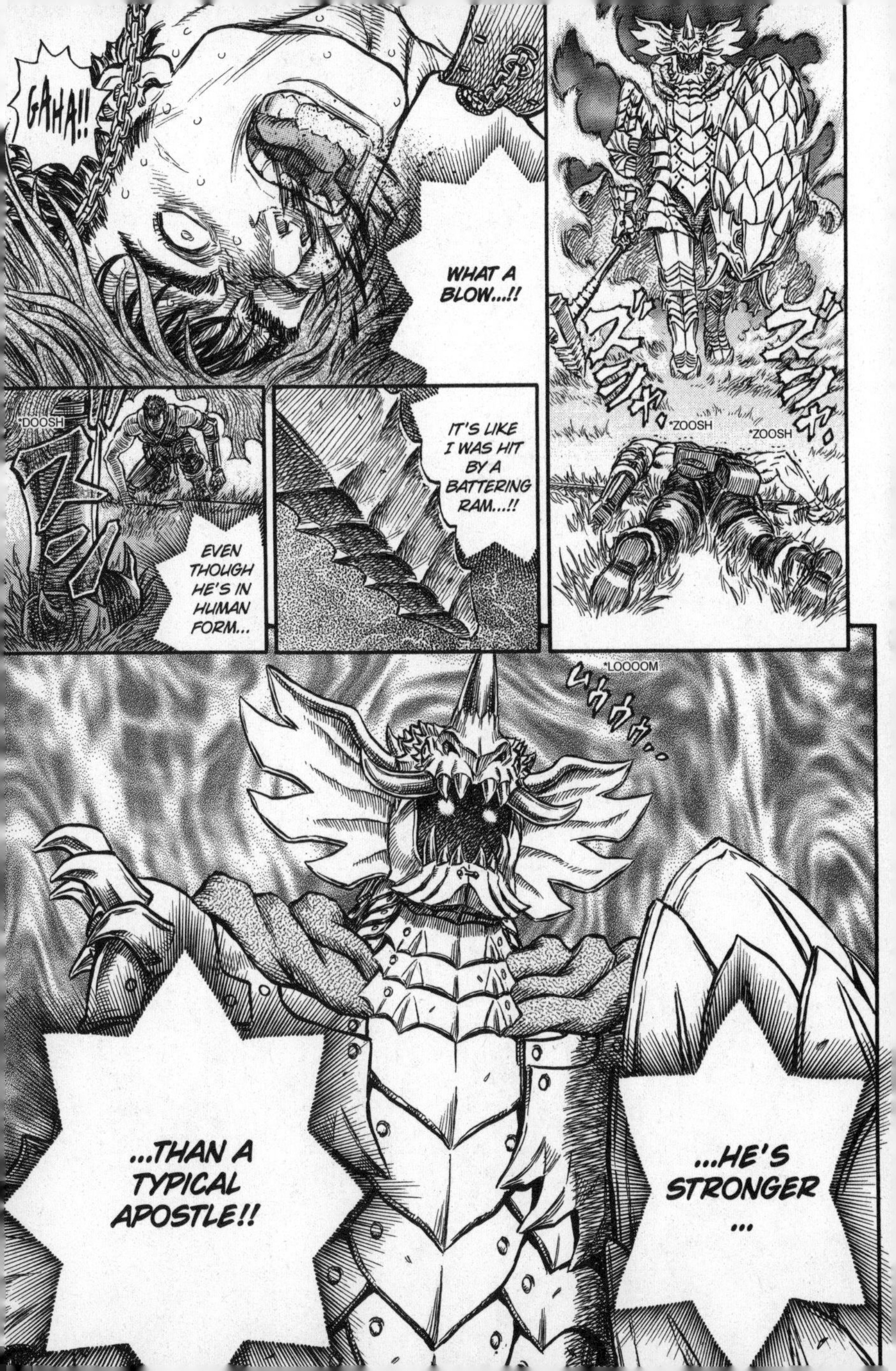
*ZOOSH
*ZOOSH
GAHA!!
WHAT A BLOW...!!
IT'S LIKE I WAS HIT BY A BATTERING RAM...!!
*DOOSH
EVEN THOUGH HE'S IN HUMAN FORM...
*LOOOOM
...HE'S STRONGER ...
...THAN A TYPICAL APOSTLE!!

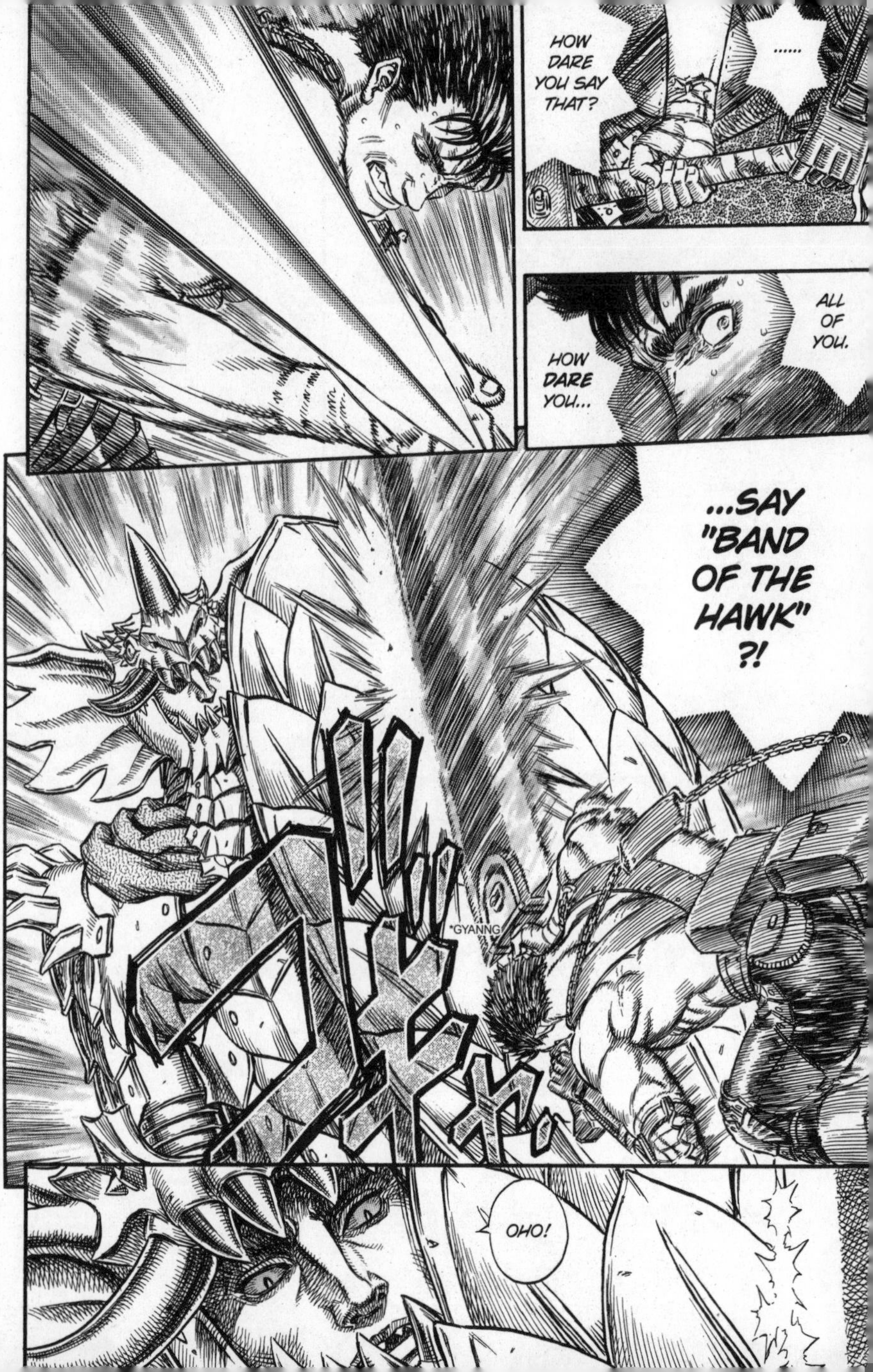

......
HOW DARE YOU SAY THAT?
ALL OF YOU.
HOW DARE YOU...
...SAY "BAND OF THE HAWK"?!
*GYANNG
OHO!

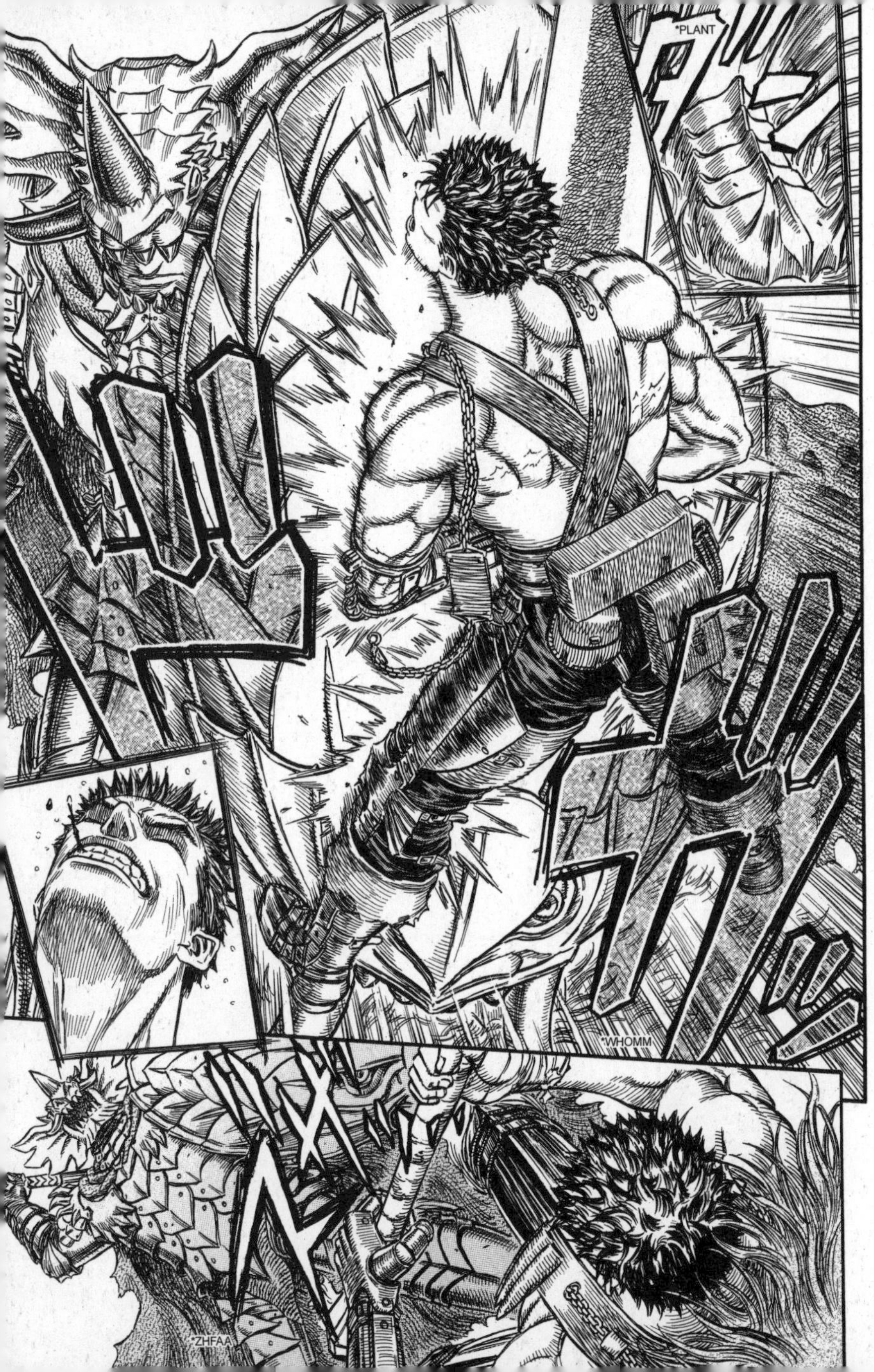
*PLANT
*WHOMM
*ZHFAA

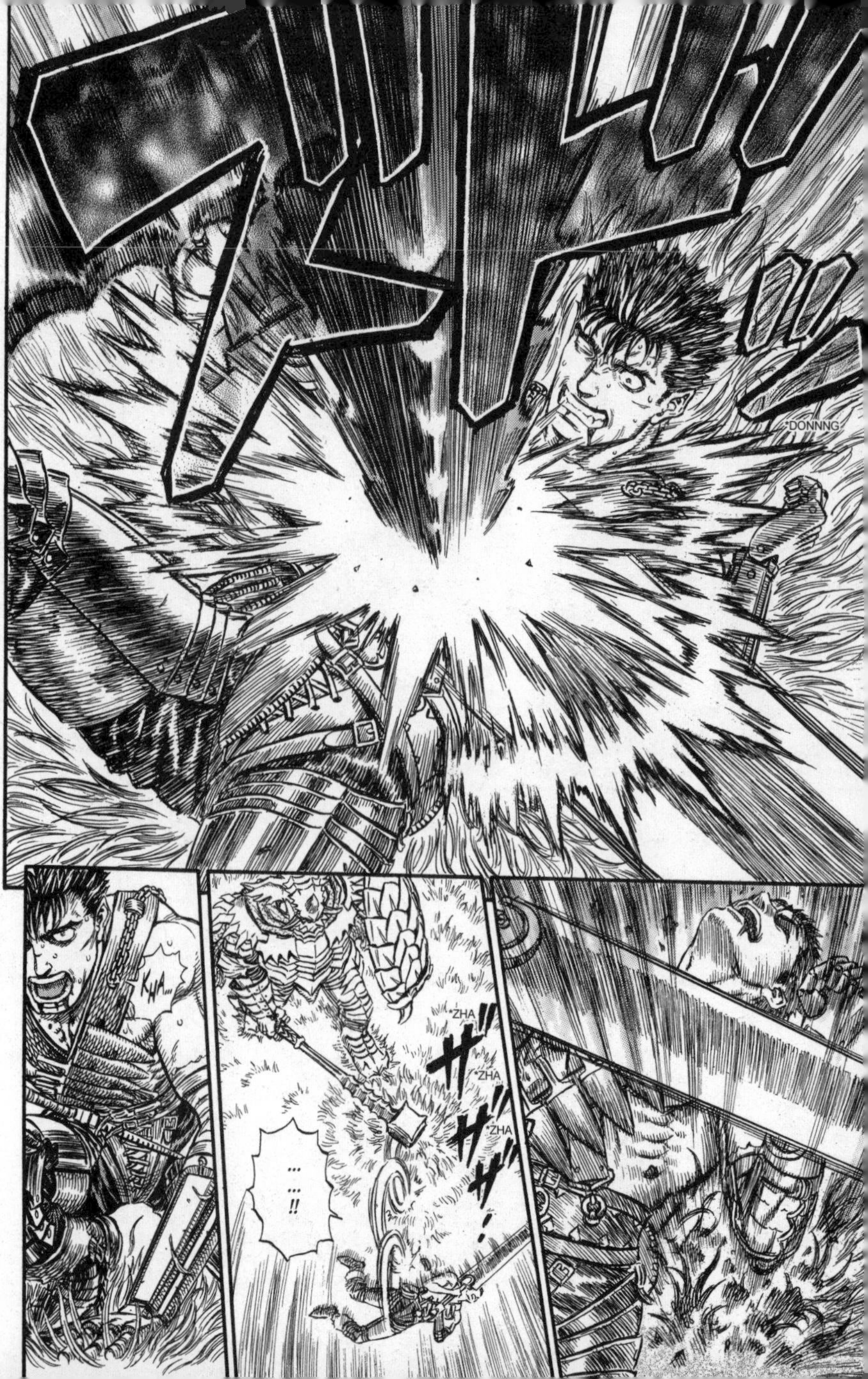
*DONNNG
*ZHA
*ZHA
*ZHA
……!!
KHA...

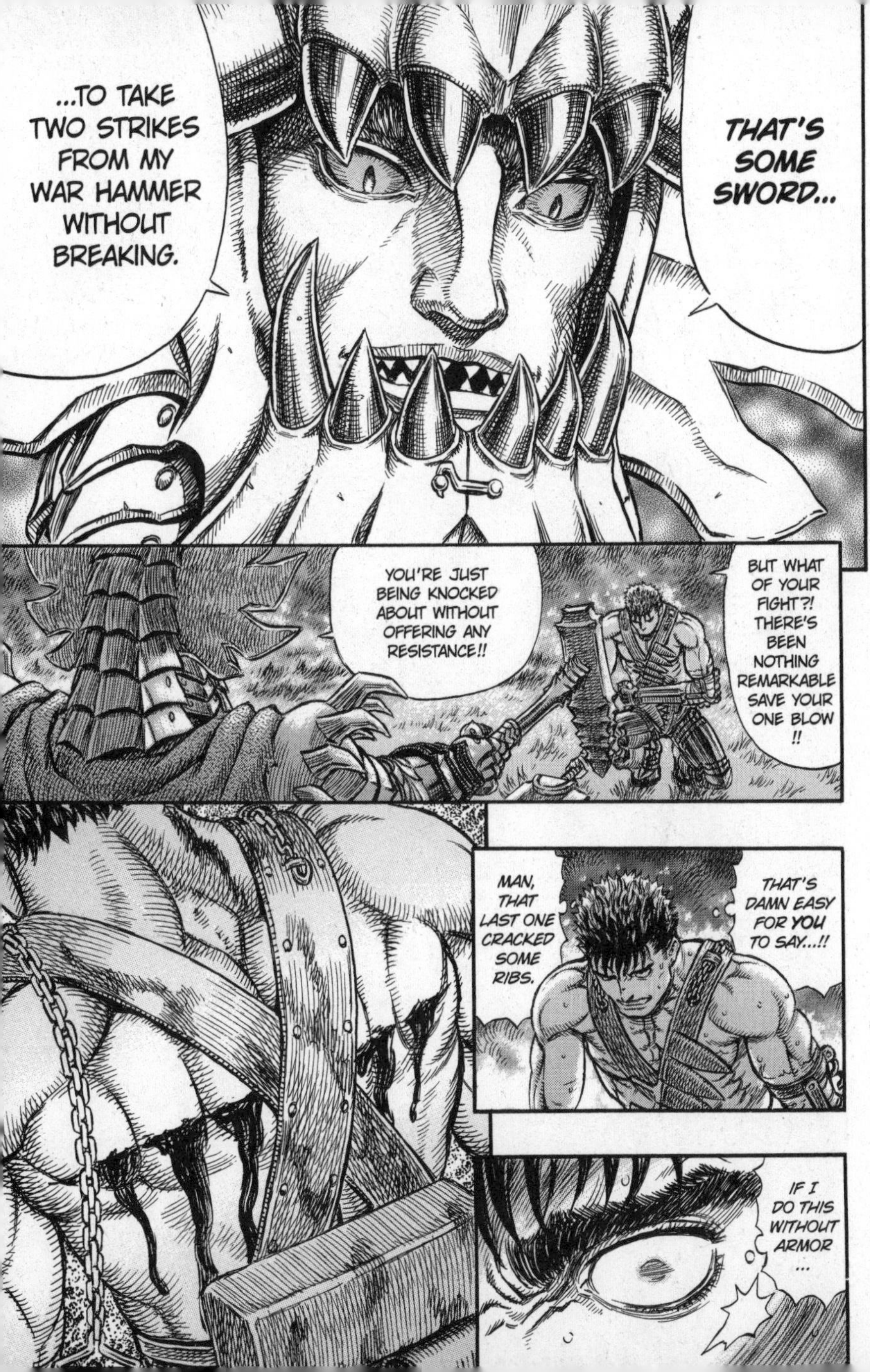
THAT'S SOME SWORD...
...TO TAKE TWO STRIKES FROM MY WAR HAMMER WITHOUT BREAKING.
BUT WHAT OF YOUR FIGHT?! THERE'S BEEN NOTHING REMARKABLE SAVE YOUR ONE BLOW !!
YOU'RE JUST BEING KNOCKED ABOUT WITHOUT OFFERING ANY RESISTANCE!!
THAT'S DAMN EASY FOR YOU TO SAY...!!
MAN, THAT LAST ONE CRACKED SOME RIBS.
IF I DO THIS WITHOUT ARMOR ...

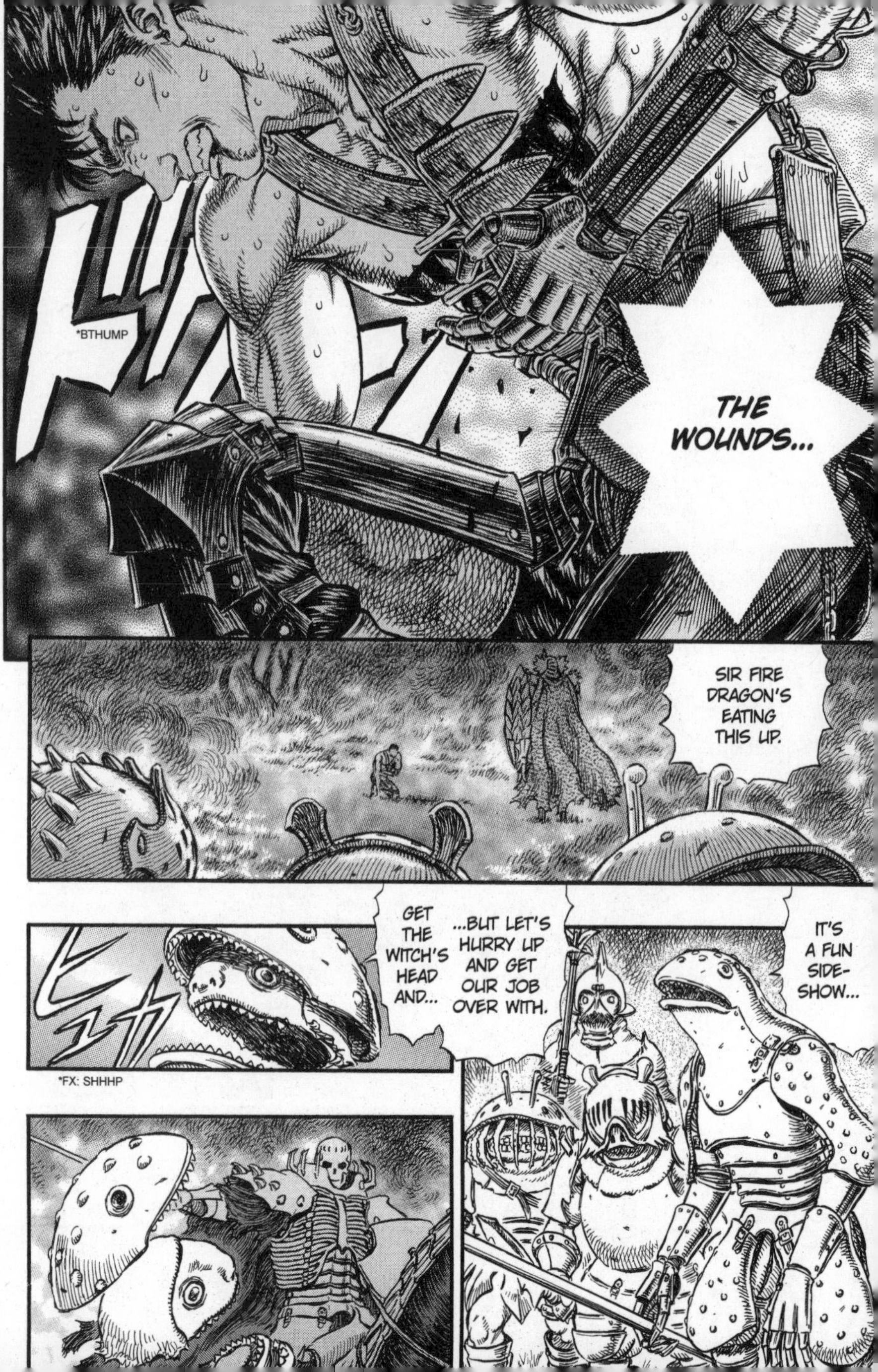
THE WOUNDS...
*BTHUMP
SIR FIRE DRAGON'S EATING THIS UP.
IT'S A FUN SIDE-SHOW...
...BUT LET'S HURRY UP AND GET OUR JOB OVER WITH.
GET THE WITCH'S HEAD AND...
*FX: SHHHP

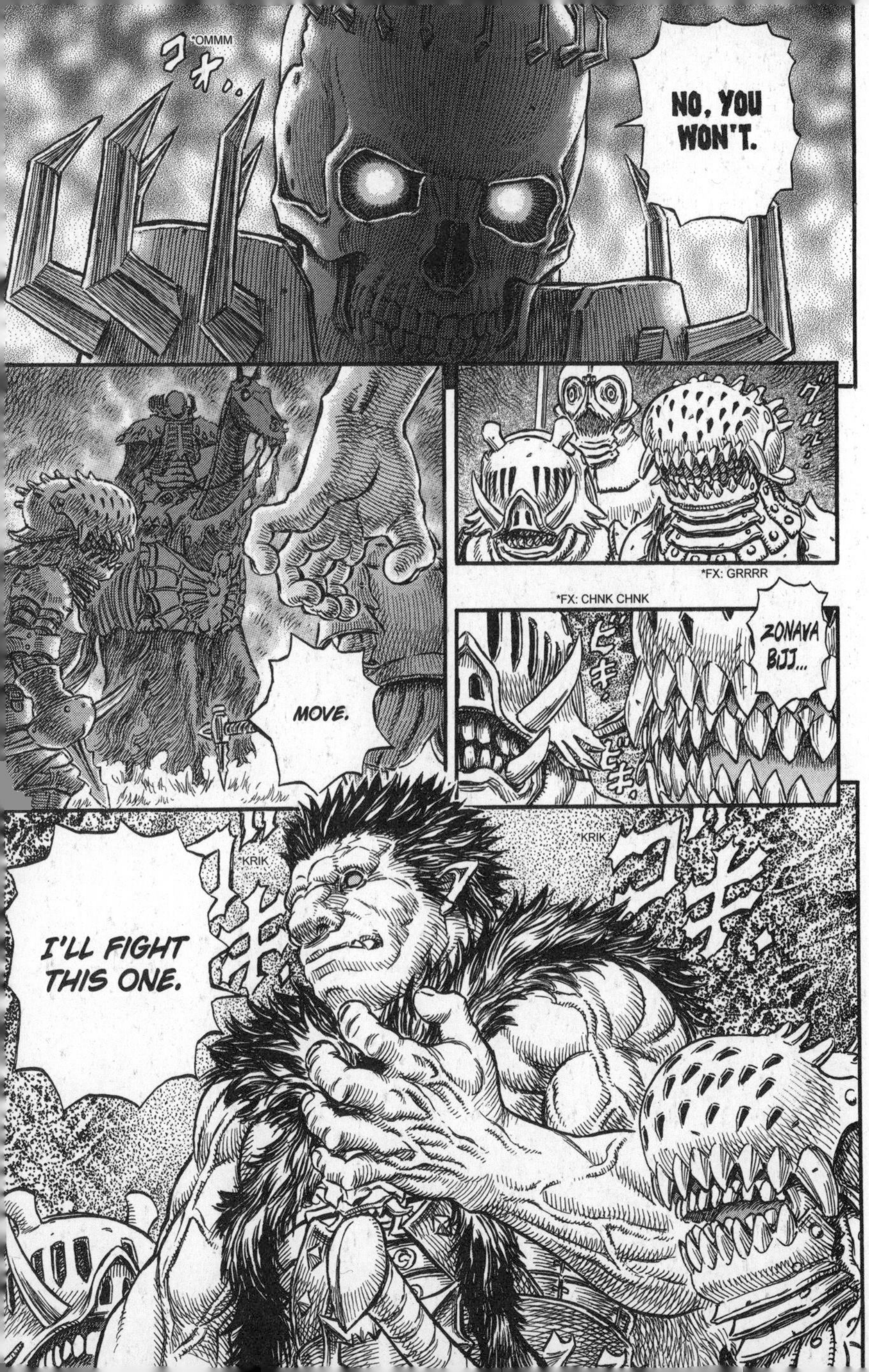
*OMMM
NO, YOU WON'T.
*FX: GRRRR
*FX: CHNK CHNK
ZONAVA BIJJ...
MOVE.
*KRIK
*KRIK
I'LL FIGHT THIS ONE.

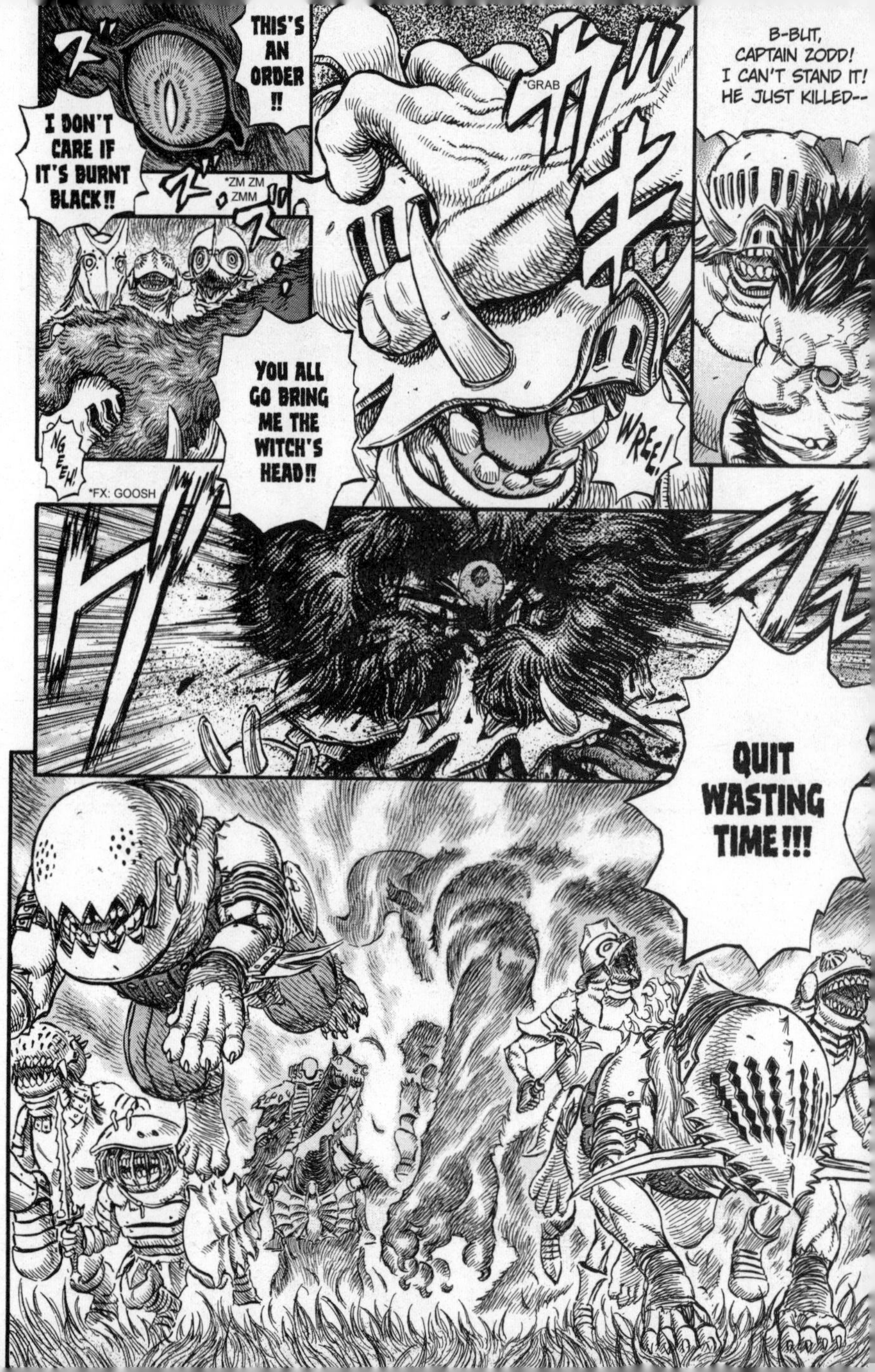
B-BUT, CAPTAIN ZODD! I CAN'T STAND IT! HE JUST KILLED--
*GRAB
YOU ALL GO BRING ME THE WITCH'S HEAD!!
WREE!
THIS'S AN ORDER!!
I DON'T CARE IF IT'S BURNT BLACK!!
*ZM ZM ZMM
NGEEH!
*FX: GOOSH
QUIT WASTING TIME!!!

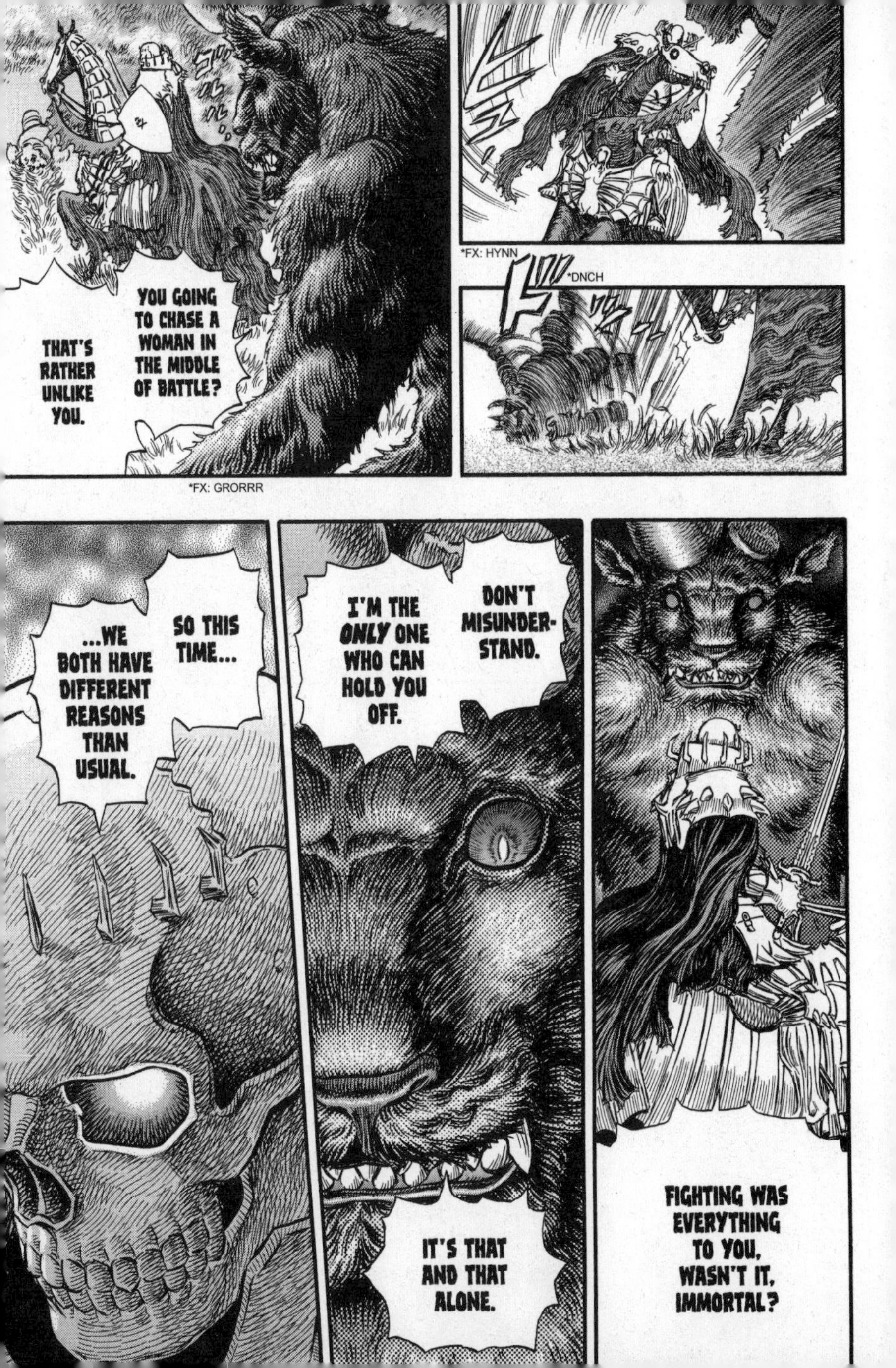
*FX: HYNN
*DNCH
YOU GOING TO CHASE A WOMAN IN THE MIDDLE OF BATTLE?
THAT'S RATHER UNLIKE YOU.
*FX: GRORRR
FIGHTING WAS EVERYTHING TO YOU, WASN'T IT, IMMORTAL?
DON'T MISUNDERSTAND.
I'M THE *ONLY* ONE WHO CAN HOLD YOU OFF.
IT'S THAT AND THAT ALONE.
SO THIS TIME...
...WE BOTH HAVE DIFFERENT REASONS THAN USUAL.

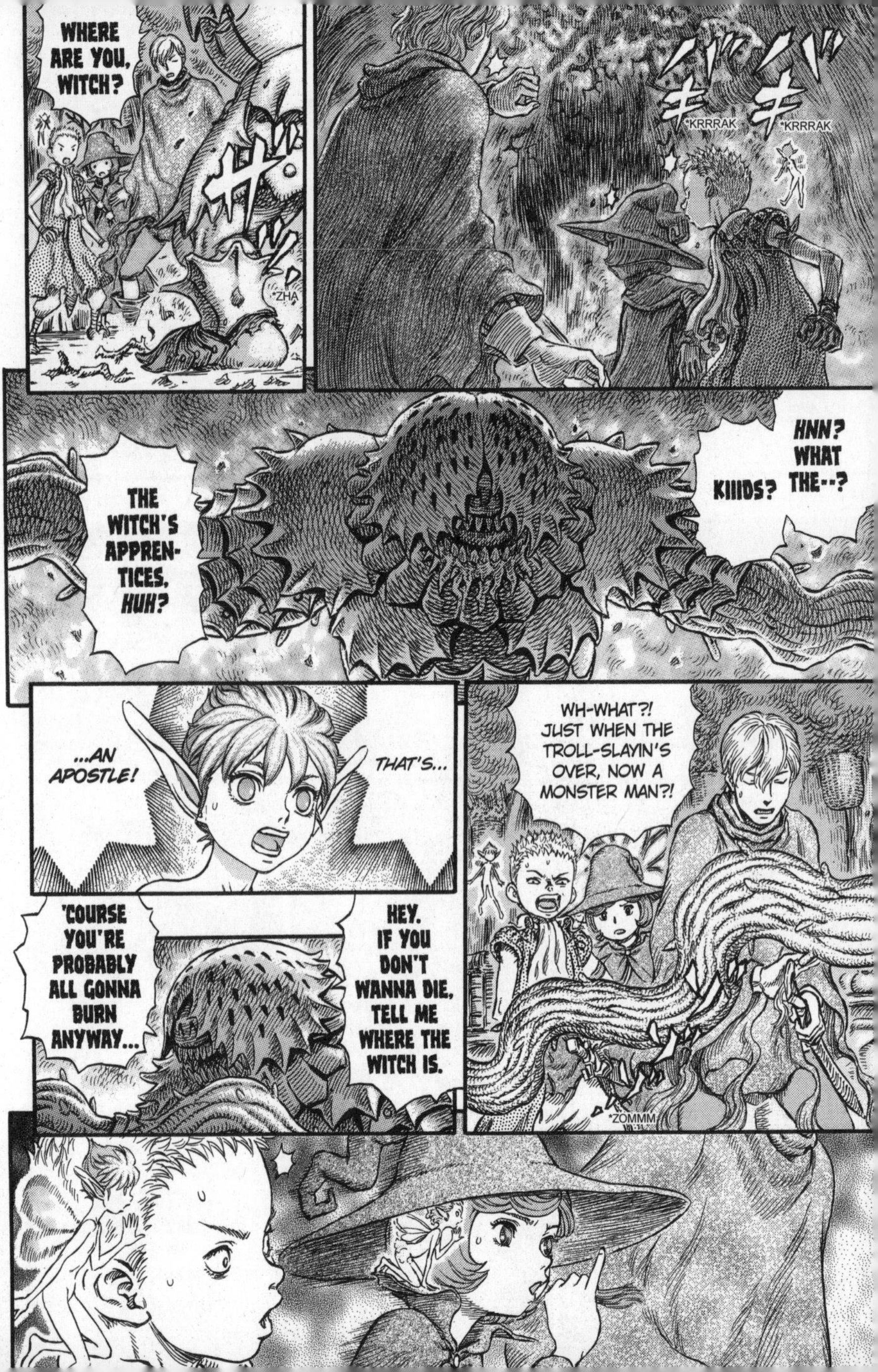
*KRRRAK
*KRRRAK
WHERE ARE YOU, WITCH?
*ZHA
HNN? WHAT THE--?
KIIIDS?
THE WITCH'S APPREN-TICES, HUH?
WH-WHAT?! JUST WHEN THE TROLL-SLAYIN'S OVER, NOW A MONSTER MAN?!
*ZOMMM
THAT'S...
...AN APOSTLE!
HEY. IF YOU DON'T WANNA DIE, TELL ME WHERE THE WITCH IS.
'COURSE YOU'RE PROBABLY ALL GONNA BURN ANYWAY...

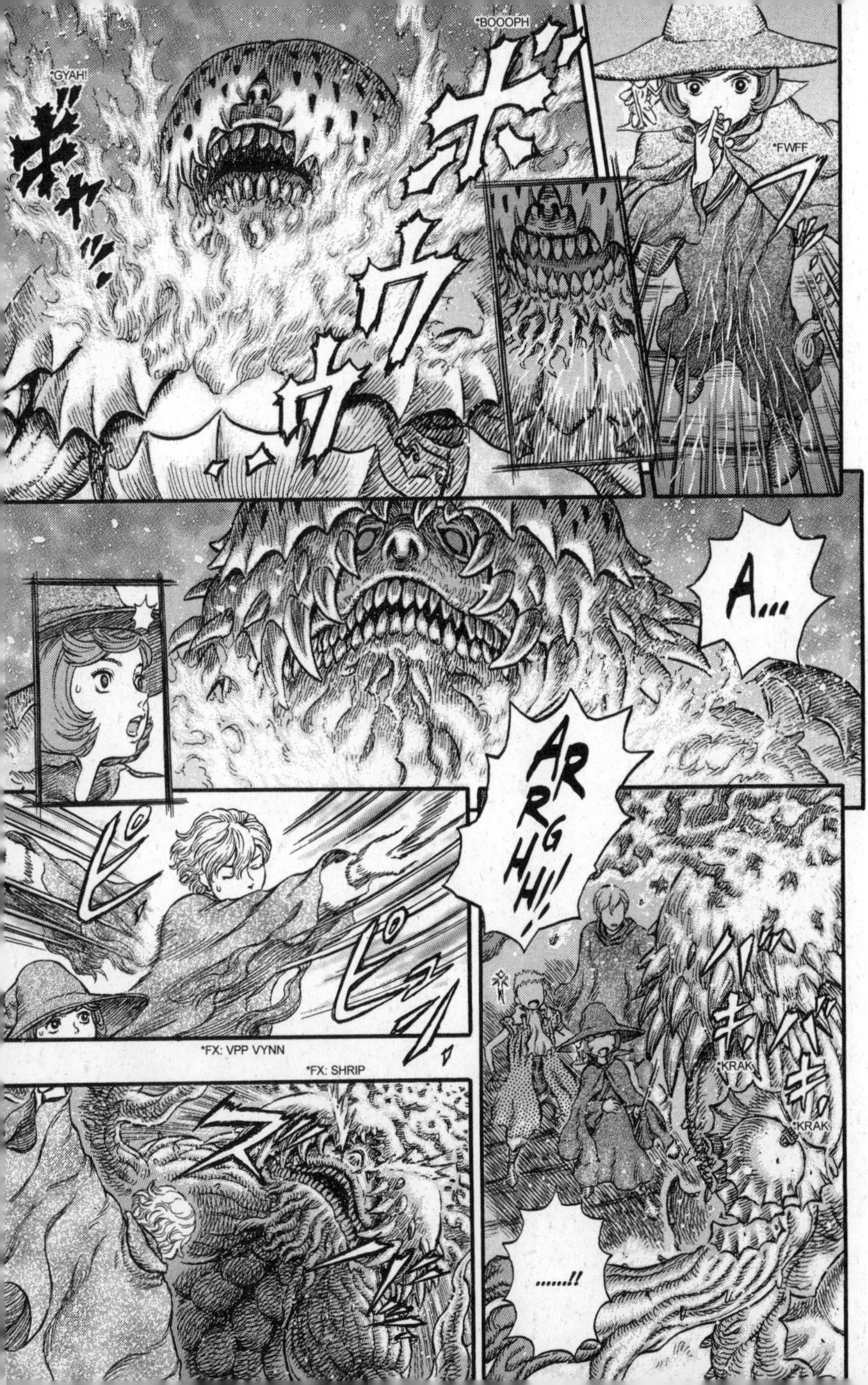
*FWFF
*BOOOPH
*GYAH!
A...
ARRGHH!!!
*KRAK
*KRAK
......!!
*FX: VPP VYNN
*FX: SHRIP

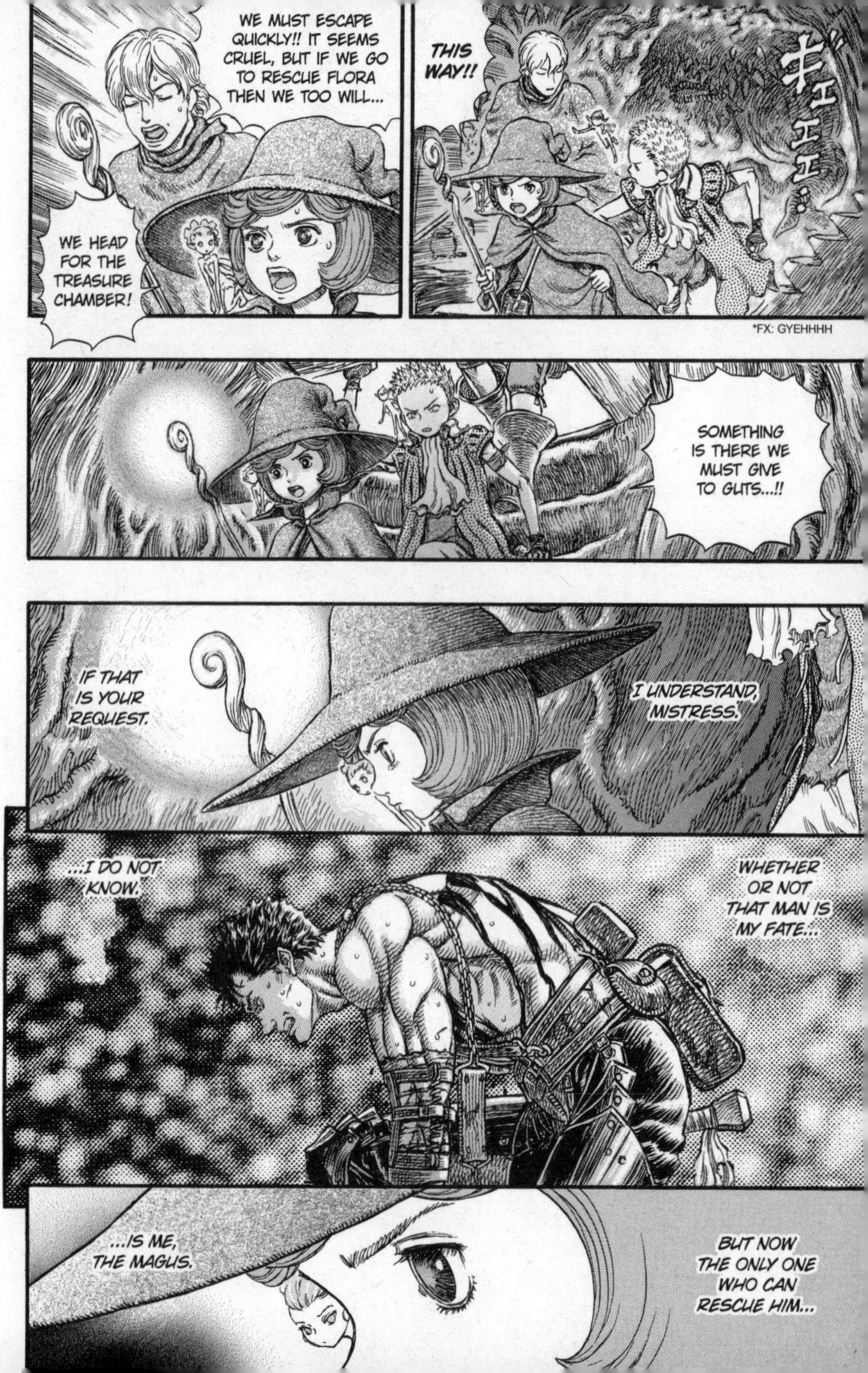
THIS WAY!!
ギェェェ
*FX: GYEHHHH
WE MUST ESCAPE QUICKLY!! IT SEEMS CRUEL, BUT IF WE GO TO RESCUE FLORA THEN WE TOO WILL...
WE HEAD FOR THE TREASURE CHAMBER!
SOMETHING IS THERE WE MUST GIVE TO GUTS...!!
I UNDERSTAND, MISTRESS.
IF THAT IS YOUR REQUEST.
WHETHER OR NOT THAT MAN IS MY FATE...
...I DO NOT KNOW.
BUT NOW THE ONLY ONE WHO CAN RESCUE HIM...
...IS ME, THE MAGUS.

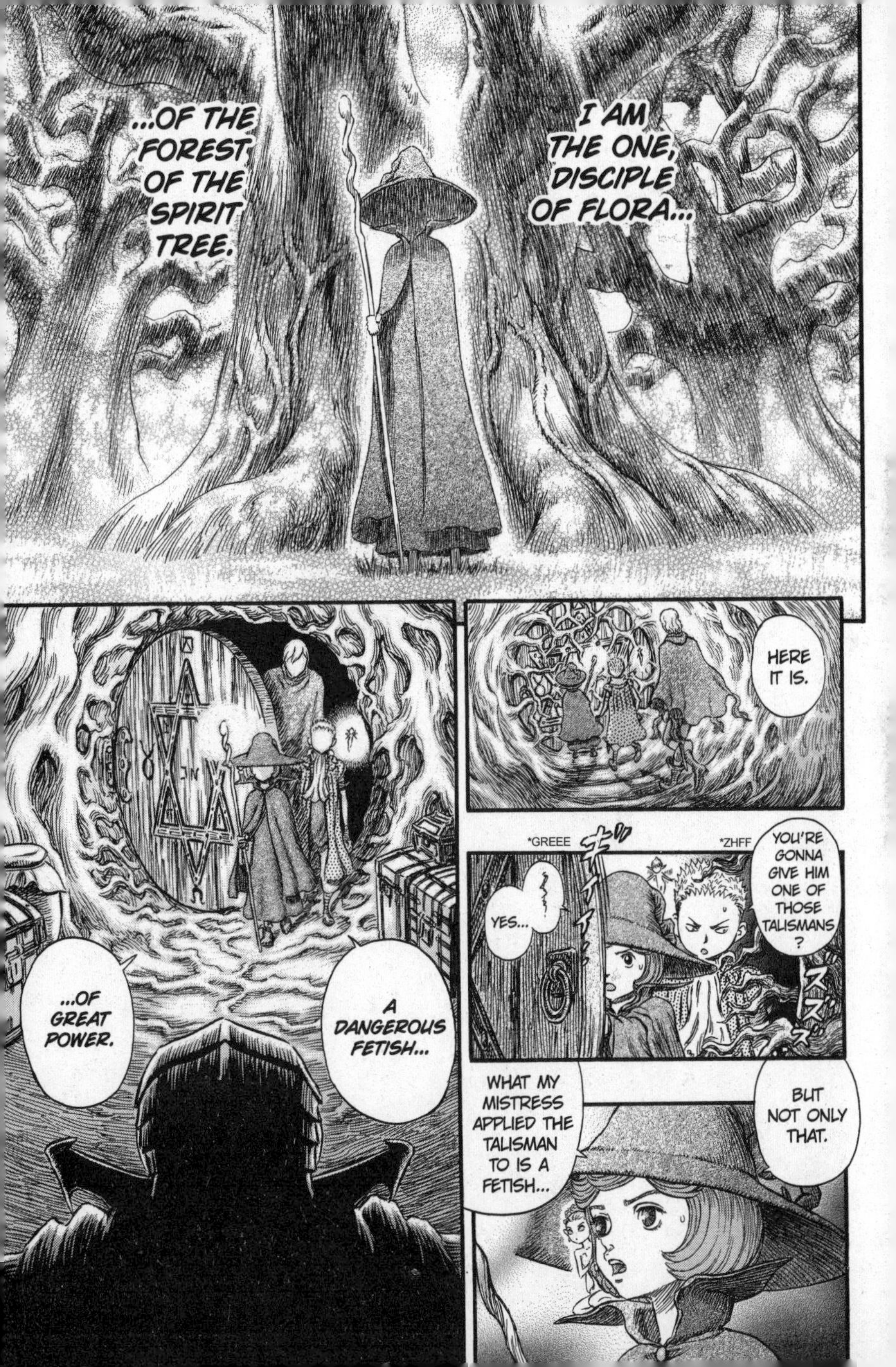
I AM THE ONE, DISCIPLE OF FLORA...
...OF THE FOREST OF THE SPIRIT TREE.
HERE IT IS.
*ZHFF
*GREEE
YOU'RE GONNA GIVE HIM ONE OF THOSE TALISMANS?
YES...
BUT NOT ONLY THAT.
WHAT MY MISTRESS APPLIED THE TALISMAN TO IS A FETISH...
A DANGEROUS FETISH...
...OF GREAT POWER.

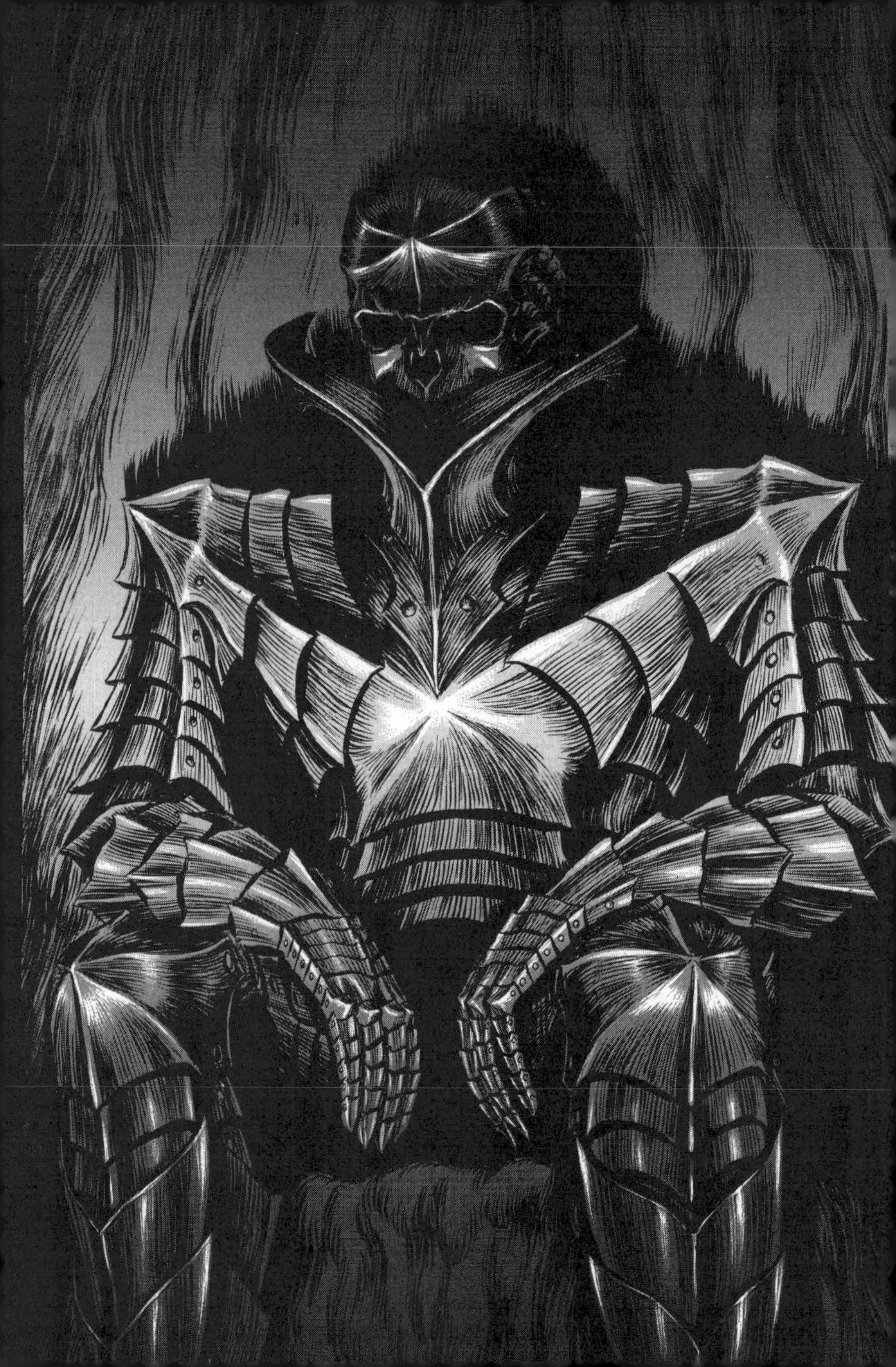

THE BERSERKER ARMOR, PART 1

狂戦士の甲冑①

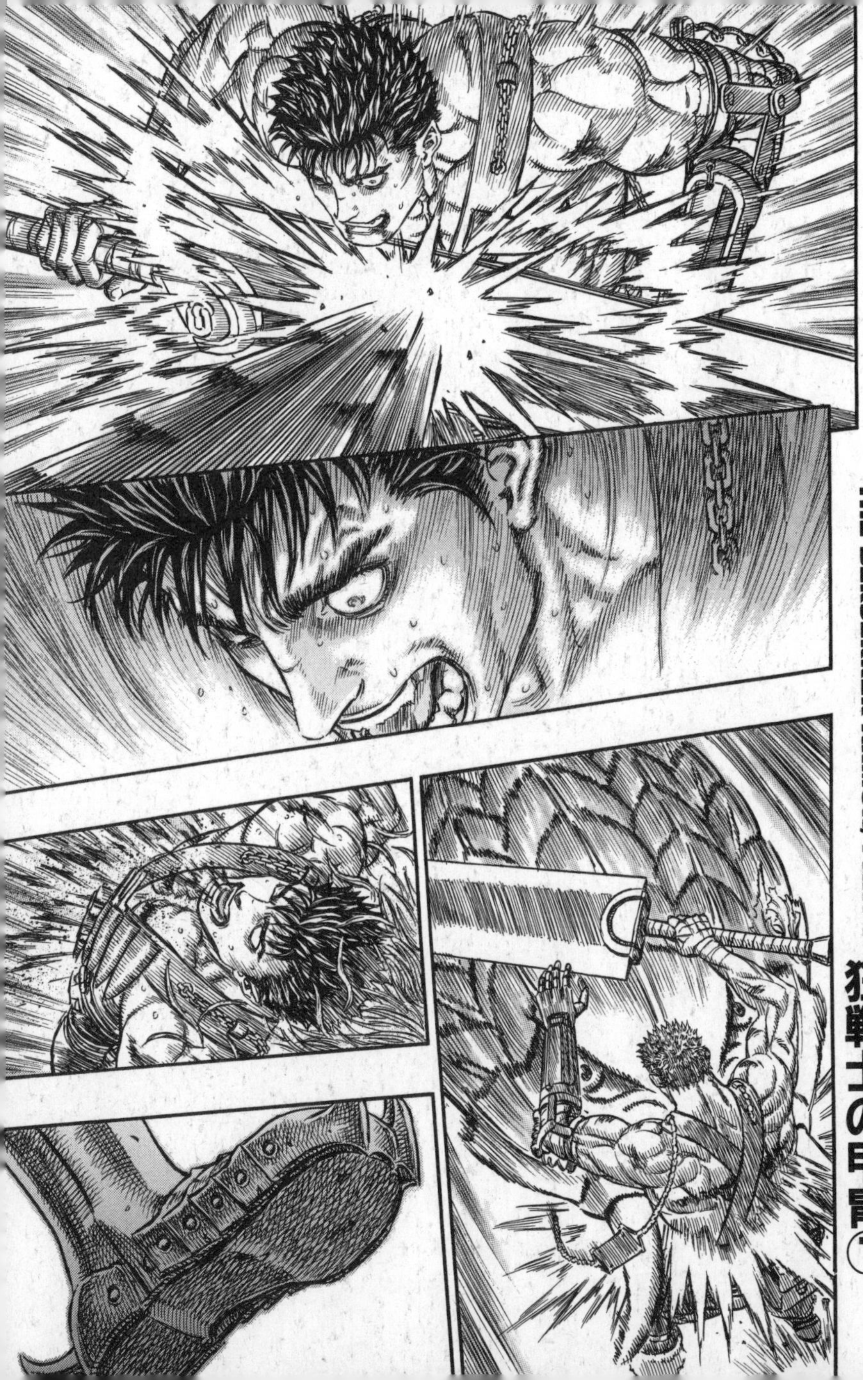

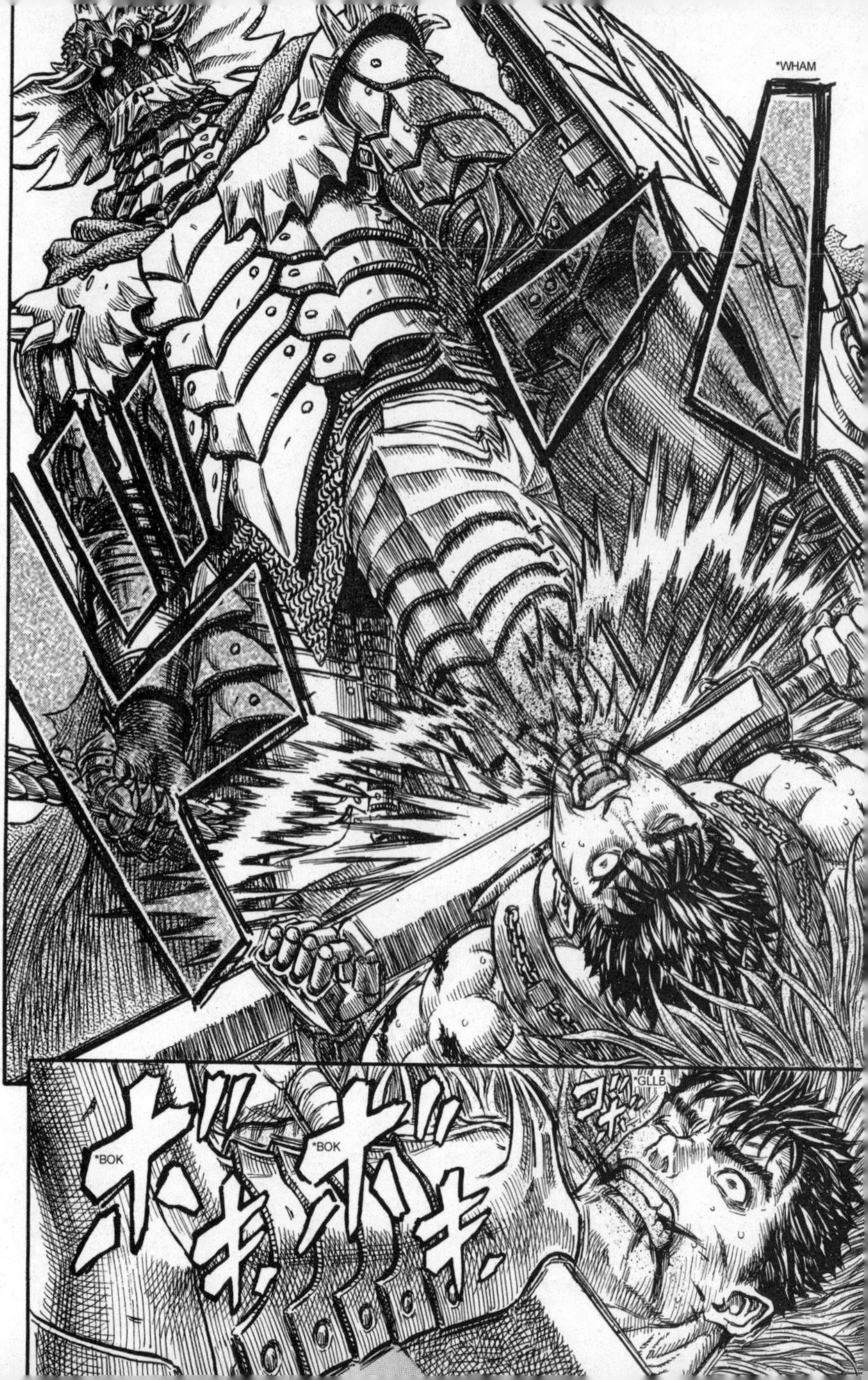
*WHAM
*GLLB
*BOK
*BOK

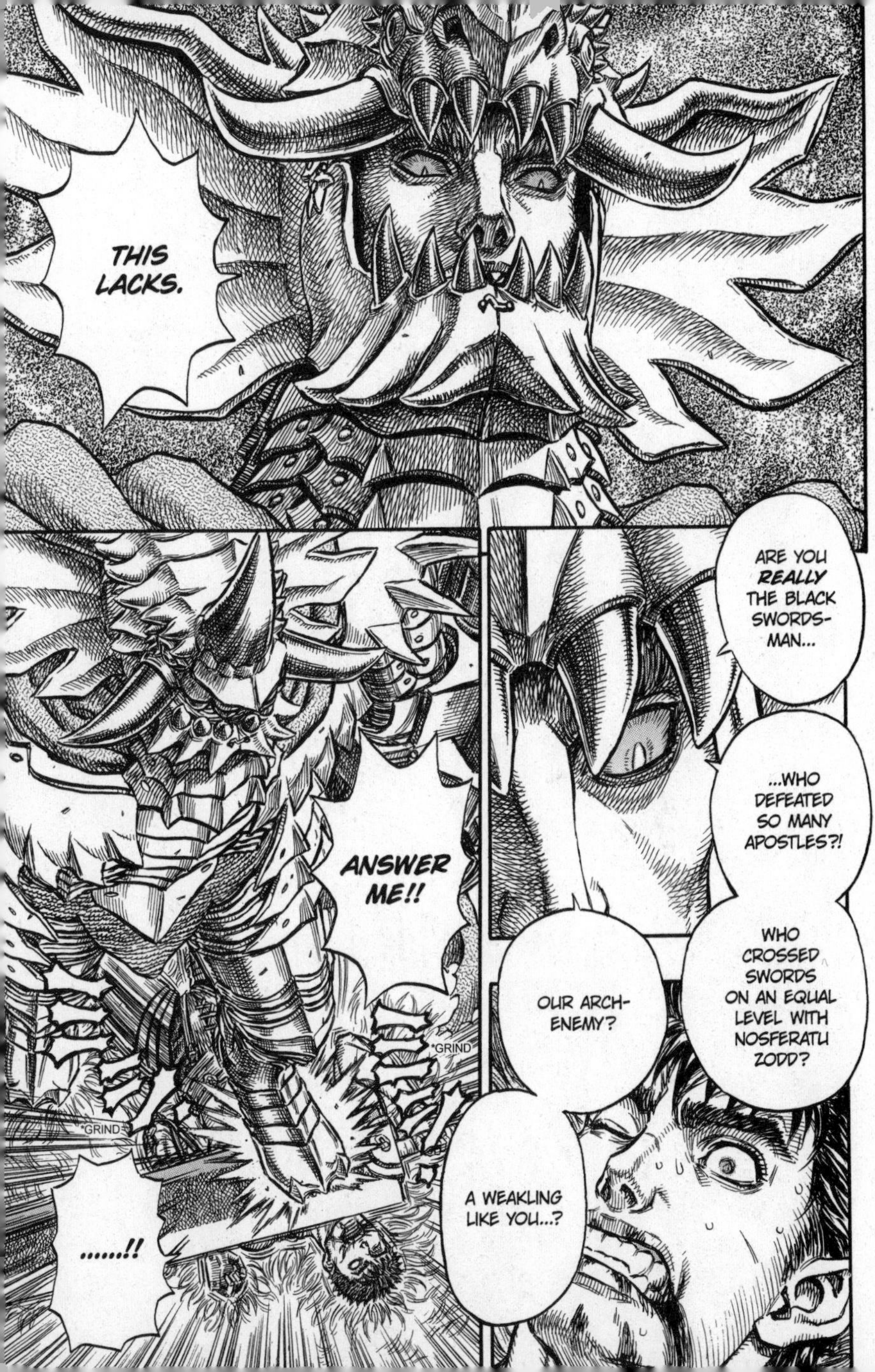
THIS LACKS.
ARE YOU REALLY THE BLACK SWORDSMAN...
...WHO DEFEATED SO MANY APOSTLES?!
WHO CROSSED SWORDS ON AN EQUAL LEVEL WITH NOSFERATU ZODD?
OUR ARCH-ENEMY?
A WEAKLING LIKE YOU...?
ANSWER ME!!
*GRIND
*GRIND
......!!

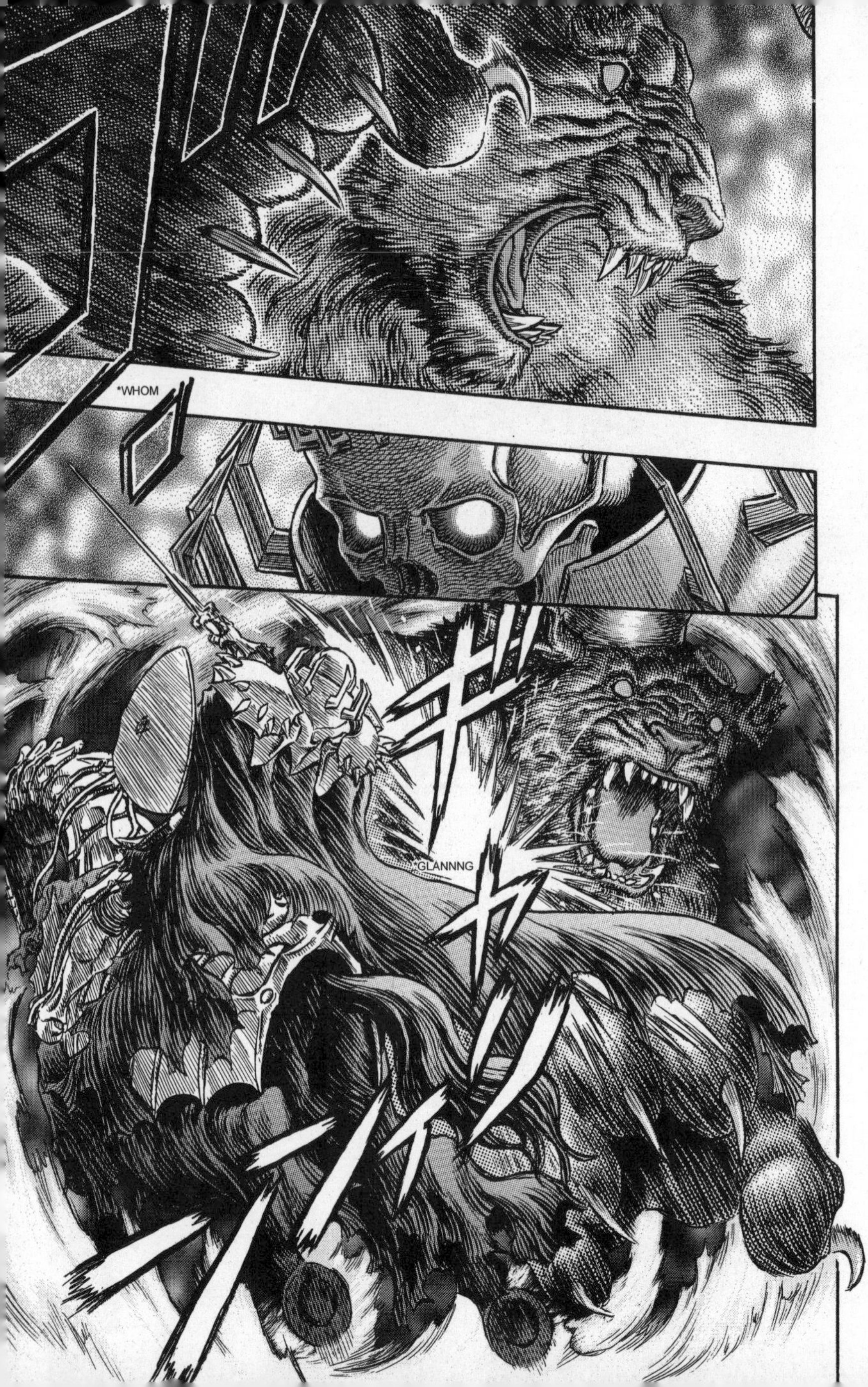
*WHOM
*GLANNNG

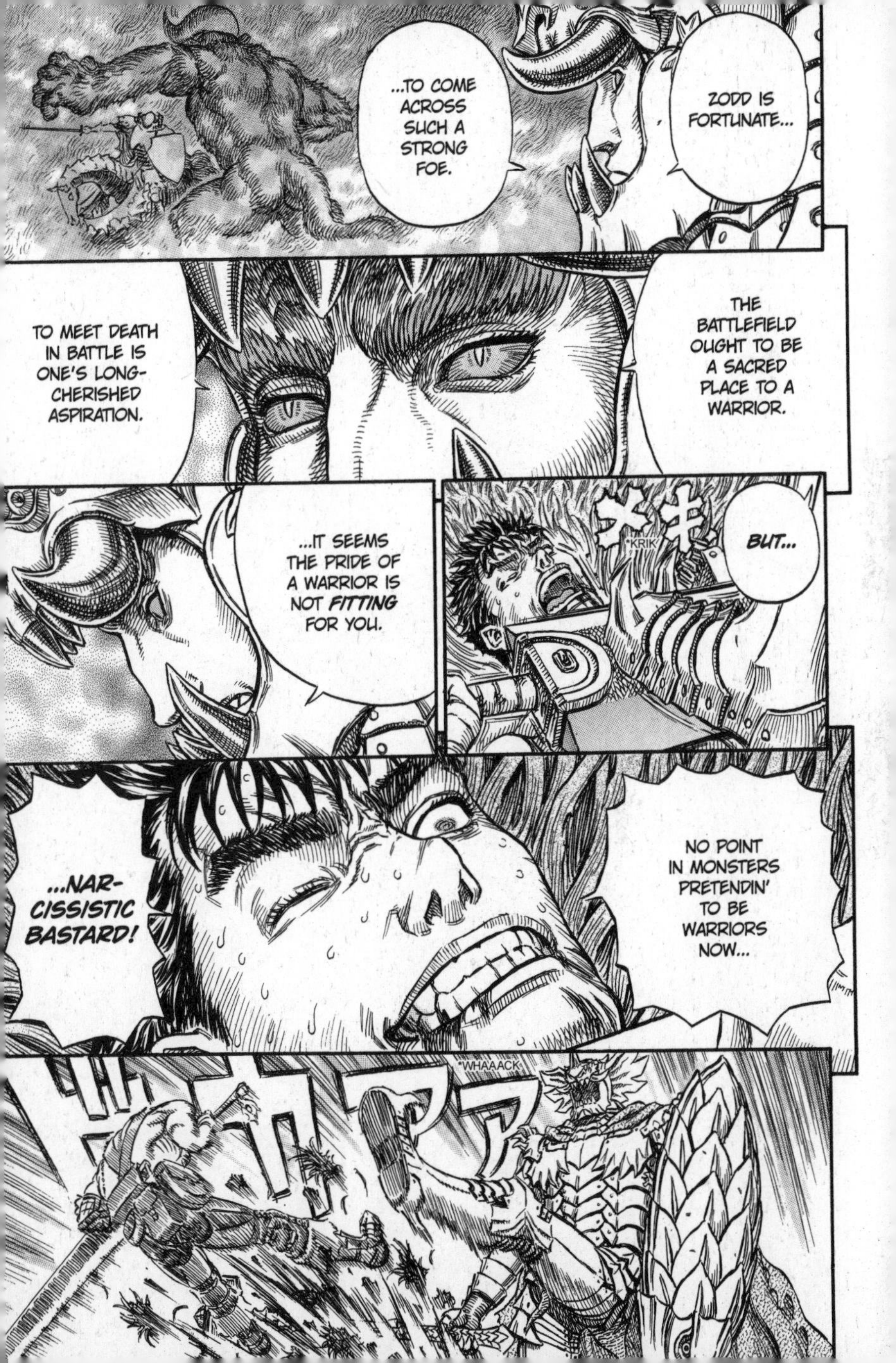

ZODD IS FORTUNATE...
...TO COME ACROSS SUCH A STRONG FOE.
THE BATTLEFIELD OUGHT TO BE A SACRED PLACE TO A WARRIOR.
TO MEET DEATH IN BATTLE IS ONE'S LONG-CHERISHED ASPIRATION.
BUT...
*KRIK
...IT SEEMS THE PRIDE OF A WARRIOR IS NOT *FITTING* FOR YOU.
NO POINT IN MONSTERS PRETENDIN' TO BE WARRIORS NOW...
...NAR-CISSISTIC BASTARD!
*WHAAACK

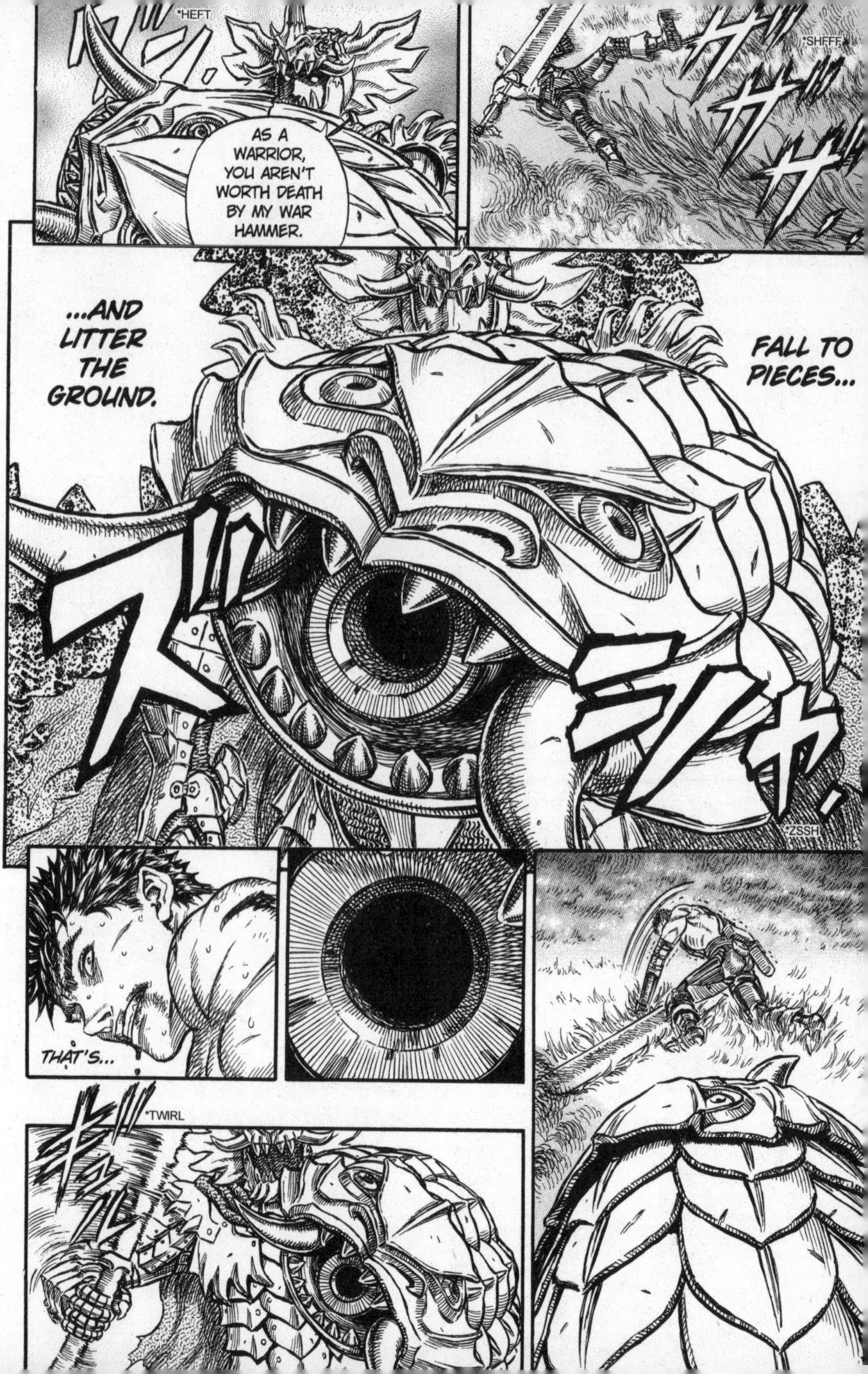
*SHFFF
*HEFT
AS A WARRIOR, YOU AREN'T WORTH DEATH BY MY WAR HAMMER.
FALL TO PIECES...
...AND LITTER THE GROUND.
*ZSSH
THAT'S...
*TWIRL

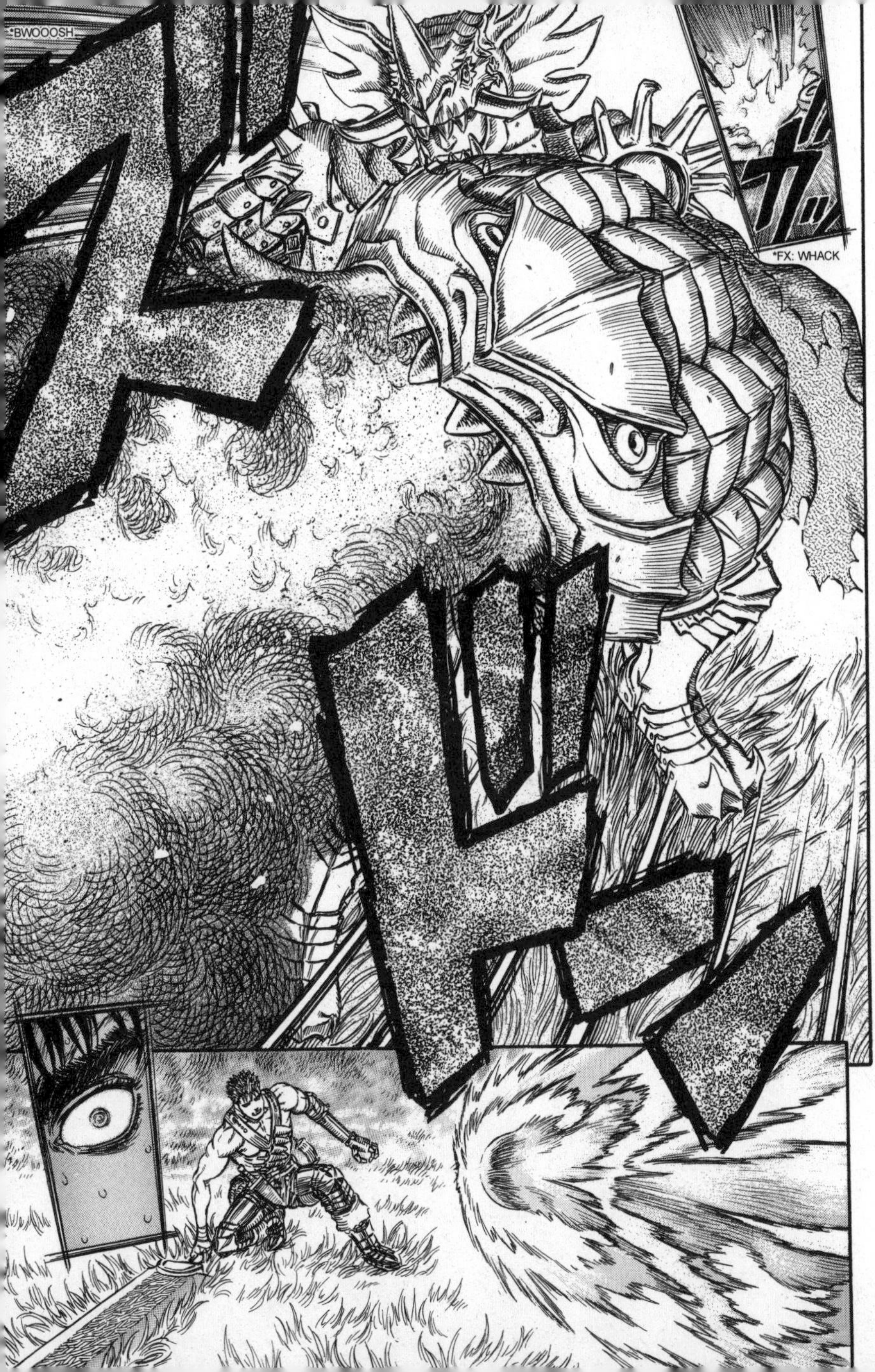
*FX: WHACK
*BWOOOSH

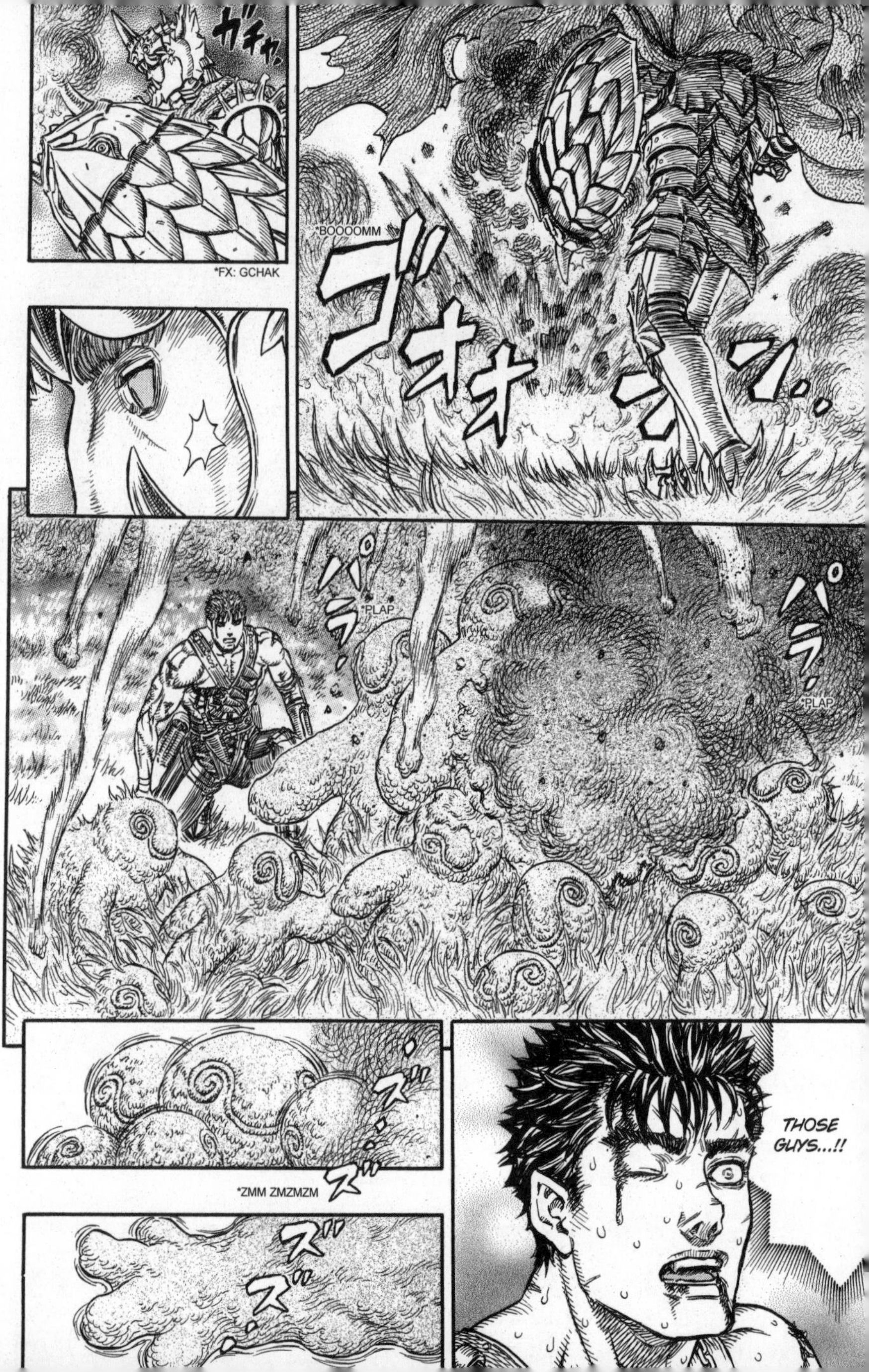
*BOOOOMM
*FX: GCHAK
*PLAP
*PLAP
THOSE GUYS...!!
*ZMM ZMZMZM

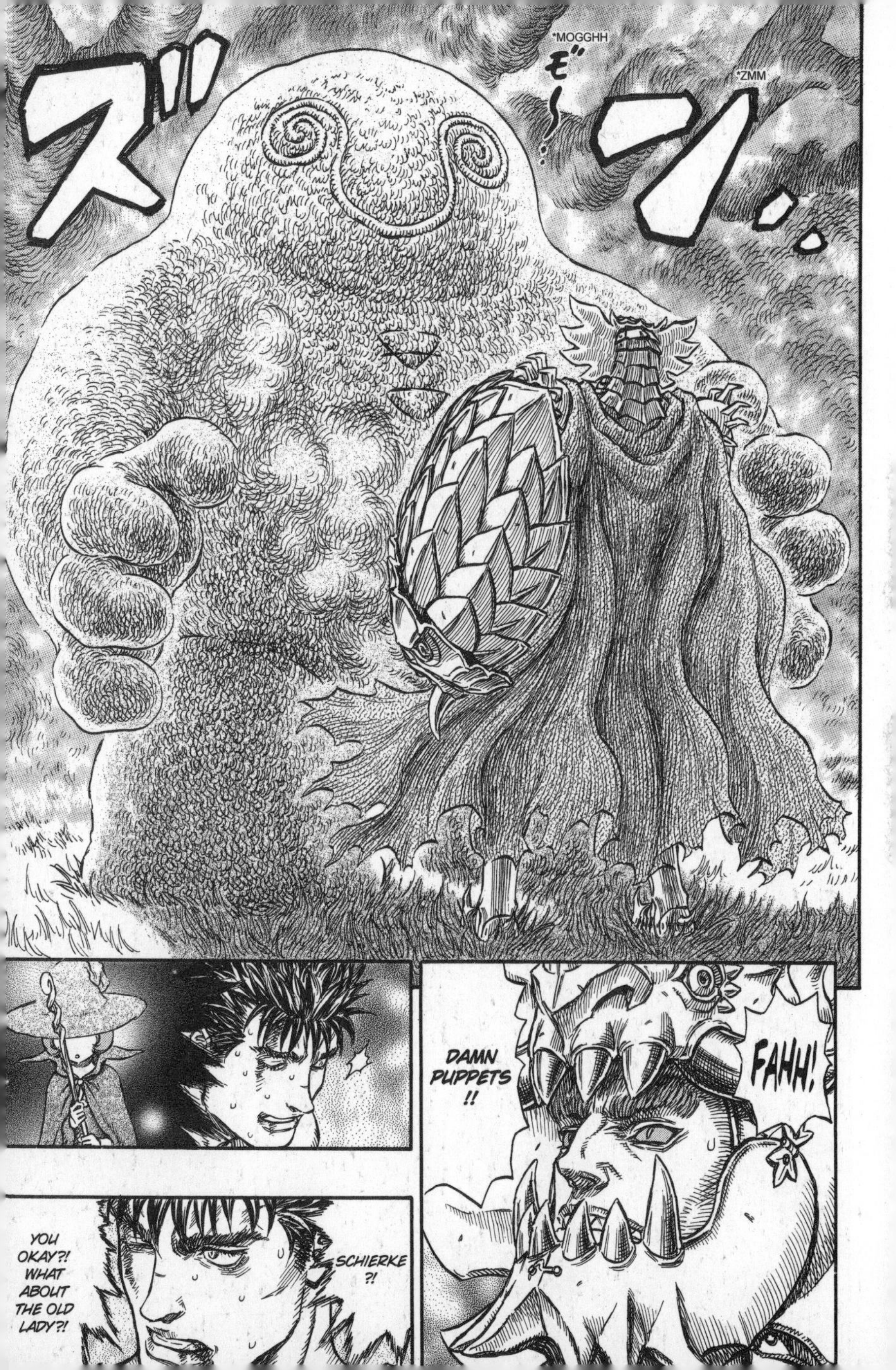

ズン
*ZMM
モ~
*MOGGHH
FAHH!
DAMN PUPPETS!!
SCHIERKE?!
YOU OKAY?! WHAT ABOUT THE OLD LADY?!

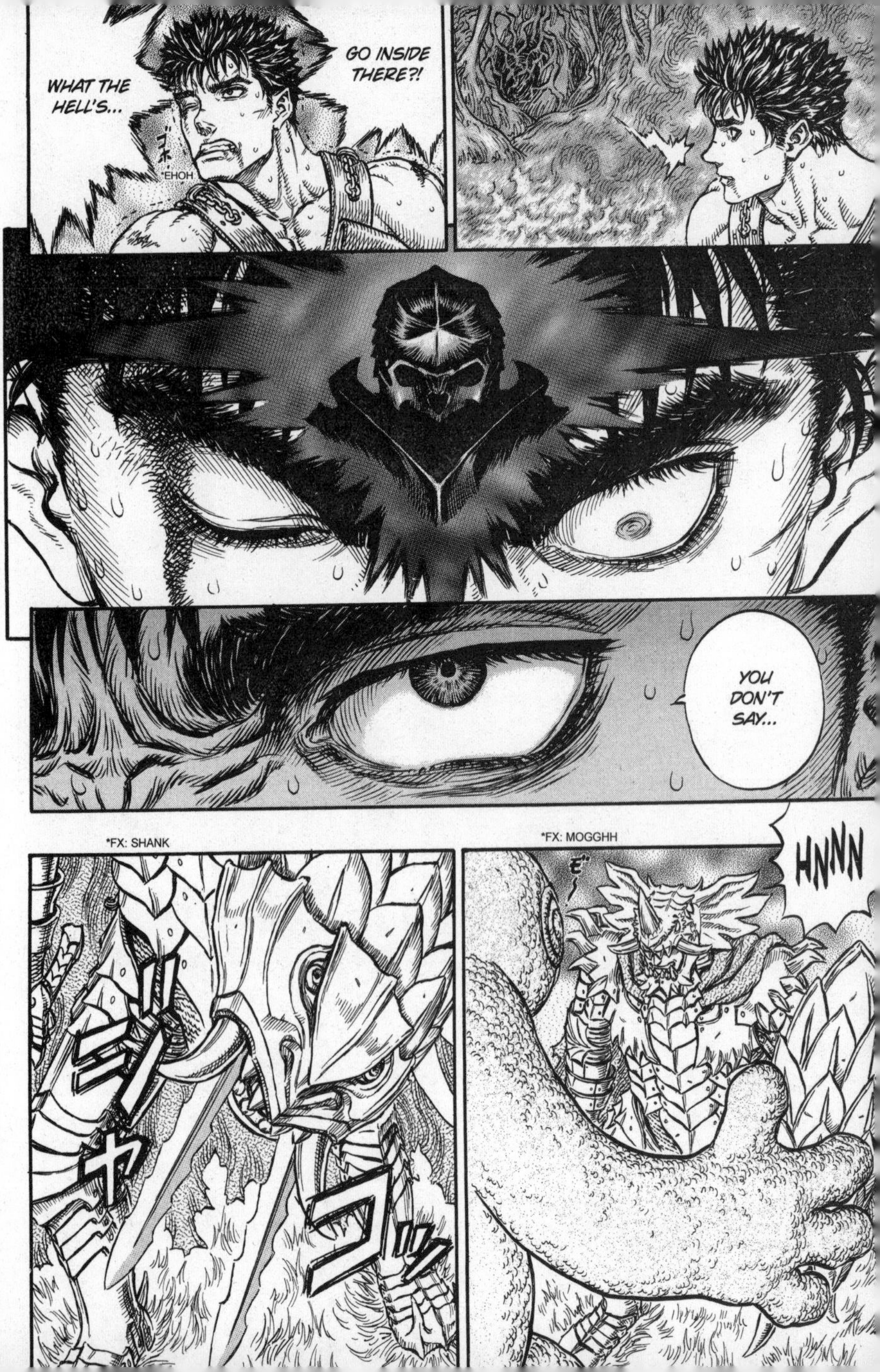
GO INSIDE THERE?!
WHAT THE HELL'S...
*EHOH
YOU DON'T SAY...
*FX: MOGGHH
HNNN
*FX: SHANK

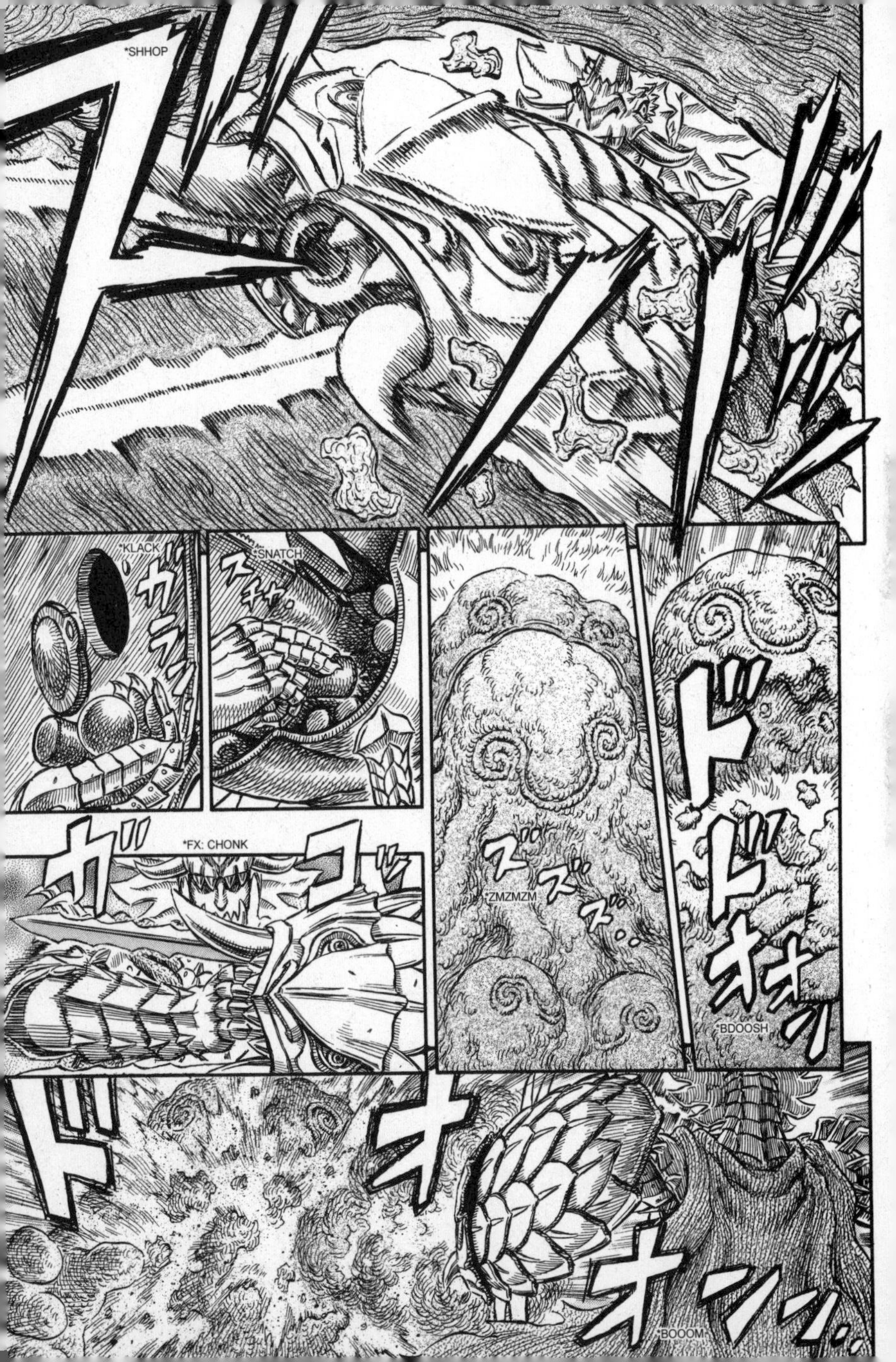

*SHHOP
*BDOOSH
*ZMZMZM
*SNATCH
*KLACK
*FX: CHONK
*BOOOM

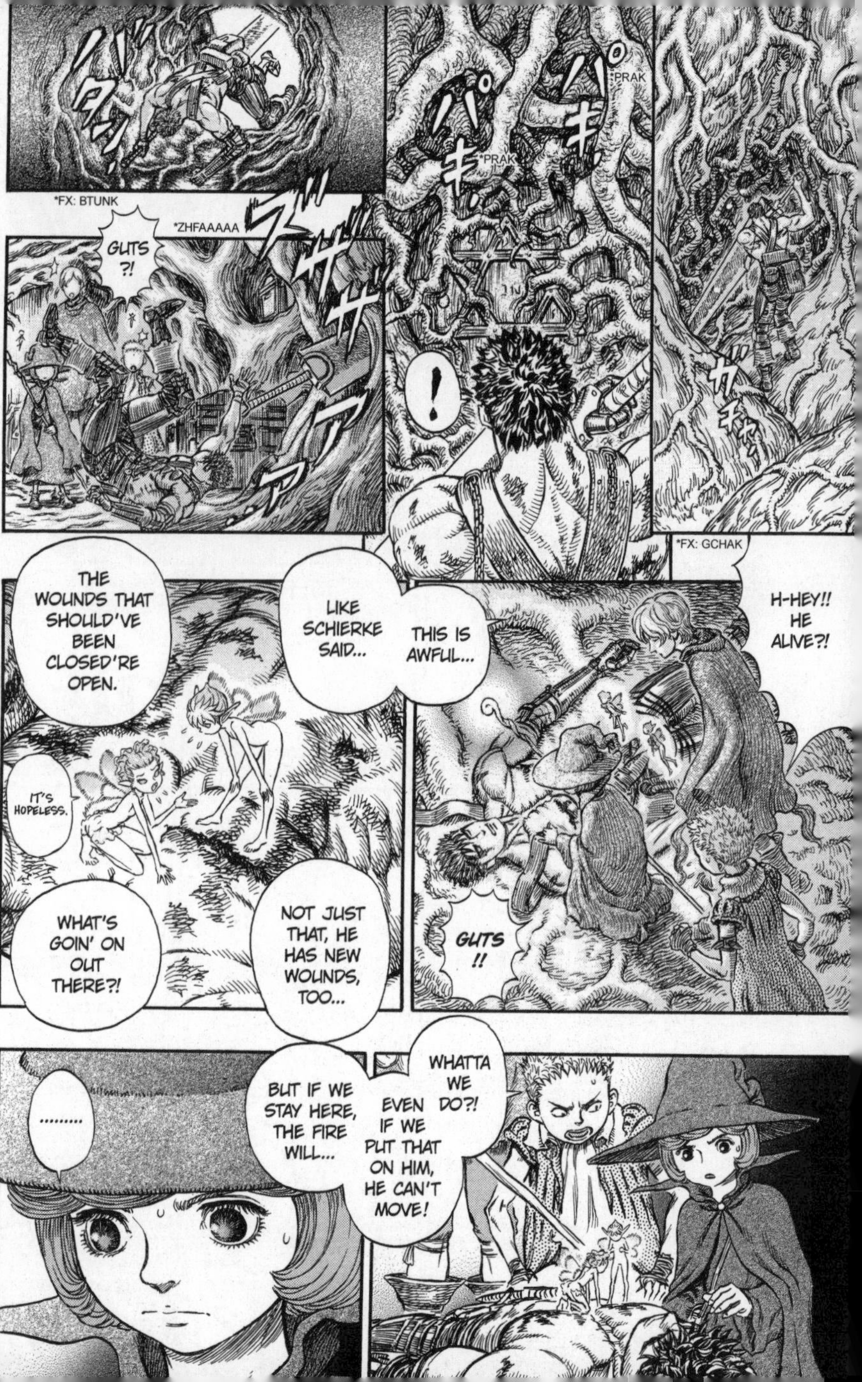
*FX: GCHAK
*PRAK
*PRAK
!
*FX: BTUNK
*ZHFAAAAA
GUTS ?!
H-HEY!! HE ALIVE?!
GUTS !!
THIS IS AWFUL...
LIKE SCHIERKE SAID...
THE WOUNDS THAT SHOULD'VE BEEN CLOSED'RE OPEN.
NOT JUST THAT, HE HAS NEW WOUNDS, TOO...
IT'S HOPELESS.
WHAT'S GOIN' ON OUT THERE?!
WHATTA WE DO?!
EVEN IF WE PUT THAT ON HIM, HE CAN'T MOVE!
BUT IF WE STAY HERE, THE FIRE WILL...
....

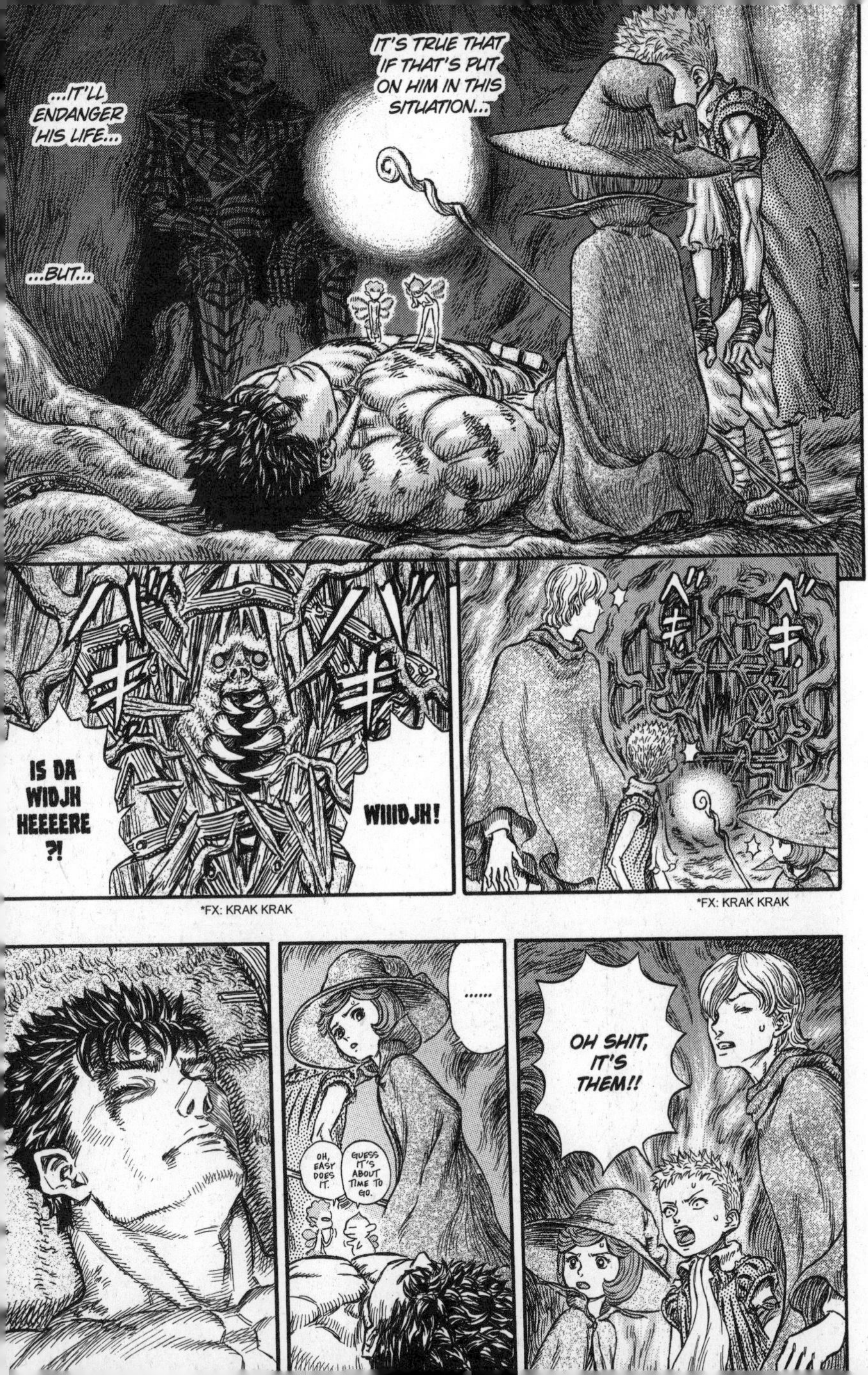
IT'S TRUE THAT IF THAT'S PUT ON HIM IN THIS SITUATION...
...IT'LL ENDANGER HIS LIFE...
...BUT...
*FX: KRAK KRAK
WIIIDJH!
IS DA WIDJH HEEEERE ?!
*FX: KRAK KRAK
OH SHIT, IT'S THEM!!
......
GUESS IT'S ABOUT TIME TO GO.
OH, EASY DOES IT.

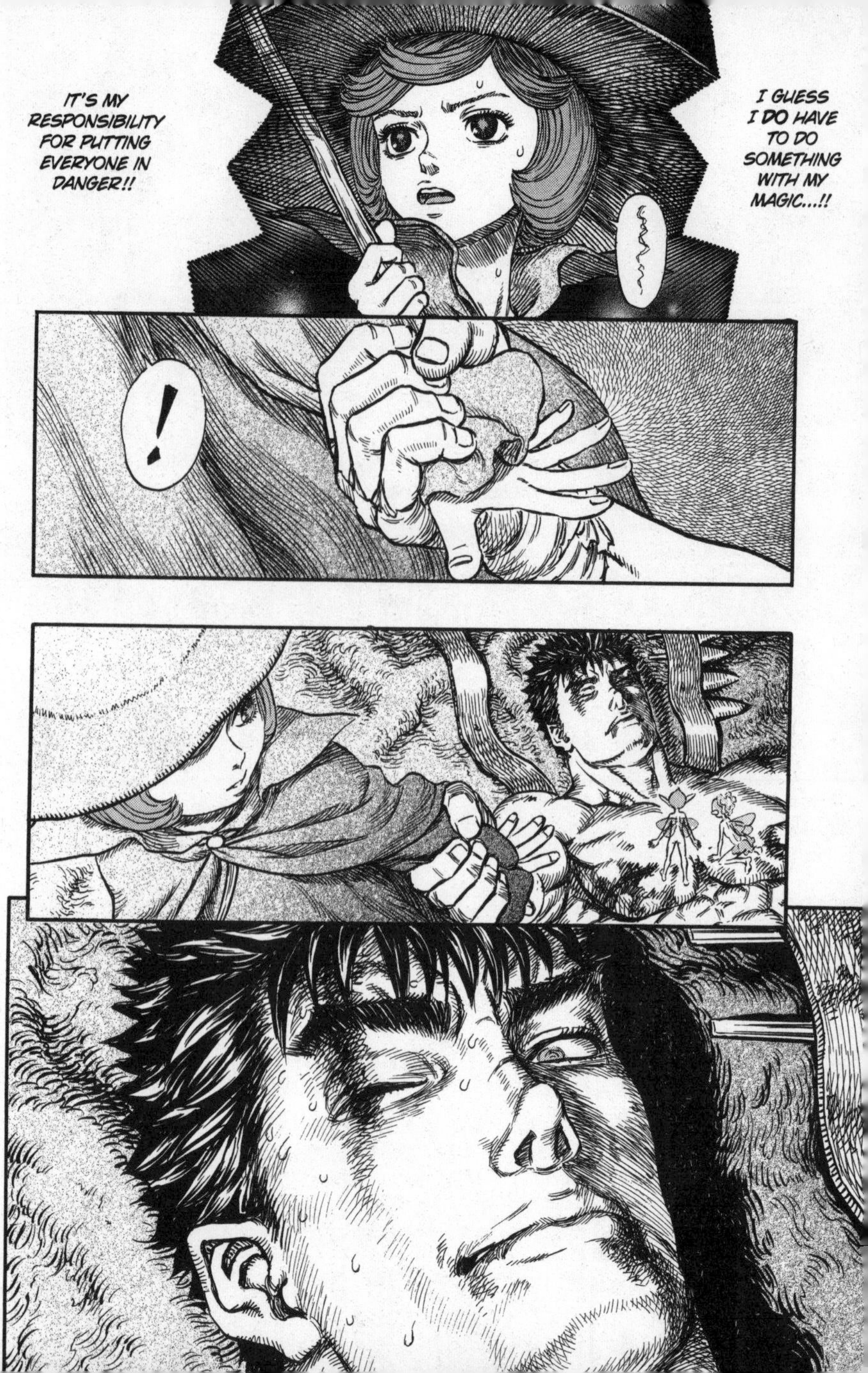
I GUESS I DO HAVE TO DO SOMETHING WITH MY MAGIC...!!
IT'S MY RESPONSIBILITY FOR PUTTING EVERYONE IN DANGER!!
!

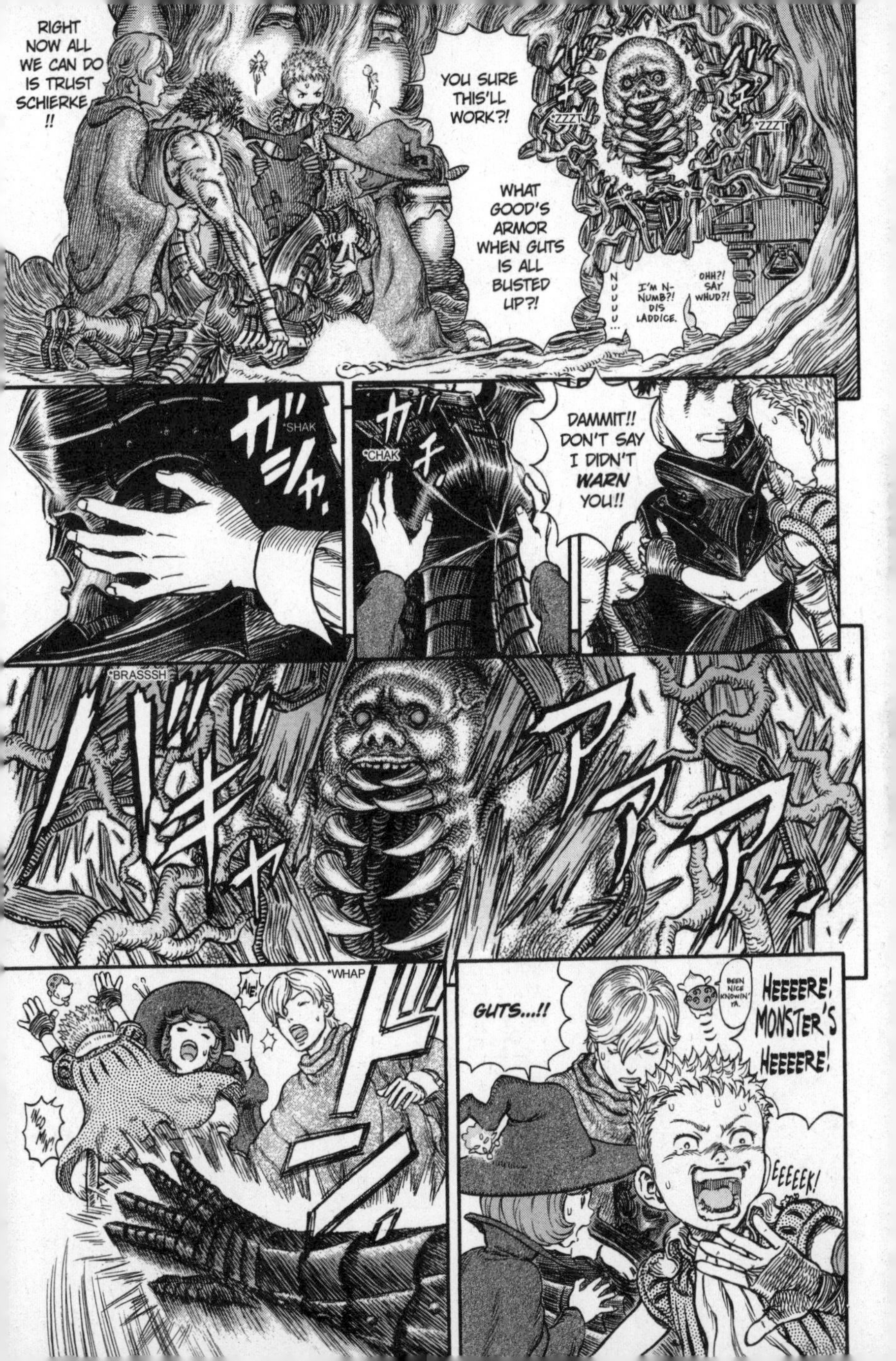
*ZZZT
*ZZZT
OHH?! SAY WHUD?!
I'M N-NUMB?! DIS LADDICE.
NUUUUU...
YOU SURE THIS'LL WORK?!
WHAT GOOD'S ARMOR WHEN GUTS IS ALL BUSTED UP?!
RIGHT NOW ALL WE CAN DO IS TRUST SCHIERKE!!
DAMMIT!! DON'T SAY I DIDN'T WARN YOU!!
*CHAK
*SHAK
*BRASSSH
HEEEERE! MONSTER'S HEEEERE!
BEEN NICE KNOWIN' YA.
GUTS...!!
EEEEEK!
*WHAP
AIE!
INCO MIN'!

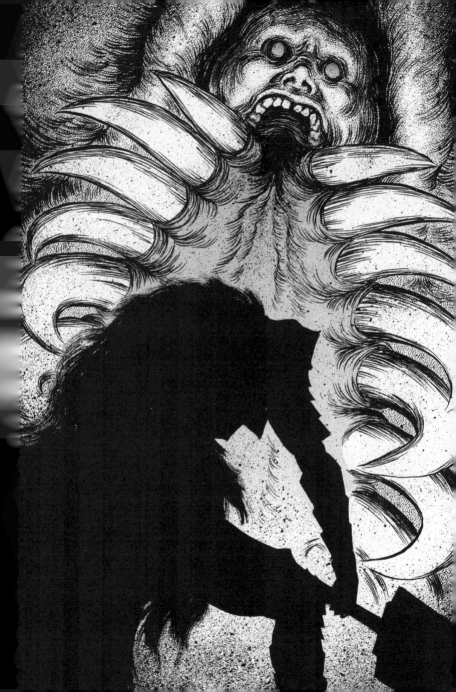

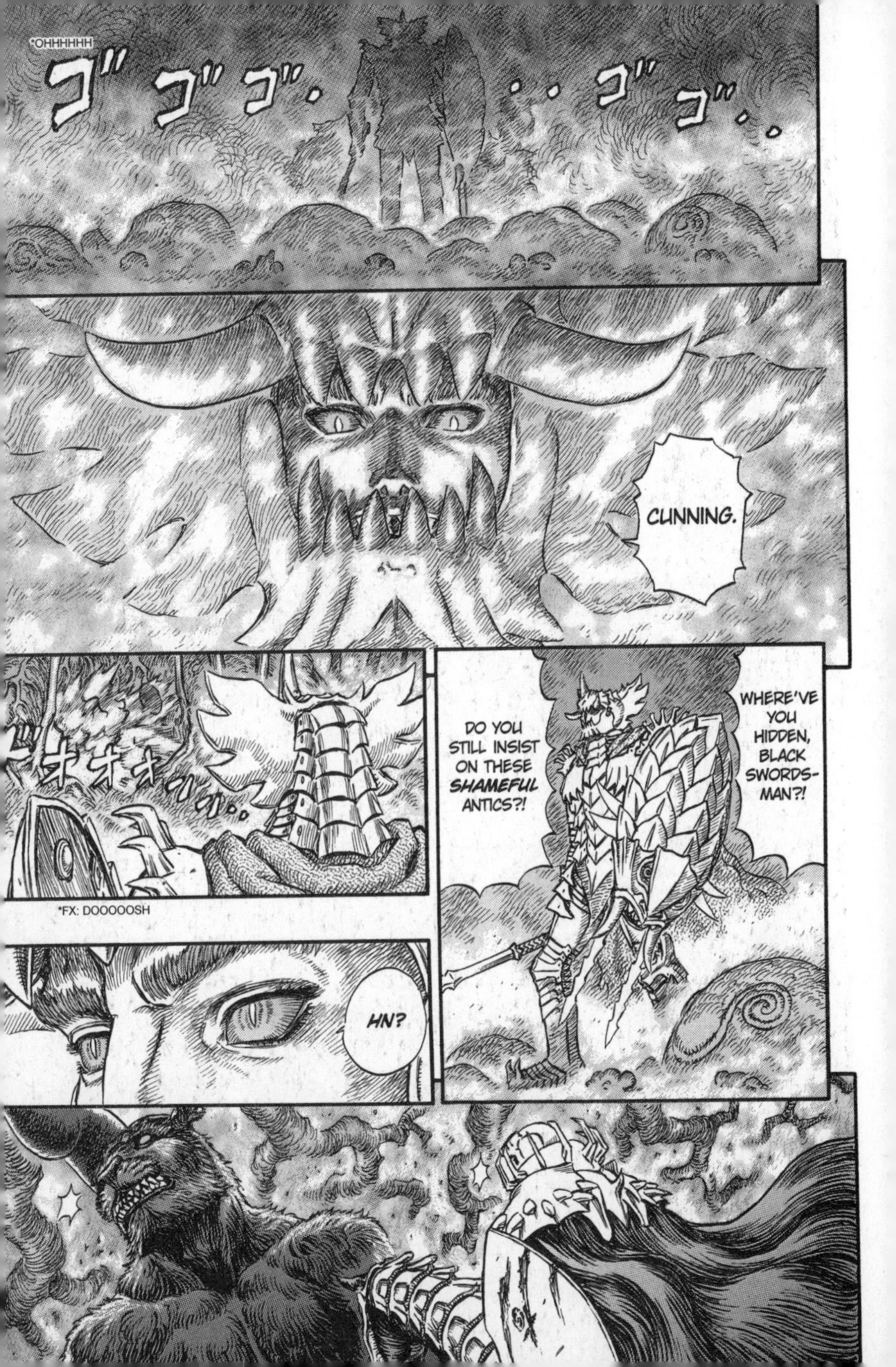

*OHHHHHH
ゴゴゴ・・・ゴゴ・・
CUNNING.
WHERE'VE YOU HIDDEN, BLACK SWORDS-MAN?!
DO YOU STILL INSIST ON THESE *SHAMEFUL* ANTICS?!
*FX: DOOOOOSH
HN?

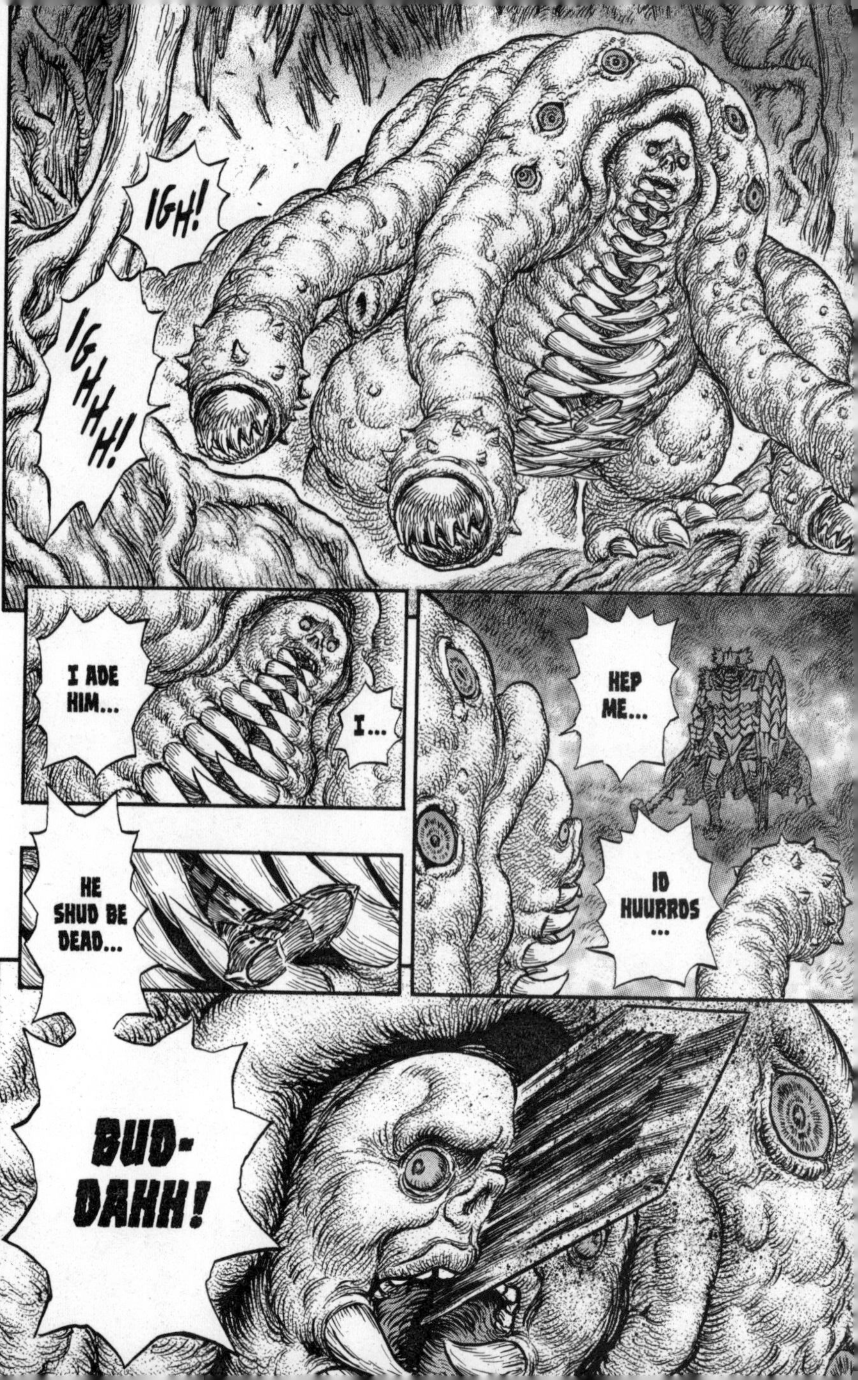
IGH!
IGHHHH!
HEP ME...
ID HUURRDS...
I ADE HIM...
I...
HE SHUD BE DEAD...
BUD-DAHH!

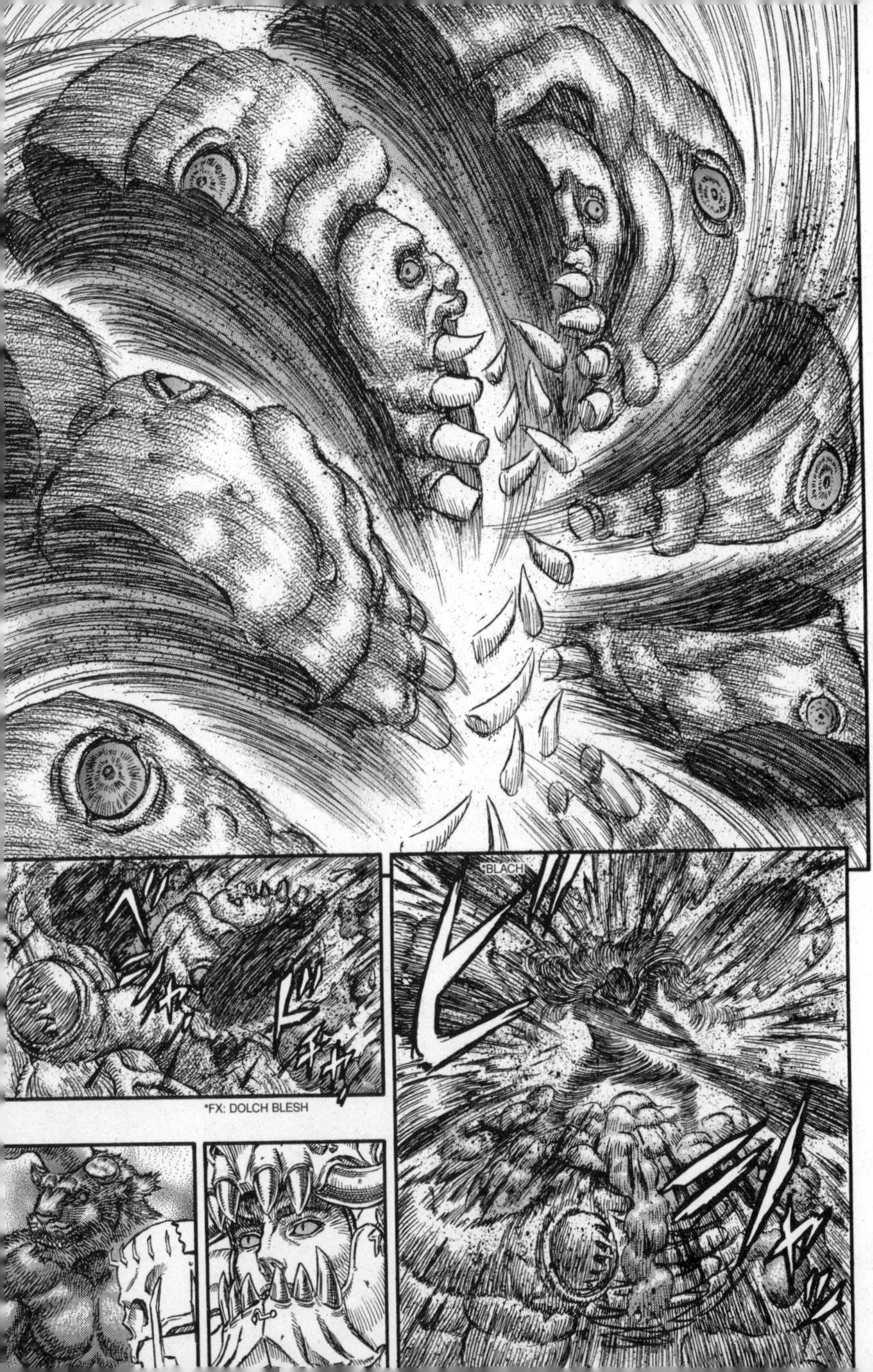
*BLACH
*FX: DOLCH BLESH

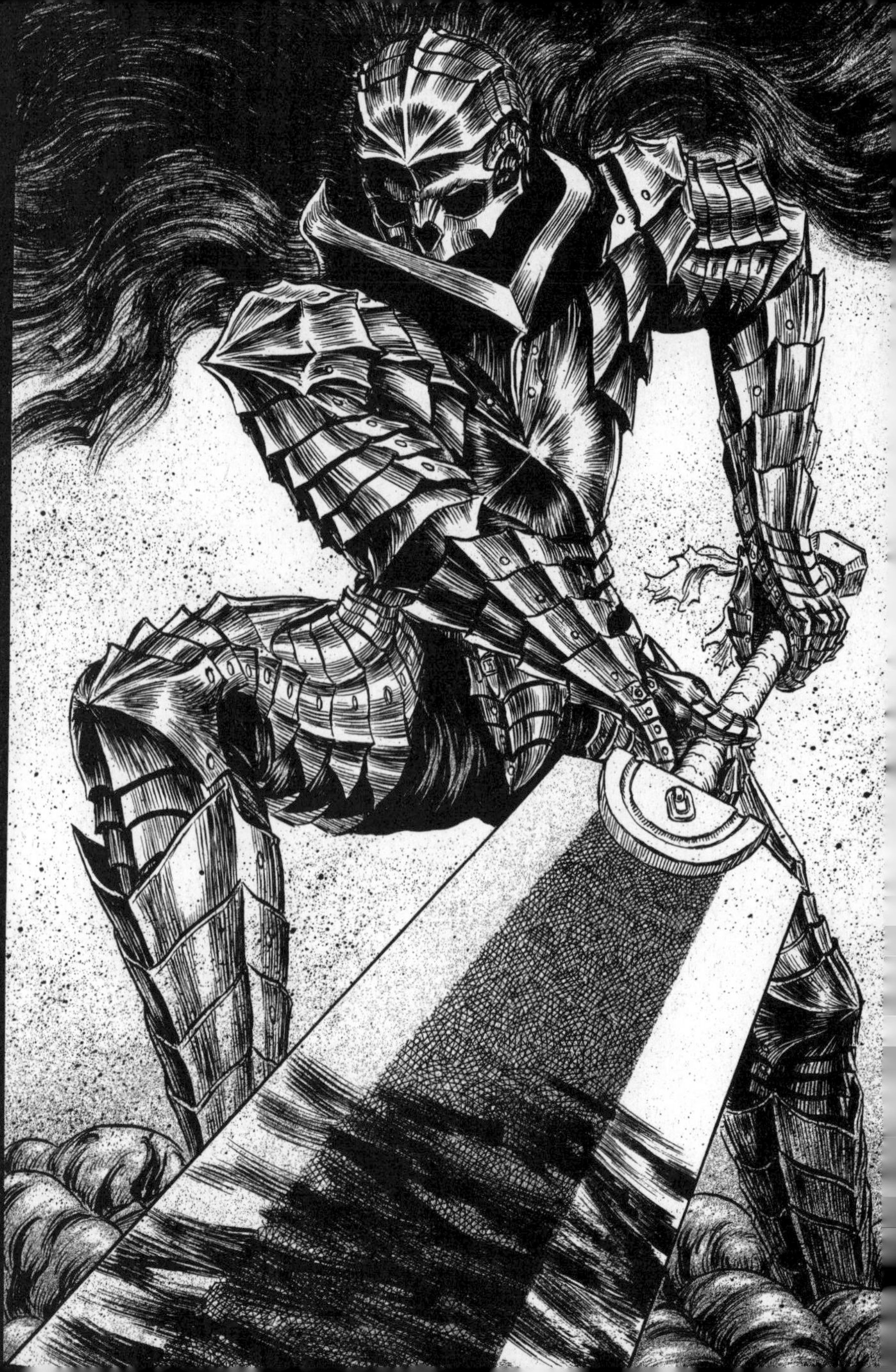

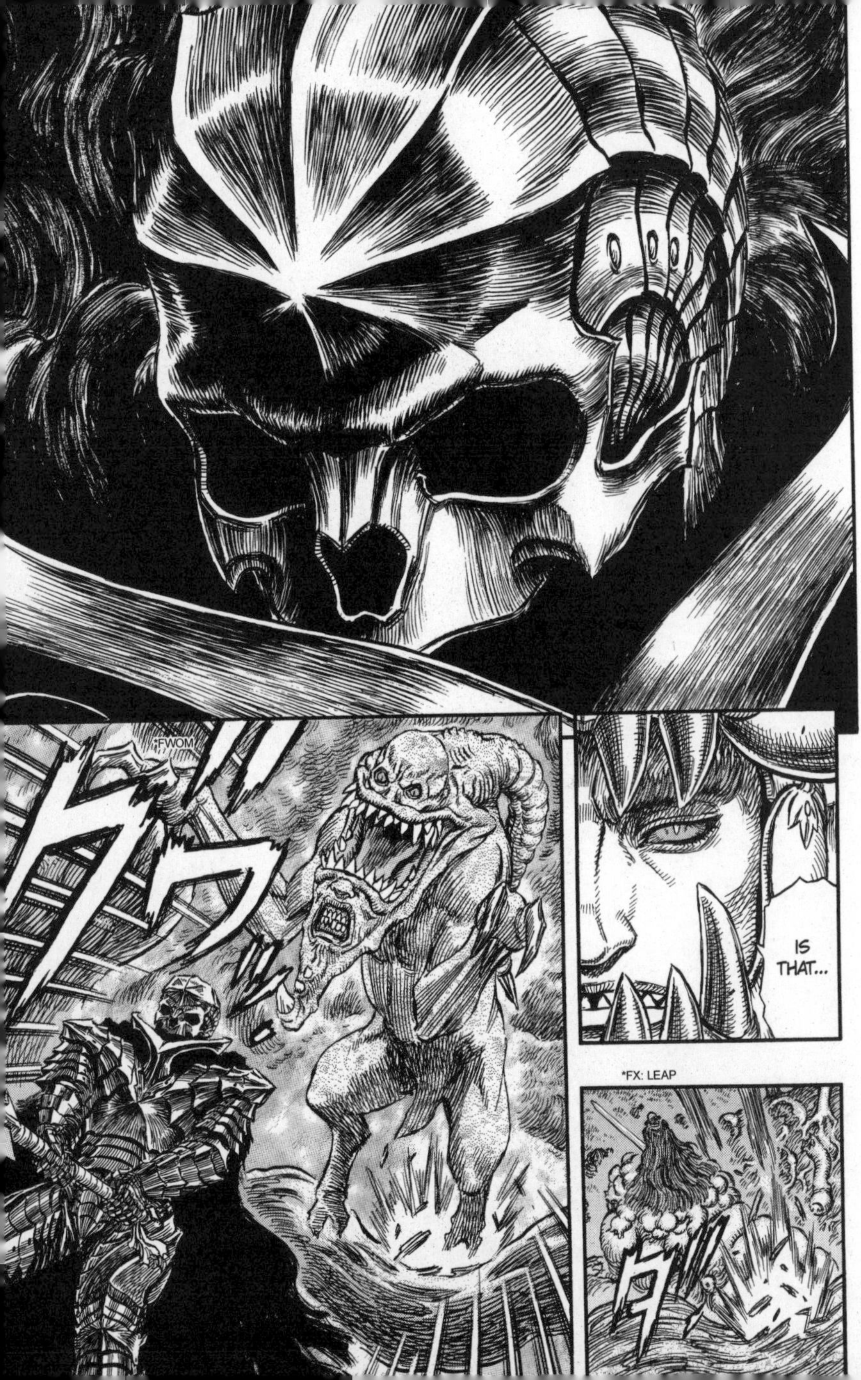
IS THAT...
*FX: LEAP
*FWOM

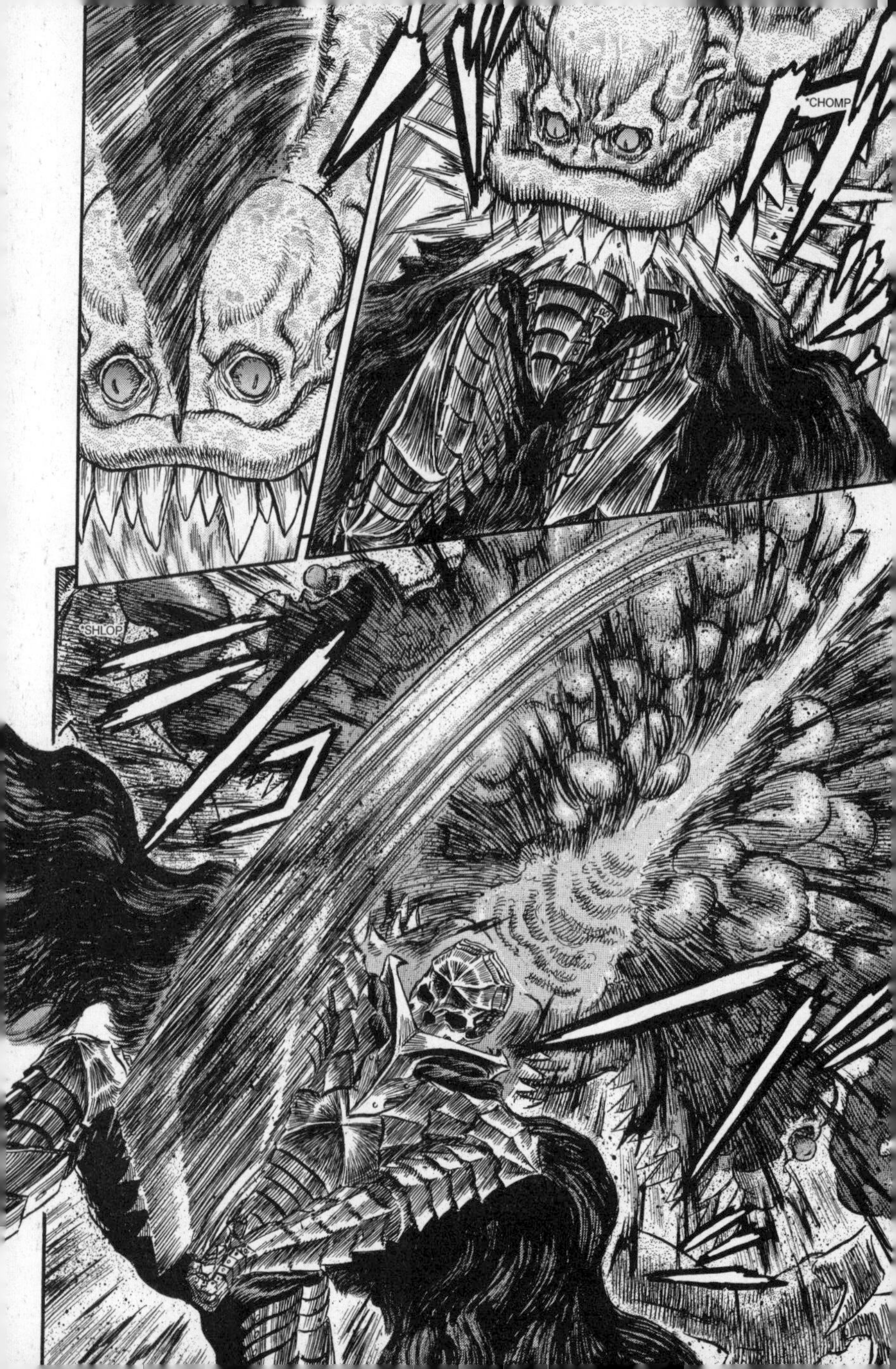
*CHOMP
*SHLOP

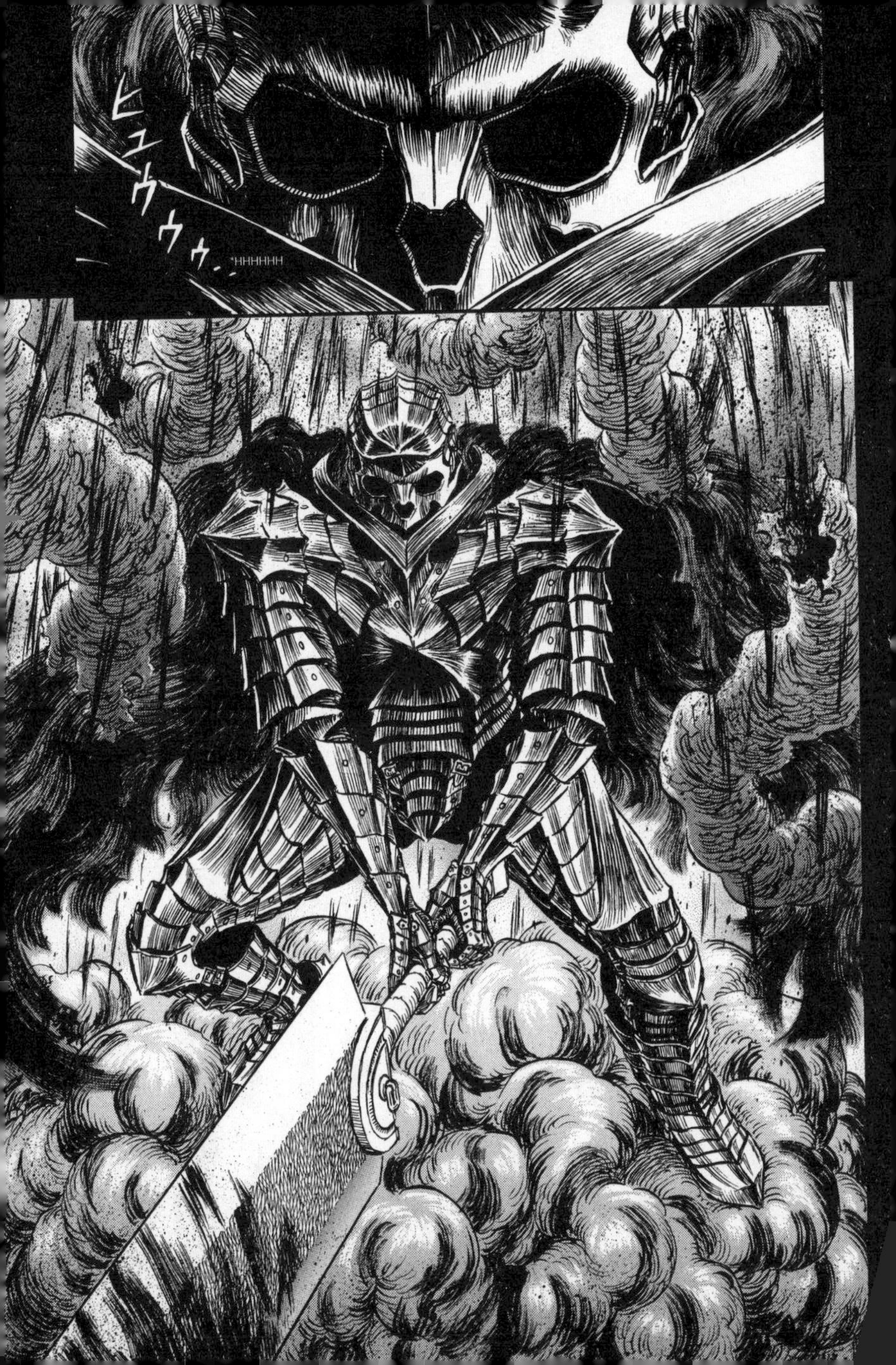
ヒュウウゥ…
*HHHHHH

THE BERSERKER
ARMOR, PART 2
狂戦士の甲冑②

BERSERK

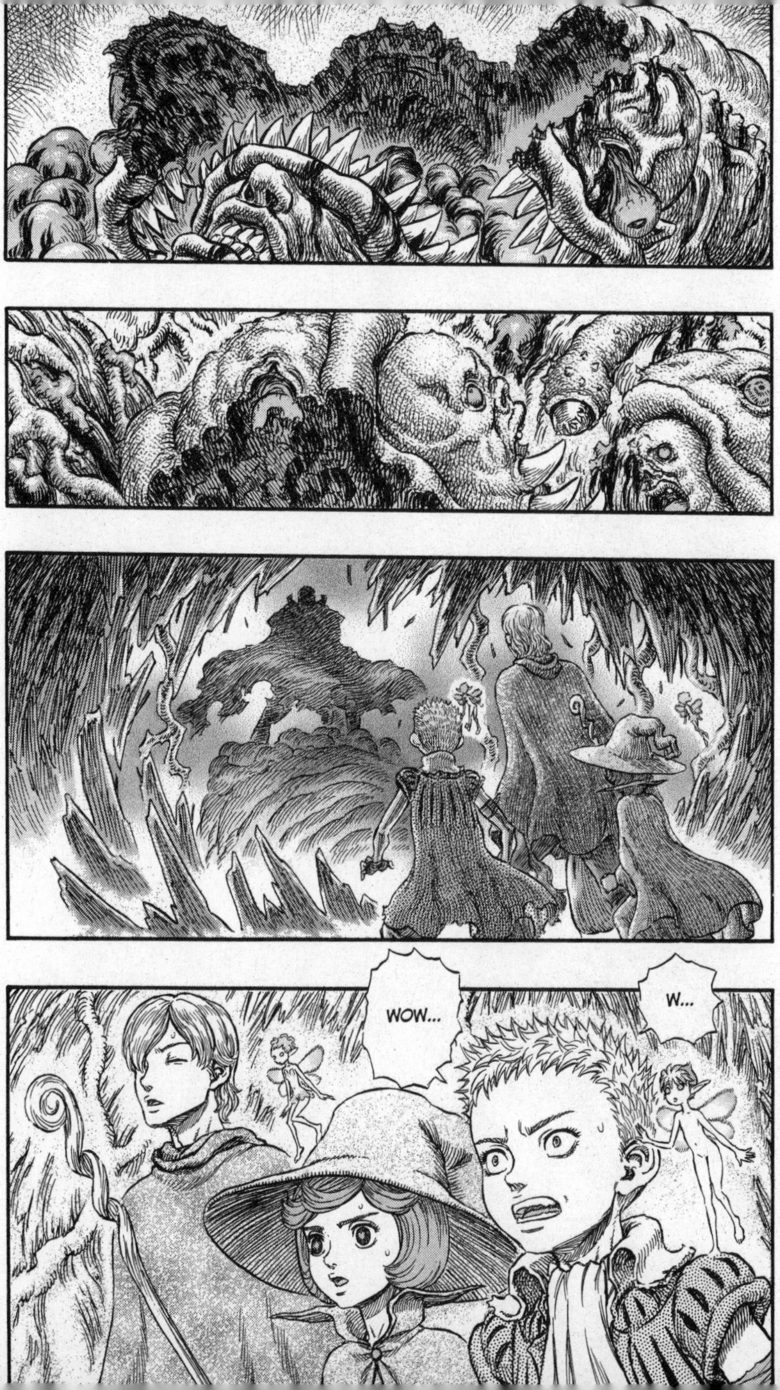
W...
WOW...

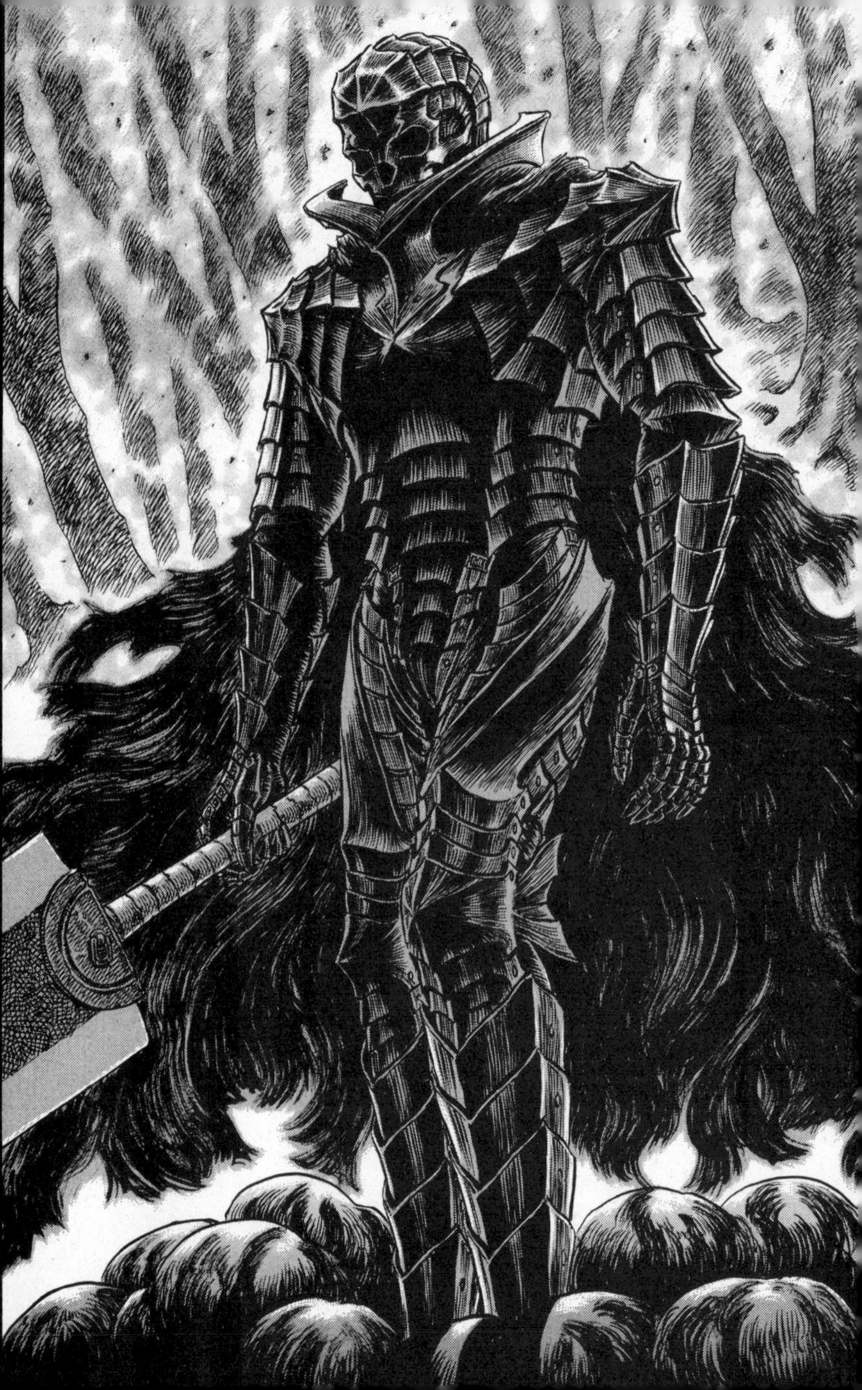

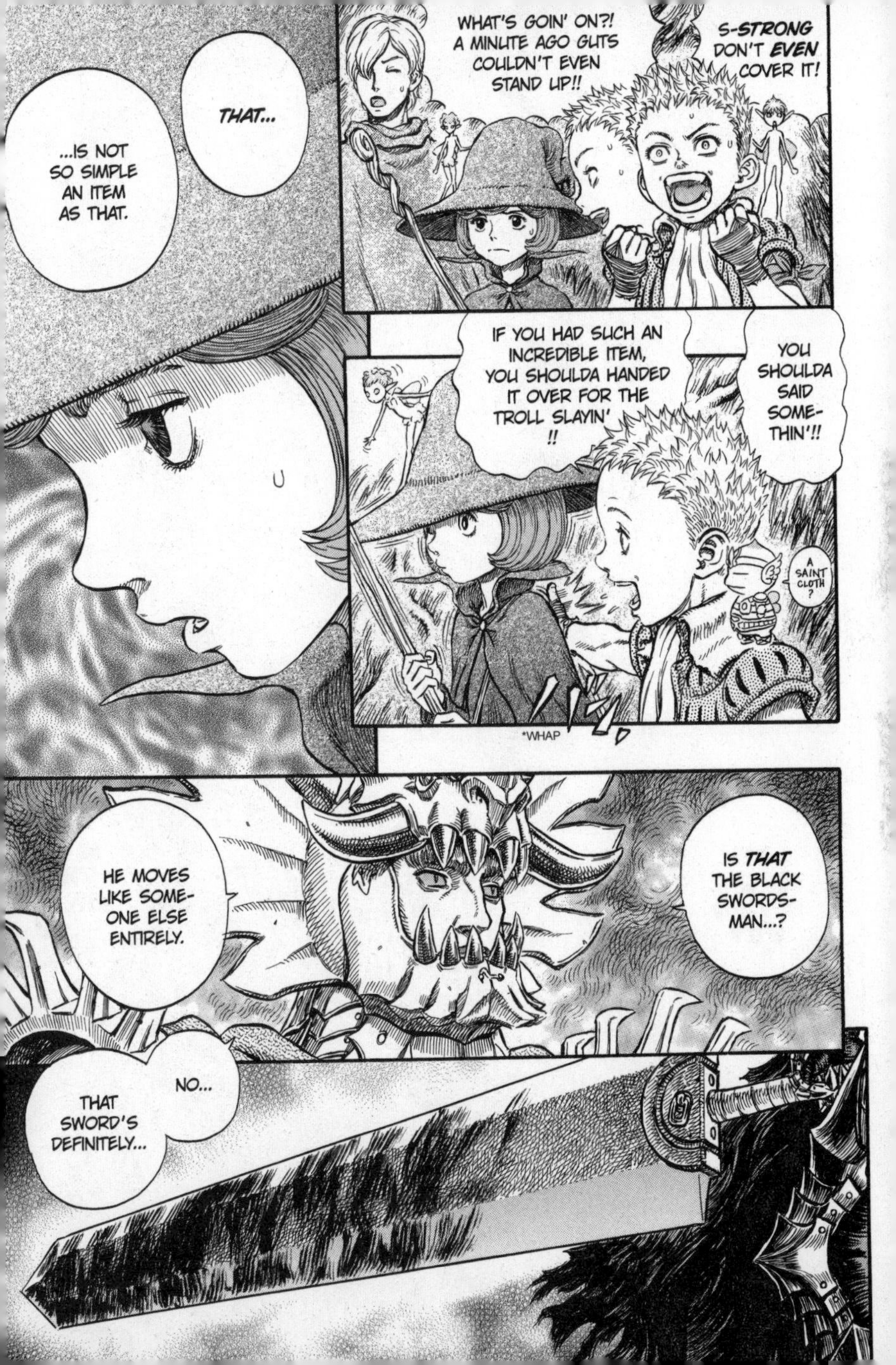
S-STRONG DON'T EVEN COVER IT!
WHAT'S GOIN' ON?! A MINUTE AGO GUTS COULDN'T EVEN STAND UP!!
YOU SHOULDA SAID SOME-THIN'!!
IF YOU HAD SUCH AN INCREDIBLE ITEM, YOU SHOULDA HANDED IT OVER FOR THE TROLL SLAYIN' !!
A SAINT CLOTH ?
*WHAP
THAT...
...IS NOT SO SIMPLE AN ITEM AS THAT.
IS THAT THE BLACK SWORDS-MAN...?
HE MOVES LIKE SOME-ONE ELSE ENTIRELY.
NO...
THAT SWORD'S DEFINITELY...

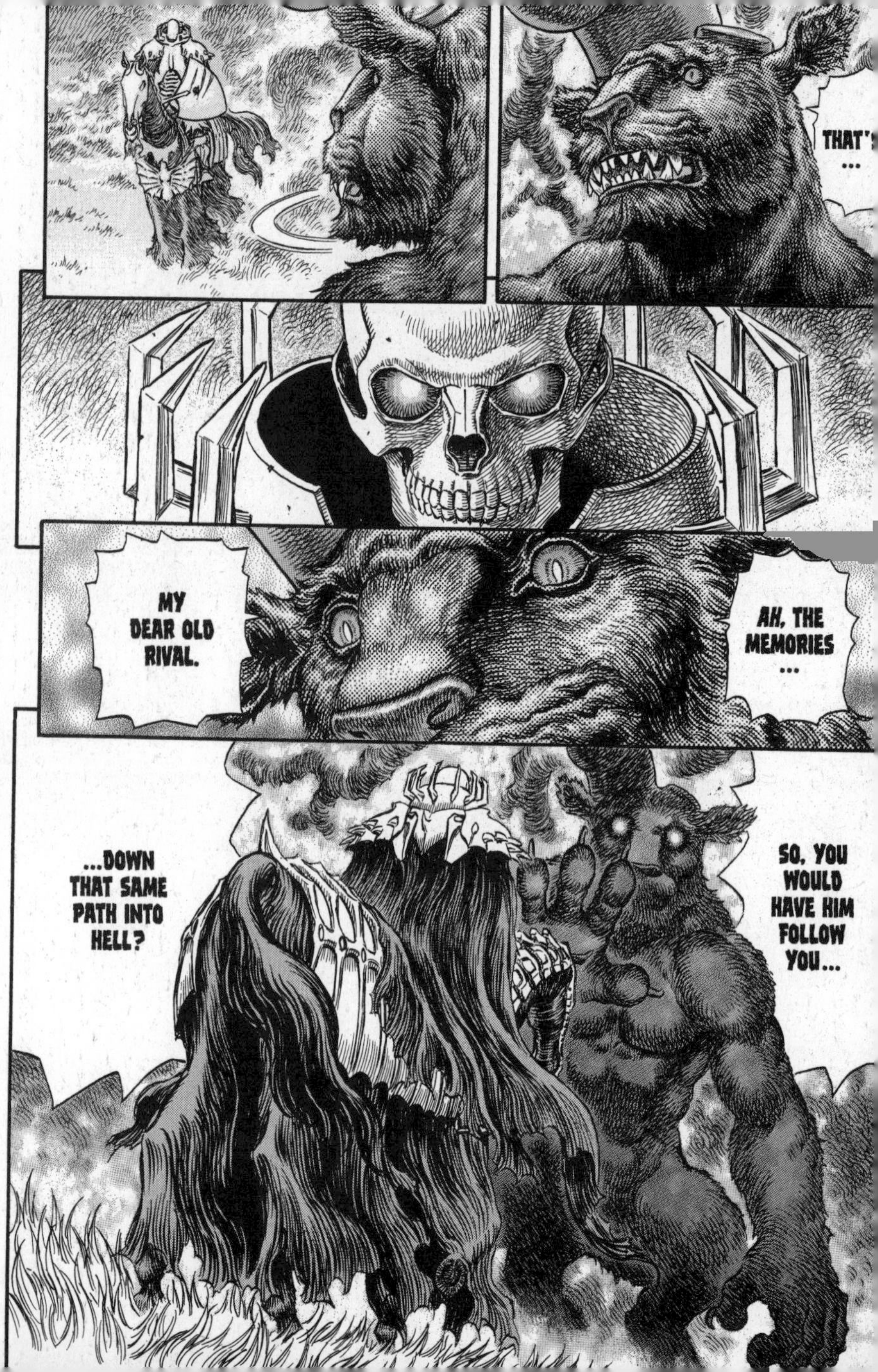
THAT'S ...
AH, THE MEMORIES ...
MY DEAR OLD RIVAL.
SO, YOU WOULD HAVE HIM FOLLOW YOU...
...DOWN THAT SAME PATH INTO HELL?

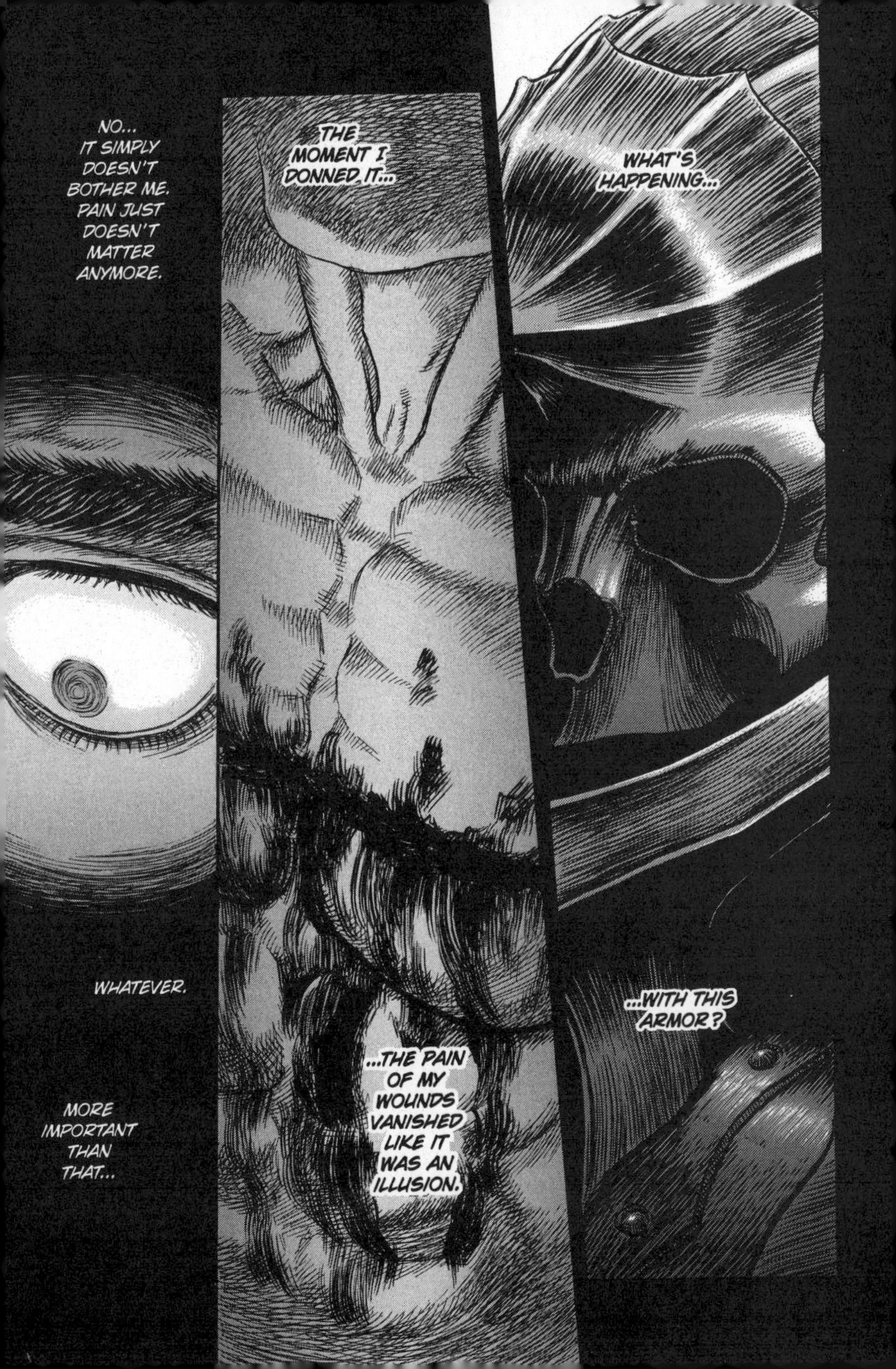
WHAT'S HAPPENING...
...WITH THIS ARMOR?
THE MOMENT I DONNED IT...
...THE PAIN OF MY WOUNDS VANISHED LIKE IT WAS AN ILLUSION.
NO... IT SIMPLY DOESN'T BOTHER ME. PAIN JUST DOESN'T MATTER ANYMORE.
WHATEVER.
MORE IMPORTANT THAN THAT...

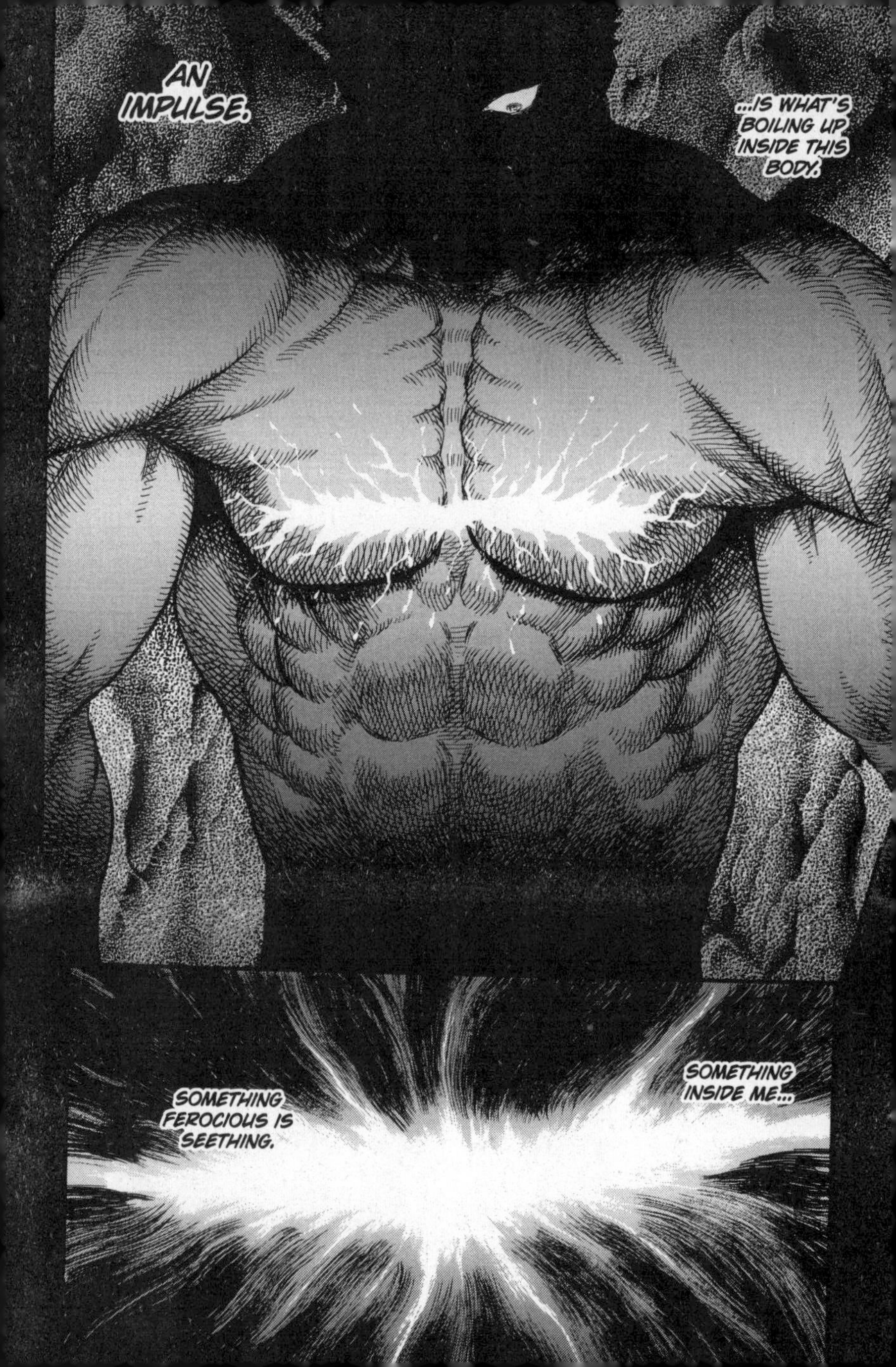
...IS WHAT'S BOILING UP INSIDE THIS BODY.
AN IMPULSE.
SOMETHING INSIDE ME...
SOMETHING FEROCIOUS IS SEETHING.

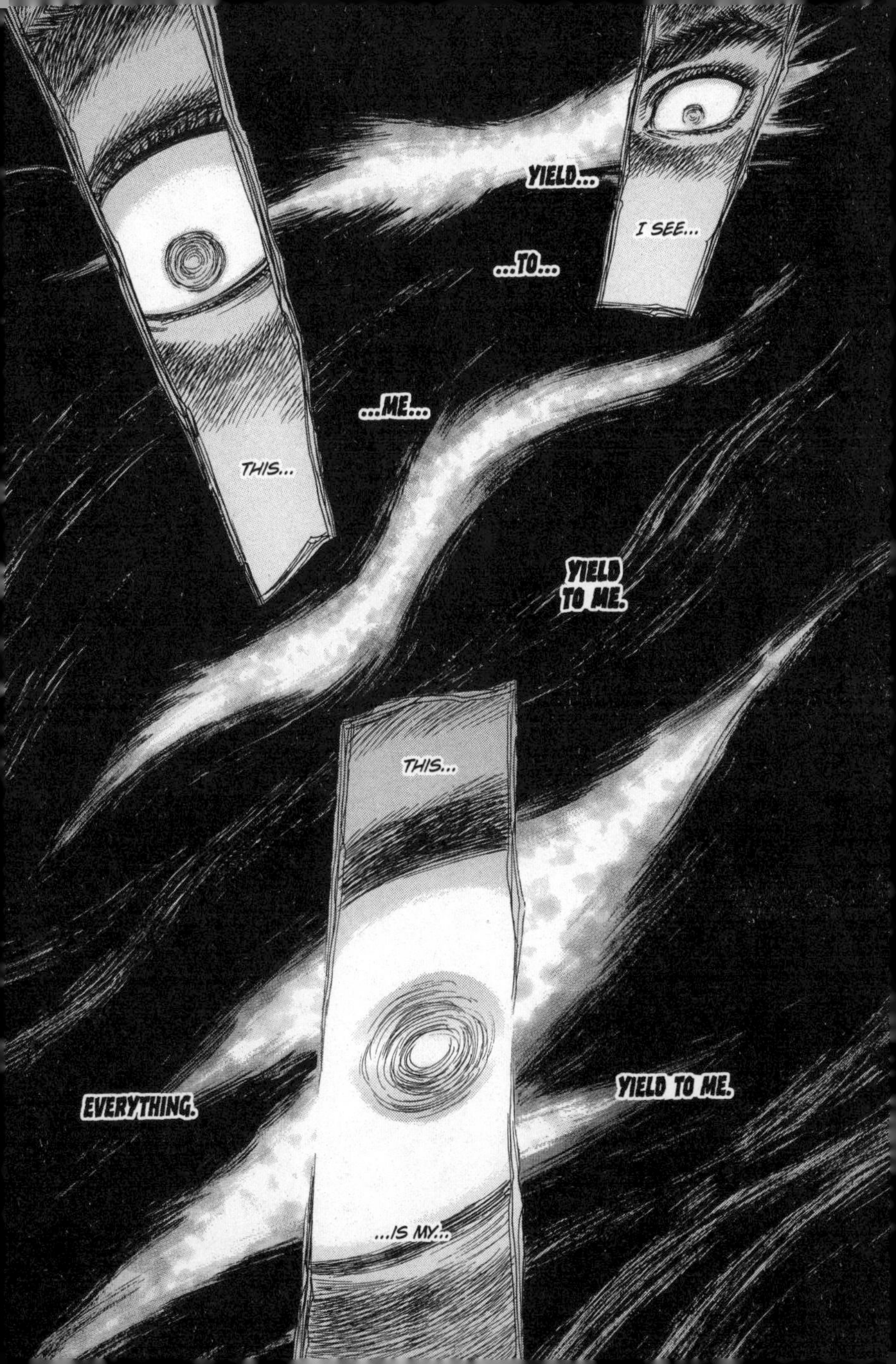
I SEE...
YIELD...
...TO...
...ME...
THIS...
YIELD TO ME.
THIS...
YIELD TO ME.
...IS MY...
EVERYTHING.

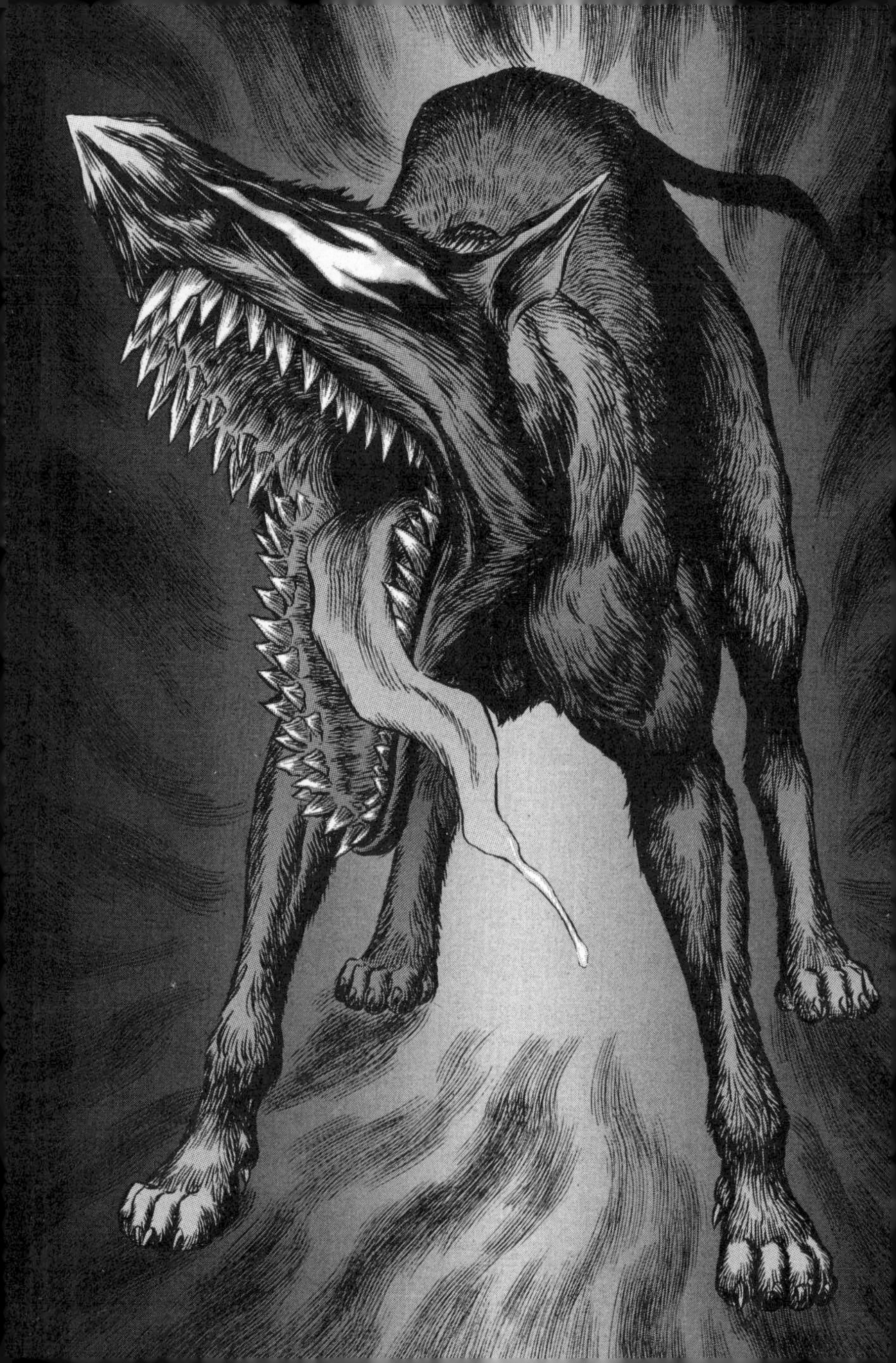

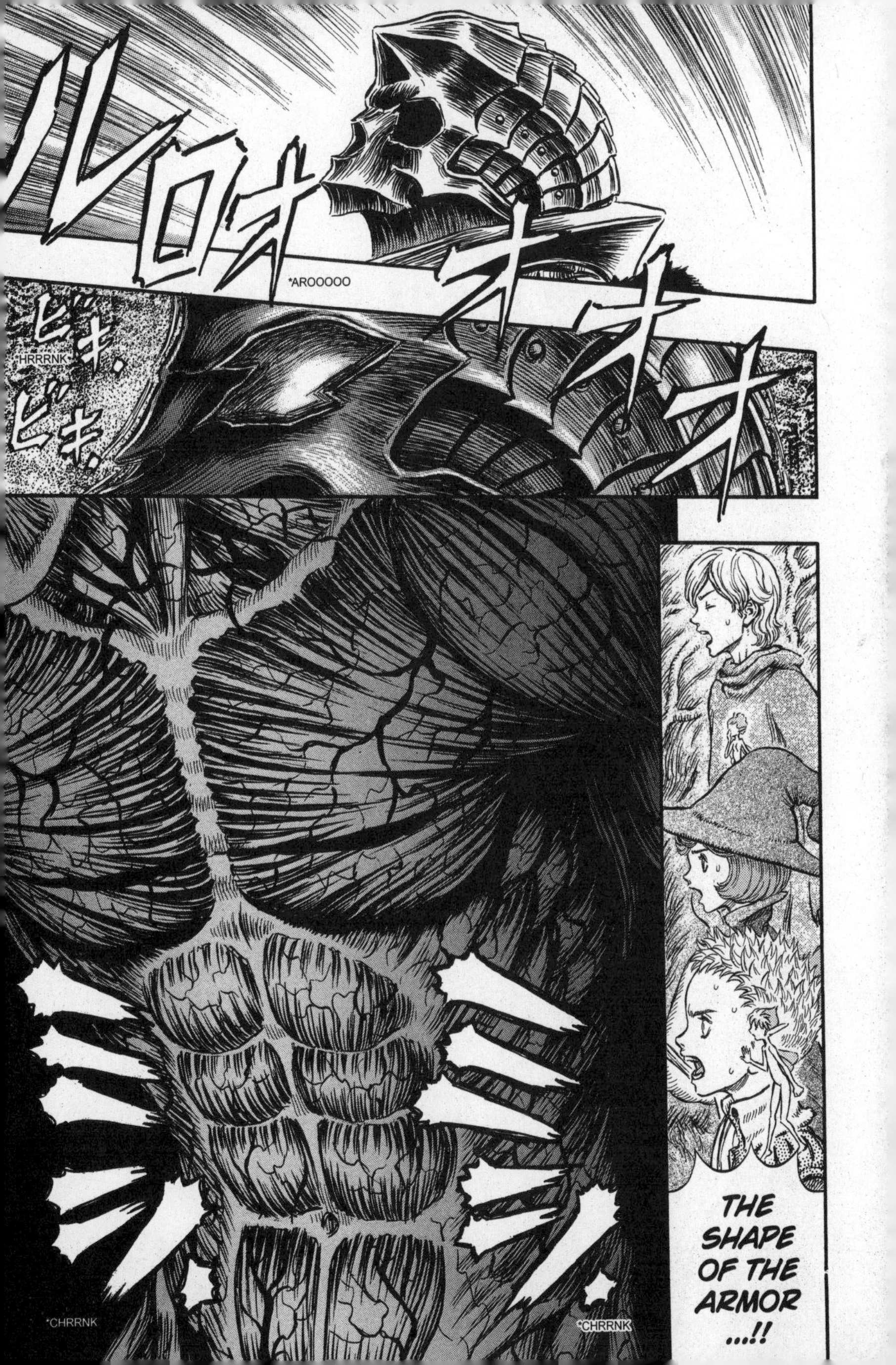
ルロオオオオ
*AROOOOO
ビキ、ビキ。
*HRRRNK
*CHRRNK
*CHRRNK
THE SHAPE OF THE ARMOR ...!!

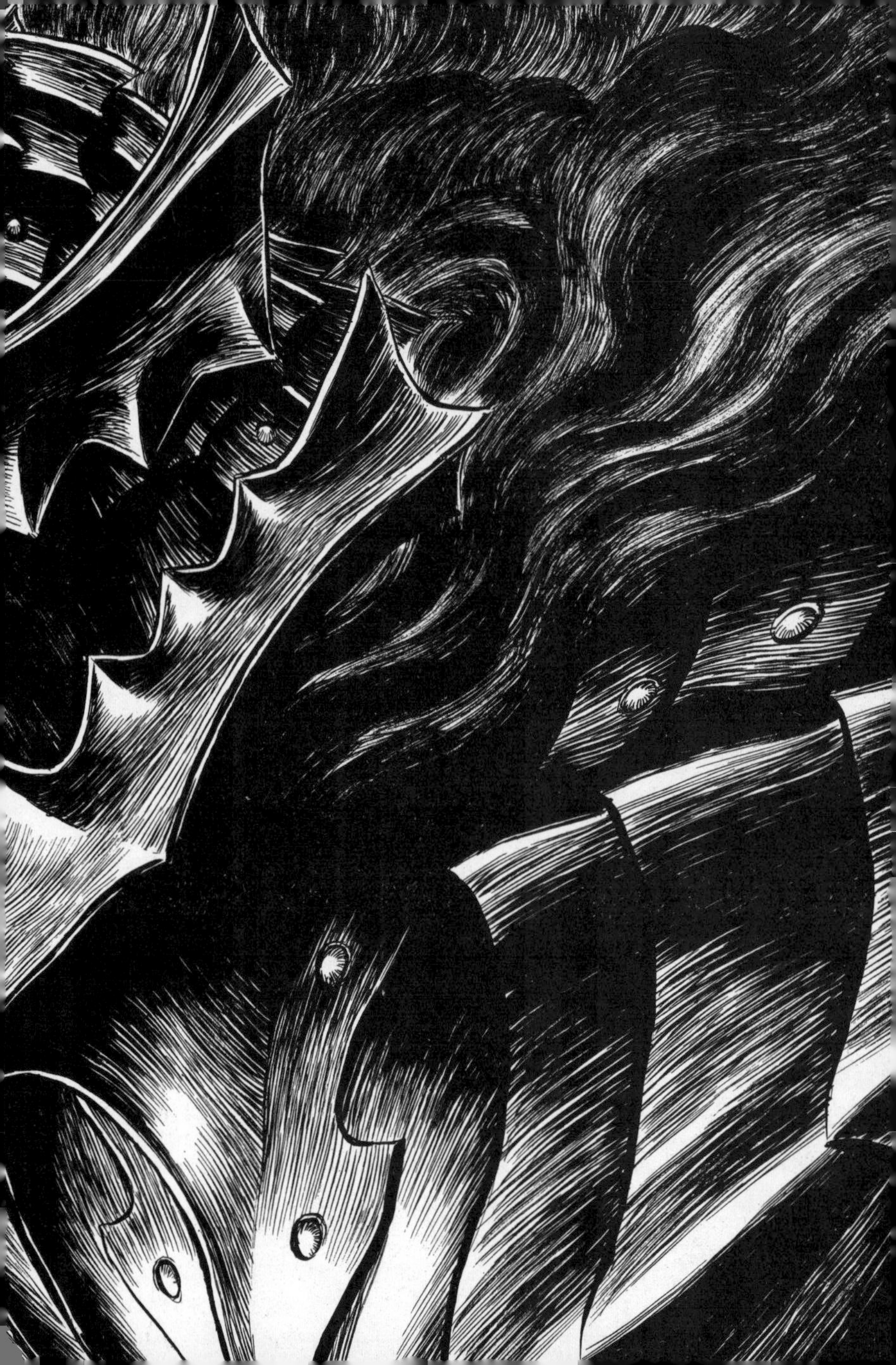

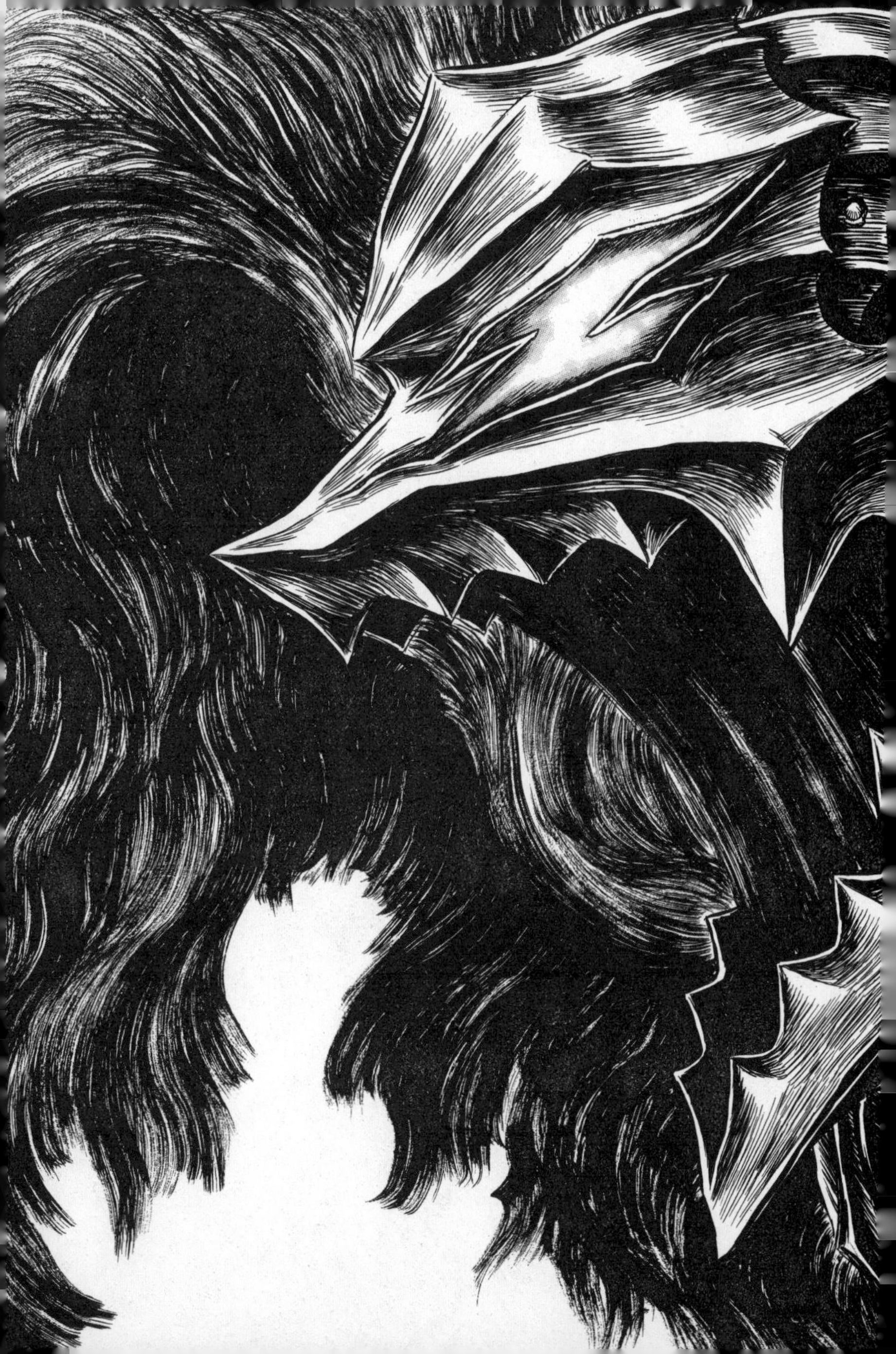

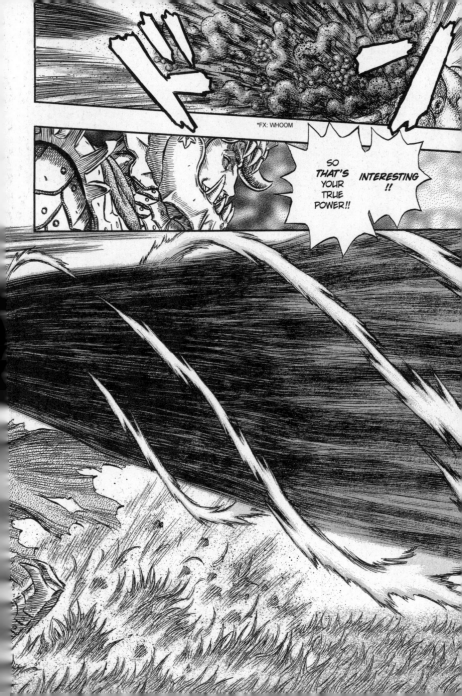

*FX: WHOOM

SO *THAT'S* YOUR TRUE POWER!! *INTERESTING!!*

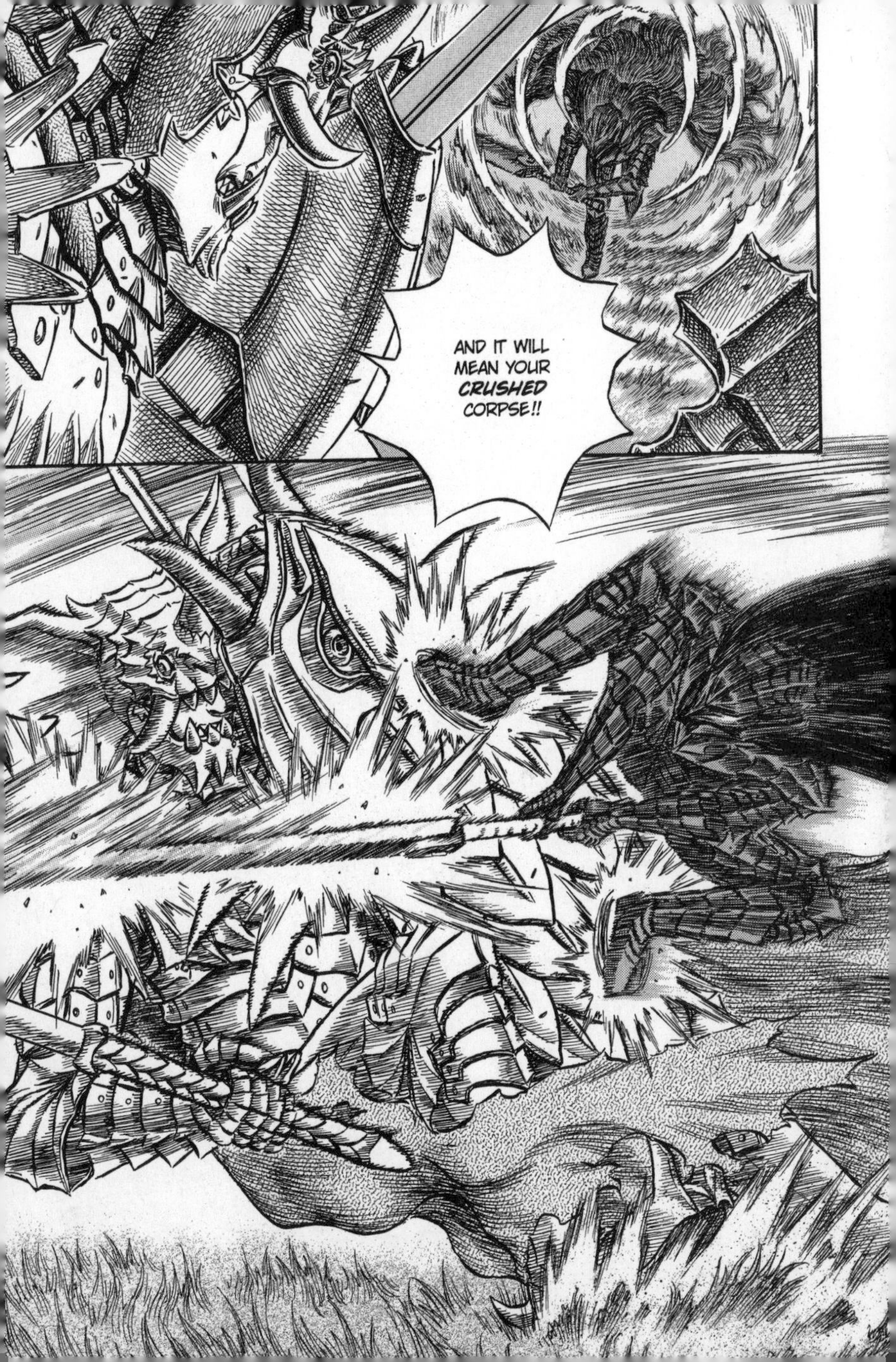
AND IT WILL MEAN YOUR CRUSHED CORPSE!!

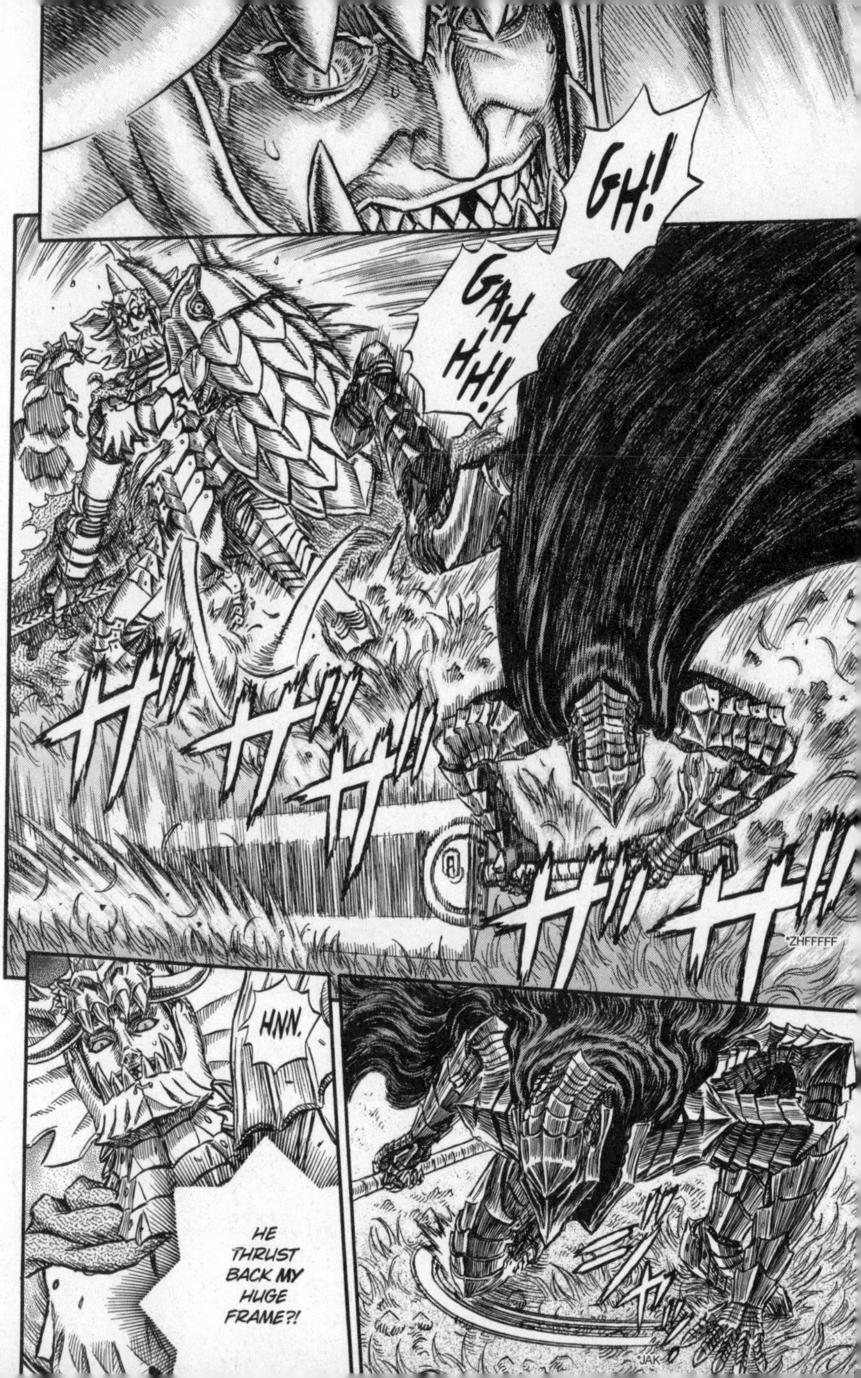
GH!
GAHHHH!
ザザザザ
ザザ
*ZHFFFFF
JAK
HNN.
HE THRUST BACK MY HUGE FRAME?!

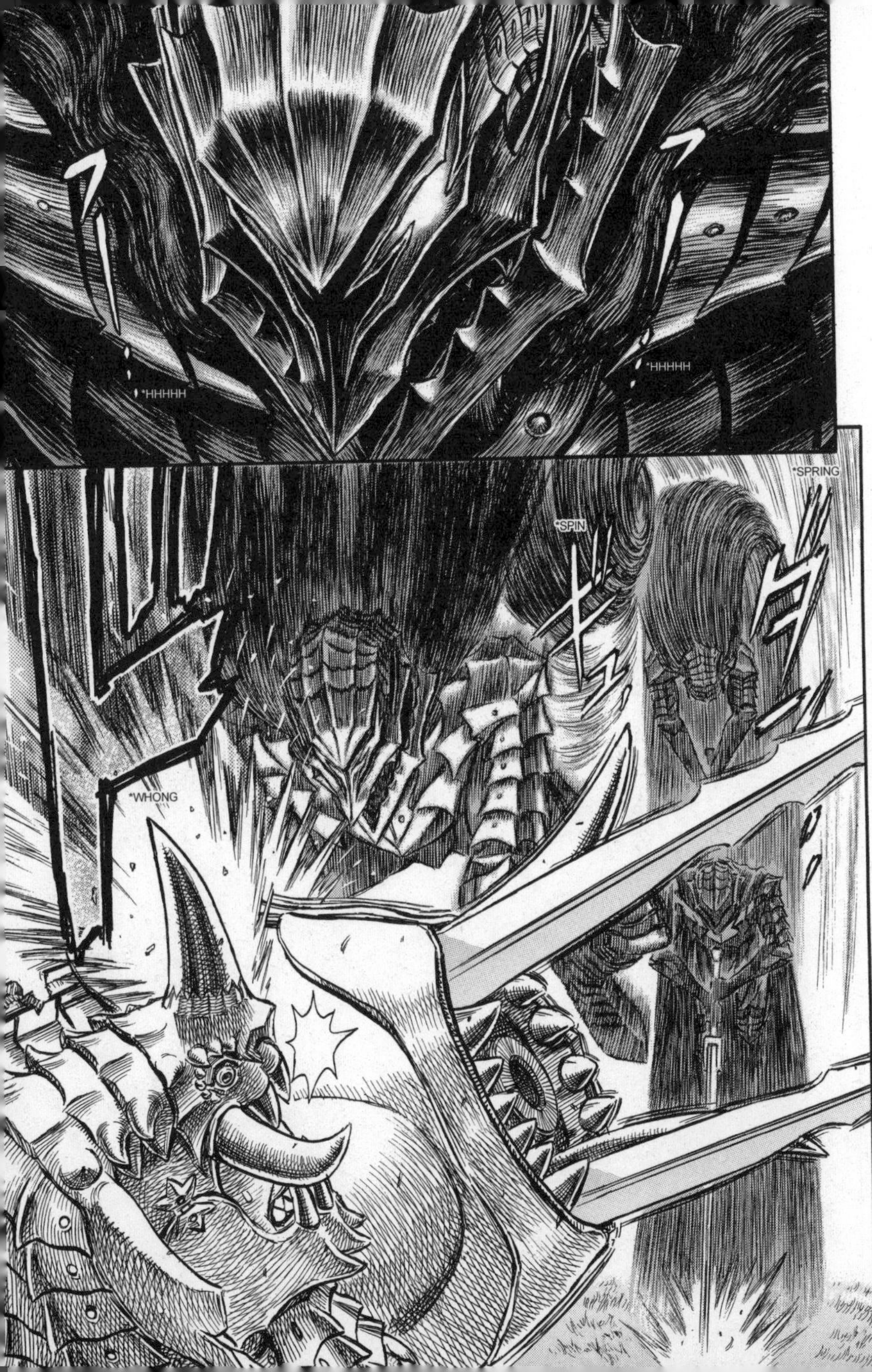
*HHHHH
*HHHHH
*SPRING
*SPIN
*WHONG

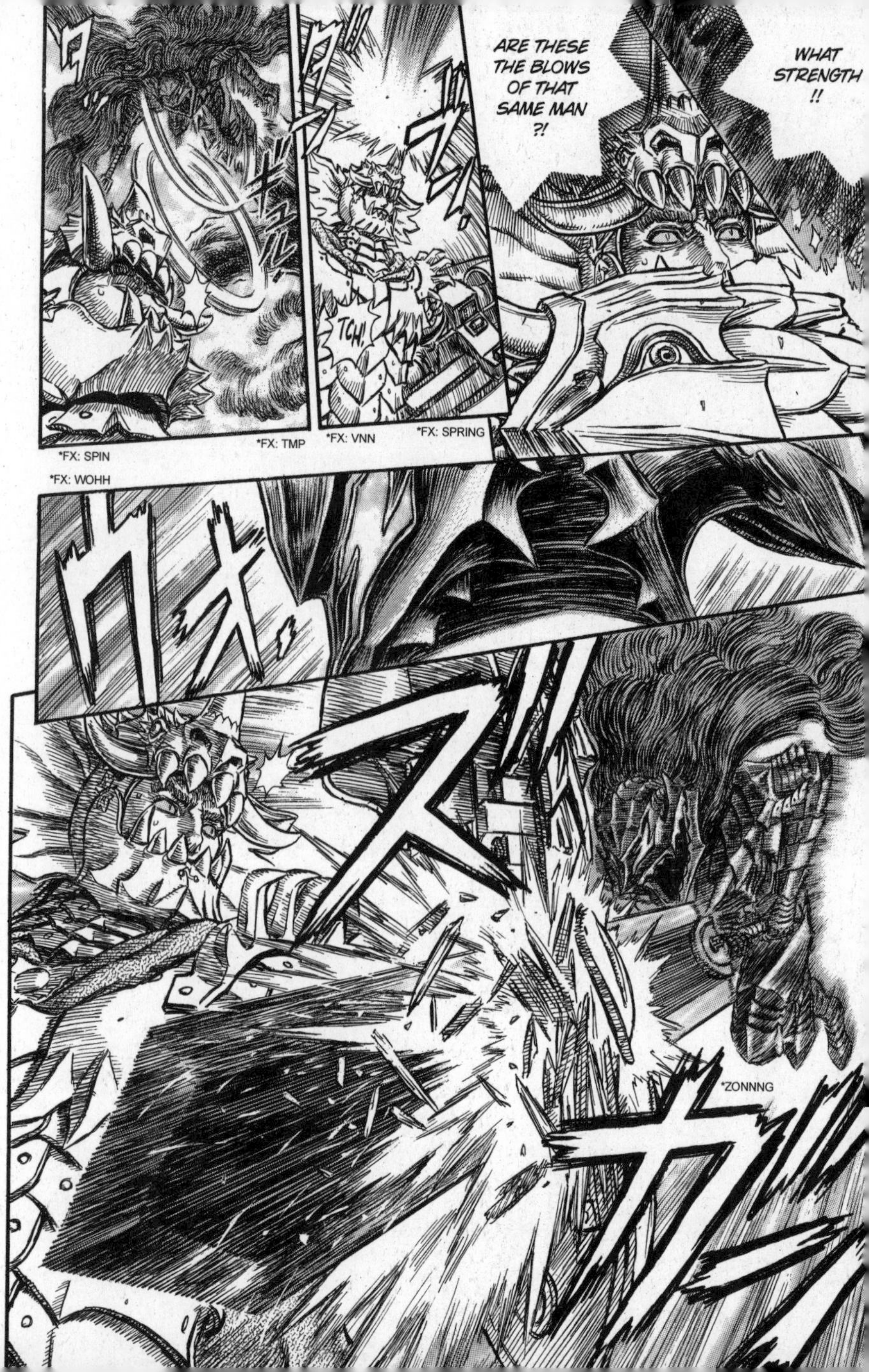
WHAT STRENGTH !!
ARE THESE THE BLOWS OF THAT SAME MAN ?!
*FX: SPRING
TCH!
*FX: VNN
*FX: TMP
*FX: SPIN
*FX: WOHH
*ZONNNG

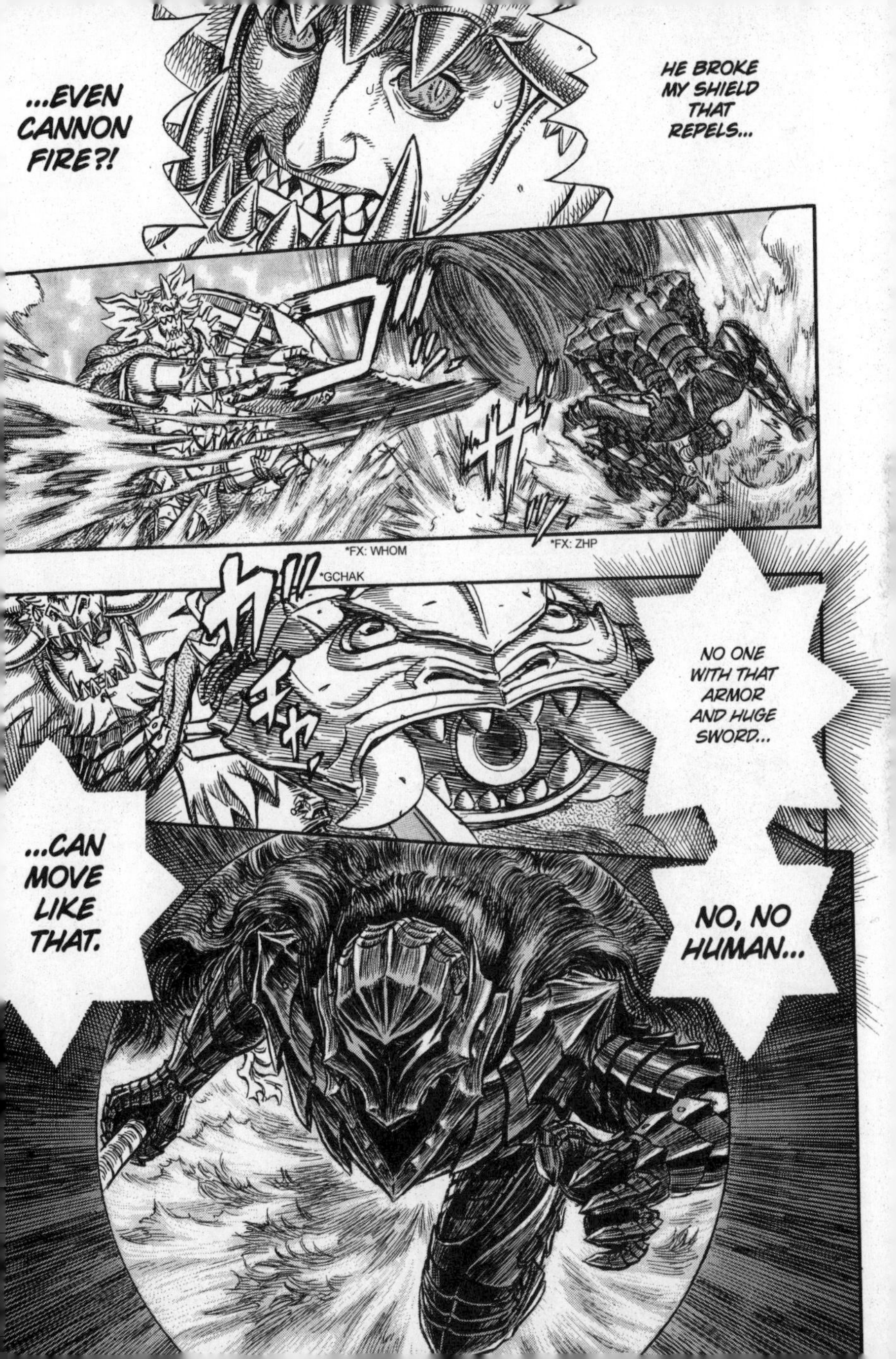
HE BROKE MY SHIELD THAT REPELS...
...EVEN CANNON FIRE?!
*FX: ZHP
*FX: WHOM
*GCHAK
NO ONE WITH THAT ARMOR AND HUGE SWORD...
NO, NO HUMAN...
...CAN MOVE LIKE THAT.

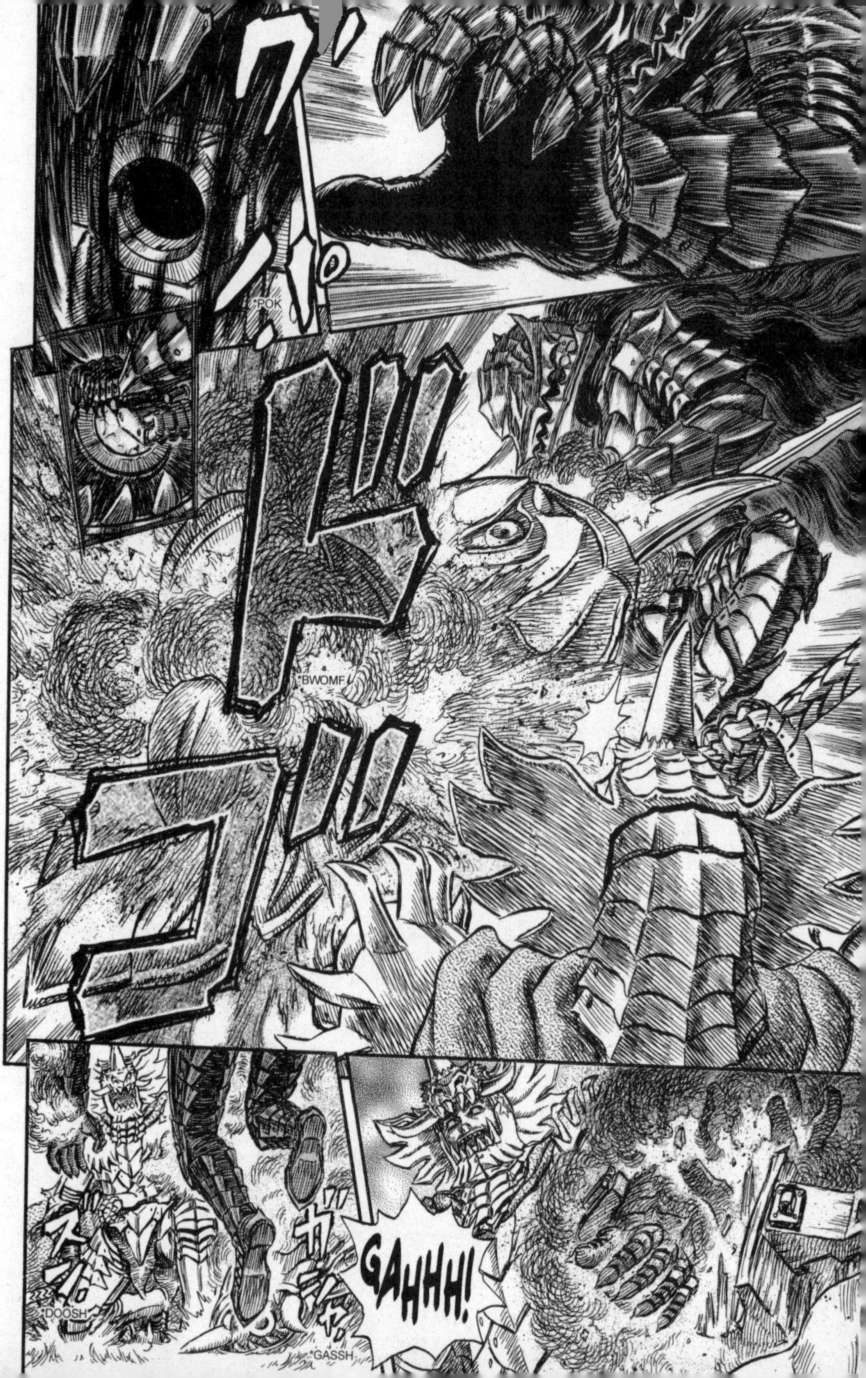
*POK
*BWOMF
GAHHH!
*GASSH
*DOOSH

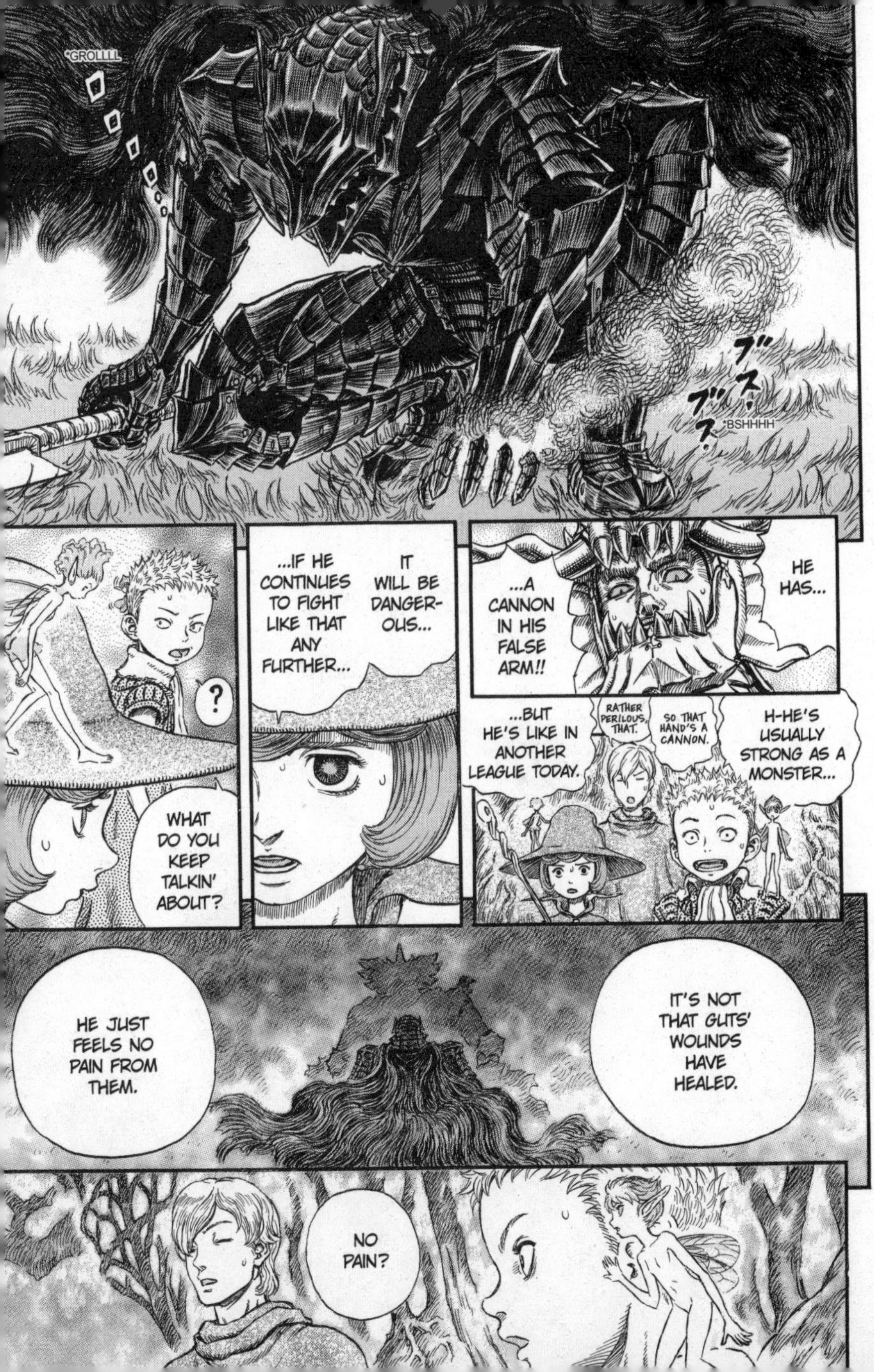
*GROLLLL
ブズ
ブズ
*BSHHHH
HE HAS...
...A CANNON IN HIS FALSE ARM!!
H-HE'S USUALLY STRONG AS A MONSTER...
SO THAT HAND'S A CANNON.
RATHER PERILOUS, THAT.
...BUT HE'S LIKE IN ANOTHER LEAGUE TODAY.
IT WILL BE DANGER-OUS...
...IF HE CONTINUES TO FIGHT LIKE THAT ANY FURTHER...
?
WHAT DO YOU KEEP TALKIN' ABOUT?
IT'S NOT THAT GUTS' WOUNDS HAVE HEALED.
HE JUST FEELS NO PAIN FROM THEM.
NO PAIN?

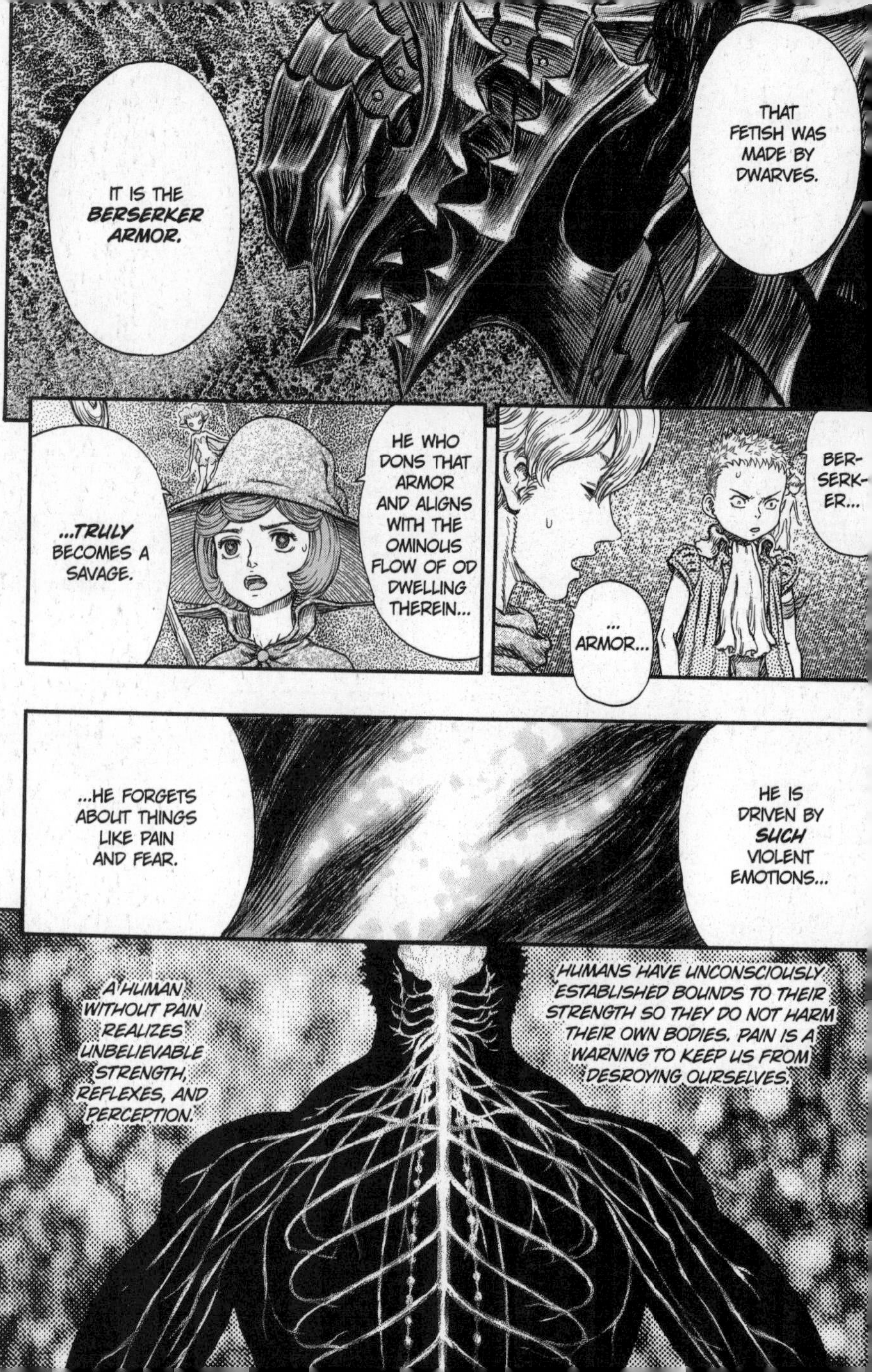
THAT FETISH WAS MADE BY DWARVES.
IT IS THE BERSERKER ARMOR.
BER-SERK-ER...
...ARMOR...
HE WHO DONS THAT ARMOR AND ALIGNS WITH THE OMINOUS FLOW OF OD DWELLING THEREIN...
...TRULY BECOMES A SAVAGE.
HE IS DRIVEN BY SUCH VIOLENT EMOTIONS...
...HE FORGETS ABOUT THINGS LIKE PAIN AND FEAR.
HUMANS HAVE UNCONSCIOUSLY ESTABLISHED BOUNDS TO THEIR STRENGTH SO THEY DO NOT HARM THEIR OWN BODIES. PAIN IS A WARNING TO KEEP US FROM DESROYING OURSELVES.
A HUMAN WITHOUT PAIN REALIZES UNBELIEVABLE STRENGTH, REFLEXES, AND PERCEPTION.

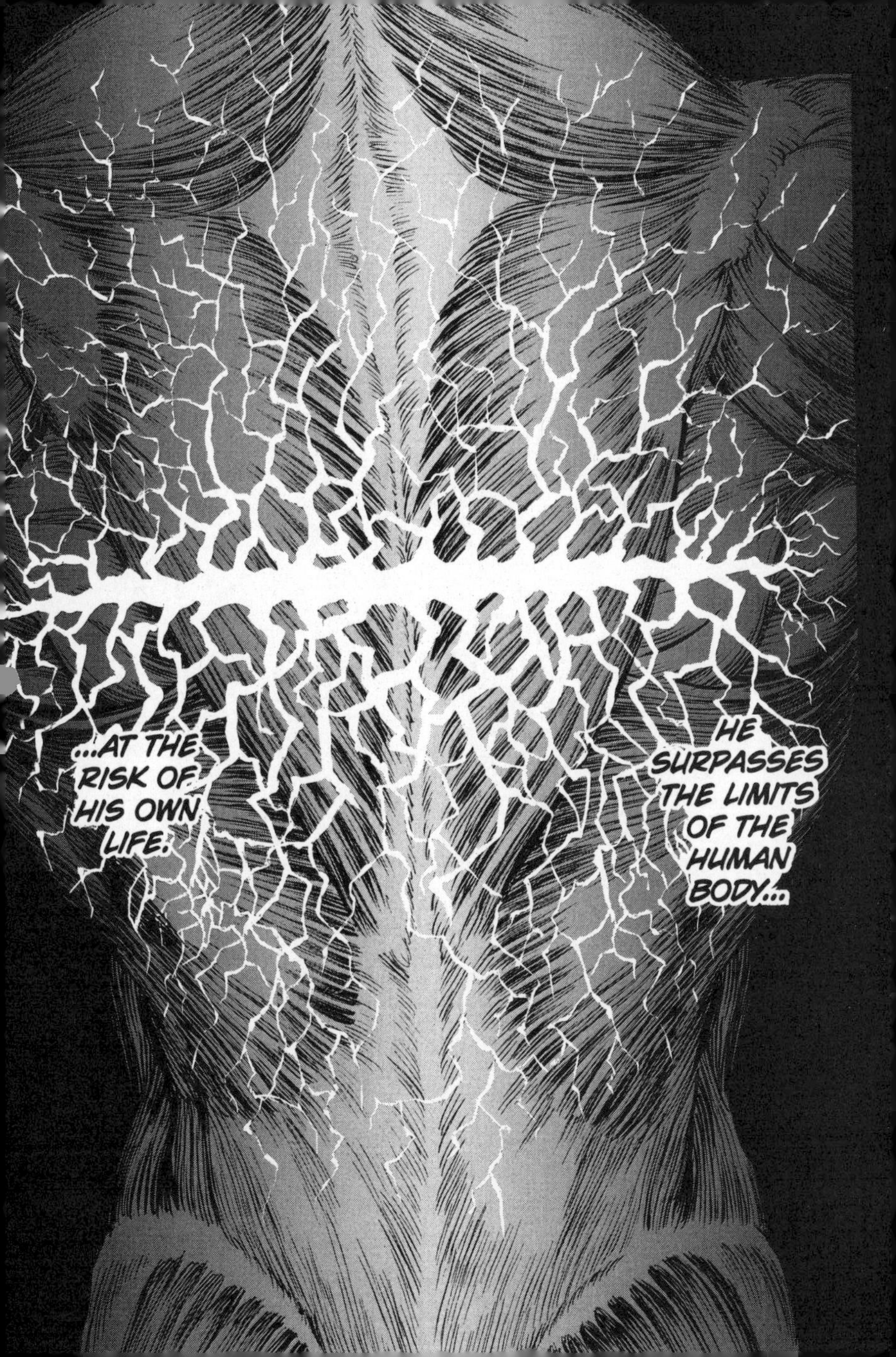
HE SURPASSES THE LIMITS OF THE HUMAN BODY...
...AT THE RISK OF HIS OWN LIFE.

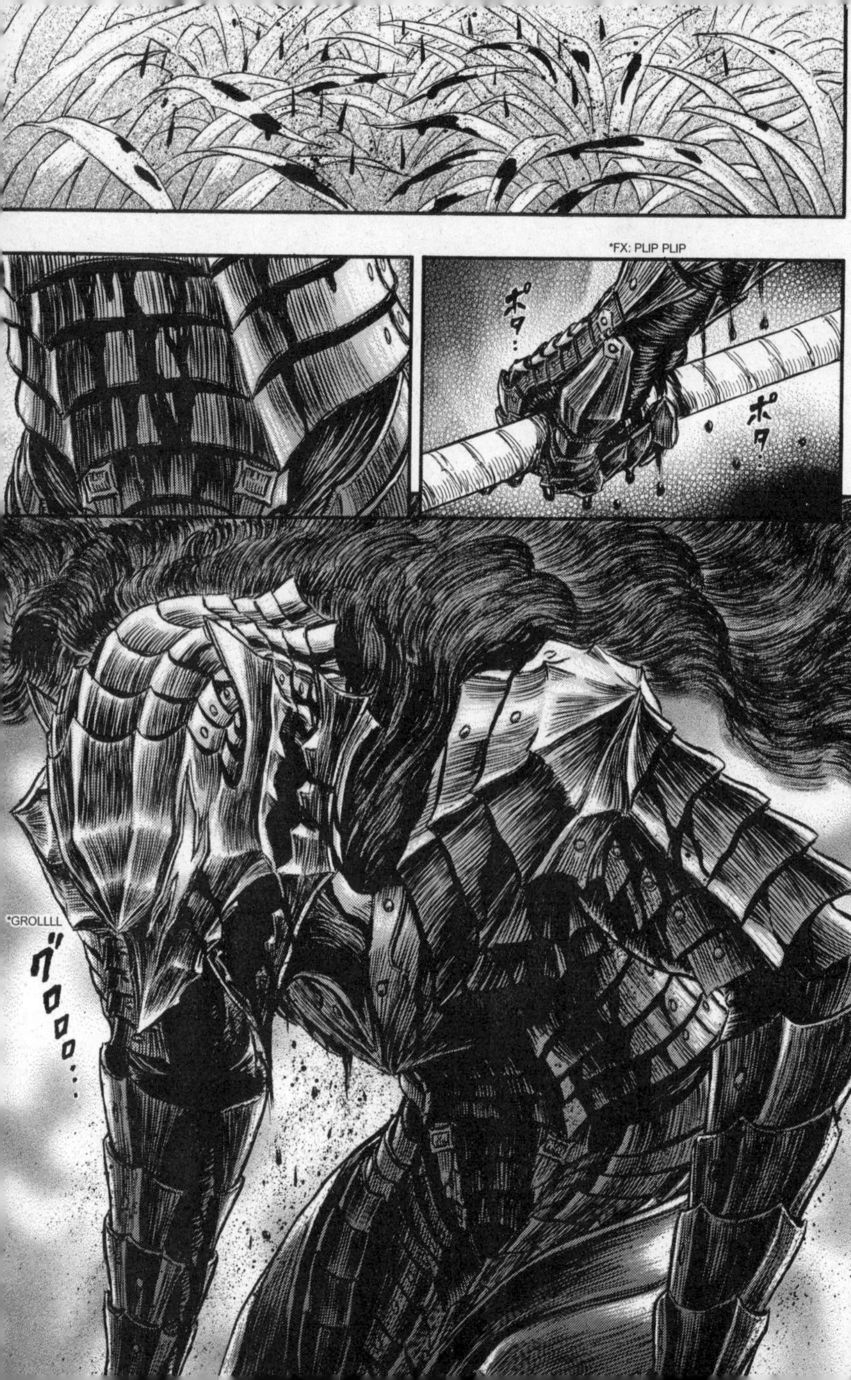
*FX: PLIP PLIP
ポタ…
ポタ…
*GROLLLL
グロロロ…

BERSERK

Created by Kentaro Miura, *Berserk* is manga mayhem to the extreme—violent, horrifying, and mercilessly funny—and the wellspring for the internationally popular anime series. Not for the squeamish or the easily offended, *Berserk* asks for no quarter—and offers none!

Presented uncensored in the original Japanese format!

$14.99 EACH!

AVAILABLE AT YOUR LOCAL COMICS SHOP OR BOOKSTORE
To find a comics shop near your area, visit comicshoplocator.com. For more information or to order direct: On the web: darkhorse.com | E-mail: mailorder@darkhorse.com | Phone: 1-800-862-0052 Mon.–Fri. 9 a.m. to 5 p.m. Pacific Time.

DARK HORSE MANGA

DARKHORSE.COM